Understanding Latin America's Economy in the Twenty-First Century

Diálogos Series
KRIS LANE, SERIES EDITOR

Understanding Latin America demands dialogue, deep exploration, and frank discussion of key topics. Founded by Lyman L. Johnson in 1992 and edited since 2013 by Kris Lane, the Diálogos Series focuses on innovative scholarship in Latin American history and related fields. The series, the most successful of its type, includes specialist works accessible to a wide readership and a variety of thematic titles, all ideally suited for classroom adoption by university and college teachers.

Also available in the Diálogos Series:

Armed Frontier: Warfare and Military Culture in the Texas–Northeastern Mexico Borderlands, 1686–1845 by Luis Alberto García-García

Driving Terror: Labor, Violence, and Justice in Cold War Argentina by Karen Robert

Frontier Justice: State, Law, and Society in Patagonia, 1880–1940 by Javier Cikota

Anti-Catholicism in the Mexican Revolution, 1913–1940 edited by Jürgen Buchenau and David S. Dalton

The Struggle for Natural Resources: Findings from Bolivian History edited by Carmen Soliz and Rossana Barragán

Viceroy Güemes's Mexico: Rituals, Religion, and Revenue by Christoph Rosenmüller

At the Heart of the Borderlands: Africans and Afro-Descendants on the Edges of Colonial Spanish America edited by Cameron D. Jones and Jay T. Harrison

The Age of Dissent: Revolution and the Power of Communication in Chile, 1780–1833 by Martín Bowen

From Sea-Bathing to Beach-Going: A Social History of the Beach in Rio de Janeiro, Brazil by B. J. Barickman

Gamboa's World: Justice, Silver Mining, and Imperial Reform in New Spain by Christopher Albi

For additional titles in the Diálogos Series, please visit unmpress.com.

Understanding Latin America's Economy in the Twenty-First Century

JEFF DAYTON-JOHNSON

UNIVERSITY OF NEW MEXICO PRESS | ALBUQUERQUE

© 2025 by the University of New Mexico Press
All rights reserved. Published 2025
Printed in the United States of America

Library of Congress Cataloging-in-Publication Data
Names: Dayton-Johnson, Jeff, author.
Title: Understanding Latin America's economy in the twenty-first century / Jeff Dayton-Johnson.
Description: Albuquerque: University of New Mexico Press, 2025. | Series: Diálogos series | Includes bibliographical references and index.
Identifiers: LCCN 2025006427 (print) | LCCN 2025006428 (ebook) | ISBN 9780826368614 (cloth) | ISBN 9780826368621 (paperback) | ISBN 9780826368638 (epub)
Subjects: LCSH: Latin America—Economic conditions—21st century. | Economic development—Latin America—History—21st century.
Classification: LCC HC125 .D36927 2025 (print) | LCC HC125 (ebook) | DDC 330.98—dc23/eng/20250228
LC record available at https://lccn.loc.gov/2025006427
LC ebook record available at https://lccn.loc.gov/2025006428

Founded in 1889, the University of New Mexico sits on the traditional homelands of the Pueblo of Sandia. The original peoples of New Mexico—Pueblo, Navajo, and Apache—since time immemorial have deep connections to the land and have made significant contributions to the broader community statewide. We honor the land itself and those who remain stewards of this land throughout the generations and also acknowledge our committed relationship to Indigenous peoples. We gratefully recognize our history.

Cover illustration: photograph by Parker Hilton on Unsplash
Designed by Felicia Cedillos
Composed in Adobe Jenson Pro

For Jan Knippers Black (1940–2021) and
Jeffrey William Cason (1962–2022)
Great Middlebury teachers, accomplished Latin Americanists, dear friends

> *No hay nada aquí:*
> *Sólo unos días que se aprestan a pasar*
> *Sólo una tarde en que se puede respirar*
> *Un diminuto instante inmenso en el vivir*
> *Después mirar la realidad*
> *Y nada más*

Contents

List of Figures — ix

List of Tables — xiii

Acknowledgments — xv

Abbreviations and Acronyms — xvii

Introduction. News Dispatches from the Twenty-First Century Latin American Economy — 1

PART ONE. HISTORICAL BACKGROUND

Chapter One. An Introduction to Latin America — 15

Chapter Two. High Developmentalism and Its Aftermath (1949–1999) — 25

PART TWO. GROWTH

Chapter Three. *O Milagrinho*: The Latin American Decade (2000–2007) — 53

Chapter Four. The Jazz Effect: The Global Financial Crisis in Latin America (2008–2009) — 75

Chapter Five. Hurricane Season (2010–2019) — 91

Chapter Six. Growth in the Time of COVID-19 (2020–2024) — 111

Chapter Seven. The Pandemic's Inflationary Coda (2021–2024) — 128

PART THREE. DEVELOPMENT

Chapter Eight. Structural Transformation Delayed   145

Chapter Nine. Declining Inequality   167

Chapter Ten. Improved Fiscal Policy   191

Chapter Eleven. Better Economic Statecraft   213

Chapter Twelve. Lessons from This Century   233

Notes   249

References   265

Index   287

Figures

Figure 2.1. Growth averages by decade, Latin America, OECD, world, 1960s–2020s — 38

Figure 2.2. Growth averages by decade, LAC-7 countries, 1960s–2020s — 40

Figure 2.3. GDP per capita, Latin America, Caribbean, and world, 1960–2022 — 48

Figure 3.1. GDP per capita, LAC-7 economies, 2000–2008 — 54

Figure 3.2. Cumulative growth of GDP per capita, LAC and other economies, 2003–2008 — 55

Figure 3.3. Per capita income as a share of OECD countries (%), 2000–2022 — 59

Figure 3.4. Commodity price indices, 1992–2024 — 61

Figure 3.5. Growth and commodity intensity of exports, 2003–2008 — 63

Figure 3.6. Cumulative GDP per capita growth and exports to China, 2003–2008 — 65

Figure 4.1. Economic growth 2007–2009, selected regions and countries — 77

Figure 4.2. GDP per capita indices, LAC-7 and OECD, 2006–2011 — 78

Figure 4.3. Current account balances in 2007 and 2009, LAC-7 countries — 87

Figure 4.4. Financial/capital account balances in 2007 and 2009, LAC-7 countries — 87

Figure 5.1. Income per capita, selected countries and country aggregates, 2010–2019 — 93

Figure 5.2. Income per capita, LAC-7 economies, 2010–2019 — 94

Figure 5.3. Cumulative growth in per capita income,
Latin America and selected economies, 2010–2019 — 95

Figure 6.1. Economic growth rates 2020 and 2021, selected
regions and countries — 119

Figure 6.2. Economic growth rates 2020 and 2021, LAC-7 countries — 120

Figure 6.3. Economic growth rates 2020 and 2021, Latin American
countries other than LAC-7 — 121

Figure 7.1. Rates of inflation, major economic aggregates, 2000–2024 — 130

Figure 7.2a. Rates of inflation, LAC-5 countries, 2020–2024 — 134

Figure 7.2b. Rates of inflation, Argentina and Venezuela, 2020–2024 — 135

Figure 8.1. Commodity and natural resource-based manufactured exports
(% of goods exports), developing regions, 1990–2016 — 148

Figure 8.2. Industry and manufacturing value added, as a share of GDP,
four Latin American countries 1960–2022 — 152

Figure 8.3. Manufacturing value-added as a share of GDP, LAC-7
countries, 1960s–2020s — 154

Figure 8.4. Changes in manufacturing value-added (% of GDP)
1970s vs. 2010s — 155

Figure 9.1. Gini coefficients for Latin American and
selected economies, 2021 — 171

Figure 9.2. Gini coefficients over time, LAC-7 and
comparator economies, 1980s–2020s — 172

Figure 9.3. Changes in Gini coefficients between the 1990s
and the 2020s, selected economies — 173

Figure 9.4. Share of total net personal wealth held by bottom
half of national wealth distribution, LAC-7 countries, 1990s–2020s — 180

Figure 9.5. Share of total net personal wealth held by top 1%
of national wealth distribution, LAC-7 countries, 1990s–2020s — 181

Figure 10.1a. Fiscal deficit/surplus (% of total government revenue),
LAC-7 countries (exc. Venezuela), 1999–2023 — 195

Figure 10.1b. Fiscal deficit/surplus (% of total government revenue), Venezuela, 1999–2022 — 195

Figure 10.2a. Tax revenues (% of GDP), Latin America and OECD, 1990–2021 — 196

Figure 10.2b. Structure of tax revenues, Latin America and OECD, 2020 — 196

Figure 10.3a. Government debt (% of GDP), LAC-5 countries, 2001–2023 — 206

Figure 10.3b. Government debt (% of GDP), Argentina and Venezuela, 2001–2023 — 206

Figure 10.4. Gini coefficients of market and disposable income, selected Latin American and European countries, early 2000s — 211

Tables

Table 2.1. Elements of the Washington Consensus	43
Table 4.1. The Colombian Balance of Payments, 2007	80
Table 5.1. Indicators of Current Account Exposure and Resilience, Hurricane Season	98
Table 5.2. Indicators of Financial/Capital Account Exposure and Resilience, Hurricane Season	101
Table 6.1. Covid-19 Mortality Indicators	113
Table 6.2. Covid-19 Mortality Indicators, Latin American and Caribbean Countries	115
Table 8.1. Latin American Firms in the Fortune Global 500, 2008	159
Table 8.2. Top Ten Non-Financial Latin American Firms	161

Acknowledgments

Though I wrote this book in a relatively short span of time, it draws upon many decades of academic and professional work, and as such it draws upon many important relationships and friendships. I want to acknowledge an unavoidably partial number of those relationships: some recent, some deep in the past, and some in between.

My writing of this book was greatly stimulated by opportune short-term visits to Sciences Po Bordeaux (where I also met with faculty from other nearby Bordeaux universities), Instituto Tecnológico y de Estudios Superiores de Monterrey, and the Universidad Iberoamericana. My thanks to Anthony Amicelle, Delphine Gorostidi, Carol Lin and the members of the "Assomérica Latina" student group in Bordeaux, for facilitating the Bordeaux stay. And to Pablo Cotler Avalos and Irving Rosales Arredondo at the Ibero; Pablo de la Peña Sánchez and Carlos Lugo Contreras at TEC; and to Mario López Roldán of the OECD Center in Mexico City, for their help in organizing the Mexico visits. These encounters allowed me to meet with faculty and students and to make various presentations, formal and informal, related to the material in this book. I am also grateful to colleagues at the Middlebury Institute of International Studies at Monterey, who participated in an informal seminar, and to participants in a panel at the 2023 meetings of the Latin American Studies Association in Vancouver, for their feedback.

For helpful conversations and feedback during the drafting of this book, my thanks to William Arrocha, Edgardo Ayala Gaytán, Éric Berr, Matías Bianchi, Jan Knippers Black, Jeff Cason, Pablo Cotler Avalos, Fernando DePaolis, Mario Luis Fuentes Alcalá, Jason Gagnon, Fernando Gómez Zaldívar, Claudio González Chiaramonte, Alejandro Guevara Sanginés, Gabriel Guillén, Tonatiuh Guillén López, George Henson, David Heres del Valle, Katiuska King Mantilla, Jeffrey Knopf, Alice Klozer, Mario López Roldán, Cassio Luiselli Fernández, Gabriela Luna Ruíz, Ángel Melguizo Esteso, Margaret Miller,

Sebastián Nieto-Parra, Pablo Oliva, René Orozco, Laurie Patton, Kate Petrich, Diana Piloyan Boudjikanian, Martha Areli Ramírez Sánchez, Gary Richman, Alejandro Rodríguez Arana, Antulio Rosales, Irving Rosales Arredondo, Henri-Bernard Solignac-Lecomte, Isidro Soloaga, Ernesto Stein, and Felix Zimmermann.

My thanks also to coauthors and collaborators from across the twenty-first century, who may well detect their influence in the pages that follow: Rolando Avendaño, Francesca Castellano, Bárbara Castelletti, Tess Cyrus, Rita da Costa, Juan de Laiglesia, Hamlet Gutiérrez, John Hoddinott, Johannes Jütting, Louka Katseli, Barry Lesser, Juliana Londoño Vélez, Lars Osberg, Mario Pezzini, Anna Pietikäinen, Gabriela Ramos, Javier Santiso, Juan Vázquez Zamora, and Carol Wise among them. And thanks, finally, to teachers and mentors who are also, implicitly or explicitly, present in these pages: Pranab Bardhan, Daniel Cohen, Alain de Janvry, Albert Fishlow, Tulio Halperín Donghi, Richard Salvucci, Alex Saragoza, Irene Tinker.

Michael Millman of the University of New Mexico Press has been an engaged and supportive ally in the process of writing and publication, and Kris Lane, series editor of the Press's excellent *Diálogos* series on Latin America, was an early supporter of my idea.

The writing of this book might have been possible without the sabbatical leave from my position as dean of the Middlebury Institute of International Studies, but it would have been neither as rich nor as gratifying an experience as the sabbatical allowed it to be. I am particularly beholden to the then Middlebury president Laurie Patton not only for agreeing to, but actively encouraging me to take, a sabbatical leave; as well as for providing invaluable writer-to-writer feedback all the while. Laurie is a consummate scholar-administrator whose example I take great delight in seeking to emulate. My warmest thanks to my colleagues Provost Michelle McCauley and Vice President for Academic Affairs Stephen Snyder for so ably taking over my administrative responsibilities during my leave.

Finally, my gratitude to my beloved family, each of whom has been patient and encouraging and made space literally, temporally, and figuratively, for me to work on this, from Boise to Brooklyn to Nevada City and back again: heartfelt thanks to Allie, Nell, my in-laws Al and Joan, and of course Jennifer, most of all.

Abbreviations and Acronyms

ALBA	Alianza Bolivariana para los Pueblos de Nuestra América [Bolivarian Alliance for the Peoples of Our America]
AMLO	Andrés Manuel López Obrador, Mexican political figure
APEC	Asia-Pacific Economic Cooperation
APRA	Alianza Popular Revolucionaria Americana [American People's Revolutionary Alliance], Peruvian political party
Bancomer	Banco de Comercio, Mexican bank (now part of BBVA México)
BBVA	Banco Bilbao Vizcaya Argentaria, Spanish bank
BNDES	Banco Nacional de Desenvolvimento Econômico e Social [National Bank for Social and Economic Development], Brazilian public development bank
CAF	Corporación Andina de Fomento; now CAF Development Bank of Latin America and the Caribbean
CARICOM	Caribbean Community
CCTs	Conditional cash transfers
Cemex	Cementos Mexicanos, Mexican construction firm
CEPAL	Comisión Económica para América Latina; after 1984, Comisión Económica para América Latina y el Caribe; the United Nations Economic Commission for Latin America and the Caribbean
CHN	China
CIAT	Centro Interamericano de Administraciones Tributarias [Inter-American Center of Tax Administrations]
CORFO	Corporación de Fomento de la Producción [Corporation to Promote Production], Chile
Covid-19	Coronavirus disease 2019
CPI	Consumer price index

DFID	United Kingdom Department for International Development
ECG	Exports' Contribution to Growth
Embrapa	Empresa Brasileira de Pesquisa Agropecuária [Brazilian Agricultural and Livestock Research Company]
EU	European Union
EZLN	Ejército Zapatista de Liberación Nacional [Zapatista Army for National Liberation], Mexico
FEMSA	Fomento Económico de México, S.A. de C.V., Mexican corporate conglomerate
FONTAR	Fondo Tecnológico Argentino [Argentinian Technological Fund]
FTA	Free trade agreement
GDP	Gross domestic product
GNI	Gross national income
Gruma	Grupo Maseca, Mexican food company
HHI	Herfindahl-Hirschman Index of Export Concentration
IBRD	International Bank for Reconstruction and Development (formal name of the World Bank)
ICT	Index of competitive threat
IDB	Inter-American Development Bank
IEA	International Energy Agency
IFC	International Finance Corporation, World Bank
IMF	International Monetary Fund
ISI	Import-substituting industrialization
ISIC	International Standard Industrial Classification of All Economic Activities
JHU	Johns Hopkins University
LAC-5	Five large economies in Latin America and the Caribbean (the LAC-7 without Argentina and Venezuela)
LAC-7	Seven largest economies in Latin America and the Caribbean (Argentina, Brazil, Chile, Colombia, Mexico, Peru, and Venezuela)
LAC-18	The LAC-7 plus Bolivia, Costa Rica, the Dominican Republic, Ecuador, El Salvador, Guatemala, Honduras, Nicaragua, Panama, Paraguay, and Uruguay.

LAC-19	The LAC-18 plus Cuba.
LCN	Latin America and the Caribbean (World Development Indicators aggregate)
LMY	Low- and middle-income countries (ISO)
MAS	Movimiento al Socialismo [Movement toward Socialism], Bolivian political party
Mercosur	Mercado Común del Sur [Southern Common Market]
MIT	Massachusetts Institute of Technology
Morena	Movimiento de Regeneración Nacional [Movement for National Regeneration], Mexican political party
NAFIN	Nacional Financiera, Mexican public development bank
NAFTA	North American Free Trade Agreement
NGO	Non-governmental organization
OECD	Organisation for Economic Co-operation and Development
PAN	Partido de Acción Nacional [National Action Party], Mexican political party
PDSB	Partido da Social Democracia Brasileira [Brazilian Social Democratic Party], Brazilian political party
PDVSA	Petróleos de Venezuela S.A., Venezuela's state-owned petroleum and natural gas company
Pemex	Petróleos Mexicanos, Mexico's state-owned petroleum and natural gas company
Petrobras	Petróleo Brasileiro, Brazil's state-owned petroleum and natural gas company
PNR	Partido Nacional Revolucionario [National Revolutionary Party], twentieth-century Mexican political party
PRI	Partido Revolucionario Institucional [Institutional Revolutionary Party], Mexican political party
PRM	Partido de la Revolución Mexicana [Party of the Mexican Revolution], twentieth-century Mexican political party
PT	Partido dos Trabalhadores [Workers' Party], Brazilian political party
R&D	Research and development
Selic	Sistema Especial de Liquidação e de Custódia [Special System for Settlement and Custody], Brazilian policy interest rate

Telmex	Teléfonos de México, Mexican telecommunications firm
TFP	Total factor productivity
UNCTAD	United Nations Conference on Trade and Development
UNDP	United Nations Development Programme
UNSD	United Nations Statistics Division
USAID	United States Agency for International Development
VEF	Bolívares fuertes, onetime Venezuelan currency
WDI	World Development Indicators
WEO	World Economic Outlook, IMF report
WHO	World Health Organization
WTO	World Trade Organization

INTRODUCTION

News Dispatches from the Twenty-First Century Latin American Economy

"LATIN AMERICA'S PROSPECTS DIM, Again."

So read a headline in the 26 August 2019 issue of the *Wall Street Journal*, the premier financial daily in the United States. The title encapsulates, almost perfectly, a widely observed attitude regarding the possibility of economic good times in Latin America, an attitude of pessimism, of resignation. The fatalism contained in the comma, followed gloomily by "... again," is a fatalism frequently encountered in the business press in the United States, and just as frequently in Latin American media.[1]

It is the contention of this book that the economic history of Latin America in the twenty-first century, though as checkered as the pessimists might suggest, nevertheless contains several encouraging inflection points, some more consolidated, others still incipient. Twenty-some years into the new century, those ever-promised economic good times still lie more in the future than in the present, but this history is meant to provide a case for guarded optimism.

To provide a sense of the ups and downs of Latin America's economies in this period, let's scan fifteen news flashes to complement that baleful August 2019 dispatch.

20 December 2001: Argentina's President Declares a State of Emergency Amidst Unrest. As political protests and widespread looting of supermarkets broke out in the cities of Córdoba, Rosario, Concordia, Mendoza, and several neighborhoods of the capital, Buenos Aires, President Fernando de la Rúa declared a state

1

of emergency, giving the government extraordinary powers. In some cities there were reports that police stood by as protestors pillaged stores; in others, the authorities' response was harsh, and news of fatalities circulated. "We are stealing because we have to," an out-of-work custodian told a reporter. "The looting is not about hunger," a government minister countered, "they are stealing alcoholic beverages. This is a political matter." The backdrop for the unrest was economic decline, including high unemployment and a series of increasingly desperate measures taken by economy minister Domingo Cavallo, including wage cuts for government workers and capital controls in hopes of averting a banking crisis. Cavallo abruptly stepped down at midnight the night before, and signs that the government was not meeting interest payments on its public bonds, presaged a possible default on its $132 billion debt (Krauss 2001).

26 November 2004: Chinese President Hu Jintao Makes State Visit to Argentina, Brazil, Chile, and Cuba, Emphasizing Economic Ties. En route to the Asia-Pacific Economic Cooperation (APEC) summit meeting in Santiago, Chile, Chinese president Hu Jintao met with leaders in Argentina, Brazil, and Cuba. The emphasis was on increasing trade and investment ties, just a few short years after China's entry into the World Trade Organization (WTO). Hu announced as much as $30 billion of Chinese investment in infrastructure, mining, and agricultural development in Latin American countries, with a view to securing reliable access to supplies of soybeans, copper, and other commodities. Argentina and Brazil, the largest economies among the countries Hu visited, agreed to classify China as a "market economy," allowing freer movement of goods and services among those trading partners. It was also announced that Chile and China would begin the negotiation of a bilateral trade agreement, the first between China and a Latin American country. Foreign Minister Li Zhaoxing, who accompanied Hu, declared that "distance cannot separate true friends who feel so close even when they are thousands of miles apart" (Casey 2004; Rohter 2004; Ministry of Foreign Affairs, China, 2004).

1 March 2005: Leftist Physician Tabaré Vázquez Elected Uruguay's President, Indicative of a "Pink Tide." Tabaré Vázquez, candidate of the left-wing Frente Amplio, was elected president, wresting power from the long-standing Colorado Party (founded in 1836), which had governed continuously since the end of the military dictatorship in 1985. Frente Amplio senator José "Pepe" Mujica (who would succeed Vázquez as president) offered this assessment of the new government's ideology: "We have changed because the world has changed. We live in a unipolar world in which attempts at socialism have failed and there are no alternatives. We have to take a pragmatic line." The *New York Times* noted that Dr. Vázquez's election followed a succession of elections of left-leaning governments to power across the region, in countries including Venezuela, Chile, Brazil, Argentina, Ecuador, and Bolivia. In what would become a label for this historic movement, *Times* reporter Larry Rohter mused, prophetically, that this represents "not so much a red tide as a pink one" (Rohter 2005).

29 October 2006: Leftist Lula Reelected as Brazil's President, Global Capital Markets Do Not Blink. Luiz Inácio Lula da Silva, incumbent presidential candidate for the left-wing Workers Party in Brazil, faced off against a roster of contenders, led by Geraldo Alckmin, former governor of São Paulo, representing the centrist[2] Brazilian Social Democratic Party (PDSB). Polling put Lula ahead of Alckmin through the summer, and the two headed to runoff following their first- and second-place finish in the first round of voting on 1 October. Lula's lead in the polls climbed steadily after the first round, and he won the second round handily with 60.8 percent of the vote on 29 October. Throughout the lead-up to the elections, global investment banks were unfazed by the prospect of a second Lula government. Citigroup wrote to its customers that "whoever wins the election, the broad tenets of macroeconomic policies, including fiscal responsibility, inflation targeting, and a floating exchange rate, likely will remain in place." The average of the banks' recommendations to their customers regarding Brazilian government bond remained positive (that is, "overweight") and steady, and these recommendations improved in the months following Lula's reelection. This stood in stark contrast to the banks' recommendations leading up to Lula's first election in 2002. Goldman Sachs warned its customers at that time that "the incoming administration is poorly prepared to tackle the hard challenges of restoring confidence, stabilizing the stock of net public debt, and simultaneously engineering a recovery of economic activity." Investment banks' average recommendation on Brazilian bonds plunged into negative ("underweight") territory throughout 2002 and fell further in the early months of the PT government, placing significant constraints on the government's capacity to issue new debt.[3]

24 January 2008: Argentina's President Calls the Global Recession "The Jazz Effect," Points Finger at United States. Argentina's leftist president Cristina Fernández de Kirchner, addressed the global financial crisis, and located its roots in the US economy: "We could call this crisis the 'jazz effect.' We've seen the tequila effect, and the caipirinha effect, depending on the origins of the market movement. Today it comes from the North—what used to be a model." The *tequila effect* refers to the 1994 financial crisis in Latin America unleashed by a botched devaluation of the Mexican peso; the *caipirinha effect*, to the contagion unleashed by a Brazilian financial crisis in 1998. Rather than emanating from Latin America northward as in the past, the *Jazz Effect* spread from the United States to the south. President Fernández de Kirchner furthermore held up her leftist economic strategy, meanwhile, as a saner alternative to the precarious US economic model, pointing to vigorous growth, surging exports, and declining unemployment. "In the face of the jazz effect lashing the world," she noted, Argentina offered "the consistency of a model in which, in addition to exporting and building, is giving shape to our own vision and a means of engaging with this globalized world" (*La Nación* 2008).

7 February 2009: Bolivia Promulgates a New Constitution Which Grants Rights to Mother Earth. In the city of El Alto, President Evo Morales led a ceremony to mark the entry into force of a new constitution. Morales, the first Indigenous executive of a country with one of the largest Indigenous minorities in Latin America, and a former coca farmer, declared the new constitution a "new independence for Bolivia." Among the most striking and novel elements of the new charter was its Article 33, which granted constitutional rights to Mother Earth, echoing Morales's frequent evocation of "Pachamama," the Earth divinity of Inca cosmology. The rights of nature would be further clarified by laws passed in 2010 ("Rights of Mother Earth") and 2012 ("Framework of Mother Earth and Integrated Development to Live Well"). According to the 2010 law, "Mother Earth [la Madre Tierra] is the dynamic living system made up of the indivisible community of all life systems and living beings, interrelated, interdependent, and complementary, that share a common destiny." Together with a new 2008 constitution in Ecuador, which similarly granted rights to nature, the Bolivian charter departed in significant ways from the more common granting of rights to individuals (or to firms) and represented an attempt to incorporate Indigenous ideals into national law (Vaca 2009; Harris 2021).

16 December 2009: Moody's Qualifies Peru's Foreign Debt as Investment Grade. The credit-rating agency Moody's, following earlier upgrades by Fitch and Standard & Poor's, rated Peruvian dollar-denominated bonds and loans at investment grade. "As with other sovereigns that have been recently upgraded, the decision to raise Peru's foreign currency ratings was driven by indications of increased shock-absorption capacity relative to similar or higher-rated sovereigns," according to Moody's. The improved assessment of Peru's government finances pointed to the successful initiative of President Alan García's finance minister Luis Carranza to accelerate the reduction of the country's foreign indebtedness, and to promote macroeconomic stability in the midst of the global financial crisis. This was a far cry from President García's first term as executive in the 1980s, when the country was beset by hyperinflation and defaulted on its foreign debt. Minister Carranza indicated that the higher credit ratings would lower the country's borrowing costs and foster economic growth (Velez 2009).

24 January 2011: Colombian President Santos Predicts a "Latin American Decade" in an Address to the OECD. Colombian President Juan Manuel Santos made the case that the world was witnessing the dawn of a "Latin American Decade." Abundant natural resources, reformed and stable financial sectors, and coherent fiscal and monetary policy making added up, in Santos's reckoning, to a positive prognosis for the region in a global context of lingering recession in the United States and Europe. He pointed out that Latin American governments had managed the global financial crisis more ably than many European countries, as they had "already put in place many of the regulations and controls that Europe had never had to put in place, because it had never experienced any crisis, or the crises had been very weak, very small. We, on the other hand, have experienced very deep crises, and we learned the hard way." Santos foresaw vigorous inflows of portfolio and investment capital and bolstered trade relationships that would maintain historically high growth rates and transform Latin American societies in beneficial ways. The setting for Santos's speech—at Bercy, the French Finance Ministry, at a gathering convened by the Organisation for Economic Co-operation and Development (OECD)—was significant. Santos made no secret of his ambition that Colombia be invited to join the OECD, a confirmation of gaining admission to the ranks of the high-income industrial democracies, or, in unfortunate shorthand, the "rich countries' club" (Colombia would become the thirty-seventh member of the OECD in April 2020) (Delcas 2011; Santos 2011; OECD n.d.).

2 July 2012, Mexico's Partido Revolucionario Institucional Elected to Power Following Two Terms by the Long-Time Opposition Party. Former governor of Mexico State Enrique Peña Nieto took an early lead in voting for the Mexican presidency, nudging out rival candidate Andrés Manuel López Obrador (known as "AMLO"). Peña Nieto was criticized for citing the early projections by the official elections agency as confirmation of his victory. López Obrador would meanwhile bring forward claims of irregularities, with the support of protestors, and a recount would confirm Peña Nieto as the contest's winner. These controversies aside, the presidential election of 2012 marked a milestone in the peaceful transition of power. Peña Nieto's party, the PRI, had held power continuously between 1929 and 2000, when Vicente Fox, Guanajuato governor and candidate of the long-time conservative opposition party, the Partido de Acción Nacional (PAN), was elected president. Fox was succeeded by another PAN president, Felipe Calderón, who served until Peña Nieto. Thus the 2012 elections witnessed the transfer back from the PAN to the PRI. In the next presidential elections, in 2018, AMLO would be elected at the head of an entirely new party, known as Morena. While all of these changes in political platforms generated their share of debates and rancor, the twenty-first century has been one of consolidation of democratic practices, notably the peaceful transfer of power, in what was, not long before, effectively a single-party state (Ellingwood and Wilkinson, 2012).

22 May 2013: Fed Chief Ben Bernanke Tells US Congress that the Central Bank Will Taper its Purchases of Financial Assets, Setting Off "Taper Tantrum." Appearing before the US Congress's Joint Economic Committee, Federal Reserve System Chair Ben Bernanke stated that "If we see continued improvement [in economic conditions] and we have confidence that that's going to be sustained then we could in the next few meetings . . . take a step down in our pace of purchases." This was the first signal that the Fed intended to move away from its aggressive "quantitative easing" policy. Pursued by the Fed and other rich-country central banks, quantitative easing centered on huge central-bank purchases of financial assets, which had the effect of increasing the money supply, lowering interest rates, and—it was hoped—promoting economic recovery from the global financial crisis. The threat of slowing (not reversing) this expansionary monetary policy led to a sudden sell-off in bonds and stocks in the United States, and tighter financial conditions. The International Monetary Fund (IMF) warned that this "Taper Tantrum" would reverberate in emerging economies, including in Latin America and the Caribbean: Bond yields in Latin America fell even more steeply in response to the 2013 Tantrum than did US bond yields, and capital inflows into the region also fell substantially (Reuters 2019b; Klemm et al. 2014).

20 June 2013: Across Brazil, One Million Protest Rises in Public Transport Fares. On 2 June 2013, the fare for riding a bus or the subway in São Paulo was raised from R$ 3 to R$ 3.2, a move met with immediate protest. Four days later, 2,000 protesters voiced their disapproval along the Avenida Paulista; by 17 June, the protest swelled to 65,000 in São Paulo, blocking major arteries, while in Brasília, protestors occupied the National Congress. On the 19th, the fare increase was reversed (and fares in Rio de Janeiro reduced as well), but too late to stem the growth of the movement the initial price rise engendered. Approximately one million Brazilians—300,000 in Rio alone—marched on 20 June in various cities of the country. Before long, protesters linked their demands with condemnation of sizeable public spending to host the 2014 World Cup and the 2016 Summer Olympics; the opening of the World Cup in June 2014 would be met with renewed demonstrations.[4]

17 December 2014: US President Obama Moves to Normalize Relations with Cuba. US President Barack Obama shocked the political world internationally and domestically, when he announced that the United States and Cuba had been engaged in secret negotiations for eighteen months, and were poised to reestablish diplomatic relations, which had been severed in the aftermath of the Cuban Revolution in 1959. "These 50 years have shown that isolation has not worked," Obama told the American people, from the White House: "It's time for a new approach." For his part, Cuban president Raúl Castro told Cubans he looked forward to dialogue on "profound differences" between Cuba and the United States, "particularly on issues related to national sovereignty, democracy, human rights and foreign policy." Indeed, the two countries stood at opposite ends of an economic policy spectrum, between a liberal market orientation and a Communist command economy. The American blockade of Cuba was furthermore a central component of the country's Cold War foreign policy in Latin America, emblematic of US hostility to revolutionary socialism in its "backyard," and a perpetual source of criticism for political parties and political actors of many orientations throughout the region (DeYoung 2014).

3 April 2020: The Covid-19 Dead Pile Up in the Streets of Guayaquil. Only weeks after the novel coronavirus appeared in Ecuador, it quickly overwhelmed the capacity of the public health system in Guayaquil, the country's largest city. With hospitals and morgues beyond capacity, people in Guayaquil were forced to abandon their dead in the city streets. Guayaquil's mayor, Cynthia Viteri, despaired: "What is happening in the country's public health system? They are not taking away the dead from houses, they're leaving them on the sidewalks, they're falling in front of hospitals. No one wants to pick them up . . . we need to know the causes of why people are dying in their homes." It is not clear how many of the dead succumbed to Covid-19 or were unable to receive treatment for other fatal maladies. President Lenín Moreno was frank about the lack of information: "It's important to tell the truth . . . both the number of cases and deaths, the records fall short" (Gallón 2020).

7 October 2021: Satellite Imagery Reveals the Extent of Amazon Deforestation for Commodity Extraction. Nature magazine reported the results of analysis of thirty-six years' worth of Google Earth Engine data by an academic/private sector/NGO group called MapBiomas. Deforestation is led by illegal mining operations (particularly gold) and clearing for cattle raising, activities symptomatic of the *"reprimarization"* of the Brazilian and other Latin American economies in the twenty-first century. Illegal mining incursions increased fivefold (in terms of land area affected) in the ten years prior to the publication of the report. "We kind of knew that this was happening, but to see numbers like this is scary even for us," said the lead scientist of the MapBiomas team. Deforestation of the Amazon has been met with street protests and legal challenges by the Indigenous people whose land and livelihoods have been affected by deforestation and encroachment of mining and cattle raising. The pace of incursions shot up sharply under the government of far-right populist president Jair Bolsonaro, whose stated position was that Indigenous people in Brazil controlled "too much" land (Tollefson 2021).

11 January 2024: Argentinian Inflation Tops 200 Percent, as an "Anarcho-Capitalist" Assumes the Presidency. Argentina skirted into hyperinflationary territory during the 2023 electoral cycle, and inflation was exacerbated by the first measures enacted by "anarcho-capitalist" President Javier Milei. These included a sharp devaluation (which raised the price of imports for Argentinians), and an elimination of some price controls put in place by his predecessors. In contrast to the IMF's October 2023 forecast for end-of-year 2023 inflation of 136 percent annually, official data suggested that the 2023 rate was in fact 211 percent, the highest in Latin America, surpassing the rate of inflation in Venezuela. In December 2023, prices of goods and services rose 30 percent; health costs, 32.6 percent; transport costs 31.7 percent; and food, 29.7 percent. The IMF tentatively praised the measures undertaken by the new Milei administration but cautioned that its continued support was conditional on "continuous and enduring implementation" of fiscal adjustment (Nessi 2024; Criales 2024).

Making Sense of the Twenty-First Century Latin American Economy

Even with a mere fifteen news dispatches, it is difficult to weave a simple narrative from these disparate threads. The reflexive pessimists would point out that our selection begins and ends with crippling economic crises in Argentina, in keeping with the fatalist version of the region's history. But what then to make of Argentina's left-populist president in the middle of the story, confidently boasting that its booming economy had proven superior to that of the United States, mired in the global financial crisis? Or Colombia's center-right president (and future Nobel Peace Prize winner) Juan Manuel Santos proclaiming the dawn of a "Latin American decade"? And speaking of leftist presidents, many came to power during these years, including onetime Tupamaro guerrilla leader José Mujica, quoted herein calling for pragmatism. The same pragmatism, perhaps, that led international capital markets to peaceably accept longtime firebrand Lula in the Brazilian presidency, and to rate once-hyperinflationary Peru's public debt as investment grade. An ephemeral rapprochement flickered into view between the standard-bearers of the polar extremes of models of politics and economics in the hemisphere: the globalizing United States and revolutionary Communist Cuba. Whatever the ultimate balance of steps forward and steps back, even the pessimists would have to acknowledge that this century has not been business as usual in Latin America.

The Brazilian economist Laura Carvalho wrote a book about the recent economic history of her country entitled *Valsa brasileira*: Brazilian Waltz. It's organized around an elegantly simple and delightful narrative structure. Her story unfolds as a series of dance moves in the waltz of the book's title: a step forward (the administration of President Luiz Inácio Lula da Silva, 2003–2010); a step to the side (President Dilma Rousseff, 2011–2016); and a step backward (President Michel Temer, 2016–2018).

The larger Latin American waltz analyzed in the pages that follow similarly traces a series of steps, and half steps, forward and back. At the risk of spoilers, here are the four principal elements to the story.

1. *One step forward, a half step back: Two episodes of economic growth, each ending in a global crisis.* The first growth spurt was quite rapid by historical standards (2003–2008), the second more volatile and less spectacular (2011–2019). Both ended in global crises. The first—the global financial crisis—was shorter and shallower in Latin America than it was elsewhere, notably in the rich countries of the OECD. The second—Covid-19—was sharper, deeper, and more deadly in Latin America than most other parts of the world.

2. *A half step forward, a full step back: the reprimarization/deindustrialization binary.* Many countries in the region experienced what is called locally a *reprimarización*: an increase in the share of commodities—copper, soybeans, lithium, petroleum and so on—in the export mix of many countries. This has been driven by the insatiable demand of Chinese industrialization, much more intensive in metals than other homologous processes in history. Many countries became even more exposed to the volatility of commodity prices and perhaps to the long-term tendency of commodity prices to fall relative to manufacturing prices (an argument explored in chapter 2). The commodity boom brought with it a boom in tax receipts for a while, making ambitious government projects possible. Nevertheless, a contentious political and social debate has emerged around this *neoextractivismo*, focused on the environmental degradation and political repression it engenders, among other consequences. Reprimarization, meanwhile, was accompanied by a sharpening of the decline in importance of manufacturing in national output; this trend, in turn, foreclosed opportunities for growth in incomes and productivity.

3. *One step forward, a half step back: Declining income inequality.* Many researchers have demonstrated a downward trend in economic inequality, which they attribute to a new generation of social policies, and to the reduction of the so-called "skill premium" for wages earned by higher-skilled workers. This shrinking skill premium is related to reprimarization: Labor demand for less-skilled workers (particularly in the commodity sector) has grown more rapidly than for higher-skilled workers, thus reducing the wage gap between the two groups and with it, income inequality (more on this in chapter 8). There has nevertheless been a significant uptick in inequality in the face of Covid-19, the impact of which also revealed many stark long-standing dimensions of inequality.

4. *One step forward, a half step back: Improved economic governance, particularly in fiscal policy.* This century has witnessed a complex transformation of the characteristics of governance, of the quality of public policies, especially macroeconomic and social policies. Javier Santiso (2005) has called this style of governance *possibilism*. Possibilist governments are pragmatic, and perhaps less ideological than the governments in previous decades. Possibilism in its classic form features fairly orthodox macroeconomic policy, which reassures and even encourages international investors. Alongside this macroeconomic orthodoxy, there are not-so-orthodox elements, such as ambitious social policies like the Brazilian Bolsa Família, Juntos in Peru, Progresa/Oportunidades/Prospera in Mexico, and Chile Solidario, all of which had significant impacts on reducing poverty and inequality (see above).

The book is divided into three parts. Part 1 provides historical and economic background, including a swift overview of the colonial and nineteenth-century economic history of Latin America, and a slightly less swift look at the latter half of the twentieth century. Part 2 proceeds through the phases of the economic history of the twenty-first century, with a sustained focus on economic growth and the balance of payments. Part 3 broadens the coverage from growth to consider other dimensions of development during the current century, including structural transformation of the economy, inequality, public finance, the quality of economic governance, and lessons from the first quarter of the century for the future.

For Whom Is This Book Written?

I wrote this book for people like the students I have taught over the last twenty-five years at the Middlebury Institute of International Studies at Monterey, California, at Sciences-Po campuses in Paris and Bordeaux, and at Dalhousie University in Halifax, Nova Scotia. Overwhelmingly, these have been masters-level, interdisciplinary, and professionally oriented students. Not all such students have had extensive training in economic analysis, and the pages that follow presume a lower level of technical background in economics than would be found among readers in graduate economics programs, commercial banks' research divisions, central banks, or ministries of finance.

But let me be explicit: This is a book for economists, too. Working economists will, I hope, find stimulation and the seeds of debate in the arguments I have proposed. Moreover, teachers and students of economics will find ample material for more sophisticated further reading and reflection in the notes and references. And I hope my fellow economists will appreciate an economics book attuned to politics and history and other disciplinary currents.

Part One

HISTORICAL BACKGROUND

CHAPTER ONE

An Introduction to Latin America

Five Keys to Latin America's Economic History

Mexico City's Palacio Nacional was built in the sixteenth century to house the seat of government of the viceroyalty of New Spain. Centuries later, in the aftermath of the Mexican Revolution of 1910–1917, the muralist Diego Rivera decorated the corridors of the palace's courtyard with masterful revolutionary frescoes. The Rivera murals depict the grand sweep of Mexican history, from scenes of Indigenous civilizations all the way to the struggles of the early twentieth century, with Karl Marx in the role of Moses, pointing the working classes to Mexico's future. In the northeast corner of the courtyard, in the last mural that he painted in the palace, Rivera situated a violent depiction of the Spanish conquest at Veracruz on Mexico's eastern coast. The scene illustrates many horrible cruelties of the conquistadores, led by Hernán Cortés: murdered Indigenous people swing from the trees; another is tortured in the painting's foreground, his face about to be branded with a hot iron (another man already bears the brand on his cheekbone); still other Indigenous men are marched off under the weight of some of the huge, felled trees that lie about. Mounted Spaniards drive all manner of Old-World livestock through the scene, while others of their compatriots inspect samples, apparently of mineral wealth, borne by pick-wielding Indigenous men. A lone African man in irons is held by a group of soldiers, presaging the generalized enslavement of Africans in the New World to come. A baby bundled on the back of an Indigenous woman looks directly at the viewer with blue-green eyes, representing the mixed-race population that would dominate the formerly Indigenous geographies of Central and South America, and hinting at sexual violence. A syphilitic Cortés, accompanied by a Catholic priest, stands aside a large cross, a reminder of the evangelizing mission that went hand in hand with military conquest. Rivera's mural is part of a larger movement in Latin American artistic and intellectual history, underscoring the brutality of the conquest, and its long-lasting consequences for the peoples of the region.[1]

Standing before Rivera's mural, one can muster some sympathy for the reflexive Latin America pessimists encountered in this book's introduction: those who are resigned to eternally poor economic performance in the region. Indeed, many of the economic ills we debate today, in the twenty-first century—a colonial overhang, a dependence on commodities, vast inequalities, antidemocratic governance—were all there, back in the sixteenth century. The vigor of Rivera's representation, executed in 1951, suggests that he considered many of those same ills to be present in the middle of the twentieth century too. Surely, the reflexive pessimists will conclude, the region will never overcome these obstacles.

This book argues, in contrast, that many actors in the twenty-first century—leaders, governments, parties, social movements, businesses, working people, researchers—made important strides forward in the long struggle to address and transform the Latin American ills decried by the reflexive pessimists. To gauge more accurately this forward progress, a clearer depiction of the long-standing historical background will be useful. This introductory chapter accordingly provides a lightning-fast overview of five fundamental themes that course through the region's history, with a view to informing the more detailed look at the current century that comes later. The chapter closes with a specification, historical in part, of what exactly is meant by "Latin America" as a geographical term, in the pages that follow.

Key #1: The Colonial Heritage. As an economic, social, political region, "Latin America" was born of the conquest of the Indigenous populations of Meso- and South America by the Iberian powers beginning in 1492 (as illustrated in part by Rivera's mural in the Mexican Palacio Nacional). Iberian dominance would remain in place until the struggles for independence in the early nineteenth century. Latin America's insertion in the world economy therefore was not intended to promote the region's—or its peoples'—economic and social progress, but rather to extract wealth for the metropoles, Spain and Portugal. This extractive model stands in contrast to modern understanding of international trade, which proposes a model of exchange with mutual benefits for all participating economies. Princeton historians Stanley and Barbara Stein's masterful and still-useful

1970 synthesis of the colonial legacy, *The Colonial Heritage of Latin America: Essays on Economic Dependence in Perspective*, illustrates that the long colonial centuries witnessed the creation of formal and informal institutions with very long half-lives. The legacies of those institutions recur in the description of the four remaining keys below.

An important part of Latin America's colonial legacy are the scars of the considerable violence involved in shaking off the mantle of colonial rule in the early nineteenth century. This involved armed struggles pitting criollo armies against imperial forces. But it extended to decades of within-Latin America wars and domestic conflicts, as well as repeated foreign invasions and interventions, an aftermath of colonialism, as new political forces sought to take shape and control of the territory. Historian John Coatsworth (1978) provides telling statistics of the economic toll of the tumultuous nineteenth century, comparing the United States and Mexico. In 1800, prior to its independence, Mexico's national income was just over half that of the United States, and its income per capita—an indicator explained in greater detail in the following chapter—was just under a half of the US level. By the end of the century, Mexico's national income was a meager 2 percent of that of the US, and its income per capita stood at one-tenth its northern neighbor's. A big part of the divergence in standards of living between the United States and Mexico—and to varying degree, other parts of Latin America—stems from the ruinously costly struggles for independence and their aftermath over the course of the nineteenth century.

Latin America's independence from Spain and Portugal preceded the liberation of European colonies in Asia and Africa by more than a century. Nevertheless, even without a formal imperial metropole, Latin American countries suffered under the neocolonial power of the United Kingdom, first, and the United States subsequently. Corporations from the Anglo-American countries, backed by the implicit and explicit exercise of power by their governments, derived lopsided benefits from trade and investment relationships with Latin American countries.[2]

Key #2: Inequality. The colonial period was marked by a concentration of landed property—the principal form of wealth—in few (Spanish and Portuguese) hands, which gave rise to a concentration of wealth higher than in virtually all parts of the world and throughout the modern era. At the same time, the colonial powers deployed severely repressive forms of labor mobilization, some of them painted by Rivera in the corridors of Mexico's Palacio Nacional, ranging from the enslavement of Africans to systems of forced labor of Indigenous peoples, to varieties of serfdom of European immigrants in the nineteenth century.

Economic historian Rosemary Thorp (2012) of Oxford University argues that the historical sources of contemporary inequality in Latin America derive from differing political and economic responses to labor shortages in the region's nineteenth-century export-oriented growth era. Thorp's taxonomy includes three groups of countries. Argentina, Chile, and Uruguay attracted European immigrants. Brazil, Mexico, Cuba, as well as parts of Peru, also relied on immigrant labor, but under more brutal working conditions than in the first group of countries. A third group, including Andean countries and Guatemala, deepened abusive systems of labor coercion among sizeable Indigenous populations.

In all three groups of economies in Thorp's typology, the evolution of labor-market institutions served to widen income and wealth inequality, both by depressing the returns to labor, and by increasing the value of land, held in few hands. Moreover, governance processes, to the extent that they sought to affect levels of poverty and inequality, tended to *increase* both: Inequality was, in Thorp's terms, "functional" to economic growth.

In the twentieth century, there were significant movements to combat these inequalities, including land reform to redistribute agricultural land, on the one hand, and labor movements to improve workers' conditions. Even so, inequality of wealth and income remains extremely high, and the relationship between labor and capital is prone to conflict.

Key #3: Primary Products. During the colonial era, Latin America produced and exported raw materials: gold and silver from Meso-America and the Peruvian highlands, to begin with; subsequently, with the emergence of an Atlantic market economy, commodities like sisal (from the Yucatan Peninsula, Mexico); sugar (Cuba, Brazil, the Dominican Republic); other minerals; agricultural products like maize, sorghum, and wheat; and livestock. Latin American countries enjoyed a comparative advantage in the production and export of these goods, as explained by the classical economist David Ricardo (whose specter will return in the mid-twentieth century, in chapter 2). Finished products and manufactured goods were imported, first from the metropolitan Iberian economies, and later from the Northern European industrial economies, the United States, and now, China.

Key #4: Market, Reform, or Revolution? The first three keys are intimately linked to what the Steins called the colonial heritage of Latin America. For almost as long as Latin Americans have debated it, they have crafted and led the most varied social and political movements to overcome the undesirable components of that heritage, and to narrow the widening gap that separates Latin America from the industrializing North. In the twentieth century, in the economic domain, those debates pitted proponents of an activist state against champions of the free market.

On the strong-state side of the debate, Chilean development theorist Cristóbal Kay (1991) has argued that there are in fact two variants: reform and revolution.[3] He traces the origins of this division to the 1920s and 1930s in Peru, where two hugely influential intellectuals made their case for the country's future. Víctor Raúl Haya de la Torre, an accomplished politician and the founder of the Alianza Popular Revolucionaria Americana (APRA), one of the most important political parties in Latin America's history, argued for reformism, within the ambit of electoral politics. In the other corner, José Carlos Mariátegui, arguably Latin America's first major Marxist intellectual, saw no alternative to armed socialist revolution. Since then, Haya de la Torre–style reformism has predominated, often shrouded in lofty revolutionary rhetoric, especially among the early High Developmentalist and populist governments of Juscelino Kubitschek (Brazil, 1956–1961), Lázaro Cárdenas (Mexico, 1934–1940), and Juan Perón (Argentina, 1946–1955 and 1973–1974), squarely in favor of aggressive state intervention (if stopping short of revolutionary socialism). Only Fidel Castro in Cuba, whose government adopted a Soviet economic model, truly followed Mariátegui's revolutionary recipe in practice.

The reformists' true ideological adversaries were not the revolutionaries but the free-marketeers, who embodied an extreme liberalism, most markedly embraced by the Chilean military dictatorship of Augusto Pinochet. Pinochet's economic policy-making machinery was undergirded by the so-called "Chicago Boys," the general's American-trained advisors. Market liberalism was similarly embraced, with varying degrees of effectiveness, by military dictatorships elsewhere in South America. These debates unfolded against the backdrop of frequently bloody Cold War geopolitics, in which free-market positions were more closely aligned with the preferences of the US government. With the end of the military dictatorships, and of the Cold War, a new form of liberalism would be promoted in the 1980s and 1990s by international financial institutions under the moniker of the "Washington Consensus"—on which more in chapter 2.

The zigzagging historical sequence from High Developmentalist state intervention to market orthodoxy serves as a prelude for twenty-first century economic policy debates. Those debates pit the Workers Party governments of Lula and Dilma Rousseff in Brazil against their electoral opponents arrayed from the center to the far right, and Mexican president Andrés Manuel López Obrador against his opponents in the coalition of older political parties; to say nothing of the economic platforms of polemical twenty-first-century figures ranging from Hugo Chávez (Venezuela), Rafael Correa (Ecuador), Evo Morales (Bolivia) on the left, to Felipe Calderón (Mexico), Álvaro Uribe (Colombia) and Jair Bolsonaro (Brazil) on the right.

More market-oriented policy packages have tended to favor specialization in primary production—commodities (key #3)—often with slow growth of income and little economic diversification (the early twenty-first century would provide the impetus for more rapid growth). State intervention demonstrated the potential to transform the structure of the economy, as many of the reformist and revolutionary governments listed attempted to do, but often with mixed results or a downright crisis.

Key #5: Two, Three, Many Latin Americas. When we talk about Latin America as a single entity, we cover up vast differences in economic and social circumstances across time and space. Indeed, we do this even when we talk of a single country. Contemporary Brazil, for example, includes modern São Paulo, with a standard of living equivalent to that of European Union member Portugal; Brazil also includes the impoverished states of the Northeast, whose poverty indicators resemble those of some sub-Saharan African countries. There is great analytical value for students and social scientists in generalizing across Brazil, or across the Latin American continent. But we must nevertheless periodically remind ourselves of the immense heterogeneity of experiences in this vast region—within countries, between countries, and over time. Rather than one Latin America, there are, to paraphrase Che Guevara, two, three, many Latin Americas.[4]

What Is Latin America?

As a way of digging more deeply into the heterogeneity of the region that is key #5, let us ask the question: Just what does this vast region comprise? "Latin America" is a label imposed from without, just as the shared history of Iberian colonization was imposed from outside the geographic region to which it refers. Historians have averred that the label was born in France, the idea of nineteenth-century geographer Michel Chevalier.[5] Chevalier's argument was that the shared Latin cultural roots of Spanish America and France provided a connection *not* found between the north and south of the Americas. As such, Chevalier's idea provided support for French imperial ambitions toward the hemisphere, which reached its bloody climax with the installation by Napoleon III of Maximilian as Emperor of Mexico in 1864; he would be deposed by the liberal Benito Juárez in 1867.

It's curious that this French conception of the region did *not* include Brazil, despite its being Iberian and Catholic like its neighbors. Historian Leslie Bethell (2010), editor of the massive *Cambridge History of Latin America* project, argues that in the mindset of many nineteenth-century observers, Brazil—still a monarchy, overwhelmingly reliant on enslaved African-descended labor—differed too much from the former Spanish colonies to belong to the same geographic construct. (A historical irony: Centuries before France's Mexican intervention, the sieur de Villegagnon, under orders from the French monarch Henri II, set out in 1555 to establish a French colony in Brazil, in the bay of Rio de Janeiro. He failed.) Over time, Bethell continues, the Spanish-speaking countries of Central and South America did not come to consider Brazil as part of their region until the wider world did. That is, during the post–World War II era addressed in chapter 2 of this book, the geographic segmentation of the world employed by the United States and the United Nations in diplomacy and international cooperation redefined Latin America in the way it is used in this book, including Brazil.

For this book, then, which jurisdictions are in Latin America, and which are not? In general, in the pages that follow, I mean by Latin America the following nineteen countries: Argentina, Bolivia, Brazil, Chile, Colombia, Costa Rica, Cuba, the Dominican Republic, Ecuador, El Salvador, Guatemala, Honduras, Mexico, Nicaragua, Panama, Paraguay, Peru, Uruguay, Venezuela. These, minus Cuba, are sometimes referred to as the "LAC-18" in reports from international and multilateral organizations (Cuba having been left out for years during which its economic and social indicators were not systematically compiled with those of the other eighteen). I will call these the LAC-19 countries. Special attention will be paid from time to time to the seven largest economies among the LAC-19, the "LAC-7":

Argentina, Brazil, Chile, Colombia, Mexico, Peru, and Venezuela.[6] According to World Bank data, the LAC-7 countries account for approximately 88 percent of the economic output of the LAC-19, and about 82 percent of the population.

What's left off this list are, roughly speaking, Caribbean island economies. Not entirely: Cuba and the Dominican Republic, in light of their shared history with the mainland former Spanish colonies, are in. And the fates of Belize, French Guiana, Guyana, and Suriname, though attached to the mainland, are cast with the Caribbean. The geographic segmentation of the world's countries used by governments and international organizations tends to lump the Caribbean together with Latin America; the UN Economic Commission for Latin America—an agency that will be an important protagonist in chapter 2—added the Caribbean to its coverage, and to its name, in 1984. Most of the small island economies have different colonial histories, and some are still de facto or de jure colonies of distant metropoles (including Puerto Rico). The economic and social concerns of the small island economies are arguably different than most of the LAC-19, though there are countries like Haiti and Jamaica, which by dint of their size bear a stronger resemblance to the Latin American economies. I will note, inadequately, that the concerns of Caribbean development are too often left out of policy and analytical debates because of the basin's having been grouped with much larger, distinct economies. Except for Cuba and the Dominican Republic, they are not consistently part of the story that follows.[7]

But the Caribbean islands are not entirely absent, either. The World Bank's World Development Indicators (WDI), frequently used in the preparation of this study (and hundreds of others) includes an aggregate called Latin America and the Caribbean that is used in some of the figures that come later (e.g., figs. 2.1 and 2.3). This World Bank aggregate includes forty-two distinct economies.[8] Though the aggregate includes jurisdictions—mostly smaller Caribbean islands—not nominally part of this study, the quantitative effect of their inclusion in figures and tables is small.[9]

Today this group of countries has considerable quantitative heft, though it is dwarfed by several larger economies and groups of economies. Over the period 2011–2021, the combined annual gross domestic product of Latin America and the Caribbean averaged about $5.1 trillion. Compare this to a handful of other developing economies: $11.9 trillion for China, $2.8 trillion for the South Asian economies (including India), and $1.7 trillion for the sub-Saharan African economies. The Latin American economies thus sum to well under half the size of the Chinese economy, almost twice the size of the South Asian economies, and more than three times the size of sub-Saharan Africa. Over the same time frame, the average annual GDP of the United States was $18.5 trillion; the mostly rich member countries of the Organisation for Economic Co-operation and Development (OECD), meanwhile, which include the United States, Japan, and most of the European Union, totaled $48.1 trillion over the same span of years.[10]

Another way to compare the size of Latin America versus other countries and groups is in terms of population. In 2021, the population of Latin America and the Caribbean was 655 million, compared to 1.4 billion in China, 1.9 billion in South Asia, and 1.18 billion in sub-Saharan Africa. The population of the OECD countries totaled 1.34 billion, of which 332 million were in the United States.

Boundaries and definitions evolve with time. In his 2009 book, *El insomnio de Bolívar* (Bolívar's Insomnia, a contrast to the Spanish American liberator Simón Bolívar's "dream" of unification of the newly independent countries), Mexican novelist Jorge Volpi wonders whether Mexico—given its intense economic interlocking with the United States—is properly a part of Latin America at all anymore, suspecting that it belongs in North America. Volpi further observes that wide swaths of the United States and Spain are being connected or reconnected with Latin America by the millions of Southern migrants in those Northern climes. In the United States, of course, many Latin Americans have been there since before the United States itself. As the wildly popular San José, California-based conjunto Los Tigres del Norte (2001) sing in their song "Somos más americanos": "Yo no crucé la frontera—la frontera me cruzó" (I didn't cross the border—the border crossed me).[11] Volpi suggests that the northern border of Latin America—pushed south to the Rio Grande/Río Bravo river at the close of the Mexican-American War in 1848, crossing over the Tigres' narrator in the process—is now moving back northward.

Perhaps this is a sixth key to understanding the Latin American economy—that its shape, size, and character is in constant mutation. These changes sometimes happen slowly. And the objective of this book is to look more closely at some of the changes that took place during the twenty-first century. What long-horizon processes are present in the present? What historical trends have disappeared? Which, thought dead, have been rejuvenated? And what new characteristics have emerged?

CHAPTER TWO

High Developmentalism and Its Aftermath (1949–1999)

LOOKING AT LATIN AMERICA'S economy in the twenty-first century through the lens of economic history requires us to consider the lasting impact of events, processes, institutions, and structures from the past. Chapter 1 reviewed five "keys"—some of those phenomena that have endured and evolved over the course of many centuries. In this chapter and those that follow, we will assess economic performance, first in the latter half of the twentieth century, and then in greater detail in the current century.

More specifically, in this chapter, we will

1. review the concepts of *growth* and *development*;
2. introduce *High Developmentalism*, the set of public policies and growth strategies promoted by the United Nations Economic Commission for Latin America (known hereafter by its Spanish-language initials CEPAL), in theory and in practice;
3. review the *Washington Consensus*, an alternative development strategy that rose to prominence in response to the long *Lost Decade* ushered in by the Latin American debt crisis of the 1980s;
4. assess comparative economic growth rates during the High Developmentalist and Lost Decade years.

Growth, Development, and Freedom

The late French economist Daniel Cohen's posthumously published *Une brève histoire de l'économie* begins with the bold assertion that "Economic growth is the religion of the modern world."[1] Perhaps that quasi-religious regard has shrouded the concept unnecessarily in mysticism. We will frequently refer to growth as a yardstick for economic performance in the first half of this book, so it will be worthwhile to demystify it. Economic growth is a narrow and precise concept, but with enormous explanatory power. Growth refers to year-to-year expansion or contraction of the size of the economy: national output.[2] National output, in turn, is the monetary value of the sum of all production of final goods and services in an economy within a year. National output, roughly speaking, is equivalent to national income: the sum of income earned by all households in the economy during the year. National income is most frequently measured by gross national income (GNI), national output by gross domestic product (GDP), and these terms are often used interchangeably, including in this book, which can be a little confusing. The principal insight here is that the monetary value of everything produced must be matched by payments to people to produce them (including workers and owners of the means of production). The "size of the economy," then, can be measured through output data or through income data and should always arrive at (roughly) the same magnitude.

Growth can then be measured as the increase or decrease in the value of GNI or GDP. But a couple further adjustments need to be made. The first is to correct for the effects of inflation. It could be that GDP in Paraguay, say, as defined above, is 3 percent higher in 2023 than in 2022. But it may be that the economy was subject to sharp generalized price increases—inflation—in 2023, as was in fact the case in many countries in 2023. If so, the value of GDP may rise not because more was produced, but because the price of everything went up. *Nominal* GDP is said to increase, but *real* GDP is adjusted (downward) to account for the effects of inflation. If the Paraguayan rate of inflation was 2 percent, then the rate of growth of real GDP was 1 percent (or 3 percent minus 2 percent, the difference between nominal GDP growth and inflation).

A second adjustment to national income has to do with population growth. To do this, we consider growth of *per capita income* (or average income). To return to our running Paraguayan example, if real GDP rises by 1 percent, but

Paraguayan population increases by 1 percent, then the rate of growth of per capita income is zero. By definition, average income growth is equal to the rate of real GDP growth minus the rate of population growth. Alternatively, you can take the measure of aggregate Paraguayan GDP in 2022 and 2023 and divide those numbers by Paraguay's population at midyear in each year. That provides average income in 2022 and 2023 and you can calculate the rate of growth (which in principle could be positive, zero, or negative) between the two points in time.[3]

If aggregate GDP grows more slowly than population growth, then the average command over resources in the economy has in fact shrunk. Looked at another way, growth of income per capita indicates that on average there has been an increase in command over resources, as measured by GDP or national income. For that reason, growth of (real) per capita income is frequently the growth measure of preference among economists.

We will make ample use of growth of average income in the chapters that follow. We will use it to distinguish different phases of recent economic history in Latin America and the Caribbean, and to contrast the experiences of different countries within Latin America and beyond (e.g., China or the rich countries that are members of the Organisation for Economic Co-operation & Development, or OECD).

Though per capita growth rates may vary from year to year and country to country, over the very long term, variation is far more muted—and growth rates might be lower than you would guess. Piketty (2013, graphique 2.4) synthesizes an enormous amount of historical research in this regard. There is an enormous amount of imprecision about data from hundreds, or thousands, of years ago, so take these broad trends with an appropriately large grain of salt. Before 1700, worldwide, global GDP growth did not exceed population growth, so the growth of average income was zero. Beginning in the eighteenth century, average income grew at a rate barely above zero. In the nineteenth and the first half of the twentieth centuries, average income worldwide grew just under 1 percent annually. In the second half of the twentieth and the early twenty-first century, average income worldwide grew at about 2 percent annually. Projections formulated by the United Nations suggest that global average income growth might approach 2.5 percent through the middle of this century and subside to about 1.5 percent thereafter.

A major driver of these global growth patterns is the diffusion of the technological innovations of the Industrial Revolution. Industrialization raised growth of average income over a relatively small part of the Earth during the nineteenth century, and therefore raised global average income only modestly. The spread of industrial growth across the North Atlantic economy, and then, in waves, across the so-called developing world, raised growth rates in more countries of the world, and with them, the global rate of average income growth. At the same time, a typical industrialization process raises the growth rate of average income precipitously at first, only to see it decline thereafter (though not to the preindustrial zero rate). As more of the world enters into industrial maturity, the global average growth rate declines as well. (Needless to say, such broad generalizations mask many important variations; and predictions about the future should be interpreted with caution.)

Such long-term patterns provide a useful context for the Latin American story told in this book. In the middle of the twentieth century, for example, Latin America outperformed the global growth average; in the latter part of the century, the region underperformed relative to the rest of the world. In the first decade of the century, some parts of Latin America again outperformed global growth rates of average income while dipping below global rates in the second decade.

Almost as soon as governments, media, and civil society began to pay attention to economic growth—particularly in the wake of the Great Depression of the 1930s—observers have criticized the sufficiency of growth of average income as a measure of economic performance. To be fair, economics textbooks generally do not argue that growth is synonymous with expansion of well-being, and indeed explicitly say as much. But then again, many textbooks will equate GDP with "pie" in explanatory examples—as in, "a larger pie means there can be bigger slices for everyone in the economy." And who doesn't like pie? This kind of rhetorical sleight of hand helps promote the incorrect notion that GDP is equivalent to social well-being. From this perspective, it is a short step to adopting the shorthand notion that GDP is best thought of as something good.[4] Cohen's labelling of growth as a religion speaks to this confusion between growth as an expansion of command over resources that might allow societies to pursue the things they value—freedom, say, or other measures of well-being—and growth as something that should simply be pursued for its own sake. In recent decades, a host of qualifiers have been added to growth to denote the growth objectives of a society: "growth with equity," "inclusive growth," and "green growth."

Alongside such qualifications and critiques of growth as a societal objective, the concept of *development* arose, among policy makers, economists, and in society at large. Unlike the relatively precisely defined concept of growth, development has enjoyed a proliferation of definitions, not all of them mutually compatible. What most definitions of development share is that they are multidimensional: They include but are not limited to growth of average income. And unlike average income growth, development is meant to be a measure—a multidimensional measure—of increases in societal well-being. I would argue that most definitions of development add to growth an explicit reduction of poverty and income inequality, on the one hand, and transformation of the structure of the economy, on the other.

Critiques of a narrow growth focus are relevant to the Latin American experience. Among these is the problem that "average income" is an *average*: If average income rises, we cannot necessarily infer that everyone's command over resources has increased. This is particularly true in highly unequal economies, and as we shall see, Latin America has been, for at least a couple centuries, the most unequal region of the world economy. As such, we will devote considerable attention here to the roots and historical evolution of income inequality in Latin America. Chapter 9 will analyze the reasons behind the surprising fall in Latin American inequality during the period under study—as well as the work still to be done.

A second critique of "average income" as a measure of development is that it measures only *income* (or *output*). Many of the incomes earned in an economy constitute recompense for goods and services that, arguably, do not enhance well-being. These include the production and sale of lethal weapons, for example. Growth also ignores environmental degradation as a by-product of other production processes. National income, or GDP, is a mishmash of good and bad things, and the expansion of supply of the aggregate is not all good.

At the same time, there are many things to which people devote time and other resources to "supply" to others that are not counted, or only partially counted, in national income, including many forms of care and mutual support. These and other aspects of the good life are central to emerging conceptions rooted in Andean Indigenous notions of *sumak kawsay* (Quechua) and *suma qamaña* (Aymara), which are in turn used as the basis of critiques of economic growth and colonial patterns of economic development.

The Nobel Prize-winning economist Amartya Sen, in his 1999 book *Development As Freedom*, offers a philosophical framework for development that goes beyond the "growth-plus-this or that" style of thinking. Sen argues compellingly that the goal of development should be understood as a broadening of the *freedoms* enjoyed by people in society. Sen's conception of freedom, furthermore, departs from libertarian uses of "freedom" common in economics, which are associated with an earlier Nobel economics laureate, Milton Friedman (1962): "free markets," "free trade," "free enterprise," "freedom of choice." The narrow libertarian freedoms championed by Friedman are recognized by Sen as part of the package of freedoms that people value; the freedom to exchange goods and services in markets, to participate in markets for labor or credit, are good things. But they are a small slice of a larger set of freedoms that matter to people and societies. Sen's notion of freedom is more akin to that developed by Martin Luther King Jr. (a Nobel Peace Prize winner), in his last book, *Where Do We Go From Here?* (1967), in which he writes, "in speaking of freedom I am not referring to freedom of a thing called *the will*."[5] Many of the freedoms that development must pursue in Sen's view (and King's) involve collective goals like health care, public education, civil liberties, and political rights. And clearly, stark income inequality abridges the freedoms of segments of society, just as an economy dependent upon the extraction of natural resources limits freedoms.

The term "development," whether one follows Sen's conception or not, is necessarily multidimensional by design and contested in practice; it is not defined with the same precision as economic growth. Debates surrounding growth versus development have moved from a view that growth is necessary but not sufficient for development, to a view that growth, especially in light of its environmental consequences, might in fact be *destructive to* development, if the latter is taken to mean enhanced well-being or freedoms. A primarily European discourse has explored the notion of *de-growth* as a social objective.

Moreover, development has by now acquired a host of qualifiers and adjectives, just as growth did: International organizations and governments aspire to "sustainable development," "human development," and other variations that suggest that development, like growth, has not been equal to the task of enhanced freedom and well-being. A school of Latin American critics write about "maldevelopment" and "post-development" (Ojeda Medina and Villarreal Villamar, 2020).

High Developmentalism in Theory and Practice

High Developmentalism is both a diagnosis of the structure of the global economy as well as a set of development strategies that flow from that diagnosis. High Developmentalism in practice led to rapid growth and structural transformation of many Latin American economies. But it also set up economic and political tensions that contributed to dire economic performance in the last two decades of the last century. In addition to the internal causes of the crisis of the 1980s and 1990s there were external shocks, emanating especially from global capital markets, that hurt the region's economic prospects, and in so doing, hurt the livelihoods and well-being of millions in the region.

The ideas behind High Developmentalism, the growth they engendered when operationalized as public policy, as well as the trauma of the debt crisis of the 1980s and the painful adjustments of the 1990s, are all critical components of Latin America's economic memory in the twenty-first century—memories that condition the decisions made by policy makers, voters, firms, and households in the history we will study in the remainder of this book.

In 1949, Raúl Prebisch, a free-trade economist and former director general of Argentina's Central Bank, authored a report for the newly created United Nations Economic Commission for Latin America. The Commission would become widely known in the region for its initials in Spanish, CEPAL. Alongside CEPAL, the UN founded economic commissions for other regions of the developing world and for the war-torn European continent, to encourage fresh development strategies for the postwar global economy. The creation of these new institutions in the global governance architecture was paralleled by the advent of a new area of academic study known as development economics. CEPAL would play an important role in Latin America's international relations, and, to a lesser degree, in the scholarly realm of economics. (At times I will also use the Spanish adjective *cepalino* to label some of the economists and the ideas that arose from this school of thought.)

Entitled *El desarrollo económico de la América Latina y algunos de sus principales problemas* (The Economic Development of Latin America and Some of Its

Principal Problems), Prebisch's 1949 CEPAL report sketched an explanation for Latin America's relative economic backwardness based on its role in the global economy. Using the analytical methods of the then mainstream economics, Prebisch argued that adherence to liberal ("free") trade with the rich countries of the North would only widen the gap in income and development between Latin America and its trading partners. The key innovation of Prebisch's and CEPAL's thinking from the very beginning is that the global economy has a structure, with a Center and a Periphery. National economies' prospects, furthermore, are conditioned by whether they are central (like the United States or the United Kingdom) or peripheral (like the postcolonial economies of Africa, Asia, and Latin America).

The economies, and particularly the export baskets, of most Latin American countries were dominated by raw materials production (key #3 from chapter 1). To simplify Prebisch's argument, consider two economies, "Periphery" and "Center," and two goods: food and automobiles.[6] The poorer Periphery produces food and imports automobiles from the rich Center. The richer Center, meanwhile, produces automobiles and imports food from the Periphery. Each economy has a comparative advantage in the good it produces. As the classical economist David Ricardo pointed out in *On the Principles of Political Economy and Taxation* (1817), a country benefits from specializing in the production of the good in which it has a comparative advantage, exporting its excess production to import other goods. Ricardo's eye-opening example considered the exchange of wines for textiles between England and Portugal, which would be in the interest of consumers in both countries, even if Portugal (whence the English Ricardo's ancestors) could produce *both* commodities more efficiently than England. Ricardo's insight provides the intellectual underpinning for the flourishing of trade liberalization of the North Atlantic economy in the nineteenth century. Prebisch argued that while Ricardo's logic is sound in a static sense, over time, such specialization might not be the best strategy for all countries—especially for peripheral economies like Latin America's.

Say that incomes are rising among consumers in both the Center and Periphery; consumers' demand for imports from the partner country rises with their incomes. But there is a wrinkle introduced by something called Engel's law. Ernst Engel, a nineteenth-century statistician, found from survey research in Germany that richer households devote a lower share of their income to food purchases than relatively poorer households do; his eponymous law proposes that, as a household's income rises, it will devote a declining *share* of its income to food, even if it spends more on food. A corollary is that as these households' incomes rise, they will devote a larger share of their income to manufactured goods (cars, in our simple illustration). Over time, in the dynamic conception critical to Prebisch's argument, the global demand for food rises more slowly than that of automobiles. A critical consequence of this asymmetry in the growth path of demand for the two goods in question is that the *price* of food will fall relative to the price of automobiles (even if both prices are rising over time).

For the Peripheral economy, this process means that the price of the good it imports (automobiles) is rising relative to the price of the good it exports (food). In the parlance of international trade, the Peripheral economy faces *declining terms of trade*. A country's terms of trade denote the ratio of its export prices to import prices. In order to import a constant volume of automobiles (to say nothing of rising quantities), the Periphery must export ever larger quantities of food every year. Under the circumstances, the average incomes in the two trading partners will diverge: The gap between higher Center and lower Periphery incomes will widen.

Faced with such a prospect, Prebisch and the CEPAL recommended that economies like the Periphery would do well to foster the development of domestic automobile production. The problem is that the Center produces automobiles relatively more efficiently than the Periphery; a Peripheral automobile start-up would have to price its cars at a level that could not compete with the imported Central cars. Government intervention in the Periphery, to restrict Central car imports and allow the price of cars in the Periphery to rise temporarily, might bring about what the free play of supply and demand would not: namely, the emergence of domestic car production in the Periphery.

Prebisch's declining-terms-of-trade argument fed into a broader current of what might be called Commodity Pessimism. Not only would commodity-exporting countries see their average income grow more slowly than that of manufactures-exporters; other ills might befall the former set of countries. The volatility of commodity prices acted as an ever-present external threat beyond the control of Peripheral economies: High world prices for copper or oil, for example, might ensure frothy government revenues, ebullient public spending, and better pay for working people; a sudden crash, however, and all these positive indicators are reversed—and cash-strapped governments now find themselves unable to lend aid to impoverished households. Being subjected to the vicissitudes of commodity price swings is one of the key dimensions of "dependency" that High Developmentalists would deplore.

Commodity Pessimism takes other forms: There is, for example, the well-known case of "Dutch Disease," so named in reference to the consequences of the natural gas boom in the Netherlands in the late 1970s. The phenomenon had already been observed by Caribbean economist W. Arthur Lewis (whose insight as a development theorist we will get to know better in chapter 9) in the Jamaican bauxite industry in the 1950s (Lewis 1964). The Dutch Disease refers to the unfortunate side effects of even successful commodity exports. In Lewis's Jamaican case, the bauxite industry was able to pay wages substantially above the national average, putting upward pressure on Jamaican wages generally. As a result, labor costs for non-bauxite producers were increased, reducing their competitiveness in external markets (if they were exporters), and reducing their demand for workers whether or not they exported. In the case of the Netherlands, the natural-gas boom drove up demand for the Dutch guilder (to purchase natural gas, and for foreign firms to invest in the sector); this led to an appreciation of the guilder, which reduced the competitiveness of Dutch non-gas exports.

Commodity Pessimism, finally, is evinced in the celebrated "Natural Resource Curse" hypothesis, which highlights the ironic paradox that countries endowed with valuable commodities or other natural resources appear to have less successful, or even disastrous, experiences with economic growth. Examples include the violence surrounding "blood diamonds" mined amidst civil war in a number of sub-Saharan African countries, as well as the lopsided economic progress of many oil-exporting countries. We will revisit the Natural Resource Curse in chapter 8, where we will argue that the macroeconomic evidence is weak, though there are important qualitative exceptions across and within countries.

It followed, the CEPAL insisted, that economic policy makers in Latin America ought to erect barriers to imports as a means of promoting domestic manufacturing, thereby transforming the structure of Latin American economies and the role they played in the global economic system. So-called import-substituting industrialization (ISI) was a wildly popular policy package, adopted far beyond (and sometimes with more successful results than in) Latin American countries.[7]

ISI required a non-liberal conception of the state (where "liberal" is understood in its nineteenth-century sense): a strong state, intervening in the functioning of the free market, changing prices, and creating markets. States raised import tariffs to protect domestic manufacturers; they directed subsidized credit to those firms; they created state-owned enterprises in strategic industries, including energy and commodities; and they created national development banks—domestic World Banks, if you will—to drive investment in infrastructure and other areas complementary to private investment. Perhaps no country embraced these principles more assiduously than Brazil, in the guise of *desenvolvimentismo*—"developmentalism," of which pioneer CEPAL economist Celso Furtado was a leading theorist and practitioner.

CEPAL's contributions to economic thought were not limited to the declining terms of trade and ISI, though these are the commission's signature findings. A host of other leading thinkers worked alongside Prebisch and led the CEPAL school of thought even after Prebisch left to be the first Secretary-General of the United Nations Conference on Trade and Development (UNCTAD) in 1964; among the leading lights in and around CEPAL were Fernando Fajnzylber, Celso Furtado, Juan Noyola, Aníbal Pinto, Osvaldo Sunkel, and Maria da Conceição Tavares.

Moreover, while CEPAL was critically influential to policy making in Latin America and beyond, a host of authors, many but not all of whom overlapped with CEPAL, developed related analyses of the region's economic reality (these included "structuralist" theories of inflation). Most visible and influential was a decidedly more radical "dependency theory." Dependency theory owed to CEPAL the critical distinction between Center and Periphery, the key element of the global economic structure that constrained development possibilities in the peripheral Latin American economies; the theory added a more explicit Marxian analysis to the CEPAL school's approach. The most celebrated exponents of dependency theory were Fernando Henrique Cardoso, a radical Brazilian sociologist, who, like others in this drama, will appear in a vastly different guise later in the story, and his Chilean coauthor, sociologist Enzo Faletto (dependency theory would attract adherents and theorists from the world outside Latin America, including Samir Amin, Arghiri Emmanuel and Andre Gunder Frank[8]). I refer to the heterogeneous mix of approaches and theory of the early CEPAL, its surrounding penumbra of collaborators, and dependency theorists as "High Developmentalism."

In the early 1960s, differences between the views of the more institutionalist *cepalinos* and the radical *dependentistas* loomed much larger than the common elements, as Margarita Fajardo (2022) recounts in her history of CEPAL, and the two camps appeared more like warring ideological parties than streams of a single body of thought. From the perspective of this century, however, I argue that the commonalities of CEPAL and dependency-theory analyses matter more.[9]

Together with the aggressive development strategies of the newly independent Indian state (like the Latin American countries, historically skeptical of the benefits of free trade with the rich North), the CEPAL way of thinking contributed significantly to the birth of contemporary economic-development policy. Development economics was the application of methods of economic analysis to the problems of poorer countries, but CEPAL offered something more than merely a new domain of application, however vast: The Latin Americans arrived at bold policy prescriptions that upended conventional wisdom.

The African American poet and feminist theorist Audre Lorde famously stated that the "master's house cannot be dismantled with the master's tools."[10] Prebisch and the CEPAL economists in his wake—to borrow and simultaneously quibble with Lorde's well-known phraseology—arguably used the master's tools to dismantle the master's house. The tools: a classical economics education, and experience at a central bank—the epitome of conservative economic policy prudence and probity.[11] The house: a world economic structure that prevented the progress and development of the South. Prebisch would later author a book entitled *Peripheral Capitalism* (1981); a key contribution of this Argentinian is that he helped move the center of creative economic thinking from the global Center to the erstwhile Periphery. Northern realms of privilege in knowledge creation were thereby invaded from the South. More to the point, economic tools and methods required contextualization if they were to be imported from the rich Northern countries to the South.

Mexican philosophy professor Gerardo de la Fuente Lora (1994, 59) captured the kernel of the CEPAL's contribution, as well as the attendant excitement for thinkers in the South: "An extraordinary contribution, this: an economy with structure and, from it and through it, a theory of economic policy; that is, not merely a construction of economic variables, but action that implied a correspondence with something real: the structure of the economy discovered at long last."

The examples of Prebisch and his High Developmentalist confrères would inspire would-be development theorists across the global South. The celebrated Bombay-born, Columbia University international economist Jagdish Bhagwati wrote the following in an appreciation of Prebisch in 1984:

> For my generation of economists in the developing countries, preeminence of Raúl Prebisch in a field of obvious importance was a major source of inspiration. To see that one's own can be innovative, ingenious, and important is always, and was then especially, a matter of considerable psychological significance. For, among the colonial attitudes which afflicted our societies in those days was the belief that fundamental thinking required that one belong to the center, not the periphery, in Raúl Prebisch's splendid terminology. Prebisch and Lewis, among a few key figures, helped to shatter that myth decisively ... in the 1950s development economists traveled in numbers to the periphery to "advise the natives"; now the same flow is substantially to collaborate with them in dispensing the research funds of the center on the problems of the periphery!

Latin American Economic Performance During and After High Developmentalism

Development economics, the subdiscipline of economics that sought to apply its tools and methods to the problems of the vast majority of humankind, was not, however, founded by the CEPAL or the practitioners of High Developmentalism. Like every other subfield of economics, development economics arose almost exclusively in the universities of North America and Europe, with close ties to, and fundamental influence upon, a new set of global institutions that included the International Monetary Fund, the International Bank for Reconstruction and Development (IBRD, more commonly known as the World Bank), and the bilateral aid agencies of the rich countries. The more orthodox brand of development economics practiced at Harvard and Oxford, and in the United States Agency for International Development (USAID) or the UK Department for International Development (DFID), often found fault with High Developmentalism, but the latter indelibly marked the character of the former nonetheless.

The 1960s and 1970s were, roughly speaking, the heyday of ISI, though it is of

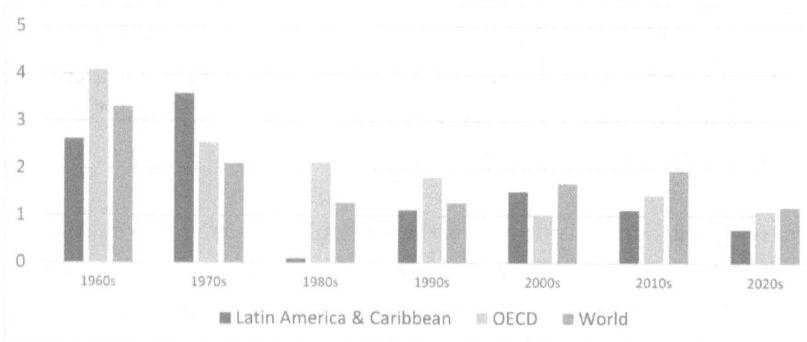

Figure 2.1. Growth averages by decade, Latin America, OECD, world, 1960s–2020s. Decadal averages of annual percentage growth rate of GDP per capita based on constant local currency. Series ends in 2022. *Source:* WDI database, World Bank.

course complicated to attribute the economic performance of the region to the impact of High Developmentalist policies alone. In the 1960s, the economies of Latin America and the Caribbean as a region grew, on average, at a rate of 2.6 percent per year, lower than the world growth rate of 3.3 percent during the same decade, and lower than the 4.1 percent growth rate of the high-income OECD area (refer back to the introduction for a primer on economic growth measurement). During the 1970s, in contrast, Latin America's 3.6 percent growth outpaced both the world and OECD rates (fig. 2.1). The region's growth in the 1960s and 1970s, moreover, exceeded any of its subsequent decadal averages, including the boom years of the first decade of the current millennium.

A few observations about these long-term growth numbers are in order. First, the decadal segmentation of data in fig. 2.1 is arguably arbitrary and masks important episodes of acceleration or contraction of growth that are shorter than a decade, or that straddle two decades. For example, Latin America and the Caribbean's average annual per capita growth rate during the decade from 2000–2009 was 1.5 percent, but if we restrict attention to the export boom years 2003–2008, the average rises to 3.2 percent annually.

Second, economists likely expected Latin America's growth to outpace that of the OECD. Most theories of economic growth—at least, first-wave growth models like Nobel laureate Robert Solow's celebrated theory (Solow 1956, 1957)—predict that poorer economies will grow more quickly than richer ones.

The principal rationale is that the former are comparatively "capital-poor," which means that the rate of return to capital is higher in poorer economies than in rich ones. *Capital* in this case refers to the economic concept by that name: machines, buildings, and inventories, which are generally used together with labor to produce other goods. Changes in the level of the capital stock, meanwhile, are referred to as *investment*. Think of the rate of return to capital as what the owner of a machine could earn by renting that machine to a business.

Given the different rates of return to capital in the Center and Periphery, our machine owner could earn more renting her machine to business owners in the Periphery than in the Center. As such, owners of machines (or, again, other forms of capital, including financial assets) will disproportionately move capital to the poorer countries. Given that economic growth is almost synonymous with investment, the flow of capital from rich to poor countries will accelerate growth in the latter relative to the former. Therefore, many economists would have an a priori expectation that Latin American growth should generally exceed that of the richer OECD economies, something in fact observed only in the 1970s and the 2000s. This phenomenon is sometimes referred to as "convergence," namely, that average income levels in poorer economies will, by growing more quickly, converge over time toward average income levels observed in richer economies.

There is a problem with this well-founded logic: Empirically speaking, capital does *not* flow from rich to poor countries, at least not as readily as basic economic logic would predict. Researchers suggest that other factors in the Periphery—that is, average levels of education among workers—depress the rate of return to capital there, weakening the incentive for capital to flow from rich to poor countries (Lucas 1990; Alfaro, Kalemli-Ozcan and Volosovych 2008). The point being made here is that a development economist in the 1970s looking at a chart like fig. 2.1 would ask why growth rates in Latin America didn't exceed those in the OECD in *every* decade.

Third and finally, the Latin American regional average, needless to say, masks a range of country-level growth performance. Among the seven largest Latin American economies, Mexico and, especially, Brazil were the growth all-stars of the ISI years between 1960 and 1980 (fig. 2.2). Brazil's average annual per capita growth rate was a heady 6.2 percent in the 1970s; Mexico's healthy 3.2 percent growth seems small only by comparison. Observers at the time

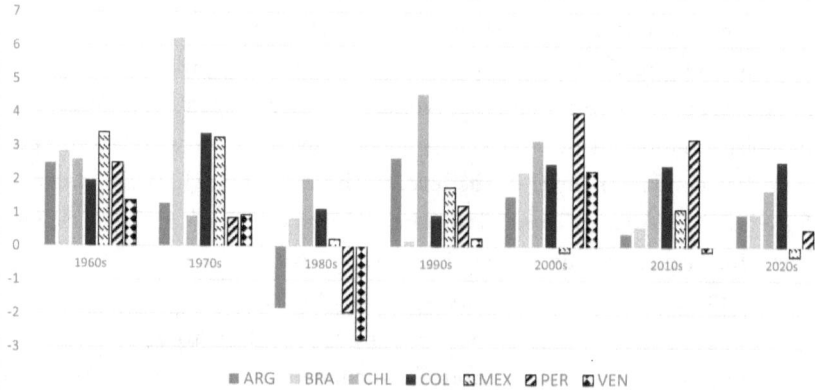

Figure 2.2. Growth averages by decade, LAC-7 countries, 1960s–2020s. See the information in the note to fig. 2.1 for the measure of average income used. Series ends in 2022; Venezuelan data end in 2014. *Source*: WDI database, World Bank.

referred to both countries' growth rates as "miracles." Brazil and Mexico were particularly well suited to the ISI strategy, given that they had (and have) the largest domestic markets in Latin America to purchase the goods produced by new manufacturing industries. Smaller countries would face a limit on the size of internal demand for consumer products whose production was subject to scale economies. Once again, comparative figures are provided for the twenty-first century, as a prelude for the discussion in the remainder of this book.

Taken together, the economic growth data illustrated in figs. 2.1 and 2.2 suggest a periodization of Latin American economic performance in the second half of the last century:

1. Accelerated growth during the High Developmentalist phase (1960s to 1982);
2. Volatility, decline, and stagnation during the debt crisis of the 1980s;
3. Moderate (at best) growth during the Washington Consensus years of the 1990s.

Growth would resume—interrupted by the global financial crisis of 2008–2009 and the economic impact of Covid-19 in 2020—in the new millennium, as we will see in the remainder of the book. For now, I emphasize the long shadow cast by the faster growth, never subsequently recaptured, of the High Developmentalist era in Latin America.

The Debt Crisis of the 1980s

High Developmentalism, and ISI in particular, foundered on the shoals of the Latin America debt crisis, unleashed by Mexico's cessation of debt service payments in August 1982. The prelude to the crisis prominently featured fatal flaws in the implementation of the policy package, which led Latin American governments to seek ever greater volumes of foreign borrowing. This, unfortunately, coincided with a glut of global credit, aggressively marketed by (primarily) US banks.

ISI was executed by means of a variety of mechanisms, some of which were detailed in our discussion of the 1949 CEPAL report. Chief among these was tariff protection for industrial sectors that would produce substitutes for previously imported goods. Another was the establishment and promotion of state-owned enterprises, particularly in infrastructure and energy. Both state-owned and privately owned industries were supported by subsidized credit and tax exemptions. With the exception of the tariffs themselves, what unites all these measures is that they require financial resources: investment to build and maintain state-owned railroads, for example, fiscal resources to bridge the gap between loans expensively obtained and re-lent more cheaply to national industrial firms, or to cover lost revenues from tax breaks. These were in principle economically sound uses of these resources. Such investments would pay off if they sped the transition from commodity-producing to manufacturing-led economies, with higher capacity to generate tax revenues for the state. Even more so if the "infant industries" born during ISI came of age and became internationally competitive, no longer requiring tariffs and subsidies to exist. Indeed, Nobel economist Kenneth Arrow argued that under certain conditions, producers would "learn by doing," reducing the unit cost of production over time (Arrow 1962).

Regardless of the long-term wisdom of investing in and spending on ISI, in the short to medium term, Latin American governments required resources that exceeded tax revenues. The alternative was issuing public debt. And during the era of High Developmentalism (and to a large extent, even today), Latin American countries did not enjoy the same density of long-term domestic lenders that rich countries do. Consequently, governments in the region turned to international capital markets.

At the same time, the ISI focus on domestic markets weakened export performance (through a variety of channels, including the effects of the policy package on exchange rates). Thus, countries ran persistent trade deficits. From a balance of payments perspective, current account deficits (dominated by trade deficits) would be offset by capital account surpluses; that is, inward financial flows (the concept of the balance of payments is introduced and explained at greater length in chapter 4).

As it happened, international capital markets were flush with resources, driven by the accumulation of dollar assets created by the two oil price increases of the 1970s; petroleum exporters channeled their export earnings into the international banking system. US banks in particular were eager to lend—on reasonably aggressive terms—to sovereign borrowers like Latin American governments with apparently good growth prospects.

When international interest rates spiked in the late 1970s, however, Latin American governments found themselves holding dollar-denominated debt with ballooning debt service obligations. Mexico's suspension of payments on its debt was followed in turn by several more governments in the region (and beyond). A series of interim measures orchestrated by the US Treasury and the IMF followed in order to contain the financial crisis that followed. These financial measures provided short-term financing for Latin American governments (more indebtedness, paradoxically) in exchange for painful economic austerity measures that the international organizations supposed would make the recipient countries better able to service their debt. The economic contractions that ensued were severe. During the whole of the 1980s, Latin America's per capita GDP was essentially stagnant, growing at a near-zero average rate of 0.02 percent per year (fig. 2.1). Both Argentina and Peru contracted annually at an average rate of −1.9 percent (fig. 2.2). In short order, Latin America went, in economist Albert Fishlow's baleful phrase, from growth-led debt to debt-led growth, to debt-led debt.

The Washington Consensus of the 1990s

A new policy package emerged in Latin America, the so-called Washington Consensus, so named for its endorsement by the World Bank, the IMF, and the US Treasury, three institutions whose headquarters are within a few blocks of each other in Washington, DC, and whose support was sought to overcome the debt crisis of the 1980s (the moniker "Washington Consensus" was coined in a descriptive, rather than prescriptive, overview of the emerging policy package by economist John Williamson in 1990; even as a description, the phrase missed its mark, as there was little consensus about these policies among governments and social forces in developing economies). The canonical list of the Washington Consensus comprises ten components, summarized in table 2.1.

In global policy and political debates from the 1990s forward, the terms "neoliberal" and "neoliberalism" were almost always applied with opprobrium. The terms were not subject to a universally agreed-upon definition, and they were generally only used pejoratively. The same cannot be said of "Washington Consensus": In Latin America as elsewhere, many observers criticized the latter policy package, but many others, including influential economists at those Washington, DC-based institutions just mentioned, enthusiastically promoted and recommended the Consensus measures. The irony is that for the purposes of this economic history, an adherence to the ten-point Consensus list in table 2.1 is a good working definition of neoliberalism. And yet one will be hard-pressed to find enthusiastic self-described neoliberals in the debates of this period.[12]

TABLE 2.1. Elements of the Washington Consensus

1. Fiscal discipline
2. Redirect public expenditure priorities toward health, education, and infrastructure
3. Tax reform
4. Unified/competitive exchange rates
5. Secure property rights
6. Deregulation
7. Trade liberalization
8. Privatization
9. Eliminate barriers to foreign direct investment
10. Financial liberalization

Source: Rodrik (1996), following Williamson (1994).

Economist Dani Rodrik (1996) analyzes the ten components of the Washington Consensus and argues that there are at least two reform packages—related, but with distinct focus areas—mixed into the list. The first of these is *stabilization* (items 1, 3, 4), the package most closely associated with the advice of the International Monetary Fund. Stabilization rests upon conservative macroeconomic management, including fiscal, monetary, and exchange rate policies. The second package is *structural adjustment* (items 5–10), most closely associated with the World Bank. Structural adjustment calls for the retreat of the state from, or liberalization of, markets and sectors in which Latin American governments had exercised a more interventionist role, notably, finance, labor markets, international trade, and capital flows. Liberalization was accompanied in the Consensus by privatization of state-owned enterprises.

Rodrik points out that the two sets of policy packages do not necessarily constitute a monolithic bloc, and that successful development experiences do not rely on implementing both types of policies. Indeed, Rodrik argues that the most successful cases on the minds of international policy makers in the 1990s—South Korea and Taiwan—mostly applied the stabilization recipe, but only partially at best the structural adjustment recommendations. Latin American countries, in contrast, more studiously applied the latter, to mixed results.

At the time, MIT economist Lance Taylor (1997), meanwhile, was critical of the effectiveness of both sets of policies and went so far as to argue that the IMF and World Bank recommendations are in fact inconsistent and contradictory. A simple example of the kind of policy incoherence Rodrik was talking about: The IMF might recommend increasing tax rates (to reduce the budget deficit), while the Bank would recommend reduced tax rates (to promote investment). More complicated inconsistencies arise in the arenas of international trade and foreign exchange.[13]

The Washington Consensus did not really differ from middle-of-the-road policy orthodoxy in rich Northern countries, and that was the point: A political economy founded on the distinctive structure of Latin American economies and their role in the global economy gave way to a one-size-fits-all recipe. Politicians and policy makers who had been excited by the explicit introduction of "structure" into analyses of Latin American development were now faced with "structural adjustment." The hopeful, homegrown heuristic of the CEPAL school receded into the background.

What's worse, the economic consequences of the adoption of the Washington Consensus policies were profoundly disappointing. Economic output per capita in the region rose by less than a paltry 1 percent annually during the 1990s (fig. 2.1), two to three percentage points below the annual rates achieved during the High Developmentalist phase. It is of course possible, even likely, that economic performance would have been even worse if the ISI-CEPAL policy tool kit had been maintained during these years. An equally relevant counterfactual question, of course, is whether the region's economy would have grown as dramatically during the 1960s and 1970s had it *not* adopted the High Developmentalist policy package. Éric Berr (2017) argues that the unflinching support for the Washington Consensus among influential economists and economic organizations, in the face of damning evidence that the policy package has not improved economic well-being where it has been applied, in fact resembles a kind of religious faith. Echoing Daniel Cohen's remark regarding the religion of growth, Berr wryly recasts the ten points of Williamson's version of the Consensus in the form of biblical Ten Commandments.[14] In any case, the effects of the so-called "Lost Decade" in Latin American development further extinguished the hopes of some observers that the region would find a development path that was both successful and its own.

As a painful example of the straitened circumstances, and the high risks, of the policy environment in which Latin American countries found themselves during the Lost Decade, consider Mexico in 1994. Arguably, Mexico was at the time among the most apt pupils of the World Bank's structural adjustment prescriptions, and this in a continent full of apt pupils. The structural adjustment portion of the Washington Consensus, recall, calls for far-reaching changes in the role of the state and the market in the national economy. This includes liberalization of trade—reducing tariffs and other barriers to the flow of goods and services in and out of the country. Mexico famously pursued this goal via its entry into the North American Free Trade Agreement (NAFTA) in January 2004. Adjustment includes financial liberalization—reducing the government's influence over the flow of credit to firms in the economy, and terms of such loans, such as discounted interest rates. Adjustment also includes privatization of state-owned enterprises—selling utilities and other public firms to private hands, often through newly created or vastly expanded domestic stock exchanges. Mexico mustered the political energy to pursue many of these difficult (and generally unpopular) reforms.

When it comes to the IMF-promoted stabilization measures, which have to do with fiscal and monetary policy, Mexico was also a good student—but not quite as ardent as in the liberalization or structural adjustment reforms. In particular, Mexico fell prey to a politically difficult management of the peso-dollar exchange rate. Investors in foreign exchange markets foresaw a devaluation of the peso, which can often become a self-fulfilling prophecy. Consider a simplified explanation. To maintain a fixed peso-dollar exchange rate, the Banco de México (the central bank) commits to sell dollars to all takers at the fixed price (say, three pesos to the dollar), a practice which is limited by the bank's US dollar reserves. If an international currency speculator believes that the peso will lose value, he can fly to Mexico, borrow three million pesos from Bancomer, a Mexican commercial bank of the Washington Consensus era, take a cab over to the central bank, and demand $1 million, which the bank is bound to hand over in exchange for his borrowed pesos.[15] If enough speculators imitate the example of this fellow, the bank's reserves might fall to the point where it can no longer defend the 3:1 exchange rate and it may be forced to devalue the peso; say, to six pesos to the dollar. Now our original speculator goes back to the central bank to buy back the three million pesos that he owes Bancomer; except now it only costs him $500,000. He repays his loan, and pockets the half-million-dollar speculative profit (minus whatever interest he owes Bancomer). Once the expectation that the central bank would devalue became generalized, thus depleting the Banco de México's dollar reserves, the devaluation itself became inevitable. (Needless to say, in the real world of currency exchanges, speculators don't need to fly to Mexico or visit the physical offices of the central bank for this prophecy to be fulfilled.)

Mexican reality was more complicated than the simple example outlined in the previous paragraph. Nineteen ninety-four was a presidential election year in Mexico, and the government engaged in expansionary fiscal policy—increased government spending—to generate support for the ruling party's candidate. This required the issuance of debt (some of it dollar-denominated) to pay for roads and social programs, and as government indebtedness grew, investors' confidence about the quality of that debt began to degrade. Shockingly, in the midst of this, the ruling party's candidate, Luis Donaldo Colosio, was assassinated on the campaign trail in Tijuana, amplifying uncertainty in financial markets. Government assurances that the peso would not be devalued increasingly fell upon deaf ears among the investor class, and this despite massive injections of US dollars by the IMF and President Bill Clinton's Treasury Department. Three weeks after entering office, the new Mexican president, Ernesto Zedillo, oversaw an abrupt devaluation of the peso. Investors fled from Mexican public and private debt and equities; the contagion spread to other Latin American countries, tarnished, fairly or not, by their geographical proximity. Investors lost their appetite for purchasing and holding debt issued by the Mexican government and Mexican firms, but also Brazilian, Argentinian, and Peruvian debt. Declining demand for Latin American debt was accompanied by declining demand for Latin American currencies and imposed further pressure on dollar reserves of Latin American central banks. The spillover of negative consequences throughout Latin America of the Mexican devaluation was dubbed the "tequila effect." (In 1997–1998, a similar episode of contagion from a Brazilian exchange rate crisis was called the "caipirinha effect." Stay tuned until chapter 4 for a discussion of the "Jazz Effect." Guess where it originated?)

The time path of gross domestic product per capita illustrates in more continuous detail than the decadal averages how the region's economy grew and compares income per capita in the region to the global average (fig. 2.3). The slope of the path at any point in time reflects the instantaneous growth rate of the economy; during the High Developmentalism phase ending in 1980, the time path is steeper than at any other period in the seventy years covered by fig. 2.3—except for briefly in the early twenty-first century, to which we turn in the next chapter. It was beginning in the debt crisis of the 1980s that average income worldwide surpassed that of Latin America and the Caribbean, a gap in income levels that would only widen in subsequent decades.

After the Boom

A new generation of technocratic policy makers dismissed the ideals of their High Developmentalist predecessors. The CEPAL and the politicians and policy makers who followed its advice are not exactly forgotten today, though when High Developmentalism is recalled today, it is often in pejorative terms. Thus the Brazilian political scientist André Singer condemned Brazilian president Dilma Rousseff during her first term in office for her "ensaio desenvolvimentista"—he referred to attempts to reduce the borrowing costs faced by

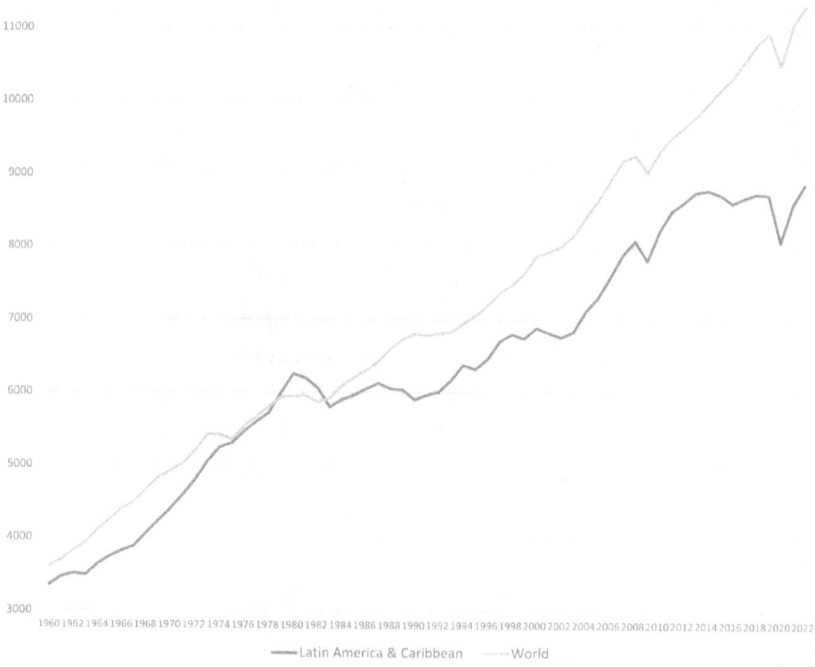

Figure 2.3. GDP per capita, Latin America and Caribbean and world, 1960–2022. GDP per capita is gross domestic product divided by midyear population. Data are in constant 2015 US dollars. *Source*: WDI database, World Bank.

manufacturers.[16] Similarly, the global business press expressed fear that Peronist presidential candidate Alberto Fernández would replace the austere macro policies of incumbent Mauricio Macri with "nationalist" or "leftist" measures during the 2019 presidential contest in Argentina. Such criticisms are based on the deep rejection among some political currents of High Developmentalism.

Along with the decline in Latin America of a domestically designed and produced development strategy, development economics itself could be said to have dissipated in the aftermath of the Washington Consensus. The influential Oxford University development economist Paul Collier (2015) argued that, while it may have been defensible to lump China, Chile, and Chad into a single category of developing countries in 1949, contrasted to the rich member countries of the OECD, no such grouping makes any kind of consistent sense today. In other words, it is not even clear what the subject matter of development economics should be. The older school of development economics seeking structural transformation has largely yielded to a politically neutral quest for greater rigor in the evaluation of various microeconomic policies and projects.

Critiques of the notion of development in the early part of this century were not limited to the realm of orthodox economists. The lively Latin American tradition of critical perspectives on development established by the CEPAL and dependency theorists was rejuvenated with a broad range of perspectives (Ojeda Medina and Villarreal Villamar, 2020); those critiques will appear from time to time in chapters 8 through 12.

Latin America's economy would rebound, perhaps to the surprise of most observers, in the new millennium, even achieving growth rates to match those of High Developmentalist days. The economic policy debates that animated the past century would likewise rebound, pitting market orthodoxy against activist policy (key #4 from chapter 1). Both the growth rebound and the policy debates, however much they might resemble their twentieth-century counterparts, took on new forms and set new political and social coalitions against each other. These are among the questions to be addressed in the remainder of this study.

Part Two

GROWTH

CHAPTER THREE

O Milagrinho

The Latin American Decade (2000–2007)

IN JANUARY 2011, COLOMBIA'S then president Juan Manuel Santos prophesied the coming of a "Latin American Decade" in a speech at an OECD forum in Paris (see the news dispatch item in the introduction). As it happens, Santos's enthusiasm had more explanatory power retrospectively than it did prospectively. The decade following his Paris speech witnessed an uneven and disappointing economic performance, as we shall see in subsequent chapters. But Santos's assessment accurately describes the factors that led to accelerated growth in the decade *before* his speech. In particular, profitable natural resource-derived exports and pragmatic policy making drove historically good development performance. Growth rates of income per capita in the region in the years 2000–2009 were higher than in any decade since the heyday of High Developmentalism, at 1.7 percent annually (fig. 2.1). The venerable heterodox economist Edmar Bacha dubbed this period "o Milagrinho" in the Brazilian context: the "little miracle," to contrast it with the full-blown miracle growth rates of the High Developmentalist era (Carvalho, 2018, p. 13).

In this chapter, we will

1. provide a descriptive and quantitative summary of the economic growth experience of Latin America during the Milagrinho years;
2. explore the role of high commodity prices in driving faster rates of growth;
3. assess the role of Chinese demand in driving up commodity prices, as well as

look closely at the changing economic relationship between China and Latin American countries;

4. discuss the surprising "Pink Tide" of left-leaning governments that came to power during the Milagrinho years.

The Short Decade of O *Milagrinho*

The little miracle in fact corresponded to a little decade: For most Latin American economies, the acceleration in growth rates began in or around 2003 and ended with the onset of the global financial crisis of 2008 (fig. 3.1). In fig. 3.1, the height of any of the seven curves represents the *level* of average income in that country at that date.[1] The slope of any of the curves, in contrast, depicts the rate of change in the level of average income, which is to say, the economic growth rate. Steep and climbing (e.g., Venezuela between 2003 and 2004) means rapid growth; falling (e.g., Venezuela between 2002 and 2003) means the economy is contracting in size.

Comparing the time path of gross domestic product per capita among the seven largest Latin American economies reveals important divergences. First, a

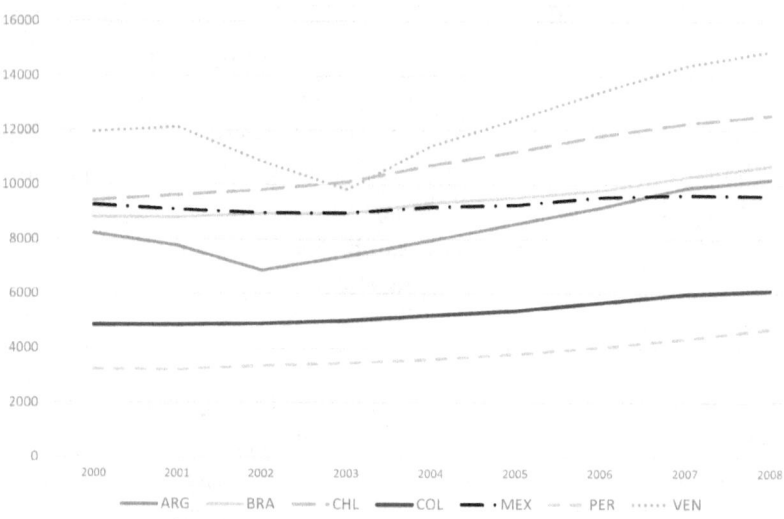

Figure 3.1. GDP per capita, LAC-7 economies, 2000–2008. Data are in constant 2010 US dollars. *Source:* WDI database, World Bank.

divergence in levels of GDP per capita: Venezuelan average income was roughly *three times* that of Peru over this period, with the other five economies arrayed between the Venezuelan and Peruvian extremes. Second, and more related to the subject of this chapter, there was a divergence in *rates of change* of GDP per capita. The steepest inclines beginning in 2003 were experienced by Venezuela, Argentina, and Peru; the shallowest was Mexico's. Mexico's GDP per capita was third highest among the LAC-7 in 2000; by 2008, it had fallen to fifth place, having been surpassed by Argentina and Brazil. Note that all these figures are in constant 2010 US dollars, which is to say they are adjusted for inflation.

A more granular comparison of growth of all Latin American economies during the Milagrinho years illustrates three performance tiers. Let us compute the cumulative growth of per capita income simply, as follows: Compare constant-dollar GDP per capita in 2008 to the corresponding value in 2003 and calculate the percentage change. Four benchmarks are highlighted: Latin America and the Caribbean, OECD member countries, China, and the world. During the Milagrinho years, Latin America grew more quickly than the world average, which in turn grew more quickly than the mostly high-income OECD members, and China grew more quickly than all of the above (fig. 3.2).

Three categories of countries emerge:

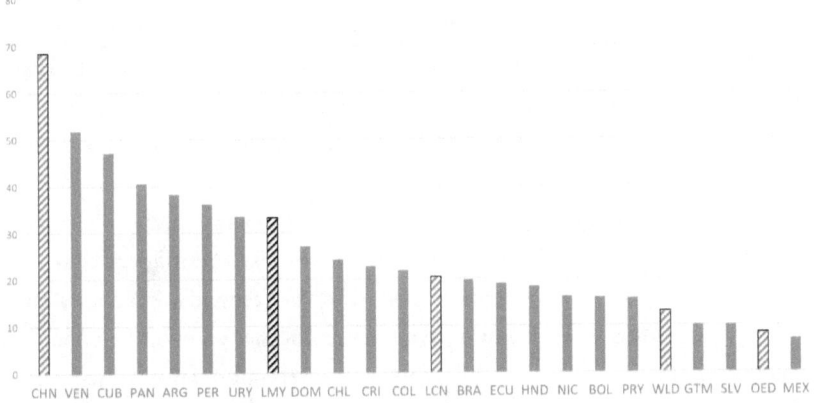

Figure 3.2. Cumulative growth of GDP per capita, LAC and other economies, 2003–2008. The difference between constant-dollar GDP per capita in 2003 and 2008 is expressed as a percentage of GDP per capita in 2003. LMY = low and middle income countries, LCN = Latin America and the Caribbean, WLD = world, OED = OECD members. *Source*: WDI database, World Bank.

1. A large group whose cumulative growth, while smaller than China's, exceeded the Latin American average (20.4 percent): Venezuela, Cuba, Panama, Argentina, Peru, Uruguay, the Dominican Republic, Chile, Costa Rica, and Colombia;
2. Those with cumulative growth lower than the Latin American average, but in excess of the global rate of growth (12.9 percent): Brazil, Ecuador, Honduras, Nicaragua, Bolivia, and Paraguay;
3. Those whose growth fell below the world rate of cumulative growth: Guatemala, El Salvador, and Mexico.

Argentina and Venezuela owe their membership in the fastest-growing club to special and noteworthy historical circumstances. Both jumped from a particularly sharp trough (fig. 3.1): Argentina in 2002, Venezuela a year later.

Venezuela's 2003 growth dip and subsequent rebound is a macroeconomic reflection of the social conflicts that marked Hugo Chávez's early years in power. Chávez (whose rise is described in greater detail later in this chapter when we consider the Pink Tide phenomenon) faced fierce opposition from certain sectors within society, notably business leaders and some labor unions. A particularly formidable foe was the nationalized oil industry, accustomed to autonomy and great power (Parker 2007). Chávez's reforms to the oil industry, including changes in the leadership of the state-owned oil firm Petróleos de Venezuela (PDVSA), provided the proximate spark for an attempted coup d'état in April 2002: Oil workers struck, and PDVSA managers stopped production. The coup failed but unrest and resistance continued, including a longer oil strike between December 2002 and February 2003. The growth slowdown occasioned by these actions can be visibly detected in fig. 3.1, as can the rapid recovery that followed the agreement reached between the Chávez government and the opposition in May 2003.[2]

Argentina too suffered a sharp economic downturn early in the century, the time path of which resembled the remark by the Ernest Hemingway character who is asked how he went bankrupt. "Two ways," he responds, "gradually, then suddenly." A gradually deteriorating economy in the last years of the twentieth century gave way suddenly to the largest-ever sovereign default in world economic history in December 2001 (violent suppression of protests against government measures are recounted in the first news dispatch in the introduction). The proximate causes during the "gradually" phase: chronic fiscal deficits, leading to rapid accumulation of foreign debt owed by national and provincial governments; appreciation of the peso-to-dollar exchange rate, exacerbated by the rigorous Convertibility Plan adopted in 1991; and the "sudden stop" in capital flows to countries like Argentina in the wake of financial crises in Mexico, East Asian countries, Russia, and Brazil during the late 1990s. The Convertibility Plan had pegged the Argentinian peso to the US dollar at a fixed rate, but with the added constraint that each peso emitted by the authorities needed to be backed one-for-one by a US dollar in the reserves held at the Banco Central de la República Argentina, the country's central bank (in contrast to the practice of most central banks, which hold only a fraction of the money supply in hard-currency reserves). This arrangement, known as a *currency board*, was meant to make investors inside and outside of Argentina confident about the stability of the exchange rate (and by extension, the macroeconomy more generally). Argentina was praised by global financial institutions for this extreme adherence to item 4 of the Washington Consensus (table 2.1).

During the "suddenly" phase of the crisis (December 2001/January 2002), a rapid deterioration in confidence led Argentinians to seek to empty their bank accounts; the authorities partially froze deposits in response. A portion of public foreign debt payments were suspended—a default. And the convertibility of the peso was abandoned. Protests and demonstrations were widespread and met with harsh responses from the government; the violence claimed many lives. In the meantime, sluggish growth was replaced by a sharp downturn, marked by high levels of unemployment.[3]

In many ways, Venezuela's and Argentina's early-millennium growth downturns can be interpreted as markers of the shift from a twentieth century to a twenty-first century Latin American political economy. Argentina's 2001 economic crisis, viewed retrospectively and hopefully from the perspective of pre-recession 2007, looked very much like the last in a long series of twentieth-century macroeconomic shocks, but the improvements that followed suggested that it might be the last such crisis of the outgoing century. That is, at least until the 2023 Argentinian crisis (addressed in the last news dispatch in the introduction) made it look instead like the *first* crisis of the incoming century. The political conflict underlying Venezuela's 2002–2003 economic shock, meanwhile, signaled the consolidation of power of a left-leaning government in that country that would signal a departure from decades, if not centuries, of unequalizing growth (key #2 from chapter 1). And a so-called Pink Tide of left-leaning governments of quite varied ideology and political behavior would sweep across the region alongside Chávez, in Argentina, Bolivia, Brazil, Chile, Ecuador, Mexico, Nicaragua, Paraguay, Peru, and Uruguay, at various points during the years covered by this book (more on this below).

The subsequent little growth miracle, visible in fig. 3.1, has less to do with solely internal political or economic factors, and more to do with the global commodity boom that affected Argentina and Venezuela, and many of their neighbors.

Chinese Industrial Growth and the Commodity Price Boom

What accounts for the broad swath of Latin American countries that outpaced global economic growth during the little miracle's little decade? And what accounts for the variation in cumulative growth over this span of time? The short answer—indeed, the short answer to so many questions posed in the domains of international economics, diplomacy, security, and more in the last forty or so years—is China. China's cumulative per capita GDP growth between 2003 and 2008—68.5 percent—amply exceeded that of all nineteen Latin America economies during the same period. As such, China came rapidly to contribute an outsized share to global growth. A country's contribution to global growth depends both on that country's rate of growth, and the size of its economy; the values of both of these variables were unusually large in China during this century. Indeed, as Steven Barnett of the IMF points out, China's contribution—currently more than one percentage point annually—will remain large even as Chinese growth slows, because its size has increased so much in recent decades (Barnett 2014). To the extent that Latin America's growth fortunes depend on global growth, China's remarkable growth is in part responsible.[4]

The comparative performance of the Latin American and Chinese economies during the current century demonstrates that China is converging toward the average income of the largely rich countries of the OECD, and more quickly, toward that of Latin America and the Caribbean. Fig. 3.3. includes average income in China (CHN) and Latin America and the Caribbean (LCN) as a share of average income in the OECD member countries over a time span that extends beyond the coverage of this chapter, through the onset of the Covid-19 pandemic. Latin America and the Caribbean's average income fluctuates in a band between 20 percent and a quarter of that of the OECD countries, rising during the commodity boom of the Milagrinho years, falling since 2013. China's average income, meanwhile, has steadily grown as a share of the rich countries', from less than 10 percent to close to 30 percent, and surpassed Latin America's in 2017.

The figure also includes average world income (WLD) and that of low- and middle-income economies (LMY) as a share of OECD average income. This comparison demonstrates that Latin America and the Caribbean countries have consistently had a higher average income than the LMY countries (essentially, all developing economies). Incomes in the latter group, meanwhile, are converging toward OECD levels consistently during this century, while Latin America and the Caribbean countries' average incomes are not.

In brief, in the twenty-first century, Latin America's growth has been weak compared to other developing economies, and especially compared to China's.

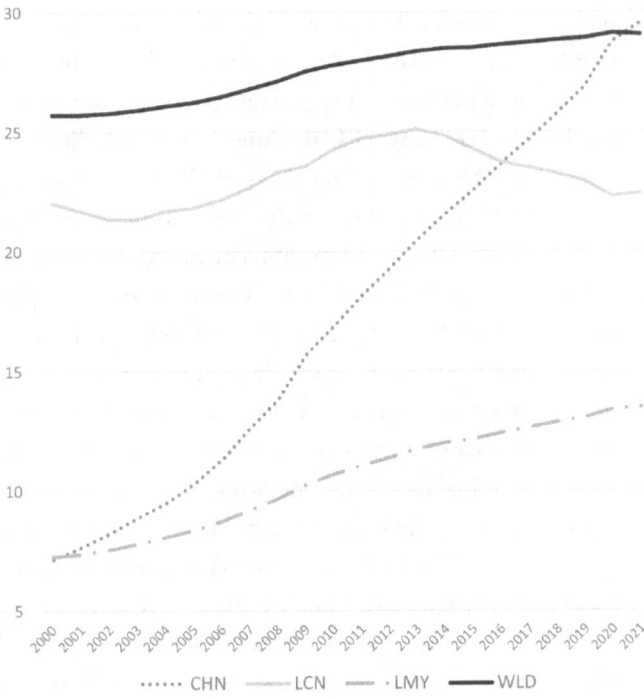

Figure 3.3. Per capita income as a share of OECD countries (%), 2000–2022. The measure on the vertical axis divides GDP per capita of all Latin American and Caribbean countries (LCN), and Chinese GDP per capita (CHN), all countries (WLD), and low- and middle-income countries (LCN) by that of all OECD countries. Original data are in constant 2015 US dollars. Source: WDI database, World Bank.

Thus, China's surging growth has fueled growth in other countries indirectly. But there are more particular and direct channels linking China to Latin America's little miracle, and they form an unusual concatenation of mutually reinforcing trends.

Chinese growth since the late 1970s has had a distinct character: It is unusually commodity intensive. In general, when primarily agricultural economies are transformed into manufacturing-based ones, their demand for commodities, particularly energy and metals, increases. China is no exception to that general temporal pattern. However, China's aggressive and focused state-led and state-encouraged investment in manufacturing and infrastructure have made its industrialization even more commodity-intensive than in other historical cases. That is, at any level of GDP per capita, China's per capita demand for commodities was higher than when earlier industrializing economies had been at the same level of GDP per capita (Roache 2012).

A study from the IMF Research Department by Yongzhen Yu (2011) summarizes the especially metals-intensive nature of recent Chinese growth. Rapid growth in construction, infrastructure, and the production of machine goods and automobiles, led to a seemingly insatiable thirst for iron ore, copper, and alumina, in particular. Add to this the use of soybean meal in the production of livestock and poultry for the growing (and increasingly prosperous) urban middle class, and the roots of Latin America's commodity boom can be readily discerned. The historically high rates of Chinese economic growth, meanwhile, meant that those large commodity demands increased at a vertiginous rate.

As a result, China became a major importer of key commodities, many of which were exported from Latin American countries (key #3 from chapter 1). Around 2000, China imported approximately 10 percent each of globally traded iron ore and soybeans; by 2008, those proportions had risen to over 60 percent and 50 percent, respectively (Roache 2012). And China became a higher-ranked trading partner of many Latin American countries, even displacing the long-dominant United States in some cases.

Moreover, the rapid rise in commodity demand led to increasing commodity prices (fig. 3.4). The IMF's all-commodity price index, on the eve of the global financial crisis, was more than three times—that is, 300 percent—higher than it was at the onset of Latin America's Milagrinho in 2003. We will analyze the roller coaster of commodity prices beginning with the global recession in the next two chapters.

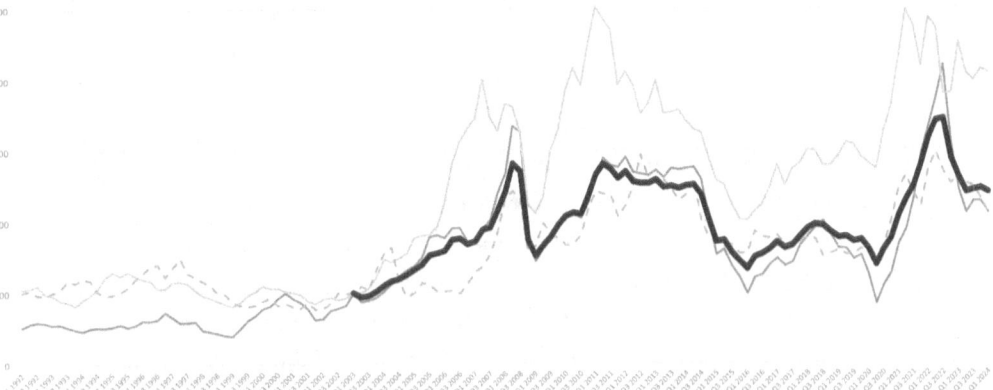

Figure 3.4. Commodity price indices, 1992–2024. Quarterly data, and the base (100) has been set to first quarter 2003, rebased from the IMF's base year of 2016. "Energy index" includes crude oil (petroleum), natural gas, coal and propane indices. "Metals index" includes aluminum, cobalt, copper, iron ore, lead, molybdenum, nickel, tin, uranium, and zinc indices. "Soybeans" index measures Chicago soybean futures contract (first contract forward) No. 2 yellow and par. "All commodities" index begins in 2003 Q1. *Source*: IMF Primary Commodity Price System.

A more disaggregated look at key Latin American commodity export categories important to Chinese industrial development reveals variations on the all-commodity pattern. Metals prices, including copper (Chile and Peru), iron ore (Brazil), and nickel (Cuba), rose swiftly during the Milagrinho years, peaking at four times their 2003 values, though faltering in mid-2007, prior to the deepest phase of the global economic downturn. Energy prices, including petroleum (Venezuela, Argentina, Brazil, and Mexico), surged nearly as high as metals, though with a lag. Soybeans (Argentina, Bolivia, Brazil, Paraguay, and Uruguay) did not witness as large an increase as metals and petroleum, but nevertheless surged to more than double their 2003 value before the 2008 recession.[5] Latin American exporters benefited from these price increases regardless of whether they exported to China in significant volumes or not; Venezuela, for example, always exported more to the United States than to China, but was singularly favored by high world petroleum prices driven in large part by Chinese demand.

Finally, for many commodity-exporting countries, rising commodity prices translated into improved terms of trade. This is a dramatic reversal of the declining terms of trade forecasted by Raúl Prebisch's 1949 CEPAL report (discussed in chapter 2). Prior to the onset of the global financial crisis, the terms of trade—the ratio of export prices to import prices, roughly speaking—in many Latin American economies had spiked dramatically.

An improvement in the terms of trade does not follow automatically from a rise in commodity export prices. In the first instance, countries with especially diversified economies (like Mexico and Brazil, for example) export many goods whose export prices did not rise as swiftly as commodity prices, even if their export baskets include some of the latter. In fact, some of those non-commodity exports (like light manufactures) might have seen their prices stagnate precisely *because* of competition with Chinese exporters in third-country markets. Venezuela, meanwhile, had an extraordinarily concentrated export basket based on petroleum, whose price surged during the Milagrinho years. Thus, the numerator of the terms of trade ratio will not rise by the same proportion for all commodity exporters. And countries have different import baskets, which determine the denominator of the terms of trade ratio. Latin American countries that are net importers of the commodities in question—most notably, petroleum—may see their terms of trade decline.

Let us return to the classification of Latin American countries during the Milagrinho in fig. 3.2. How does the Chinese-influenced boom in commodity prices help us understand the different tiers of growth? Consider first the relationship between commodity exports and cumulative growth in the LAC-19 countries (fig. 3.5). A vertical line is drawn in the figure at the average value for the cumulative growth of these nineteen economies over the 2003–2008 period, namely 24.9 percent; a horizontal line is likewise drawn to mark the average commodity share of merchandise exports over the 2002–2009 period, in this case 66.6 percent. If there is a strong positive correlation between commodity exports and growth, we would expect to find most observations in the scatter plot in the northeast (above-average values of both variables) and southwest (below-average values of both variables) quadrants. The pattern is not so neat, and brings to the surface some idiosyncrasies and peculiarities.

Six countries have above-average commodity export intensity but *below*-average growth: Bolivia, Chile, Ecuador, Honduras, Nicaragua, and Paraguay. Are the countries in the northwest quadrant exporting the "wrong" commodities—that is, commodities not subject to fast-growing Chinese demand? In some cases, yes.

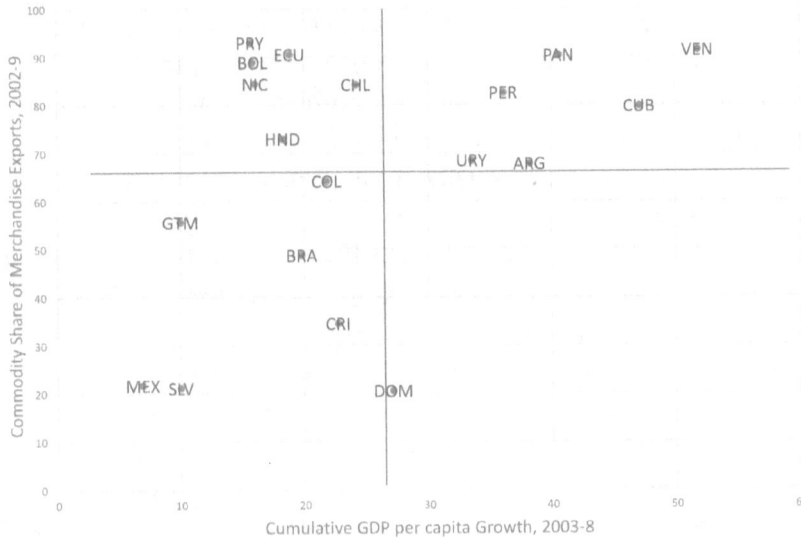

Figure 3.5. Growth and commodity intensity of exports, 2003–2008. Commodity share of merchandise exports is the sum of the following export categories: agricultural raw materials, food, fuel, ores, and metals, averaged over the years 2002–2009. Observations are missing for some years and some countries. Vertical and horizontal lines are drawn at the average value of the variables depicted. See note to fig. 3.2 for information on growth rates. *Source:* WDI database, World Bank.

This latter scenario was precisely the situation faced by most of the Central American countries during the Milagrinho years. The economies of the isthmus are important commodity exporters. But the principal commodities they export—coffee, sugar, and bananas—are not industrial inputs and as such were not affected by dynamic Chinese industrial growth. In the meantime, Central American countries saw their import costs of metals and energy increase. El Salvador and Guatemala, moreover, compete with Chinese exporters in third-country markets. The net effect was a decline in the terms of trade of Central America, particularly pronounced in Nicaragua (Avendaño and Dayton-Johnson 2015).

In other cases, lower growth is not only a matter of exporting commodities less desired by the Chinese growth model. Central American countries' trading relationship with China was complicated by the geopolitical circumstance that they were among the shrinking roster of mostly small countries that extend diplomatic recognition to Taipei and not Beijing (Costa Rica broke with Taipei in 2007; Panama ten years later, in 2017). Consider Paraguay, which, like its quadrant-mates Honduras and Nicaragua, recognized Taiwan's as the legitimate government of China. In 2006, 28 percent of Paraguay's exports were soybeans, nearly half of which were exported to its neighbors Uruguay, Argentina, and Brazil. Soybeans were nevertheless readily in demand to feed livestock in China. In the same year, China imported almost half of its soybeans—worth more than $1.4 billion—from Argentina, which, like many of the larger Latin American countries, had recognized Beijing for decades.

It is neither Taiwan, nor the type of commodity exported, that explains the weaker link between commodity exports and growth in the case of two Andean countries that extend diplomatic recognition to Beijing: Bolivia and Ecuador. In 2006, petroleum products, very much in demand in China, constituted a significant share of both countries' export value. Neither country exported much petroleum to China, however; Bolivia exported the lion's share of its petroleum gas to Brazil, while Ecuador exported the majority of its crude petroleum to the United States. That the two Andean countries did not sell directly to China, however, does not mean they would not have benefited from China's upward pressure on world petroleum prices. Other factors clearly counteracted in part those benefits in the determination of the countries' economic growth rates during the Milagrinho.

How does the relative importance of China as an export market correlate with Milagrinho growth? Countries with above-average growth rates are more likely to direct a larger share of their exports to China during these years; conversely, slower growing countries direct a lower-than-average share of exports to the Chinese market (fig. 3.6). This is illustrated by the cluster of countries in the northeast and southwest quadrants of fig. 3.6; the southwest group confirms the relative unimportance of China to some commodity-intensive exporters hypothesized in the discussion of fig. 3.5. The data demonstrate that China constituted a relatively small share of exports from Taipei's allies in Central America during these years: only 3.2 percent of export value, on average. For some Central American countries, China was a minuscule fraction of 1 percent of export value. In 2003, for example, Honduran exports to North Korea exceeded its exports to China.[6]

Venezuela's experience illustrates the extent to which an exporter can benefit from upward Chinese pressure on export prices, even if not exporting to China. China's average share of Venezuelan exports was a below average 2.6 percent, but

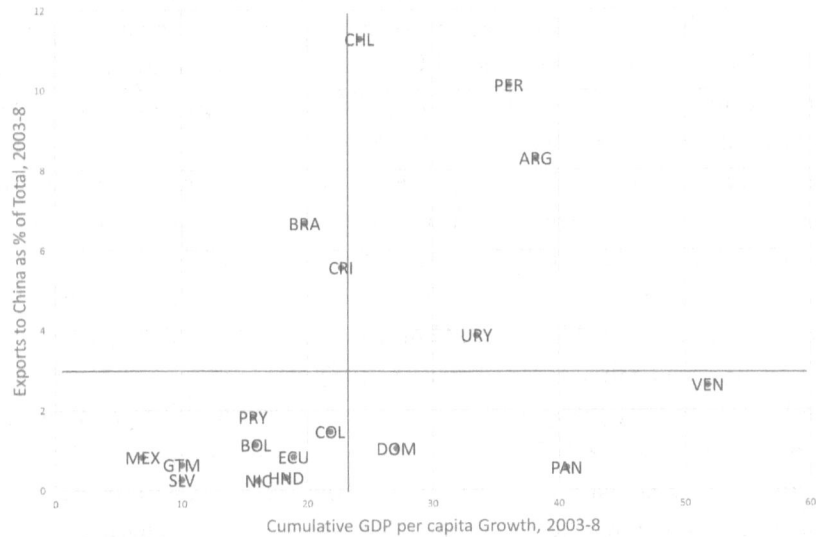

Figure 3.6. Cumulative GDP per capita growth and exports to China, 2003–2008. Exports to China as a percentage of total export value, averaged over 2003-2008. See note to fig. 3.2 for information on cumulative growth rates. *Source:* Observatory for Economic Complexity (Chinese export shares) and WDI database, World Bank (growth rates).

that did not prevent the country from enjoying the largest Milagrinho growth in the region.

A final category of countries to consider: the slower-growing cohort of countries that increasingly competed with Chinese exports in third-country markets. The largest candidate to consider in this group is Mexico. Mexico is a historically important producer and exporter of petroleum, but its economy had sufficiently diversified that by 2006, crude petroleum constituted only 14 percent of the value of Mexican exports (by 2017, the number had declined further to 4.7 percent). By 2006, Mexico increasingly produced and exported manufactured goods, including machinery of various kinds (the marvelously detailed and incongruous trade statistics include categories like video displays, computers, and insulated wire, in all of which areas Mexico excels), as well as automobiles and parts. Much of this export pattern had to do with Mexico's closer integration to US-based value chains that developed in the wake of the North American Free Trade Agreement (NAFTA), which went into effect in Mexico in 1994.

How much of a competitive threat was China to Mexico during the Milagrinho years? The evidence is mixed. The OECD (2007, fig. 4.4) computed an index to measure this threat, based on the similarity of a country's export structure to that of China during the years 2000–2005. The higher the index, the greater the Chinese threat; the lower the index, the more complementary a country's productive structure, and hence the greater the potential for mutually advantageous trade with China. By this measure, Mexico faced a higher threat from China than any other Latin American country, and globally found itself in a group of threatened exporters that included Thailand, Hungary, South Korea, Malaysia, and the United States. El Salvador and Honduras, also in the southwest quadrant of fig. 3.6, were by this measure significantly less threatened by Chinese export competition, in the neighborhood of Pakistan, Colombia, and Brazil.

Rolando Avendaño and I looked more closely at Latin American countries that had appeared to benefit less from Chinese growth, using alternative measures of the competitive threat (Avendaño and Dayton-Johnson 2015, fig. 7). These rely on an *index of competitive threat* (ICT) measure proposed by Rhys Jenkins (2008), who emphasized not merely the similarity with China's productive structure, but the relative magnitude of an economy's activity in sectors where China's export growth exceeds the global average: In brief, is a given country competing with growing sectors in China? This adds a dynamic element to the OECD's static comparison of China to a given economy's export sector. With this modification, China's threat to Mexico was actually *lower* than the Latin American average. That is, Mexico was competing with more stable sectors of the Chinese economy. Among the countries that faced the highest ICT from China: Honduras, Peru, Paraguay, Ecuador, Nicaragua, and Chile, many of which are in the puzzling northwest quadrant of fig. 3.5. Rising competition with China might explain why some of these countries' growth was lower than that of their neighbors.

As ever, there is an enduring diversity of experiences across Latin American economies (the ever-present key #5 from chapter 1) during the Milagrinho years. Note, finally, that the scatter plots in figs. 3.5 and 3.6 do not capture the degree to which China's economic dynamism raised the growth rates of *all* countries—including all Latin American countries—above the levels that would have been observed in the absence of China's acceleration.

In terms of China's effect on Latin American growth in the years leading up to the global financial recession of 2008, in summary, four country groups emerge:

1. Some countries' economies were buoyed by China's demand for their commodity exports, as was the case of Argentina, Brazil, Chile, and Peru.
2. Others, like Venezuela, may not have sold a lot of commodities directly to China, but benefited from the higher prices of their exports, which were driven in turn, at least in part, by Chinese demand.
3. Countries like some in Central America, not producers of the commodities demanded by China's industrialization, found themselves paying higher prices for those same imports.
4. Finally, a group of countries that includes Mexico, El Salvador, and Guatemala, may have been hurt by Chinese competition in third-country markets, going toe to toe with Chinese exports of certain manufactured products.

The trade relationships between China and many Latin American countries exploded in the years following Hu Jintao's late 2004 tour of several countries in the region (see the news dispatch in the introduction). China surpassed the United States as the top destination for exports from a number of South American countries. China pursued bilateral free trade agreements with Chile (signed in 2006), Peru (2010), and Costa Rica (2011) (Wise and Myers, 2017).[7]

Carol Wise (2012) analyzed the first two of these FTAs, with Chile and Peru. Though the agreements were technically "South-South" under World Trade Organization rules—that is, deals struck between two developing countries, and not between rich and poor countries—they nevertheless function more like North-South trade based on the comparative advantages of the two countries that sign them. This means that China's role in such agreements is more like that of the manufacturing-exporter Center of Prebisch's CEPAL framework. Wise further argues that it was China's desire to secure access to minerals that drove it to pursue the FTAs with Chile and Peru. China conceded to a number of restrictions proposed by Chile and Peru, including restrictions on investment outside of mining.

As for soybeans, Argentinian researcher Mariano Turzi has analyzed what he calls the "Soybean Republic," an integrated agro-industrial network spanning several South American and Asian economies. Five members of the Mercosur trading bloc—Argentina, Bolivia, Brazil, Paraguay, and Uruguay—account for 40 percent of the global soybean trade, and more than 60 percent of the trade in soybean meal and soybean oil.[8] Turzi argues that the Mercosur soybean producers have an unexploited potential to "increase competitiveness, bolster regional integration, and play a greater role in the global economy." In the meantime, the global value chains serving the Soybean Republic became increasingly dominated by Asian multinational corporations. Market power shifted from the South American producers to Asian retailers; China, for example, had considerable leverage as the buyer of over 80 percent of Argentina's soybean exports (Turzi 2011, 2017; Castro 2012).

China's economic role in Latin America expanded beyond trade and trade agreements to include important capital flows. Gallagher and Irwin (2017) investigate Chinese lending and underscore the predominant role of two Chinese "policy banks": the state-owned China Development Bank, mostly, and the Export-Import Bank of China. During the Milagrinho years, these two policy banks' cumulative lending to Latin American governments and state-owned enterprises was similar in magnitude (roughly $70 billion) to total lending by the Inter-American Development Bank (IDB). The IDB was a longer-standing multilateral lender in the region; that the Chinese state-owned banks matched IDB levels of lending represented a major shift in development financing in Latin America. Gallagher and Irwin argue that the policy banks' lending was consistent with the behavior of a "profit-seeking neodevelopmentalist state," and was often complementary to capital flows from other lenders. China lent vigorously to Ecuador and Venezuela, for example, who received no large loans from traditional international financial institutions like the World Bank or IDB, or from the United States. Most Chinese loans required that borrowers purchase Chinese goods (in construction, oil, telecoms, satellite, railroad equipment), which allowed some of the loans to be executed in yuan. Unlike loans from multilateral lenders or the United States, however, the Chinese policy banks did not require changes in borrowing governments' policies.

Converging to Convergence?

During the decade of the 2000s, average income growth in Latin America exceeded that of the OECD countries (fig. 2.1). An alternative way of illustrating the same point is to note that Latin American average income as a share of OECD average income rose during the Milagrinho years (fig. 3.3), though not as rapidly as the Chinese average income did. In other words, average income in Latin America was *converging* to that of the OECD economies. Most of what this chapter has presented would lead us to conclude that the Chinese-demand-driven commodity boom is the principal reason for this decade of convergence. If so, it would be difficult to sustain this pace of convergence in the absence of high commodity prices; given the historical volatility of commodity prices, it was almost inevitable that convergence would slow in Latin America when commodity prices fell at some later date (as fig. 3.3 illustrates, this was the case after 2015).

But there may be other contributors to the phenomenon of convergence in the Milagrinho years. The Harvard economist Michael Kremer (co-winner of the Nobel Prize in economics in 2019), together with his coauthors Jack Willis and Yang You, undertook a statistical study of the messy problem of convergence over the period of the 1990s and 2000s (Kremer, Willis, and You 2022). As noted in chapter 2, capital historically does not flow from rich to poor countries at nearly the rate that textbook economics would predict, and consequently, average income levels across poor and rich countries have not systematically converged. Indeed, an earlier empirical study by development economist Lant Pritchett bore the blunt title, "Divergence, Big Time" (Pritchett 1997). Kremer, Willis, and You, with more recent data on growth rates around the world, explored the hypothesis that economies need to meet certain institutional prerequisites in order for the convergence logic to take hold—that is, they must "converge to convergence"—and that in the period 1990–2010, more economies worldwide have become members of the convergence club. Econometric analysis of all economies around the world may still find divergence, but not big time. With passing time, the evidence for textbook convergence becomes more and more evident. Kremer, Willis, and You's conception of what it takes to join the convergence club is broad: They cite policies, institutions, and culture. But perhaps some part of those changes trace their roots to the adoption of the Washington Consensus package in the 1990s?

Linking the convergence of developing and emerging economies' policies, institutions, and culture to those of higher income economies to the Washington Consensus is bound to be controversial. But if true, it would suggest that the growth payoff of the much-maligned neoliberal policy package took time to manifest itself. I remain skeptical of any simplistic version of this story (and Kremer, Willis, and You's study is not simplistic). First, because the overlap between the ten commandments of the Washington Consensus (table 2.1) on the one hand, and the policies, institutions, and culture needed to join the convergence club, on the other, is far from perfect. Consider the case of policy reforms during the 1990s in Mexico. Arguably, the four most fundamental were the entry into force of the North American Free Trade Agreement, the establishment of autonomy of the Banco de México (the central bank), the law granting autonomy of the Supreme Court, and the creation of an autonomous electoral authority. All of these served to reduce the relative power of the executive branch; they also allowed for the alternation of parties in power in Mexico for the first time since the revolution of 1910 (see the news dispatch about Peña Nieto's 2012 election in the introduction). NAFTA maps onto Washington Consensus item 7 (trade liberalization); the other items map loosely at best onto the rather capacious item 5 ("secure property rights"). It seems more likely that the economic crisis of the 1980s created an opportunity for some relatively profound political reform proposals to appear on the policy agenda in Mexico, proposals that would not have had as much probability of adoption in previous decades. Some of the reform proposals appeared thanks to the champions of the Washington Consensus; others, as I have argued, were more tenuously related to that policy package. The second reason for my skepticism is that, as the tequila effect episode illustrated, many of the Washington Consensus items, particularly in the subset of proposals related to liberalization, had weak (at best) growth payoffs. Indeed, all of the profound changes made in Mexico in the 1990s could not prevent the country's average annual economic growth rate from falling to close to zero during the entire Milagrinho period (fig. 3.1). Nevertheless, from Kremer, Willis, and You, we retain the hopeful hypothesis that certain important political changes have been adopted in many Latin American countries, changes that have improved the quality of governance; we will return to these questions in chapters 10 and 11.[9]

The Pink Tide

The political backdrop to the economic Milagrinho was an entirely novel reconfiguration of the electoral landscape across Latin America: the so-called "Pink Tide" or "Left Turn" that swept a heterogeneous group of left-leaning governments to power. The Pink Tide can be said to have started with the election of Hugo Chávez in Venezuela in 1998. Chávez, a charismatic colonel in the military who had been imprisoned after leading an unsuccessful coup attempt by reformist officers in February 1992, drew support from voters fed up with the traditional Liberal-Conservative two-party system (oddly similar to the wave of dissatisfaction that led Chávez's ideological opposite, Álvaro Uribe, to the presidency of Colombia in 2002, running against the Colombian Liberal and Conservative candidates). Chávez also benefited from voters' rejection of Washington Consensus–style liberalization. Indeed, the brutal reaction by the government of Carlos Andrés Pérez—the "Caracazo"—to riots against liberal measures in February 1989 and which claimed hundreds of lives, was still very much in the public consciousness in the 1998 elections.

Chávez would pursue aggressive social development programs to improve health and education, dubbed "Bolivarian Missions," made possible by abundant oil revenues during the Milagrinho years. He established a particularly close relationship with Fidel Castro and Cuba, flirted with Russia, China, and Iran, encouraged other left-leaning governments in the region with alliances, and engaged in a series of diplomatic skirmishes with the United States. Political countermoves, notably the brief April 2002 coup mentioned earlier, served to consolidate his political support, and he was reelected several times. The Chávez government increasingly faced international criticism for encroaching authoritarianism, first from the Bush Administration in the United States, but later from more independent observers, including a 2008 report by Human Rights Watch, which pointed to suppression of political opponents, disregard for the separation of powers, and an anti-democratic pressure upon the courts, media, organized labor, and civil society (Human Rights Watch 2008). Chávez succumbed to cancer in 2013 and was succeeded by his vice president, Nicolás Maduro, whose presidency was marked by tumultuous macroeconomic instability.[10]

Chávez would be joined by left and left-leaning elected leaders in the years that followed his 1999 inauguration. In Chile, the Concertación governments came to power with the end of the military dictatorship of Augusto Pinochet in 1990. A coalition of center and left parties, the Concertación remained in power between 1990 and 2009, starting with Christian Democrats Patricio Aylwin and

Eduardo Frei Ruiz-Tagle (son of the ISI-promoting President Frei, whom we will meet in chapter 8). The first socialist president was Ricardo Lagos in 2000 (though Lagos was not a member of the Socialist Party), followed by Michelle Bachelet in 2006.

Luiz Inácio Lula da Silva, leader of the left-wing Workers Party in Brazil, was meanwhile elected president for the first time in 2002. Néstor Kirchner, elected president of Argentina in 2003, like Chávez, represented a rejection of the Washington Consensus liberalization earlier implemented by fellow Peronist Carlos Menem (president from 1989 to 1999); Kirchner was the first full-term president of Argentina in the wake of the economic and political chaos of the 2001 crisis. As noted in chapter 1, physician and socialist Tabaré Vázquez was elected president of Uruguay in 2005 and appointed former guerrilla leader (and future president) José Mujica a member of his cabinet. Finally, Evo Morales, an Aymara coca farmer and trade unionist, was elected president of Bolivia in 2005, marking a historic milestone in Bolivia's history and setting forth an ambitious set of economic policies.

The Chávez-Lula-Kirchner-Vázquez-Evo-Bachelet constellation captured the fancy of commentators globally and cemented the notion of a Pink Tide having swept in. These six leaders would not be the last left-leaning governments elected to power in the region: They were joined notably by former Sandinista revolutionary Daniel Ortega in Nicaragua, economist Rafael Correa in Ecuador, and Manuel Zelaya in Honduras, all of whom entered office in 2007. Some of the first wave would be succeeded by fellow partisans, like Chávez by Maduro; Kirchner by his wife Cristina Fernández de Kirchner; Lula by Dilma Rousseff, earlier a revolutionary militant during the Brazilian military dictatorship; and Vázquez by Pepe Mujica. Chávez and Lula, particularly, would foster alliances with leftist and left-ish governments in the region, including the Alianza Bolivariana para los Pueblos de Nuestra América (ALBA, Bolivarian Alliance for the Peoples of Our America) movement (Chávez) and the São Paulo Forum (Lula); these extended, at one time or another, to sympathetic Caribbean governments in Antigua and Barbuda, Dominica, Grenada, St. Kitts and Nevis, Saint Lucia, and St. Vincent and the Grenadines. A second wave of leaders would extend the Pink Tide, like Ollanta Humala in Peru (elected in 2011), Fernando Lugo of Paraguay (2013), Andrés Manuel López Obrador in Mexico (2018), Gustavo Petro in Colombia (2022), and Bernardo Arévalo in Guatemala (2024).

And there would be reversals, including the Chilean Concertación's loss to billionaire Sebastián Piñera in 2009. A throwback twentieth-century reversal was the military coup d'état that removed José Manuel "Mel" Zelaya in Honduras in 2009. Very twenty-first century reversals, in contrast, were the impeachments of Lugo in 2012 and Dilma in 2016. In an especially ugly turn, the then senator Jair Bolsonaro "dedicated" his vote for impeachment to the army officer who had tortured Dilma when she was imprisoned by the military dictatorship (Bolsonaro, of course, would become president as a Trumpian right-wing populist).

In many Pink Tide countries, the turn to the left represented more than an ideological shift; it was celebrated as part of a larger movement of democratic renewal, expansion, and consolidation. Newly elected governments, pink or not, came not long after military dictatorships in the Southern Cone, Brazil, and Central America. Elsewhere, these outcomes were voters' way of rejecting stale, limited party choices (as in the long single-party rule by the PRM/PNR/PRI in Mexico, or the back-and-forth between the Conservative and Liberal parties in Venezuela and Colombia). In Ecuador and Bolivia, and arguably in Paraguay, electoral outcomes gave voice to the political preferences of Indigenous constituencies as never before. Certainly, the end of the Cold War eliminated some of the more restrictive limitations on party platforms; in most countries of the region, it would have been unthinkable to sustainably debate, develop, and pursue the social democratic or socialist policies of many Pink Tide governments during most of the twentieth century. And the redirection of US foreign policy priorities toward the Middle East after the September 11 terrorist attacks in 2001 further loosened Cold War–style constraints emanating from the United States.[11]

In subsequent chapters, we will look in greater depth at the secondary consequences of the growth patterns assessed in this chapter. More rapid growth in many countries contributed to reductions in poverty and inequality in this century, a phenomenon that will be explored in chapter 9. Many governments enjoyed windfall tax revenues, which they were able to deploy in new and effective ways, including social assistance programs considered in chapter 10. These new forms of public expenditure featured new discipline and creativity, hallmarks of the "possibilist state" assessed in chapter 11. The great liability of the Milagrinho growth model is that it slowed and even reversed the structural transformation of economies in the region away from commodity dependence, a set of issues to which we will return in chapter 8.

CHAPTER FOUR

The Jazz Effect

The Global Financial Crisis in Latin America (2008–2009)

IN JANUARY 2008, AMIDST a global financial crisis, Argentina's president, Cristina Fernández de Kirchner, dubbed the downturn the "jazz effect," given that it originated in the United States, the birthplace of jazz (see the news dispatch in the introduction for more of her comments). American citizens—particularly American jazz fans—could feel some gratitude that a foreign leader would use "jazz" as a shorthand for "American," the way others had used "tequila" as a shorthand for "Mexican" during its 1994 crisis: A less charitable head of state might have called the recession the result of a "Mickey Mouse Effect" or a "Processed Cheese Effect." (A metaphorical challenge related to the nicknames for the financial crises of the 1980s, 1990s, and 2000s, is that they refer to pleasurable things, like tequila, caipirinha, and jazz. The financial and economic effects named after them, however, are decidedly unpleasant.)[1]

The Argentinian president underscored an important element of the global transmission of the 2008 crisis. The 1994 and 1997 financial-market disruptions had originated in Latin American countries, and spread from their points of origin, visiting financial and economic woes upon their neighbors. The Jazz Effect was different. It originated in the United States, a country President Fernández de Kirchner wryly referred to as "what was once a model."

In this chapter, we will

    1. review the two waves of the Jazz Effect—"Take Five" and "Free Jazz"—in

the United States, and their impact in Latin America, in terms of growth slowdowns and reversals;

2. introduce the economic framework of the balance of payments as a means of tracing the international transmission of the financial crisis;

3. conclude with some considerations on the comparatively robust resilience of Latin American economies in 2008–2009.²

Two Movements of the Jazz Effect

The 2008 crisis differed not only from the 1990s crises made in Latin America; it also differed from the 1982 debt crisis. During that earlier crisis, sharp increases in international interest rates, intended by the Federal Reserve to drive down US inflation, unleashed a wave of sovereign debt defaults in Latin America. It may have been this catastrophic episode that led to the oft-repeated maxim, "when the United States sneezes, Latin America catches the flu." In 1982, Latin America contracted the flu, and in 2008, something more like an unpleasant cold; but during the latter case, the United States caught a debilitating flu.

From the Latin American perspective, the Jazz Effect unfolded in two phases: The first, a liquidity crisis, dates from the summer 2007 collapse of two Bear Stearns hedge funds; the second, a global trade and income downturn, dates from the bankruptcy of Lehman Brothers in September 2008. In each phase of the global financial crisis, the Jazz Effect had different tonalities and keys. In the first, the liquidity crisis, the Jazz Effect was akin to the sinuous alto saxophone of Paul Desmond, snaking around Dave Brubeck's piano on the 1959 recording of "Take Five"; distinct and different from what had gone before, but light and steady for those paying attention. The second phase, the collapse of income and trade, resembled the jazz of another alto saxophonist, Ornette Coleman, recorded the following year with a double quartet for the album *Free Jazz*: turbulent, unsettling, and unpredictable, giving rise to a new musical grammar. After *Free Jazz*, collective improvisation would never be heard in the same way again. The same can be said of Latin American countries' understanding of the global economy following the second phase of the Jazz Effect, a prolonged and confused cognitive (as well as material) crisis.³

The aggregate growth rate for the Latin America and Caribbean region exceeded that of the OECD members as a whole in the years 2007–2009; indeed,

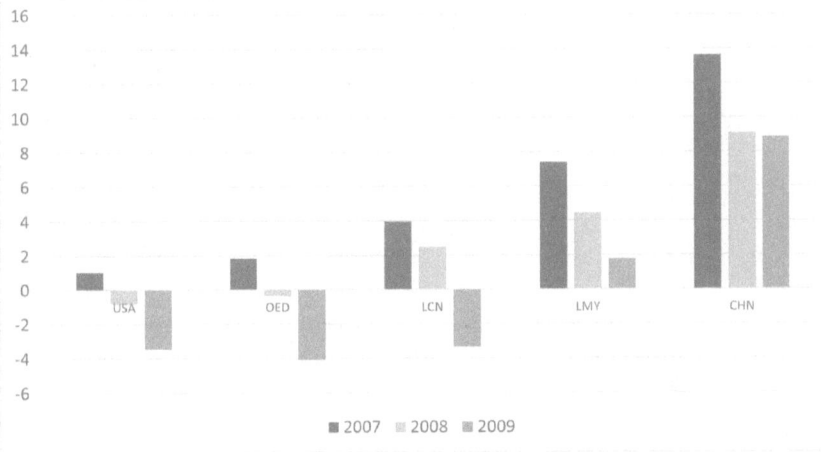

Figure 4.1. Economic growth, 2007–2009, selected regions and countries. Growth rates of GDP per capita, for the US, OECD member countries (OED), Latin America and the Caribbean (LCN), low and middle income countries (LMY), and China (CHN). *Source:* WDI database, World Bank.

Latin American growth exceeded that of the United States during this time frame (fig. 4.1). China's growth continued to outperform both Latin America and the OECD countries during the global financial crisis, as did low- and middle-income countries overall (in which aggregate China is a large component).

The growth path of the individual LAC-7 economies (fig. 4.2) illustrates the relative severity of the second phase of the Jazz Effect. For all of the seven largest Latin American economies, the trough year of national income per capita was 2009, with the exception of Venezuela, where it was 2010. The ominous economic events of 2007 and 2008, meanwhile, might have slowed growth but did not appreciably depress income per capita in these countries.

A number of other trends from the cross-country evidence on the impact of the crisis merit attention. First, and perhaps most important, all of the LAC-7 countries, with the exception of Mexico, experienced a less severe path of average income decline than did the mostly high-income economies of the OECD. That is to say, this was a crisis, as Cristina Fernández de Kirchner pointed out, that originated in Prebisch's Center, and moreover had a proportionally larger impact there than it did in the Periphery. What's more, most LAC-7 economies did not see their average income dip below their 2006 or 2007 level, unlike the OECD economies.

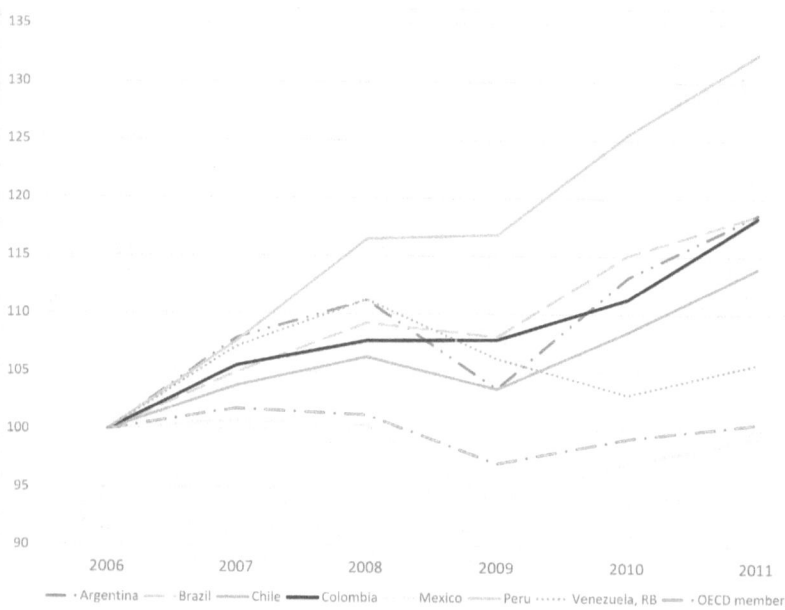

Figure 4.2. GDP per capita indices, LAC-7 and OECD, 2006–2011. The vertical axis measures an index set to equal 100 for all economies in 2006, derived from gross domestic product per capita in constant 2010 US dollars. *Source:* WDI database, World Bank.

The American flu did not spread to Latin America. Latin America's relatively better performance extends to other comparisons. For the OECD economies, and for the world as a whole, average income in 2009 was lower than in 2007. Among Latin American countries, this was true only for the following LAC-19 countries: Argentina, Chile (barely), El Salvador, Guatemala, Honduras, Mexico, Nicaragua, and Venezuela. For the other eleven economies, the crisis-related slowdown did not erase the gains in average income up to 2007. All LAC-19 economies had surpassed their 2007 average income by 2011, except for Mexico and Venezuela, which crossed that threshold the following year. The OECD economies, in contrast, barely regained their 2007 average income in 2013.

The Balance of Payments and Economic Exposure

The history of crises, panics, shocks, and other abrupt economic cataclysms in Latin America is a long one, and in modern times, as President Fernández de

Kirchner's comments illustrate, these crises are often transmitted from outside. A key part of the story is the transmission mechanism by which these contagions operate. The economic concept of the *balance of payments* provides a useful perspective from which to analyze the Jazz Effect: that is, the transmission of the global financial crisis from the United States and Europe to Latin America. And conversely, the Jazz Effect provides a rich example by which to understand the building blocks of the balance of payments.[4]

The balance of payments is a set of accounting conventions that permits the monitoring and analysis of a country's economic relationships with the rest of the world during a given year. The balance of payments is thus a kind of portrait of the position of an individual country within the wider world economy. In the interest of concreteness, let us take a closer look at the Colombian balance of payments on the eve of the financial crisis.

There are three accounts within the balance of payments: the current, capital, and financial accounts. The *current account* measures the monetary value of flows of trade of goods and services in and out of the country, as well as certain non-trade transactions of interest, notably including remittances sent home from nationals abroad (or a debit for remittances sent by migrant workers out of the country in question).

The *financial and capital accounts*, meanwhile, measure changes in the ownership of national assets; if a foreign national purchases a Colombian government bond, for example, the inflow of payment for the purchase adds positively to the Colombian financial/capital account. When Colombian companies make payments to foreign bondholders, in turn, the outflow subtracts from the balance of the financial/capital account. The Colombian financial/capital account similarly registers the records of cross-border transactions for other Colombian financial assets, including equities traded on the Colombian stock market purchased or sold by non-Colombians, and Colombian sales and purchases of non-Colombian financial assets abroad. The capital account is quantitatively substantially smaller than the financial account and records the results of capital transfers (a credit might include debt forgiveness, for example); in the discussion that follows, the capital and financial accounts will be lumped together.

Finally, the balance of payments has a double-entry bookkeeping logic. A surplus in the current account in a given year is offset by a deficit in the financial/capital account; and inversely, a current account deficit is offset by a financial/

capital account surplus. A simple example: A current account deficit creates a liability in the financial/capital accounts; the excess of purchases abroad must be financed either by an increase in foreign liabilities, or a decrease in ownership of foreign assets. Deficits or surpluses in either the current or financial/capital

TABLE 4.1. The Colombian balance of payments, 2007

Current Account	
Goods exports f.o.b.	30 577
Goods imports f.o.b.	−31 173
Balance on goods	−596
Services credit	3 636
Services debit	−6 243
Balance on services	−2 607
Income credit	1 868
Income debit	−9 755
Balance on income	−7 887
Current transfers credit	5 642
Current transfers debit	−410
Balance on current transfers	5 232
Current Account Balance	**−5 858**
Capital/Financial Accounts	
Direct investment abroad	−913
Direct investment in Colombia	9 040
Net direct investment	8 127
Portfolio investment assets	−1 098
Portfolio investment liabilities	1 719
Net portfolio investment	621
Other investment assets	−2 220
Other investment liabilities	3 809
Net other investment	1 589
Capital/Financial Accounts Balance	**10 337**
NET ERRORS And OMISSIONS	243
Changes In Reserve Assets	**−4 721**

Note: Figures expressed in millions of current US dollars.
Source: Derived from IMF (2008, 223–27).

accounts are, prima facie, neither good nor bad as indicators of economic performance.

On the eve of the global financial crisis, Colombia found itself with a current account deficit of some $5.9 billion (table 4.1). It is common to emphasize the importance of the trade balance to the overall current account results, and indeed, the Colombian import and export values dwarfed other components of its current account. Nevertheless, the contribution of the Colombian trade *deficit* to the current account deficit was quite small. In fact, Colombia had run a trade surplus in the years 2000–2006. A more important contributor to the current account deficit lay in the income balance (–$7.9 billion). Digging into the statistics, the lion's share of this sub-deficit was a debit in the entry for investment income, particularly dividends and distributed profits: that is, income transfers made by Colombian-based firms to holders of their bonds and securities abroad. Meanwhile, an important positive contributor to the current account was the balance on current transfers. Digging beneath the surface here, there is a large credit ($4.5 billion) for workers' remittances, money sent home by Colombians abroad. By way of comparison, the current account credit for workers' remittances in the same year for Mexico was $24 billion; for Peru, $2.1 billion.

The financial/capital accounts provide details regarding investment activity, both direct investment and portfolio investment. Direct investment differs from portfolio investment in that the former includes the creation of new fixed assets—capital, in the economic sense—while the latter measures changes in the ownership of existing capital. Thus, when the Swiss coal-mining giant Glencore established an open-pit mine in Colombia, as it did at La Jagua with important investments in 2007, that constituted direct investment in the financial/capital account. If foreign investors meanwhile purchased stocks traded on the Bolsa de Valores de Colombia, issued by Colombian oil producer Ecopetrol, that was portfolio investment. (In practice, the distinction is not always as clear as stated here; in particular, acquisitions of Colombian firms by foreigners, including the purchase of privatized enterprises formerly controlled by the state, typically count as direct investment, despite the resemblance of these transactions to portfolio investment.)

Colombia's considerable financial/capital account surplus was largely explained by the sub-account related to direct investment; foreign firms like Glencore created or acquired fixed capital in excess of $9 billion in 2007. It bears repeating that in balance of payment accounting, a surplus is not necessarily good, and a deficit is not necessarily bad. The concept of foreign direct investment bears this out: The inflow of capital into Colombia from investments like Glencore's was a credit and reflected in part the positive assessment of global investors about the country's economic potential. But it also increased foreigners' claims on Colombian resources and could set the stage for often asymmetric disputes between giant foreign firms and weak national governments.[5]

A final entry in Colombia's balance of payments (skipping over the "Net Errors and Omissions" line) is the change in reserve assets: essentially, foreign exchange like dollars or euros, as well as gold, held by the Banco de la República, Colombia's central bank. Here, a negative number represents an *increase* in the Banco de la República's reserve holdings (increased dollar holdings by the Colombian central bank can be interpreted as an increased claim by the United States). In 2007, the Banco de la República's reserves increased by $4.7 billion, nearly all of it in the form of increased foreign exchange. The considerable inflow of foreign direct investment passed in part through the central bank, exchanging US dollars (or Swiss francs, in the case of Glencore) for Colombian pesos in order to effect purchases in the country.

If you add up all the items in the lower panel of table 4.1 in boldface, the total should offset the current account deficit in the upper panel (in fact, the two differ by $1 million, a rounding error in the realm of national accounts).

Shocks beyond a country's borders might be transmitted through either the current or financial/capital accounts. Take for example the current account. A current account shock can operate through trade: A sudden downturn in the economic conditions in Colombia's principal trading partner might lead to a decline in earnings by Colombian exporters, reflected in a corresponding decline in the current account. Another current account shock is transmitted through remittances: Restrictions on movement of Latin American nationals into the United States or Spain, for example, or reduced employment prospects for workers in the diaspora, could be reflected in a current account decline. Now consider financial/capital account shocks. If Colombian bond rates remain steady but interest rates earned on bonds elsewhere drop, international investors might step up their purchases of Colombian bonds, increasing the financial/capital account.

The easier it is to undertake these kinds of transactions, the more exposed Colombia (or whatever the economy in question) is to external shocks both good and bad. High Developmentalist policy strategies sought to throw sand in the gears of many of these transactions by raising tariffs on trade, for example. This was deliberate; the import-substituting industrialization set into motion by the 1949 CEPAL report discussed in chapter 2 was inspired in part by the prior experience with "spontaneous ISI" that erupted during the world wars of the first half of the twentieth century: International trade broke down amidst the global conflict, and incipient manufacturing industries were able to develop shielded from competition from goods produced by the warring powers. High Developmentalist ISI would substitute tariffs and other protections for the protections offered by wartime disruptions in trade. Later, the Washington Consensus policy prescriptions, in contrast, generally sought to lower the barriers to flows recorded in the balance of payments, increasing exposure of Latin American economies to shocks in the current and financial/capital accounts.

Latin American economies were vastly more exposed to external shocks via the current account on the eve of the Jazz Effect in 2007 than they had been on the eve of the debt crisis in 1981. Three measures illustrate this trend. The first is *trade openness*, defined as the value of a country's exports plus imports, divided by national income. In 1981, trade was only 14.3 percent of national income in Argentina; by 2007, that indicator had grown to 41 percent. For smaller Central American and Caribbean economies, trade openness was higher still in 2007: the Dominican Republic (62 percent), El Salvador (77.6 percent), Costa Rica (86.5 percent), Nicaragua (93 percent), Honduras (135.1 percent), and Panama (149.6 percent). All of these numbers had risen since 1981, except in Costa Rica. The consequence: A sudden drop in exports or imports is more keenly felt in a more open economy.

A second measure is the *contribution of exports to growth*, which indicates the degree to which an economy's national income depends upon selling goods and services to the wider world. In the decade prior to 1981, exports had contributed just 6 percent to Argentina's growth, while in the decade leading up to the financial crisis, exports contributed 67 percent to Chile's growth. A third current account channel is *remittance flows*, which grew to important shares of national income in many Central American and Caribbean countries. A turndown in construction in the United States—which happened during the 2008 crisis—could be expected to depress employment of migrants and also depress their homeward-bound remittances.

The exposure of economies in 2007 via the capital and financial accounts is a little more complicated. On the one hand, the Jazz Effect struck Latin America as a whole while the region exhibited a current account surplus, indicating a reduced need for foreign financing as reflected in the financial/capital account. But other indicators suggested more exposure for some countries: notably, the ratio of external debt to national income, which was higher in 2007 than in 1981 in Argentina and Colombia, and lower in Chile, Mexico, Peru, and Venezuela, for example. This debt ratio, if high, implies the obligation to maintain a stream of debt service payments; if low, it might suggest the need for future financing, which could be complicated by an external financial crisis. Finally, most countries in the region had significantly reduced obstacles to capital and financial account transactions by eliminating or reducing multiple exchange rates, capital controls, and restrictions on foreign exchange transactions; these changes increased exposure.

Take Five: The Liquidity Crisis, mid-2007–mid-2008

In early 2007, the speculative bubble that had inflated the values of assets linked to the subprime mortgage market in the United States burst. By summer in the Northern Hemisphere, there was a near-complete freezing of interbank lending as banks came to realize that they had incorrectly assessed their exposure, and the exposure of their competitors, to the risky subprime mortgage market. The plummeting of interbank lending, in turn, was more broadly experienced as a liquidity crisis; firms, financial or otherwise, were unable to access credit of various maturities. A coordinated effort by the world's principal central banks injected $326 billion of liquidity into financial markets. Those central banks moreover began a protracted campaign to lower interest rates and encourage capital spending by firms and households. Governments in rich countries simultaneously expanded fiscal spending to promote economic activity. These measures nevertheless failed to avert the deepening of the credit crisis.

Meanwhile, the contagion of subprime-related risk in rich-country capital markets encouraged investors to seek more secure financial assets, the so-called "flight to quality" that characterizes every financial crisis. The historically unusual nature of the flight to quality this time is that capital flew *into* Latin American financial markets. Whereas in the past—as in the tequila and caipirinha crises—investors dumped Latin American financial assets simply because they were in the same asset class and came from the same neighborhood as Mexican or Brazilian assets, this time investors more carefully distinguished among the financial assets of emerging and advanced economies. In a development that few would have predicted in the depths of the 1980s debt crisis, Latin American bonds were regarded as high-quality instruments, even when many US and European bonds were not. (There is an interesting historical precedent. During the chaotic monetary history of the first half of the nineteenth century in the US, one of the safest and most universally accepted means of making payments was the silver Mexican peso.)

The flight to quality mitigated the global liquidity crisis in Latin America. So too did strong continued remittance flows to Mexico, the Dominican Republic, and to Central American and Andean countries. Finally, Chinese growth was proportionally far less depressed during this phase than US and European growth, and Chinese demand for Latin American commodity exports persisted; this tempered the downturn in the current account for countries whose trade with China had increased over the preceding half-decade.

Free Jazz: The Global Collapse of Trade and Income, September 2008–2011

The bankruptcy of Lehman Brothers in September 2008 signaled the onset of a far more damaging phase of the crisis. The Lehman bankruptcy was the detonator of a broader banking crisis, which further exacerbated the ongoing credit crisis. Meanwhile the effects of the financial crisis on the *real* economy (e.g., output, trade, employment, as opposed to the financial economy) became patently visible, reaching levels last seen in the rich countries during the Great Depression of the 1930s. These real-economy effects in the rich countries of what Prebisch called the Center, led to more dire impacts in the Latin American Periphery than those witnessed during the Take Five phase.

The Free Jazz effect was propagated to Latin American economies via both the current and capital accounts. Begin with the current account. The value of global trade tumbled 11 percent in 2009; Latin America as a whole saw its export volume fall by 3.5 percent. At the same time, the region's terms of trade fell 10 percent. Each of these effects reduced the purchasing power of Latin American exports, and the ability to pay for imports: The combined effect was a drop in export purchasing power of 14 percent. On the financial/capital account side, global saving—the principal source of financial institutions' capacity to extend credit—plummeted by 16 percent in 2009. Net private portfolio flows to Latin America whipsawed from a $42 billion inflow in 2007 to a $24 billion outflow by 2009. The volume of domestic assets purchased by foreign investors, which includes foreign direct investment, fell by half (OECD 2010, 29–30).

Let us consider the impact of the Jazz Effect—the transmission of the global financial crisis to Latin America—by quantifying the shock to the current and capital account balances of the region's seven largest economies. We can do this, somewhat crudely, by comparing the current account and capital account balances in 2007 to their values in 2009.

LAC-7 economies with a current account surplus in 2007 had a surplus in 2009 (Peru, Argentina, Chile, and Venezuela); those with a deficit in 2007 still had a deficit in 2009 (Mexico and Colombia). An exception is Brazil, which passed from a tiny surplus to a deficit (fig. 4.3). A best-fit line through these seven points is therefore upward sloping. But the slope of the line is about 0.5, which means that the typical LAC-7 economy saw its current account balance diminish by about half a percentage point of GDP. That is, a surplus economy's current account balance fell by 0.5 percent of GDP, while a deficit economy's deficit plunged further into deficit by an amount equal to 0.5 percent of GDP. That is not a small number. For an economy like Mexico's, the value of whose GDP was close to $1 trillion in 2007, that implies a reduction on the order of $5 billion.

In a similar pattern, those economies with financial/capital account surpluses in 2007 had surpluses in 2009 (Mexico, Colombia, Brazil, and Peru); while those in deficit in 2007 (Venezuela and Chile) remained in deficit in 2009 (fig. 4.4). Here the exception is Argentina, with a financial/capital account surplus in 2007, switched to deficit in 2009. A simple best-fit line through these points is again positively sloped—a typical economy with a financial/capital account surplus (deficit) in 2007 was also in surplus (deficit) in 2009—with a slope of 0.4, meaning that the typical LAC-7 economy experienced a decline in its financial/capital account balance equal to 0.6 percent of GDP.

These simple statistical exercises demonstrate that the Jazz Effect transmitted to LAC-7 economies was large. Of course, focusing as we do on the *balances* of these accounts masks even wider, and contradictory, swings in the line-by-line details of these aggregate accounts. Goods exports, for example, fell between these two years by nearly 4 percent of GDP in Mexico, 5 percent in Venezuela,

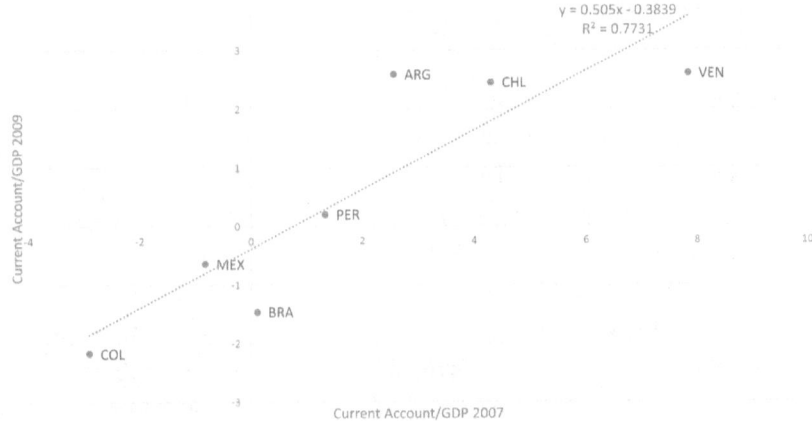

Figure 4.3. Current account balances, 2007 and 2009, LAC-7 countries. Each country's current account balance is expressed as shares of GDP in the same year.
Source: Current account balances derived from *Balance of Payments Statistics Yearbook, Part 1: Country Tables*, IMF; GDP from WDI database, World Bank.

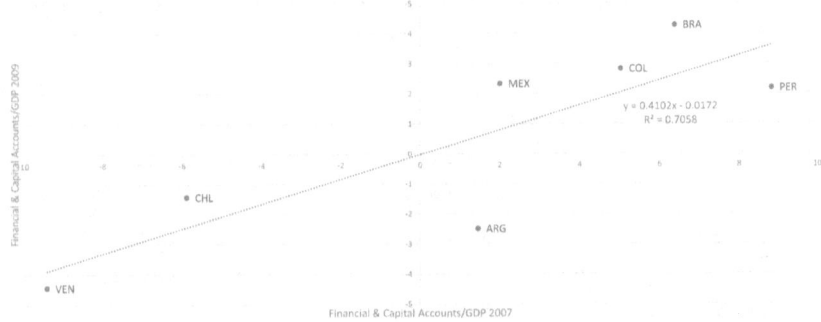

Figure 4.4. Financial/capital account balances, 2007 and 2009, LAC-7 countries. Each country's financial/capital account balance is expressed as a share of GDP in the same year.
Source: Financial/capital account balances derived from *Balance of Payments Statistics Yearbook, Part 1: Country Tables*, IMF; GDP from WDI database, World Bank.

and 8 percent in Chile: Some of these export shocks are larger than the total current account changes (which means they were offset by current account improvements elsewhere in the statistics). Moreover, the use of annual data for 2007 and 2009 only imperfectly captures the "before" and "after" of the global shock: The Take Five phase was underway during the latter part of 2007, and the Free Jazz phase was still in effect during much of 2009.

The double-entry bookkeeping logic of the balance of payments reviewed above means that changes in the current account are mirrored by offsetting changes in the financial/capital accounts. As such, we would expect the change between 2007 and 2009 in the current account balance (as a proportion to GDP) to be equal to -1 times the change in the financial/capital accounts. A review of the magnitude of these changes does indeed reveal a negative relationship between them. However, the matchup is not perfect. In accordance with our overview of the Colombian example in table 4.1, the resolution of these discrepancies must lie in changes in international reserves to balance the accounts. And indeed, the LAC-7 countries with the largest discrepancies between the sizes of their current account and financial/capital account adjustments—Peru and Chile—also have the largest movements in the size of international reserves. Remember that a negative entry for reserve holdings in the balance of payments corresponds to an *increase* in reserves in a country. What's more, comparing 2007 and 2009 is a comparison of reserve *changes* in the first year to reserve changes in the second. In the case of Chile, 2007 was marked by a decline in foreign exchange holdings of $3.2 billion, depressing the overall financial/capital account balance. In 2009, however, Chile had an inflow of reserves of nearly $1.7 billion, much of it in the form of "special drawing rights" with the IMF, a kind of reserve-quality credit granted by the Fund as part of its efforts to ameliorate the liquidity crisis. So the large change in Chile's reserve position represents a combination of market and policy-induced movements, and a shift from a net outflow of reserves in one year to a net inflow in the second.

Peru's net international reserve assets, meanwhile, rose—thanks to an increase of $10.2 billion in foreign exchange in 2007. That inflow had dwindled precipitously by 2009, to just over $700 million. The change in Peruvian reserves was bolstered in 2009, as in the Chilean case, by an infusion of some $800 million of IMF special drawing rights.

Explaining Latin America's Comparative Success: Exposed but Resilient

The foregoing statistical exercises are meant to shine a brighter light on the magnitude of the external shock, particularly in the areas of trade, remittance, and financial flows, transmitted during the global financial crisis to the LAC-7 economies, and to demonstrate the changes in particular balances. These were sizeable and could scarcely help but cause macroeconomic hardship, especially during the calamitous Free Jazz phase of the crisis. And yet, Latin America's economic performance, in aggregate, was not as severely curtailed as the rich-country OECD economies: GDP per capita in 2009 in Latin America and the Caribbean as a whole shrank by 3 percent; among OECD countries, the contraction was 4.2 percent. In 2010, OECD economic growth rebounded to a positive 2.2 percent; in Latin America and the Caribbean, the rebound was to an even more robust 4.7 percent.[6] How is it that a region more exposed to external shocks, good or bad, than in the past, should fare comparatively better than the rich countries at the Center, or indeed better than Latin America during the 1980s debt crisis? The short answer is that Latin American economies, largely more exposed, were also more resilient.

Take the case of the current account. A current account shock largely affects exporting countries, who find demand for their products depressed by a recession in the global Center, or their export earnings depressed by a drop in the world price of their principal export, or both. But Latin American current accounts were more resilient in 2007 in at least two senses. First, their export product baskets had grown more diversified; this was especially true of Colombia and Mexico. Second, their export destinations had become more diversified as well, as countries sold more to China, and smaller proportions of their exports to the United States and Europe. While Chinese growth lagged during the crisis, compared to its historical double-digit rates of increase, China's national income per capita nevertheless rose by a heady 9.1 percent in 2008 and 8.9 percent in 2009, which kept demand for many Latin American exports high even as US demand faltered. Among the countries whose export partner list had diversified: Chile, Costa Rica, and Peru. Brazil's current account resilience rose, both in terms of diversity of exported products and diversity of export markets. There were exceptions and mixed successes in creating resilience, of course: Venezuela found its export basket even more concentrated on petroleum in 2007 than it was in the past, and its export destinations were less diverse as well. While Mexico's export products were more diverse at the onset of the crisis, its dependence on the United States as a market had increased, exposing it to the sharp American economic downturn proportionally more than its South American neighbors.

Capital and financial account exposure is a matter of not finding external financing when needed, with the risk that domestic firms and governments cannot secure loans, or issue bonds or equities to finance investment and operations. Such "sudden stops" in external finance had exacerbated economic crises in the region's past.[7] Financial/capital account resilience had increased in the meantime. First, as seen in the exploration of the LAC-7 economies, fewer had current account deficits—which imply a need for financing those deficits—in 2007 than had surpluses. Second, the ratio of external debt to GDP had fallen for some, though not all, countries in the region during the Milagrinho years; Chile and Peru are exemplary cases. Such countries are less subject to "rollover risk," or the inability to refinance short-term external debt if fresh capital inflows are cut off. Moreover, the accumulation of reserves during the Milagrinho period meant that reserves were sufficient to refinance a much larger share of shorter-maturity debt than in the past. Finally, Latin American external debt, both sovereign debt issued by governments and private debt issued by firms, had longer maturities, and were more likely to be financed in local currencies rather than dollars or other international currencies, than in the past. All of these changes in the structure of indebtedness made Latin American economies more resilient in the face of financial/capital account shocks like those experienced in the 2008 crisis. While the Latin American financial sector withstood the global financial shock, it is also true that before, during and after the crisis, observers continued to bemoan the lackluster performance of the sector to provide financial intermediation: the movement of resources from savers to investors.

The central question posed by Latin America's Jazz Effect history is how so many countries in the region were simultaneously more exposed to external shocks—like shrinking export demand or "sudden stops" of needed capital—and yet also more resilient. The logic of the Center and the Periphery remained as salient as ever. But in this crisis, at least, internal economic conditions in the Periphery had evolved to equip peripheral countries to weather the economic storm. This chapter has presented and summarized the trends in some quantitative detail. An explanation for the greater resilience of so many Latin American countries lies in better economic governance than in the past; an assessment of this will be provided in chapter 11, when we look more closely at the phenomenon of the "possibilist" state.

CHAPTER FIVE

Hurricane Season (2010–2019)

IN JUNE 2022, JAMIE Dimon, the CEO of JPMorganChase, the largest bank in the United States, warned of a coming economic "hurricane": "You'd better brace yourself," he cautioned. Dimon was raising the alarm regarding interest-rate hikes by the Federal Reserve System in the United States.[1] My point here is unrelated to the particular hurricane he was forecasting, but rather to assert that "economic hurricanes" happen, and companies—and households, and communities, and countries—exposed to hurricanes are well-advised to increase their resilience to such shocks before they occur. Latin American growth during the decade assessed in this chapter weathered its share of economic hurricanes, including the knock-on effects of a round of tightening of US monetary policy like the one Dimon warned of. In many ways, the period 2010–2019 was a Hurricane Season for the region.[2]

The story of Latin America in the midst of the Jazz Effect is one of an increasingly open and exposed economy—a region vulnerable to economic hurricanes, by dint of cross-border flows of goods, services, capital, and people—but at the same time a region newly and increasingly *resilient* in the face of such shocks. The global financial crisis brought the Milagrinho growth boom to an abrupt stop, transmitting shocks via the current and financial/capital accounts, as recounted in chapter 4. The Jazz Effect ushered in two years of painful contraction. But Latin America's growth slowdown was less marked, and its economies quicker to recover, than in the rich countries where the crisis originated, in stark contrast to the region's historical experience with economic hurricanes. Latin America's resilience was in part the result of conscious policy choices made by governments in the region, notably in terms of macroeconomic discipline. In the long- and slow-growth interim between the Jazz Effect and the Covid-19 pandemic, how well did Latin America's economic resilience to hurricanes stand up? How much of that resilience was worn down by economic hurricanes?

In this chapter, we will

1. review the comparative growth experience of Latin American countries during the Hurricane Season;
2. survey some of the economic hurricanes that beset the region and the world;
3. chart the evolution of exposure and resilience to current account shocks in the region;
4. similarly, review the evolution of exposure and resilience to capital/financial-account shocks in the region.

The last two of these topics will draw extensively upon the balance of payments framework introduced in chapter 4 and will use a variety of measures of exposure and resilience.

Slowing Growth

Latin American economies grew more slowly in the 2010s than they did in the 2000s, even accounting for the financial crisis in the earlier decade: Latin America's average annual growth from 2000 to 2009 was 1.7 percent; in the subsequent decade, it was scarcely 1.1 percent, similar to growth rates observed during the "Lost Decade" of the 1990s (fig. 2.1).

Not only did Latin America's growth performance in the 2010s lag behind the previous decade's, it lagged behind that of other economies after 2010. Latin America was converging toward the world's average income level until 2013 but has grown more slowly ever since (recall that we say Economy A is *converging* toward Economy B, if the former is poorer and is growing more rapidly than the latter). Between 2010 and 2019, average income worldwide rose from about $13,600 to $16,600, a 21.7 percent increase over ten years. The corresponding increase among low- and middle-income countries (LMY)—the developing world—was 37.4 percent, or a rise from $7,500 to $10,400 (fig. 5.1): The more rapid growth of developing economies between 2010 and 2019, compared to the world overall, is consistent with the logic of economic convergence. During the same decade, cumulative growth in the rich OECD economies was lower than the global average, at 13.5 percent.³ Of course, the most spectacular growth observed among developing economies during this period was that of China, still below the world average income level, but visibly converging toward it in fig. 5.1, and marking a cumulative ten-year growth rate in excess of 80 percent. Latin America's ten-year cumulative growth, meanwhile, was a paltry 7.7 percent, slower than developing countries as a whole, slower than the global rate of growth, and far behind China's still-breakneck growth (visually, these comparisons can be seen as differences in the slope of the various lines in fig. 5.1).⁴

Among the LAC-7 economies, two groups emerge with respect to growth performance (fig. 5.2): those with relatively smoother and steeper growth rates (Chile, Colombia, Mexico, and Peru), on the one hand, and those with more erratic growth paths (Argentina, Brazil, and most notably, Venezuela), on the other.

Extending the comparison to all Latin American economies illustrates that the LAC-7 countries' fortunes depicted in fig. 5.2 diverged in this decade from

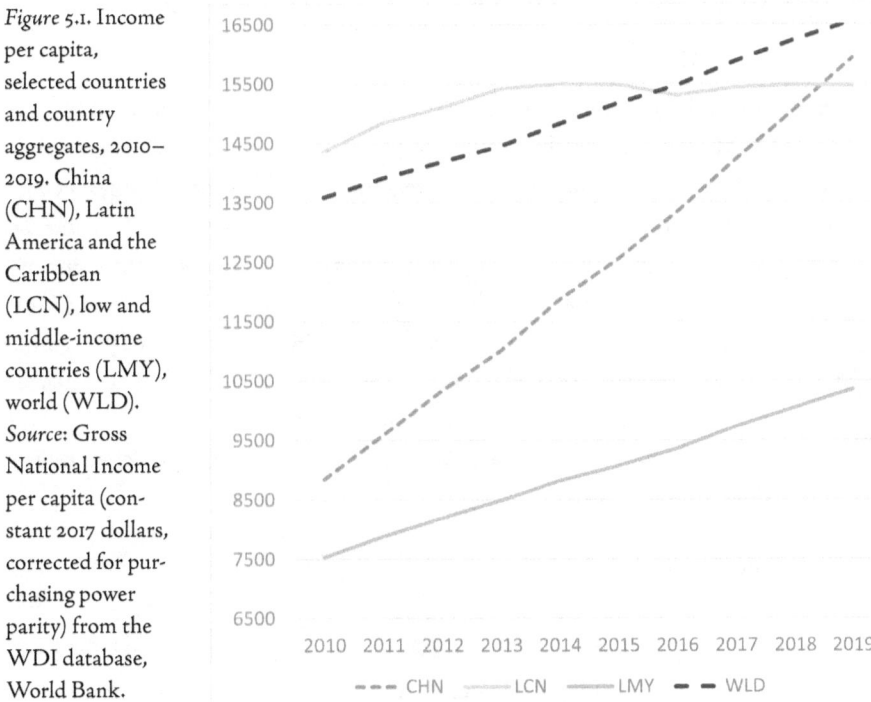

Figure 5.1. Income per capita, selected countries and country aggregates, 2010–2019. China (CHN), Latin America and the Caribbean (LCN), low and middle-income countries (LMY), world (WLD). *Source:* Gross National Income per capita (constant 2017 dollars, corrected for purchasing power parity) from the WDI database, World Bank.

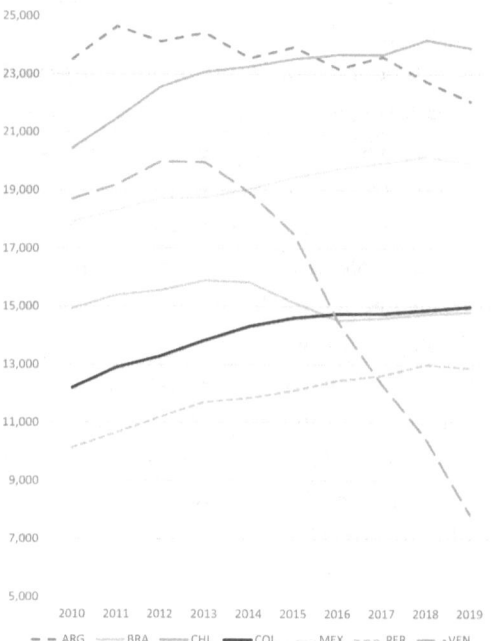

Figure 5.2. Income per capita, LAC-7 economies, 2010–2019. GDP per capita (constant 2017 dollars, adjusted for purchasing power parity), WEO database (April 2023 version), IMF.

those of smaller economies in the region (fig. 5.3). Indeed, the low cumulative growth of the region overall in fig. 5.3—just over 8 percent cumulative growth—is weighed down by the unusually poor performance of four of the largest economies in the region: Argentina, Brazil, Mexico, and Venezuela. In contrast, Bolivia, Costa Rica, and El Salvador saw growth in the range of the comparatively spritelier LAC-7 members Peru and Colombia. Paraguay, Uruguay, Guatemala, Nicaragua, Honduras, and Cuba, meanwhile, were in LAC-7 member Chile's growth neighborhood. Panama and the Dominican Republic experienced growth that exceeded that of low- and middle-income countries as a whole (LMY), though no Latin American countries' growth rate approached that of China during this decade.

Economic Hurricanes

Looking more closely at Latin America's growth and its links to the global economy during the dour Hurricane Season, across countries and over time, resembles a remix of the elements of the earlier decade's experience, from the boom of

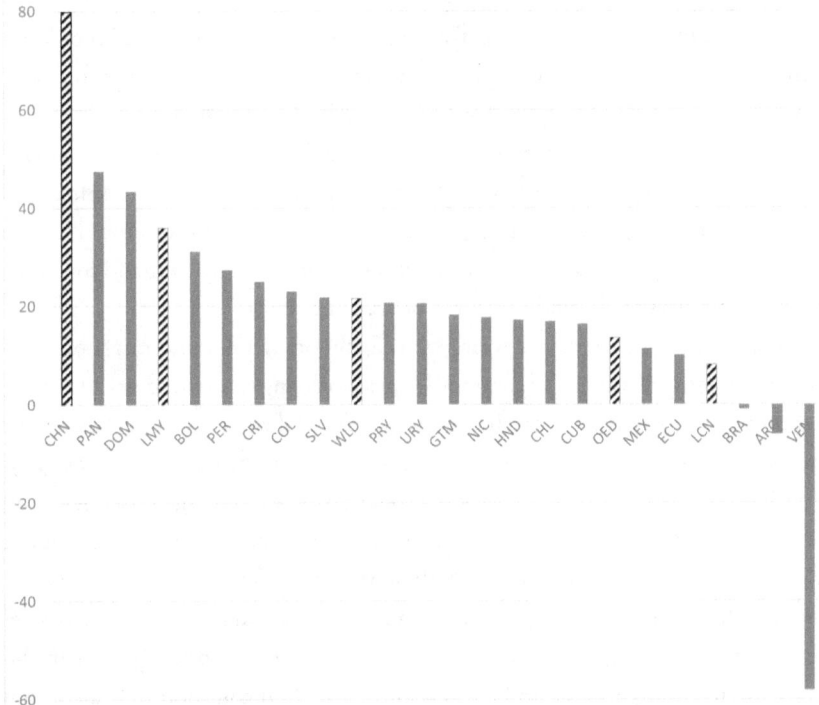

Figure 5.3. Cumulative growth in per capita income, Latin America and selected economies, 2010–2019. Calculated as the proportional increase (or decrease) in GDP per capita between 2010 and 2019. GDP per capita (constant 2017 dollars, adjusted for purchasing power parity) from the WDI database, World Bank. Cuban data only through 2017 (accessed July 2019 and no longer in the WDI database four years later). Venezuelan data from the IMF WEO database.

the Milagrinho to the crisis of the Jazz Effect. Take Brazil, the region's largest economy. Brazil experienced economic growth (of per capita income) in excess of 6.5 percent in 2010 on the heels of the global financial crisis. This was called by some in Brazilian media a "PIBaço": This translates roughly, and less poetically, as something like a "GDP blowout." This rate of growth of GDP exceeded, if briefly, the country's Milagrinho growth rate. A few short years later, however, Brazil embarked on a historically deep and protracted recession, beginning in the second quarter of 2014. The deteriorating performance of the macroeconomy contributed to the political pressures that would lead, in a startling turn of events, to the impeachment of President Dilma Rousseff in 2015.

From country to country, over the Hurricane Season, the same kind of current account and capital/financial account shocks that had marked the global financial crisis beset the region again, though in a variable-speed, staggered, and in many cases, muffled remix. Several negative shocks—economic hurricanes—stand out. First, growth slowed growth in China: The country's average annual GDP per capita growth went from 8.8 percent in the 1990s to 9.7 percent in the 2000s, dropping to 7.1 percent in the 2010s. Together with slower growth in the United States and Europe, this translated into more sluggish demand for Latin American exports of all kinds—a current account shock.

Second, commodity prices were volatile, shooting up sometimes, but frequently plunging. The path of commodity prices during the second decade of the twenty-first century traces out the whipsaw effects of the Hurricane Season, in three up-and-down phases (these can be seen on the right-hand side of fig. 3.4). In mid-2008, commodity prices stood at nearly three times their 2003 level; by the start of 2009, they had fallen to about one and a half times the 2003 level. Prices thereafter climbed briskly to their pre-crisis levels by early 2011, and remained high until mid-2014, falling and flitting around twice their 2003 level thereafter. This aggregate pattern is reflected in the prices of subgroups of the aggregate, including metals and energy, and individual commodities, including soybeans, produced and exported by Latin American countries.

In part, the ups and downs of commodity prices had to do with the corresponding accelerations and decelerations of economic growth in economies like China's, already mentioned. In addition to these demand-side factors, there are supply-side factors as well; notably, in the energy sector, increased capacity in shale production and other unconventional methods in the United States and elsewhere increased competition and depressed prices for energy, including petroleum and gas.

And third and finally, governments and firms in Latin America responded to cheap global credit, notably by increasing their foreign indebtedness, a consequence of rich countries' monetary stimulus to recover from the global recession.

Exposure and Resilience during the Hurricane Season

The big question that we will pose in the remainder of this chapter is: How did exposure and resilience evolve in the long, slower-growth interregnum between the Jazz Effect and the Covid-19 crisis? Chapter 4 drew upon many measures that help track exposure and resilience, in the current account and in the financial/capital account. We will synthesize trends in nine of these indicators: four related to the current account, five to the financial/capital account. In the interest of legibility of the storyline, this chapter will not present detailed graphics or tables of the year-to-year evolution of these seven indicators for all nineteen countries in the region. Instead, I have summarized key information—the interpretation of the variables, the central trend in each, as well as noteworthy exceptions—in tables 5.1 and 5.2.[5] Each of these tables can be viewed as a sort of high-level dashboard for monitoring these trends in the region. (Note that the indicators in these tables are not always expressed in intuitively understood units; nevertheless, I will provide guidance throughout about what higher or lower values of these indicators mean.)

Let us begin with the current account (table 5.1), which records import and export flows, as well as other income flows, including remittances sent home by a country's migrants abroad. An economic hurricane can be transmitted through the current account if one of your country's major trading partners experiences an economic crisis and buys fewer goods and services from you; or if your access to critical imports is interrupted; or if members of your diaspora in that country are thrown out of work and are less able to send money home to their families.

Trade Openness, defined as the ratio of the sum of exports plus imports to national income, declined slightly between the Milagrinho years and the Hurricane Season, among all nineteen countries, by a little more than a percentage point of GDP; it rose by about the same percentage among the LAC-7 countries. Note that there is a substantial range of trade openness exhibited among Latin American countries in each period. The value of trade exceeded national income in Panama, Honduras, and Nicaragua during the Hurricane Season; at the other end of the spectrum, trade constituted less than 40 percent of national income in economies as disparate as Argentina, Colombia, Cuba, and Brazil. In general, one would expect smaller countries—like those in Central America—to rely proportionally more on international trade, and larger countries—like the LAC-7—to rely on their larger internal markets, hypotheses that would lead the smaller economies to be more open by this measure. There were counterexamples: larger countries that were more open than average (like Chile) and smaller countries that were more closed (like Cuba).

In sum, exposure, as measured by trade openness, was little changed before

TABLE 5.1. Indicators of current account exposure and resilience, Hurricane Season

Indicator	Definition	Interpretation	Means and Country Extremes	Milagrinho-to-Hurricane-Season Trend
Trade Openness	Value of imports PLUS the value of exports, expressed as a percentage of national income (can be higher than 100 percent).	**Exposure:** Greater openness subjects a country to greater risk of a trade-related downturn.	Average openness: 62.7; Average LAC-7 openness: 46.3; Top Five: PAN (125), HND (109.3), NIC (102.2), SLV (76.4), PRY (72.6); Bottom Five: BRA (25.6), ARG (29.6), CUB (35.2), COL (37.2), PER (49.1)	Average openness fell slightly (64.3 to 62.7, 1.6 pp of GDP); Average openness among LAC-7 rose slightly (45.2 to 46.3, 1.1 pp of GDP); Noteworthy: Openness rose in MEX from 53.1 to 70.1
Exports' Contribution to Growth (ECG)	Growth rate of exports multiplied by the ratio of exports to national income.	**Exposure:** A pattern of growth more responsive to exports means growth is more vulnerable to sluggish or declining exports.	Average ECG: 1.13; Average LAC-7 ECG: 0.76; Top Five: NIC (2.7), HND (2.2), MEX (2.1), CRI (1.9), PRY (1.6); Bottom Five: CUB (−0.1), ARG (0.3), BRA (0.4), CHL (0.4), COL (0.5)	Average ECG unchanged (1.14 to 1.13); Average LAC-7 ECG fell slightly (0.82 to 0.76); Noteworthy: CUB fell from 1.8 to −0.1; DOM rose from 0.2 to 1.6; MEX rose from 0.7 to 2.1
Remittances	Workers' remittances as a share of national income.	**Exposure:** Higher relative value of remittances makes current account vulnerable to sudden stops in remittances.	Average: 4.5; Average LAC-7: 0.8; Top Five: SLV (19.0) HND (17.7), GTM (11.0), NIC (10.2), DOM (7.5); Bottom Five: CHL (0.03), VEN (0.03), ARG (0.10), BRA (0.14), URY (0.19)	Average unchanged (4.5); Average LAC-7 down (0.96 to 0.81); Noteworthy: Central America-plus (CRI, DOM, GTM, HND, NIC, PAN, SLV) > 2× regional average: 9.6
Herfindahl-Hirschman Index (HHI) of Export Concentration	A measure of dispersion of trade value across an exporter's partners. A country with trade (export OR import) concentrated in a very few markets will have HHI close to 1. A country with a perfectly diversified trade portfolio will have HHI close to 0.	**Resilience:** Higher diversification of trading partners (lower HHI) lowers the relative impact of a trade shock from any single partner.	Average: 0.19; Average LAC-7: 0.19; Top Five: ARG (0.06), PAN (0.07), BRA (0.08), URY (0.09), PER (0.10); Bottom Five: MEX (0.53), NIC (0.37), HND (0.32), DOM (0.32), VEN (0.27)	Partners less concentrated on average (0.19 from 0.25) and for LAC-7 (0.19 from 0.22)

Indicators modelled on analysis in OECD (2010, Macroeconomic Overview). Statistics are decadal averages (for 2010–2019), or differences in decadal averages (2000–2009 vs. 2010–2019, final column). pp = percentage points. VEN and PAN missing from ECG. CUB missing from Remittances and HHI. Full graphs with indicators available from the author. Source: Indicators summarized here calculated from data drawn from the World Development Indicators and World Integrated Trade Solutions (WITS) databases (both from the World Bank).

and after the Jazz Effect. But this scant change should be placed in the context of the marked increase in openness since the depths of the debt crisis. During the 1980s, the average value of the index of openness was 47.9 among all nineteen countries, and 32.1 among the LAC-7.

Exports' Contribution to Growth (ECG) measures the exposure of an economy's growth rate to fluctuations in exports. ECG is calculated for an economy by multiplying the growth of exports by the ratio of exports to national income. Take Uruguay as an example. Uruguay's exports of goods and services grew by 8.5 percent in 2008, and the value of exports made up 30.2 percent of Uruguayan GDP in that year. Then we estimate exports' contribution to Uruguayan economic growth in 2008 to be equal to 8.5 times 0.302, or about two and a half percentage points. Exports' contribution is therefore twofold: by means of the speed at which export value changes from year to year, and by means of the relative importance of exports to national income. Uruguay's growth of GDP per capita, as it happens, was 6.9 percent in 2008, so that exports, roughly speaking, account for more than a third of measured growth.

Since the 1990s, exports have been growing, on average, as a share of national income in Latin American economies. The growth rate of export value, however, has been slowing. Thus exports' contribution to growth is the product of a number that's going up and another that's going down over time; ECG, the composite indicator, has fallen from a high of nearly 1.5 in the 1990s, to 1.14 in the 2000s, and 1.13 in the 2010s (Uruguay's 2008 value, computed above, was therefore above average). The stability of ECG between the Milagrinho and Hurricane Season years masks variation from country to country. Some declined sharply, especially among countries that had been commodity boom leaders in the first decade: Uruguay, Paraguay, Bolivia, Cuba, Chile, Peru, Ecuador, and Argentina.

Remittances is measured as the value of workers' remittances as recorded in the current account of the balance of payments, expressed as a share of national income. As such, a higher remittances-to-national income ratio indicates greater exposure to the global economy through the current account. Awareness among policy makers and analysts of the pan-Latin American nature of international migration grew markedly during the twenty-first century. This was illustrated by the 2010 OECD *Latin American Economic Outlook* (OECD 2009), which showed that the phenomenon extended beyond the Mexico-to-US and Andean countries-to-Spain corridors that commanded so much attention in the Center economies. The report documented important flows within Latin America (e.g., Nicaragua to Costa Rica, Haiti to the Dominican Republic, several countries to Argentina and Chile, and more). But while Latin American diasporas are found in many places, the remittances indicator in table 5.1 demonstrates that Latin American economies are quite unequally exposed via remittances. Remittances totaled more than 10 percent of national income in El Salvador, Honduras, Guatemala, and Nicaragua, small countries with large diasporas in the United States and elsewhere; by contrast, remittances were less than one-fifth of 1 percent of national income in Chile, Venezuela, Argentina, Brazil, and Uruguay. Table 5.1 also shows little change in the macroeconomic significance of remittances before and after the Jazz Effect.

Finally, for the current account indicators, the *Herfindahl-Hirschman Index (HHI) of Export Concentration* measures concentration of a country's trading partners. The HHI ranges from zero to one: The lower the HHI, the less concentrated the country's portfolio of trading partners. The lowest HHI during the Hurricane Season was found in Argentina (0.06); in 2021, Argentina's leading export destinations were Brazil (15.1 percent of the total), China (7.9 percent), the United States (6.4 percent), India (5.5 percent), and Chile (5.4 percent). By way of contrast, Mexico's HHI averaged (0.53) during the Hurricane Season years; fully 78 percent of its exports in 2021 flowed to the United States (the number two slot is occupied by "unspecified" in the dataset, with 4.6 percent). The HHI is interpreted as an indicator of resilience in an exposed economy: The more trading partners you have, the lower the risk of a falloff in export demand from any one of them.

Now let us turn to indicators of exposure and resilience related to the financial/capital account. The *Current Account Deficit*, perhaps counterintuitively, can be interpreted as an indicator of financial/capital account exposure: Current account deficits signal an ongoing need for external financing, and therefore a vulnerability to sudden stops in external capital flows.

Some countries—notably Argentina, Bolivia, Brazil, and Chile—spent most of the Milagrinho years with current account surpluses; most countries had current account deficits, including quite large deficits in the Central American countries. But most saw their current account balances fall after the Jazz Effect, either switching from surplus to deficit, or falling further into deficit: The average fell from −1.56 percent of national income in the Milagrinho years to −2.87 percent

TABLE 5.2. Indicators of financial/capital account exposure and resilience, Hurricane Season

Indicator	Definition	Interpretation	Means and Country Extremes	Milagrinho-to-Hurricane-Season Trend
Current Account Deficit	Ratio of current account deficit to national income.	Exposure: A deficit signals ongoing need for external financing, and vulnerability to sudden stops in capital inflows.	Average: -2.9; LAC-7 average: –2.2; Top Five: PAN (–9.2), NIC (–7.5), HND (–5.6), COL (4.0), SLV (–3.8); Bottom Five: VEN (1.9), PRY (0.4), BOL (–0.5), ECU (–0.7), GTM (–1.2)	Average fell from –1.6 to –2.9; LAC-7 average fell from 1.2 to –2.2
Chinn–Ito Index	Measure of de jure capital account openness based on restrictions on cross-border financial transactions reported in IMF's Annual Report on Exchange Arrangements and Exchange Restrictions.	Exposure: Higher Chinn–Ito index indicates fewer restrictions on capital movements (USA 2021 = 2.31; ZWE 2008 = –1.93).	Average: 0.81; LAC-7 average: 0.12; Top Five: GTM, NIC, PAN, PER, URY (all = 2.31); Bottom Five: VEN (–1.93), HND (–1.23), ARG (–0.85), BRA (–0.67), COL (–0.16)	Average fell from 1.1 to 0.81; LAC-7 average fell from 0.5 to 0.12; Noteworthy: VEN fell from –0.17 to –1.93; CRI rose from 1.11 to 2.07
External Debt/GDP	Total external debt stocks (sum of public, publicly guaranteed, and private nonguaranteed long-term debt, use of IMF credit, and short-term debt) to gross national income.	Exposure: Proportionally larger external debt signals greater vulnerability to sudden stops in capital inflows, interrupting the servicing or rollover of that debt.	Average: 41.9 percent; Top Four: BRA (24.4), ECU (30.5), BOL (31.0), PER (33.1); Bottom Four: NIC (95.2), SLV (68.4), PRY (46.6), MEX (42.9)	Average fell from 49.0 percent to 41.9 percent
Short-Term External Debt/Total External Debt	Short-term external debt stocks (original maturity less than one year) as a share of total external debt stocks (public and private).	Resilience: Shorter-term average maturity of external debt subjects a country to greater vulnerability to sudden stops.	Average: 12.3 percent; Top Four (most resilient): ECU (3.9), BOL (4.3), GTM (6.6), HND (7.1); Bottom Four: PRY (28.9), ARG (22.5), CRI (15.6), NIC (14.1)	Average fell from 15.8 to 12.3 percent

Indicator	Definition	Interpretation	Means and Country Extremes	Milagrinho-to-Hurricane-Season Trend
Reserves/Short-Term External Debt	Ratio of central bank reserves to short-term external debt.	**Resilience:** The greater the sufficiency of central bank reserves to service short-term external debt, the more resilient the economy to the threat of sudden stops.	Average: 6.1; Top Four: BOL (33.1), PER (8.0), GTM (7.9), HND (7.7); Bottom Four: ARG (1.3), PRY (1.4), NIC (1.5), SLV (1.9)	Average rose from 3.3 6.1; Noteworthy: Without Bolivia's unusually high values, the decadal averages drop to 2.6 (Milagrinho) and 4.0 (Hurricane Season)

Note: Statistics are decadal averages (for 2010–2019), or differences in decadal averages (2000–2009 vs. 2010–2019, final column). Choice of indicators modelled on analysis in OECD (2010, Macroeconomic Overview). Full graphs with indicators available from the author. CUB and VEN (after 2015) missing from current account balance. No external debt data available for CHL, CUB, PAN, PRY, URY, and VEN. Because of large number of missing countries from WDI debt data, only top and bottom FOUR countries listed in those cells. CUB missing from Chinn–Ito index.

Source: Indicators summarized here calculated from data drawn from the World Development Indicators (World Bank) and Balance of Payments and International Investment Position Statistics (IMF) databases.

in the Hurricane Season. But note that the average current account deficit was even deeper in earlier periods: −4.5 percent in the 1980s and −3.8 percent during the 1990s. As such, most countries were less exposed via current account deficits on the eve of the Jazz Effect than they were at the onset of the 1980s debt crisis. While some countries had slightly deeper current account deficits in 2019 than in 2007 (e.g., Peru, Colombia, and Panama), and others slightly lower (e.g., Uruguay, Mexico, and the Dominican Republic), all were less exposed in 2019 than in 1981.

The *Chinn–Ito index* compiles information on de jure restrictions on capital movements based on IMF reporting (Chinn and Ito 2006; Ito and Chinn 2023). These include, in the IMF's words, "restrictions on international trade and payments, capital controls, and measures implemented in the financial sector, including prudential measures that may affect capital flows for all IMF members," as well as "information on the classification of their exchange rate arrangements, operation of foreign exchange markets, restrictions on current international payments and transfers and multiple currency practices" (IMF 2023a). The Chinn–Ito index is therefore a measure of financial/capital account openness; it ranged from a high of 2.31 in the United States in 2021 to a low of

−1.93 in Zimbabwe in 2008 (plenty of other countries are tied with the United States and Zimbabwe at those values). In Latin America, the Chinn–Ito index is lower, on average, in LAC-7 economies than in the region as a whole. This is not surprising, given that smaller economies may be expected to impose fewer restrictions on capital movements, in part because their trade openness—and the need for financing that accompanies trade openness—is usually higher. The degree of openness for Latin American economies of all sizes rose nevertheless, by the Chinn–Ito index, from −0.91 in the 1980s to 0.01 in the 1990s to 1.09 in the 2000s, thereafter falling to 0.81 in the 2010s. The Chinn–Ito index fell for both LAC-7 economies and for the region as a whole between the Milagrinho years and the Hurricane Season, indicating greater recourse to the types of restrictions that are discouraged by the IMF.

Measures of financial/capital account resilience focus on the dynamics of external indebtedness. By late in the 2010s, low interest rates and high liquidity in the rich countries of the Center had created strong incentives for public and private indebtedness in developing countries. In the years just prior to the Covid-19 pandemic, banks and international organizations began to express concern about the sustainability of foreign debt in developing countries. A 2020 United Nations report, motivated by the effects that the pandemic might wreak upon highly indebted countries, sketched the main contours of the vulnerability of the developing world, in particular, and worried whether the emerging Covid-19 crisis would find such countries with too little policy space to respond (UNCTAD 2020). As we will see, foreign indebtedness in Latin America traced a somewhat less risky path than was the case in other developing and emerging economies detailed in the UN report.

External Indebtedness as a Share of National Income is an indicator of exposure and resilience in the face of economic hurricanes. More indebted countries are more exposed to such shocks: Rising international interest rates, as in 1981 (and again in 2023, as we will consider in the next chapter), complicates countries' capacity to keep up payments on their debt, or to undertake new borrowing. Less indebted countries, meanwhile, are more resilient in the face of economic hurricanes, as they are able to use public spending to address such shocks, as they did during the Jazz Effect, rather than diverting public spending toward debt service. (Unfortunately, the World Bank dataset that we will use includes no data on this measure for Chile, Cuba, Panama, Uruguay, and Venezuela, which limits the possibilities for the comparative analysis.) During the Milagrinho years, the ratio of public and private sector foreign debt to national income fell swiftly in the countries for which data are available. For all the countries with available data, foreign debt as a share of national income fell by about thirty percentage points of national income, a significant drop. It is not surprising that debt-to-national income should fall during a rapid growth episode; for a given stock of foreign debt, economic growth raises the value of the denominator of the ratio, reducing the value of debt-to-national income as long as growth continues. At the same time, economic growth may slow the growth of some debt stocks, particularly for governments. During the Milagrinho years, sources of government revenue associated with commodity exports increased; this reduced the need for governments to make use of new government debt to cover public expenditures (this goes for both foreign and domestic government debt alike). Some governments, like Peru's, undertook deliberate action to reduce the amount of foreign debt during these years. Others, such as Argentina, found themselves shut out of international capital markets, which constrained their capacity to take on new foreign debt.

Once the Milagrinho boom ended, however, one might have expected foreign indebtedness to rise, as economic growth—and the steady income from commodity exports—slowed. But in seven of the countries for which data are available, average foreign debt was lower during the Hurricane Season than during the Milagrinho, in some cases substantially so (e.g., Bolivia, Argentina, and Paraguay). Point-in-time measures of this debt ratio, nevertheless, reveal that ten countries here had higher foreign debt ratios by 2019 than they did in 2007; this in turn reflects that by 2007, debt levels had been dropping for years, and by 2019, they had been rising. Most countries, furthermore, saw their debt levels fall between 1981 and 2007, to rise again by 2019, tracing a U-shaped pattern (for some countries the left-hand side of the U is higher; for others, the right-hand side).

The U-shaped evolution of external debt stocks in some Latin American countries describes the rise, then fall, of "policy space" available to governments to address economic downturns. Policy space in this reckoning refers largely to *fiscal* policy space. Fiscal policy, in turn, is defined as the use of taxation, public spending, and public debt, to achieve economic goals including the smoothing out of business cycles or the promotion of certain development goals (fiscal policy is the subject of chapter 10). In the context of the volatile macroeconomic weather of the Hurricane Season, fiscal policy space is the capacity to counteract the threat of a recession by reducing taxes, increasing spending, or taking on more debt (or to counter the threat of inflation by increasing taxes, decreasing spending, or reducing indebtedness). Examples of such expansionary, recession-fighting, fiscal spending include spending on transfers to poor and economically vulnerable households, or on low-interest mortgages for them to purchase houses. Spending on infrastructure like roads and utilities could likewise promote economic growth in a recessionary environment. Lower debt at the onset of the Jazz Effect in 2007 left governments with comparatively capacious policy space. In response to the global crisis, however, that debt drawdown was arrested and reversed, and policy space shrank correspondingly.

As external debt rose subsequently, governments needed to divert a larger share of government spending toward debt service—interest payments and reduction of the principal—and less toward other, more expansionary forms of spending. This constriction of the possibilities for combatting a recession applied to all government debt. If that debt was denominated in US dollars, and not local currency units, growing debt impeded government action in additional ways. Suppose that we are considering the case of Brazil. In order to service foreign, US-dollar-denominated debt, the Brazilian fiscal authorities needed access to US dollars, which meant that fiscal policy intersected uneasily with Brazilian monetary policy, housed in the Banco Central do Brasil, the country's central bank. This interaction can happen in a couple of ways, all of them imposing additional constrictions on policy space. With rising foreign debt, the Brazilian treasury's purchases of US dollars on the foreign exchange market might reduce the value of the Brazilian real given a floating (not fixed) exchange rate between the local currency and the dollar. That, in turn, raised the cost of imported goods and lowered the cost of Brazilian exports to foreign buyers. While the boost to exports was good for growth, the rising cost of imported inputs would depress investment by businesses in Brazil and could create inflationary pressures by raising local businesses' costs.

Alternatively, Brazil (in this illustrative example) might seek to attract US dollar inflows through the capital and financial accounts by encouraging foreign direct and portfolio investments. These inflows would increase the availability of US dollars on Brazilian foreign exchange markets, helpful in turn for the fiscal authorities' efforts to service foreign debt. The central bank could encourage such inflows by keeping Brazilian interest rates high: International capitalists seeking the highest rate of return on their capital would shift their wealth from markets with low interest rates to Brazil (during the Hurricane Season, international interest rates were ultra-low, as the Fed, the European Central Bank, and other rich-country central banks sought to promote economic growth at home). But higher interest rates depress investment spending by raising the cost of capital to Brazilian firms. Indeed, this simple Brazilian illustration bears some resemblance to the actual constraints on economic management in Brazil during the period covered by this book; in particular, these dynamics explain in part the unusually and persistently high headline interest rate in Brazil: the Selic (e.g., see Carvalho 2018, 171ff).

Note finally that the indebtedness under discussion here includes both private and public debt. The foregoing example considered only the latter, which is appropriate given that public foreign debt generally exceeded private foreign debt in Latin American economies during the twenty-first century. Public debt includes external obligations taken on by national and subnational governments, and state-owned enterprises, like Petrobras in Brazil or Pemex in Mexico, development banks like the Mexican NAFIN and the Brazilian BNDES, as well as external obligations of private debtors that are guaranteed for repayment by a public entity. The ratio of public to private external debt during the twenty-first century has ranged from a value of 2 (Colombia, Argentina, and Peru) to a ratio of 3 (Mexico and Venezuela) or even higher (Costa Rica). Brazil is an exception, in that its private foreign debt has generally exceeded public debt.

How does rising private foreign indebtedness—largely taken on by businesses—affect policy space? Less directly than its public counterpart, but in two principal ways. First, to the extent that businesses in, say, Peru have US-dollar-denominated debt, they must compete with Peruvian government authorities for US dollars in order to service their debts, further depreciating the Peruvian sol and exacerbating the constraints on policy makers described above. Second, the existence of a private foreign debt overhang further constrains the choices of policy makers; they must weigh the consequences of fiscal and monetary policy decisions on an indebted business sector. The negative consequences of decisions by the Ministry of Finance or the Banco Central de Reserva del Perú that affect exchange rates, interest rates, or other macroeconomic variables can be amplified by a higher foreign indebtedness in the private sector.

The final two measures of financial/capital account resilience provide further insight into the dynamics of external debt in the region during the Milagrinho and Hurricane Season years. The *Ratio of Short-Term External Debt to Total External Debt* measures the prevalence of short-term debt—defined as debt with a maturity of one year or less—within a country's public and private debt stock. The higher the share of short-term debt, the lower the resilience, and the more vulnerable a country is to the risk that a sudden stop of capital inflows will render governments and firms unable to make payments on their foreign debt. As it happens, most Latin American countries saw the short-term share of their foreign debt fall, on average, between the 1990s (16.3 percent), the Milagrinho years (15.8 percent) and the Hurricane Season (12.3 percent).

A short-term debt equal to 18.4 percent of the total (Guatemala during the Milagrinho years) leaves an economy more exposed to risk of a financial crisis than a short-term debt equal to 6.7 percent of the total (Guatemala during the Hurricane Season). But a short-term-to-total debt of even 6.7 percent may be too risky if it becomes impossible to service that debt due to a sudden stop to capital inflows. In such a case, the reserves held in the Banco de Guatemala, the country's central bank, may be the only means to service public and private external debt obligations. The role of central bank reserves is at the root of what is known as the "Guidotti–Greenspan rule," named after the former Argentinian deputy minister of finance Pablo Guidotti and former US Federal Reserve Chairman Alan Greenspan, both of whom articulated it around the turn of the twenty-first century. The Guidotti–Greenspan rule says simply that the ratio of a central bank's reserves to its short-term external debt should equal one. If the ratio is equal to one, then the foreign exchange held by the central bank is sufficient to meet the external financing needs of the country, even if the country should be hit by a sudden stop. Of course, a central bank may face competing demands for the use of its foreign-exchange holdings, so a more conservative version of the Guidotti–Greenspan rule might require a reserves-to-short-term debt ratio of two or more. Between the Jazz Effect and the Covid-19 pandemic, the Guidotti–Greenspan ratio had improved, on average, meaning that countries were more resilient in the face of a financial crisis at the later date. In the 2000s, the average ratio of reserves to short-term foreign debt was 3.3; during the 2010s, the average ratio had risen to 6.1. On the eve of the Jazz Effect, the average ratio of reserves to short-term debt was about three for the thirteen countries for which debt data are available in the World Development Indicators, and only Nicaragua and Paraguay fell below one. On the eve of the Covid-19 pandemic, the thirteen-country average had risen to over four: Nicaragua and Paraguay found themselves with ratios below two. Argentina's ratio in 2019 was 0.7, and this presaged the financial crisis that indeed struck that country in the midst of the pandemic.

Summary: Exposure and Resilience during Hurricane Season

In comparison to the arc of rising, then falling, rates of economic growth in the first decade of the century, Latin America experienced a bumpier economic ride in the second. A recovery from the global recession, followed by rising commodity prices, followed in turn by commodity price declines, underlain by weaker growth in the United States, Europe, and China—all of these factors buffeted the region like a series of economic tropical storms. Growth slowed (especially in the larger economies). These economic factors were exacerbated by a series of political and social disruptions that will be considered in later chapters of the book.

In summary, neither exposure nor resilience to economic hurricanes transmitted via the current account changed drastically during the Hurricane Season. Trade openness declined slightly, but there was little change in exports' contribution to growth or in the importance of remittances. Countries were more resilient to current account shocks insofar as their portfolio of trade partners became more diversified during the 2010s.

As for the financial/capital account, some measures of exposure rose (e.g., deepening current account deficits), while others fell (like the de jure restrictions tracked by the Chinn–Ito index). Indicators of resilience linked to countries' external indebtedness, if anything, improved on average. The relative magnitude of external debt, the share of foreign debt that was short-term, and the sufficiency of central bank reserves to meet short-term foreign debt obligations all improved, on average, during the Hurricane Season. (In chapter 10 we will look more closely at the management of public debt—both domestic and foreign—which tells a slightly different story.)

It is tempting, and easy, to attribute greater balance of payments resilience during the Milagrinho to the period's high growth rates. It is worth emphasizing that, on balance, the Jazz Effect, and the global recession of which it was a part, did not fundamentally break the hard-won economic resilience that most Latin American economies had constructed earlier in the century. Perhaps even more striking, measures of resilience did not degrade appreciably on average in the lower-growth Hurricane Season. To some extent, that persistent resilience to shocks in the current and capital/financial accounts bears witness to reasonably well-managed monetary and fiscal policies (as always—key #5 from chapter 1—there are wide variations in country performance around the average). Resilience persisted even with disappointing growth, and reasonably responsible management of public finances was not enough, on its own, to accelerate growth.

This combination of public policies—reasonably responsible, indeed orthodox, monetary and fiscal policies, together with novel social policies to reduce poverty and inequality—form the core of what we will call "possibilist governance" in chapter 11. Possibilist governments from the left to the center-right represented a historic change from past decades, both in terms of increasing resilience to the transmission of economic shocks via the balance of payments, as well as in terms of actively seeking to reduce poverty and inequality. This chapter demonstrates that the possibilist success story was not limited to the boom years of the Milagrinho.

What *did* change before and after the Jazz Effect is citizens' level of support for their possibilist governments. The social peace and political equilibrium of the Milagrinho period proved less resilient than the balance of payments of many countries. The hurricanes—massive public protests against rising public-transport prices in Brazil, against inequalities in public education in Chile, and against political impunity in Mexico—proved to be neither wholly economic nor external in nature.

Finally, countries' balance of payments resilience during the Hurricane Season proved to be insufficient to withstand the deleterious consequences of an entirely different kind of crisis: the Covid-19 pandemic. Moreover, the economic crises that followed, including global inflation in the wake of the Russian invasion of Ukraine, added new pressures to those faced by governments, companies, and households across Latin America. We turn to these and other developments in the following chapters.

CHAPTER SIX

Growth in the Time of Covid-19 (2020–2024)

SARS-COV-2, THE DISEASE CAUSED by the novel coronavirus Covid-19, took hold in Latin America about two months after the first cases were reported in Wuhan City, in the Chinese province of Hubei, in late 2019. The World Health Organization (WHO) noted concern about 59 cases of a pneumonia-like illness in Wuhan in early January 2020; a Brazilian case was reported in late February, and a death in Argentina in early March. In mid-March, the WHO declared the situation a global pandemic, and a national emergency was declared in the United States and other countries in short order. Fast-forward to mid-May, and there were now nearly 330,000 cases in Brazil alone, second worldwide only to the United States. WHO executive director Michael Ryan declared Latin America the "new epicenter" of the Covid-19 pandemic (De Sousa Pinto 2020, Schwalb et al. 2022).

Latin America and the Caribbean's long Hurricane Season (2010–2019) saw the region buffeted by a series of metaphorical disasters and near-disasters, including volatile commodity price swings; economic slowdowns in the United States, Europe, and China; and the spillover effects of monetary policies in the latter countries. By some measures, the region's economies weathered those shocks reasonably successfully, even as their resilience was successively strained. But at the close of the Hurricane Season decade, a genuine natural disaster struck and delivered a human and economic cost of a disproportionate magnitude. How and why did Latin America's Covid-19 outcome turn so negative, particularly in comparison to other countries and regions?

In this chapter, we will

1. review mortality from Covid-19 across Latin America and the Caribbean, and in relation to other economies and regions;
2. survey the economic consequences of Covid-19 and find that our usual focus on rates of growth of income per capita and balance of payments flows is less helpful than in earlier phases of this history;
3. explore the varied policy responses to Covid-19, and their economic effects.

Covid-19 Mortality in Latin America and the Caribbean from a Comparative Perspective

The Coronavirus Response Center at Johns Hopkins University (JHU) in the United States emerged early in the pandemic as a frequently consulted resource for Covid-19 data and trends. The grimmest measure of the pandemic's toll is the number of lives lost. JHU measures Covid-19 mortality in three ways: (i) total deaths attributable to Covid-19, (ii) the case-fatality rate (that is, the proportion of reported cases that end in death), and (iii) deaths per 100,000 population. Table 6.1 summarizes the ten leading countries for each of these indicators, summing information from December 2019 until JHU stopped updating its data in March 2023. The table illustrates distinctive patterns across these three indicators of Covid-19 mortality. These patterns reflect characteristics of countries' demography, health-care systems, and social and political contexts, as well as statistical record-keeping capacity.

Countries with the highest total death counts are predominantly those with particularly large populations (India, Brazil, Russia, and Mexico), relatively high average income (United Kingdom, Italy, and France), or both (United States and Germany). Larger Western European countries, where the initial impact of the pandemic in early 2020 was the most dramatic—and measures to combat its spread still undeveloped—are well represented here. If countries' experiences with Covid-19 are largely similar (and they are not), larger-population countries will have higher numbers of total deaths, which helps explain the presence of India, Brazil, Mexico, and Russia. China—the largest-population country of all—is noteworthy for its absence from this top ten list, and for having adopted very different measures in response to the pandemic than did the United States or Russia. Higher-income countries, meanwhile, were likelier to have better statistical record-keeping capacity, and therefore to capture the total number of deaths more accurately from

TABLE 6.1. Covid-19 mortality indicators

Deaths		Case-Fatality Rates		Deaths/100,000 Population	
United States	1 123 836	Yemen	18.10%	Peru	665.84
Brazil	699 276	Sudan	7.90%	Bulgaria	550.17
India	530 779	Syria	5.50%	Hungary	504.76
Russia	388 478	Somalia	5.00%	Bosnia/Herzegovina	496.22
Mexico	333 188	Peru	4.90%	North Macedonia	463.77
United Kingdom	220 721	Egypt	4.80%	Montenegro	447.09
Peru	219 539	Mexico	4.50%	Croatia	438.14
Italy	188 322	Bosnia/Herzegovina	4.10%	Georgia	425.43
Germany	168 935	Afghanistan	3.80%	Czechia	396.78
France	166 176	Liberia	3.60%	Slovakia	387.05

Note: North Korea's reported case-fatality rate in the JHU data set is 600 percent, based on one reported case and six deaths; this improbable number was not included in this table.
Source: Johns Hopkins University Coronavirus Response Center, coronavirus.jhu.edu.

Covid-19. India (population 1.4 billion) and Russia (population 144 million) may have had less capacity than France or Germany to measure total Covid-19 deaths, but even if the Indian and Russian totals were therefore undercounted, they are nevertheless comparatively large. Large-population countries with less record-keeping capacity than India or Russia do not appear here, perhaps because their death counts were dramatically undercounted. The Democratic Republic of Congo, for example, with a population of 94 million and a comparatively low income per capita level, reports only 1,464 deaths in the JHU dataset. Three Latin American countries—Brazil, Mexico, and Peru—are among the top ten countries in the left panel of table 6.1.

The highest case-fatality rates, displayed in the central panel of table 6.1, feature an almost entirely different group of countries. If one country has a higher case-fatality rate than another, it means that an infected person in the first country is likelier to die than an infected person in the second. This could be attributable to a less effective health-care system—perhaps people in outlying regions, or poorer people, are more at risk in the first country than in the second.

Record-keeping could play a role in these differences as well. It is plausible that cases of Covid-19 *infections* might be undercounted to a greater degree than Covid-19 *deaths* in countries with poorer record-keeping capacity. If so, their measured case-fatality rates will be higher than those of richer countries. A common characteristic of the countries in the central panel of table 6.1 is that many were subject not only to Covid-19, but also to varying degrees of violent conflict (Yemen, Sudan, Syria, Somalia, and Afghanistan); this surely stretched the capacity of health-care systems, so that their higher case-fatality rates reflect more than a simple undercounting of infections. Only two countries from the left panel of table 6.1 are also found in the center panel: Mexico and Peru.

The right panel of table 6.1, finally, reflects reported Covid-19 deaths as a proportion of the total population. On balance, this shifts the focus away from the large-population countries of the left panel. What is striking about this set of countries is that it is almost entirely made up of Central, Eastern, and Southeastern European countries, with upper-middle- or high-income levels. This suggests that the highest mortality *rates* are associated with a combination of reasonably good statistical record-keeping (so that deaths are well measured), early exposure to the pandemic before vaccines or best practices were understood—as in the Western European countries in the left panel—and perhaps less capable health-care systems, on average, than in Western European countries. Only one country is found in all three panels of the table: Peru, with the highest reported Covid-19 mortality rate in the world.

This overview of the countries in table 6.1 provides insight into the various ways that Covid-19's impact might be measured, the processes that might lead to higher measures of those indicators, and to how heterogeneous statistical capacity across different kinds of countries might skew measurements and complicate cross-country comparisons. The presence of Brazil, Mexico, and Peru in the table suggests that Latin America's Covid-19 experience was comparatively worse than that of other regions. This suspicion is confirmed by consulting the totality of the JHU dataset. While Latin America and the Caribbean countries represented 8.3 percent of the world's population in 2020, the region accounted for 12.1 percent of the reported Covid-19 cases (82.1 million out of 676.6 million), and fully 25.6 percent of the reported Covid-19 deaths (1.8 million out of 6.9 million), in the JHU dataset.

Let us focus more closely on differences among Latin American and Caribbean

TABLE 6.2. Covid-19 mortality indicators, Latin American and Caribbean countries

	Deaths		Case-Fatality Rates		Deaths/100,000 Population
Brazil	699 276	Peru	4.90%	Peru	665.84
Mexico	333 188	Mexico	4.50%	Chile	336.22
Peru	219 539	Ecuador	3.40%	Brazil	328.98
Colombia	142 339	Paraguay	2.50%	Trinidad/Tobago	311.18
Argentina	130 472	Haiti	2.50%	Argentina	288.68
Chile	64 273	Honduras	2.40%	Colombia	279.74
Ecuador	36 014	Trinidad/Tobago	2.30%	Paraguay	278.69
Bolivia	22 365	Jamaica	2.30%	Mexico	260.73
Guatemala	20 182	Colombia	2.20%	Suriname	239.33
Paraguay	19 878	Bahamas	2.20%	Saint Lucia	222.73

Source: Johns Hopkins University Coronavirus Response Center, coronavirus.jhu.edu.

economies. Table 6.2. restricts the three indicators from table 6.1 to countries in the region. The ranking of countries by total deaths in the left panel is largely determined by their total populations. That is, countries with higher populations reported more Covid-19 deaths. But there were three important exceptions. Peru ranks fifth in population but third in total deaths—as Peru's inclusion in the global figures in table 6.1 indicated, the country had an unusually tragic experience of Covid-19 mortality. Paraguay, meanwhile, ranked sixteenth in population in Latin America, but makes it into the top ten of Covid-19 deaths. This disparity between Paraguay's population and mortality rankings suggests that its relative poverty in the region contributed to a higher death rate. Finally, and most striking, Venezuela ranks sixth in population but is not even featured in the top ten. Indeed, the JHU dataset reports only 5,854 deaths from Covid-19, ranking thirty-first among Latin American and Caribbean countries. This astonishingly low number of deaths certainly drastically undercounts the true magnitude of Covid-19's impact in the country. The *Wall Street Journal* reported in June 2021 that the underreporting in Venezuela reflected a government suppression of statistics; it was also driven by a large proportion of people dying at home to avoid the nation's crumbling hospital system, and whose deaths were largely uncounted (Vyas and Dubé 2021).

Latin America and the Caribbean's highest case-fatality rates, seen in the central panel of table 6.2, represent inadequate or overstretched health-care systems (or both), such that infected people were more likely to succumb to the disease than was the case elsewhere. Additionally, underreporting of cases relative to deaths probably inflated these numbers. Case-fatality rates of the lowest-income countries in this ranking (Honduras, Paraguay, and Haiti) probably reflect both of these effects. The highest mortality rates, finally, are found among a particularly heterogeneous group of countries in which patterns are not immediately apparent.

Both the global data in table 6.1 and the regional data in table 6.2 highlight the particularly acute situation of Peru, which suffered the highest Covid-19 mortality rate in the world. A review by Álvaro Schwalb and Carlos Seas, entitled, "The COVID-19 Pandemic in Peru: What Went Wrong?" offers some insights into the country's poor outcomes. The authors highlight *insufficient* health-care infrastructure, already overstretched at the point when Covid-19 struck in early 2020; *fragmented* health-care infrastructure, between city and countryside and between public hospitals and social security hospitals for covered workers; poor availability and use of testing resources; and the spread of misinformation, such as the possible effectiveness of discredited treatments such as ivermectin and hydroxychloroquine. One suspects that all the Peruvian features adduced by Schwalb and Seas were present in most of the countries of the region, though in some examples, Peru's situation was certainly more acute (e.g., five ICU beds per 100,000 population, versus 26 in Argentina). CEPAL reported that the Covid-related rise in employment in Peru was much more abrupt than in other countries: In the second quarter of 2020, employment fell 34.9 percent for men and 45.3 percent for women in Peru, relative to the second quarter of 2019 (CEPAL 2021, gráfico II.8). This drop is much larger than that observed in other countries: For example, Mexico saw declines in unemployment over the same period of 6.5 percent (men) and 14.1 percent (women); Argentina, 20.5 percent (men) and 21.5 percent (women); and Colombia, 18 percent (men) and 27.2 percent (women). The much steeper drop in Peru could indicate an interaction between the mortality impact and economic impact of Covid-19 in Peru: The earlier and sharper economic impact may have exacerbated the rate of mortality in the country, and vice versa.

The reasons why most Latin American and Caribbean countries might stand out in terms of lives lost to Covid-19 were ably summarized by Harvard University professor of government Alisha Holland in an interview she gave to the *Harvard Gazette* in 2021 (Mineo 2021). First, a sizeable portion of Latin America's population worked in the so-called informal sector (more on this below), under working conditions that might find them in crowded marketplaces or workplaces. Second, many Latin Americans did not have access to adequate health-care services, whether because they lived in remote regions or underserved neighborhoods, or because their informal employment did not provide access to formal health care, or because their poverty meant they could not afford to pay for health care. Third, many Latin Americans lived in crowded circumstances. For all of these reasons, the principal public health measures adopted in the initial phases of the pandemic—lockdowns, sheltering in place, isolation, and quarantine—could not be followed by many Latin Americans. Their informal work could not be done from home, and their crowded homes meant they were not isolated. Moreover, the subsequent vaccine rollout in many countries in the region sputtered.

All the structural characteristics of Latin American and Caribbean economies underscored by Holland—informality and inequality, chiefly, as well as overstretched resources—are what might be termed vulnerabilities to a shock like Covid-19. What was perhaps surprising was the degree to which Latin American countries exhibited resilience in the face of Covid-19 after the shock had hit: not without trial and error and missteps, but evincing a readiness to act, with public health measures as well as public spending. These measures will be considered in the context of economic policies later in this chapter.

An important question is why Latin American countries' documented performance against Covid-19 looks in so many respects worse—at least in terms of mortality data—than that of Asian or African countries, who share many of the same structural weaknesses that Latin America exhibited in early 2020. There are two explanations. One points out the ways that structural weaknesses (including policy responsiveness) in fact varied between Latin American countries and other developing countries. China's public health response, it was acknowledged even by those observers doubtful of the veracity of officially reported statistics, was uniquely effective in reducing mortality from Covid-19; epidemiologist Bruce Aylward, who led the WHO team to Wuhan in February 2020, made news when he said, "If I get Covid, I'm going to China. They know how to keep people alive" (Nazaryan 2020). Other developing countries, particularly in Asia (e.g., Vietnam), though the details differed, mobilized an effective public health response. African countries, meanwhile, which had strikingly low Covid-19 mortality, had a comparatively younger population, which translated into lower rates of comorbidities like obesity, diabetes, and cardiovascular disease, comorbidities associated with higher Covid-19 mortality elsewhere. Health-care systems in some African countries may have benefited from the recent experience of having mobilized to combat other infectious disease outbreaks including HIV/AIDS, Ebola, and dengue fever (Duff-Brown, 2022, reporting on the research of Stanford Public Health student Tofunmi Omiye).

The second explanation for Latin America's comparatively poorer performance vis-à-vis Asia and Africa has to do with the quality of data. Even in rich countries with reasonably good statistical capacity, official counts of cases or deaths sometimes undercounted the true measure of the pandemic. Such was the case of New York City, which abruptly added 3,700 deaths to its count in April 2020 (bringing the total at that early date to 10,000 in the city), based on the discrepancy between "excess mortality" and measured cases of deaths from Covid-19 (Goodman and Rashbaum 2020). One can speculate how much less precise were mortality records in places poorer than New York City. It is reasonable to suspect that the undercounting of Covid-19 data across countries varied proportionately with income per capita. If so, Covid-19 mortality data from low-income countries in Africa and South Asia may understate the true extent of the pandemic's impact there. Furthermore, that understatement may be larger than in the middle-income countries of Latin America, where record-keeping systems, though far from perfect, may be more accurate. This suspicion has been borne out in studies that have found evidence of undercounting in African countries. Christopher Gill and Lawrence Mwananyanda, public health researchers at Boston University, for example, found that around 90 percent of the people who had died at a morgue in the Zambian capital of Lusaka had likely died from Covid-19, but only 10 percent of them had tested positive for the disease while alive (McKoy 2022).

Economic Effects of Covid-19

Let us now turn to economic effects of Covid-19 in the region. I measure those effects as in the preceding chapters: namely, in terms of gross domestic product per capita and its year-on-year rate of growth.

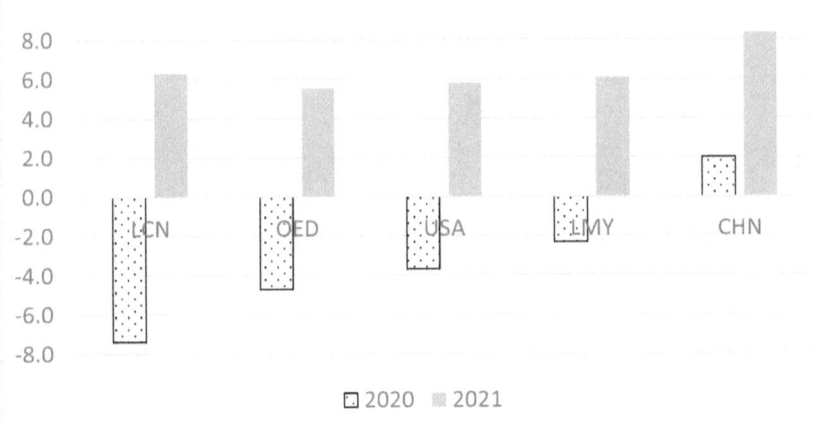

Figure 6.1. Economic growth rates, 2020 and 2021, selected regions and countries. Growth rates of GDP per capita, for Latin America and the Caribbean (LCN), OECD member countries (OED), the US, low and middle income countries (LMY), and China (CHN). *Source*: WDI database, World Bank.

Fig. 6.1 compares rates of growth in 2020 (which captures the immediate growth impact of the Covid-19 shock) and 2021 in Latin America and the Caribbean, the OECD member countries, the United States, low- and middle-income countries (the developing world), and China. They are ranked from left to right in terms of the depth of the 2020 shock. That is, Latin America and the Caribbean's aggregate contraction of 7.4 percent is larger than any of the other economies in the figure. The OECD economies had higher growth rates (or less negative contractions, as the case may be) than Latin America and the Caribbean. Contrast this with the comparative performance of Latin America and the OECD countries during the global financial crisis beginning in 2007, during which the negative shock was larger among OECD countries than among Latin American and Caribbean countries (fig. 4.1). China's economic growth—in 2020 as in 2008—was highest among all these groupings, though China's 2020 growth rate of 2 percent was among the very lowest recorded during its historic post-Deng Xiaoping expansion.

The year 2021 represented a growth rebound for the economies in fig. 6.1, and here, Latin America and the Caribbean (+6.4 percent) slightly outperformed the other economies in that year, with the exception again of China (+8.4 percent).

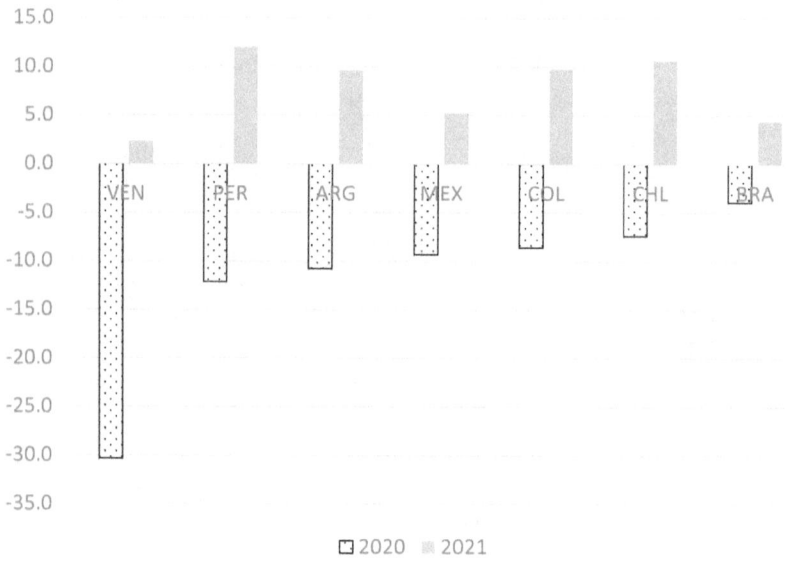

Figure 6.2. Economic growth rates, 2020 and 2021, LAC-7 countries. Growth rates of GDP per capita. *Source*: WDI database, World Bank, and WEO database, IMF (for Venezuela).

Among the LAC-7 countries, only Brazil (−3.9 percent) contracted less than the Latin American average, while Chile (−7.4 percent) roughly matched the regional average, in 2020 (fig. 6.2). The other large economies of the region witnessed large—in some cases, as with Venezuela, calamitous—economic contractions. In terms of the 2021 growth rebound, four of the LAC-7 economies (Peru, Chile, Colombia, and Argentina) exceeded the regional average (+6.3 percent).

Latin American economies smaller than the LAC-7 witnessed substantial variation in growth (fig. 6.3). Economies as varied as those of Panama, Cuba, Honduras, Bolivia, Ecuador, El Salvador, and the Dominican Republic shrank more sharply than the regional average in 2020. Those with 2020 downturns less steep than the average, meanwhile, included Uruguay, Costa Rica, Guatemala, Nicaragua, and Paraguay.[1] Some countries (Panama, Honduras, El Salvador, the Dominican Republic, and Nicaragua) rebounded briskly in 2021.

There is no clear relationship between growth downturns in 2020 and the severity of the Covid-19 health crisis. For example, the following countries had

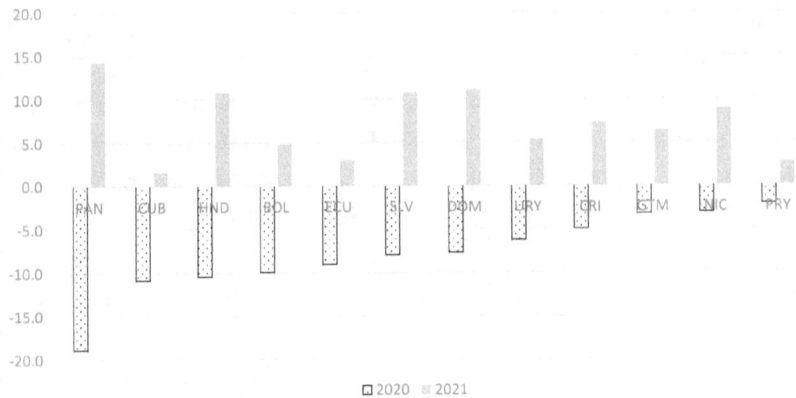

Figure 6.3. Economic growth rates, 2020 and 2021, Latin American countries other than LAC-7. Growth rates of GDP per capita. *Source:* WDI database, World Bank.

cumulative Covid-19 mortality rates per 100,000 population in the range of 180 to 220, but their growth downturns in 2020 (indicated in parentheses) varied widely: Costa Rica (−5.0 percent), Bolivia (−10 percent), Panama (−18.9 percent), Ecuador (−9.1 percent), and Uruguay (−6.3 percent). Nor were this subset of countries' 2021 rebounds similar: Costa Rica (+7.3 percent), Bolivia (+4.9 percent), Panama (+14.3 percent), Ecuador (+3 percent), and Uruguay (+5.4 percent).

It is in any case confusing to look too closely for a link between the public health emergency and economic growth, at least in the initial year of the pandemic. The economic crisis unleashed by Covid-19 was very different than that of the global financial crisis and the Jazz Effect in 2008, not least because the later crisis was a natural disaster, not a crisis with its roots in global macroeconomic trends. At some point in 2020, former Minister of the Economy David Tuesta was interviewed on Peruvian television and an economically erudite journalist asked him whether the problem required expansionary fiscal policy or monetary easing—good questions to pose about economic crises. Tuesta responded, a little exasperated, "The economy just needs to reopen!"[2] In a lockdown setting—and Peru was the first country to impose a shelter-in-place measure in the region—a good share of economic activity just stops. Getting people back to their workplaces in sufficient numbers would revive the economy more swiftly than any economic policy measure per se.

Of course, reopening the economy had to await the development and distribution of effective vaccines. The U.S. Food and Drug Administration approved the Pfizer-developed BioNTech vaccine in early December 2020, and the Moderna-developed vaccine a few days later; further vaccines developed in the United Kingdom, Russia, China, and India would come on-line in the months following. Though development of Covid-19 vaccines proceeded more swiftly than that of vaccines for any other disease in history, a full year had nevertheless passed since the first Wuhan cases were detected. And now the hurdles of production and distribution needed to be surmounted. In practice, as it happens, the vaccination effort across rich and poor countries was wildly uneven, a pattern reflected in Latin America and the Caribbean compared with other regions, and within Latin America as well.

An early 2021 study provides a snapshot of this unevenness (Mathieu et al. 2021). By early April 2021, Brazil had administered around 10 cumulative doses per 100 people, a threshold that Israel had already reached early in January, and the United States early in February; in contrast, China, India, and Indonesia had achieved even lower milestones. Chile, meanwhile, surpassed Germany's vaccination rate in early February and the United States and the United Kingdom a month later. By late 2021, upper-middle-income countries, after lagging through much of the year, had reached a rate of vaccination per 100 people of 147, virtually identical to that of high-income countries. But lower-middle-income countries fell sharply behind, at 69 doses per 100 people. Low-income countries, meanwhile, had scarcely reached 8 doses per 100 people. Most Latin American countries are middle-income by this World Bank classification, but the disparity among middle-income countries was wide, and furthermore masked vaccination disparities *within* countries—between rural and urban areas, for example (OECD 2021).

So it was that a shutdown shock, a freezing of much of economic activity by means of shelter-in-place orders, translated into a material shock. And this material shock magnified social fault lines. First and hardest hit, arguably, were informal-sector workers. This raises the question of what exactly the informal sector is. From an economic perspective, I like the definition offered by a pair of IMF economists: "activities that have market value and would add to tax revenue and GDP if they were recorded" (Deléchat and Medina, 2020). It fails to give a sense of scope of informal workers' livelihoods, often dirty, dangerous, demeaning, and difficult: street vendors, home-based workers, and people collecting garbage or combing over dumps for scraps of value; many types of sub-contracted workers in putatively formal enterprises, including security guards and restaurant workers, and even automobile assembly line workers; all kinds of rural workers, including day laborers, gleaners, and own-account farmers and their children. A resident or visitor in any Latin American or Caribbean country has a clear grasp of informal employment of these kinds.

The IMF's "if they were recorded" definition—and indeed the moniker "informal" itself—insinuates that this type of work is not standard, exceptional, or abnormal. An OECD study (Jütting and de Laiglesia 2009), however, revealed that globally, about half of all non-agricultural jobs were informal, and if agricultural work was included, that share rose to about 90 percent of jobs worldwide. Moreover, in much of the world, including in Southeast Asia and Latin America, the share of informal work is rising, not falling, with economic growth and over time. On this basis, the OECD study's authors ask, "Is informal normal?"

Of course, just because it's normal—that is, widespread and growing—doesn't make informal employment desirable, for individuals, for households, or for the larger economy (for a variety of reasons elucidated by Jütting and de Laiglesia). A principal downside to informal employment is that such workers face a vulnerability to which formal sector workers are less subject: As they are not covered by social-assistance or social-insurance schemes managed by governments, informal workers are at greater risk of falling into poverty if they lose their jobs, are injured or fall ill, or are elderly. Add to this that informal-sector wages are likely to be lower than in the formal sector, so informal workers may be poor even if they do not lose their jobs. In the context of early Covid-19, to this vulnerability to falling into poverty, or deeper into poverty, was added the greater vulnerability to falling ill with the coronavirus. Many informally employed workers were unable to give up their jobs if they could help it but had to continue working in close proximity to others, at greater risk to succumbing to Covid-19.

Our conventional focus on GDP and income per capita masks the latent vulnerability of informally employed workers during higher-growth episodes. Thus, the 2011 OECD *Latin American Economic Outlook*, which analyzed middle classes in the region, found that many middle-class (or "middle sectors") people during the Milagrinho years were informally employed. The report classified as "middle-class" those households with incomes between 50 and 150 percent of the national median income; that is, households in the middle of the income distribution. For four countries for which sufficiently disaggregated household survey data were available, the share of middle-class households employed informally ranged from 39.7 percent in Chile to 89.3 percent in Bolivia; informally employed comprised 56.7 percent of the middle class in Brazil and 66.9 percent in Mexico. Indeed, an even greater share of the "affluent" class in Chile, at 45 percent, were informally employed, though that constituted a slightly lower number of individuals (calculated based on data presented in OECD 2010, fig. 2.3).[3] That there are so many middle-class informal workers illustrates that many informally employed people had incomes above the poverty line, but were vulnerable to falling into poverty.

At the onset of the Covid-19 pandemic, 45.4 percent of Latin American households were entirely employed in the informal sector, and a further 21.6 percent had a mix of formal- and informal-sector employment; thus some two-thirds of households were directly exposed to the risks of informality (OECD/CAF/EU 2021, fig. 1.8). At the national level, the share of informal and mixed households ranged from half or fewer—Uruguay (34.6 percent), Chile (37.7), Costa Rica (48.7), and Brazil (51.3)—to over 80 percent—Peru (81.2), Paraguay (83.1), Bolivia (83.1), Honduras (88.6), and Nicaragua (89.9). And the share of those informal sector workers not covered by social-insurance and social-assistance schemes ranged from 33.7 percent in Bolivia, to 95.7 in El Salvador (OECD/CAF/EU 2021, fig. 1.11).

The upshot is that, owing in large part to the insecurity of informally employed Latin Americans and Caribbeans, as the Covid-19 shock persisted, poverty deepened sharply in the region. CEPAL estimated that extreme poverty rose from 11.3 percent of the regional population in 2019 to 12.5 percent in 2020 (CEPAL 2021, gráfico 1). Extreme poverty is defined by CEPAL (CEPAL 2018, ch. 3) as the income level at which a household can meet its caloric needs for nutritional survival, but no more: Nothing is available for clothing, housing, education, health care, saving for a rainy day, or entertainment of any kind. In absolute terms, the Covid-19 increase in extreme poverty corresponded to a rise from 70 million to 78 million people: Covid-19 eliminated the results of two decades of poverty reduction. Throughout the first year of Covid-19, CEPAL published a series of valuable special reports that focused on the unequal vulnerabilities and impacts of the pandemic. These extended beyond the fault lines of higher and lower income, or formal and informal employment; impacts on women, on the elderly, and youth (including increases in domestic violence); impacts on Indigenous people and those of African descent, and upon people with disabilities. These analyses serve as a testament to the various social cleavages that make up Latin American inequality (key #2 in chapter 1) during the Covid-19 era.

These internally driven, multidimensional poverty dynamics were amplified by the global economic crisis. As was the case during the Jazz Effect, shocks were transmitted via the current and financial/capital accounts of the balance of payments. Unlike the Jazz Effect, however, balance of payments shocks were not the primary cause of the economic crisis in 2020; the pandemic was. In the current account, trade flows plummeted in the first half of 2020: By the summer of 2020, the value of global merchandise trade was shrinking at a year-on-year rate of 20 percent, though it was growing again by the end of the year. The drastic curtailment of imports by Latin American countries even led to a short-lived current account surplus in many of them, though current accounts returned to deficits by 2021. In the financial/capital accounts, March 2020 witnessed a sudden stop in capital flows; nevertheless, the sudden stop was ameliorated by ample liquidity in financial markets, and by the strong and coordinated monetary policy response of central banks in rich countries and the IMF. The impact on commodity prices varied by type. Agricultural prices dipped slightly with the Covid-19 shock and grew thereafter. Metals and minerals prices fell more sharply than those of agricultural products, to 80 percent of their 2018 level; while energy commodities' prices fell most of all, to less than 40 percent of their 2018 levels.[4]

Policy Responses to Covid-19

Covid-19 had a disproportionately severe comparative impact in Latin America and the Caribbean, on lives lost as well as on economic growth. Despite—or perhaps because of—that, governments of the region also demonstrated a relatively agile response to the health and economic crises.[5] Most governments (national, as well as subnational in federal systems like Mexico and Brazil) early on enacted a series of measures, including lockdowns, the establishment of testing capacity, and mobilization of health-care workers (like O Brasil Conta Comigo). With time, they sought to acquire and distribute vaccines and to design reopening efforts. There was a substantial amount of variation of pace and milestones across countries, as well as considerable trial and error.

The nimble response of governments was offset in many respects by the preexisting structural weaknesses of economies and polities. Informally employed workers faced strong incentives not to respect lockdowns in the absence of alternative work or income. Economists Bargain and Aminjonov (2021) analyzed Google mobility data for hundreds of Latin American and African locations before and after lockdowns and found that the reduction in work-related mobility was significantly lower in higher-poverty locales: Poorer people were less able to stay at home. Precarious and crowded housing in many urban areas, meanwhile, limited the effectiveness of lockdowns in slowing the spread of the disease. The overstretched and unevenly deployed state of health-care systems restricted their capacity to address the influx of sick people—a situation graphically and tragically illustrated by international news reports of bodies abandoned in the streets of Guayaquil, Ecuador, in April 2020 (see the news dispatch in the introduction). As we have already remarked, asymmetries and inequities in the global vaccine development and distribution effort (arguably a component of Latin America's colonial origins—key #1 from chapter 1) slowed efforts to reopen economies safely. And low trust in governments and institutions both hampered public efforts and was exacerbated by the crisis.

Most noteworthy among the Covid-19 responses by governments were income transfer programs—some new, some redesigned—targeted at vulnerable segments of the population. These included Ingreso Familiar de Emergencia (Argentina), Auxílio Emergencial (Brazil), Ingreso Familiar de Emergencia (Chile), Ingreso Solidario (Colombia), Bono Proteger (Costa Rica), Subsidio Pytyvõ (Paraguay), and Bono Familiar Universal/Bono Independiente (Peru). Many of these provided income support to unemployed workers in the informal economy whose coverage under pre-pandemic social-assistance and social-insurance schemes was spotty or absent. These fiscal measures were complemented by transfers to firms, including small firms, to help keep them in business and keep paying their employees. Governments subsidized payrolls in Chile, Colombia, Peru, and Uruguay. Operating expenses and supplies were subsidized for agricultural-sector businesses in Guatemala, Mexico, and Panama. Lines of credit for businesses were opened or increased by governments in Brazil, Chile, Colombia, Ecuador, and Peru (OECD/CAF/EU 2021, 57–58).

A clear indicator of the effectiveness of these measures in the aggregate, particularly those that mobilized fiscal spending, can be seen in their impact on poverty. Above I cited CEPAL's estimate that extreme poverty in the region increased from 11.3 percent (70 million people) to 12.5 percent (78 million) between 2019 and 2020. In the absence of transfers to unemployed and other vulnerable people, however, it is estimated that the number of people in conditions of extreme poverty might have increased to 98 million, or 15.7 percent of the region's population (OECD/CAF/EU 2021, fig. 1.12). Perhaps this terse quantitative result—fully 8 million more people suffering from extreme poverty, while 20 million were prevented from falling into extreme poverty—best summarizes the balance of health, economic, and public-policy variables in Latin America's Covid-19 crisis.

CHAPTER SEVEN

The Pandemic's Inflationary Coda (2021–2024)

IN THE SECOND HALF of 2021, as the virulent Delta variant of Covid-19 gave way to the even more transmissible Omicron variant, a new economic threat erupted onto the global stage: inflation. Latin American and Caribbean countries were not spared from its impact.

In this chapter, we will

1. review the global inflation that followed Covid-19, and focus on how it manifested in Latin America and the Caribbean;
2. return to the High Developmentalist debates surrounding Latin American inflation to see what light they shed on our understanding of inflation today;
3. explore the hyperinflationary cases of Argentina and Venezuela in greater detail.

It is a sign of the radical differences between the economic history of Latin America and the Caribbean in the twentieth and twenty-first centuries that inflation should play a relatively minor role in a book about the latter period. Any history of the Latin American *twentieth* century, meanwhile, needs to devote considerable attention to inflation, as there was a lot of it, and a lot of debate surrounding what caused it, and what was needed to tame it.

Inflation—meaning the annual percentage increase in the overall price level in an economy and measured using a consumer price index (CPI) or other such weighted average of prices in the economy—was comparatively quite high in

Latin American economies large and small over the twentieth century, particularly in the late 1980s. At a time when the price index was rising at 2 or 3 percent annually in the United States, inflation peaked at 2,737 percent in Brazil in 1990 (and again at 2,240 percent in 1994), 3,046 percent in Argentina in 1989, and a whopping 6,261 percent in Peru in 1990.[1] Even aside from these comparatively stratospheric (and relatively rare) inflation readings, many Latin American economies ran less cataclysmic, but nevertheless damaging, double-digit or triple-digit rates of inflation over multi-year periods.

By the twenty-first century, however, persistently high inflation, much less hyperinflation, had largely vanished from Latin America (with the prominent exceptions of Argentina and Venezuela, on which more later). Throughout the current century, the average rate of inflation in Latin America was roughly equal to that of the emerging markets/developing economies category of which it was a part (fig. 7.1): Through 2020, the average inflation rate for emerging markets was 5.9 percent annually, and the rate for the Latin American subset was 5.8 percent. The advanced economies of the G7 experienced lower inflation throughout this period, with an average of only 1.7 percent annually. Indeed, for all three groups of economies, the twenty-first century, up to and including the initial phase of the pandemic, was a historically low-inflation time.

In 2021, however, inflation rose sharply, with prices up 7.1 percent in

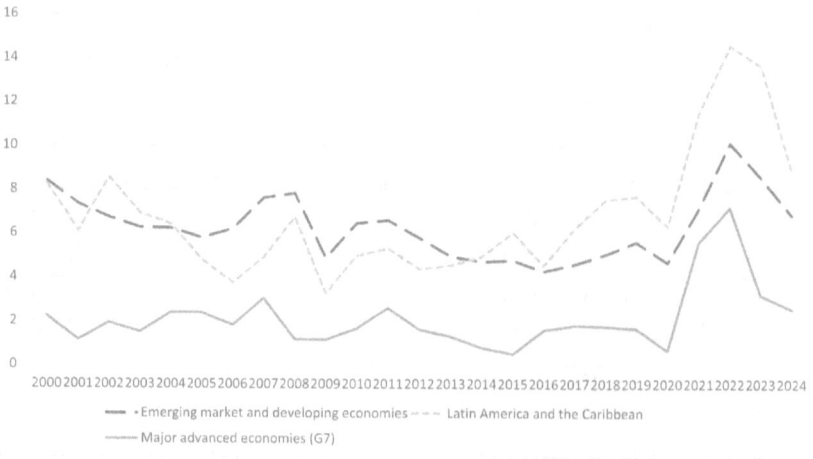

Figure 7.1. Rates of inflation, major economic aggregates, 2000–2024. Percentage change, end-of-period consumer prices. Data for 2023 and 2024 are forecasts. *Source*: WEO database October 2023, IMF.

emerging markets and 11.5 in Latin America. What is striking about the twenty-first century inflation in Latin America is how much it differs from the twentieth-century episodes, in its origins, and the policy responses it engendered.

In 2021 and 2022, there was considerable disagreement among economists and policy makers about the origins of the new Covid-19 inflation in the United States and other economies of Prebisch's Center. One camp contended that the lockdowns of 2020 that slowed global trade to a near screeching halt would take time to reverse. As governments issued stimulus transfers to their citizens and people started to buy more goods, global supply chains, rusty from having been immobilized, would be slow to revive; this would in turn drive up the cost of transport, and with it, the cost of goods. But such cost increases would be transitory, as the kinks were worked out of the supply chain, and costs—and prices—would settle back down to low, pre-pandemic levels.

An opposing camp feared that the new inflation could be longer-lasting. They saw its roots in the massive fiscal stimulus provided to consumers and firms in the rich Center economies. This transfer of income would spark new spending on goods, which would rapidly eliminate high pandemic-era unemployment, as businesses hired workers to meet the new surge in demand. Rapid hiring would lead to increased wages and salaries. Prices of goods would rise for at least two reasons. First, higher wages would push up the cost of producing goods, and some of that higher cost would be passed along to consumers in the form of higher goods prices. Second, attempting to expand production under conditions in which nearly everyone seeking employment could find work and factories and businesses were operating at full employment would be more likely to raise prices than output in the economy as a whole. As economists have frequently put it, too much money chasing too few goods results in higher prices. This kind of inflation is potentially longer-lasting than transitory, supply-chain issues: In the absence of concerted efforts by economic policy makers to slow the economy, inflation driven by a tight labor market might persist indefinitely.

As it happened, there was evidence that both effects were at work in 2021–2022: Supply-chain snarls and rising wages alike contributed to rising prices in Center and Periphery economies. Russia's invasion of Ukraine in February 2022 added additional inflationary pressure: The interruption and disruption of oil exports (from Russia) and commodity exports (from Ukraine) raised energy and food prices globally. (The increase in commodity prices beginning in 2021 is evident toward the right-hand side of fig. 3.4.) Hikes in energy and food prices meant that, in Latin America and elsewhere, the 2021–2022 inflation eroded the purchasing power of the poor disproportionately, as energy and food constituted a larger share of poor households' consumption baskets.

As late as November 2021, the Federal Reserve in the United States plumped for the transitory interpretation and opined that no action was needed to slow the economy to combat inflation. This contrasted with the reaction of Latin American central banks. The Banco Central do Brasil raised interest rates in March 2021, followed almost immediately by the Banco Central de Chile, and later by many more of the monetary authorities in the region (IMF 2021). Central banks raise interest rates to counter inflationary threats. Higher interest rates dissuade businesses from borrowing to undertake new investments, slowing economic growth. Households will similarly make fewer purchases that require credit. As output growth slows—or indeed falls—the pressure of demand on an economy operating at full capacity will subside, reducing the growth of prices. At the same time, such restrictive monetary policy can lead to increased unemployment.

Latin American monetary authorities were more aggressive, and earlier, in fighting inflation than their counterparts in the rich countries precisely because of the inflation and hyperinflation in their not-so-distant past. As a Citigroup economist put it, "Latin American central bankers basically, said, 'We've seen this movie before. We know that when inflation starts picking up, you better start acting against it quickly and forcefully.' And they did" (Dubé and Harrup 2023). Even if inflation had largely been due to transitory factors—and even if central banks in the rich countries were more accommodating of inflation initially—Latin American central banks were arguably right to treat it as permanent. This is because the history of higher and more sustained inflation in Latin American countries may make their economies more susceptible to inflation taking hold than economies in the rich countries. If consumers, businesses, and workers expect inflation to last, they are more likely to build it into their transactions; unions, for example, will insist on indexing wage agreements so that they automatically increase with inflation. These mechanisms to propagate inflation make expectations of inflation a self-fulfilling prophecy and may not be present in rich countries to the same degree that they are observed in Latin America.

Another difference between twentieth century and twenty-first-century inflation in Latin America is that in the later episode, it was largely driven by external factors.[2] IMF economists in April 2022 estimated that global factors—namely, higher prices for food and energy—accounted for more of the inflation in Latin America's five largest economies than in the United States (Appendino et al, 2022). The domestic contribution to inflation—in the United States as well as in the LAC-5—was presumed to stem from the increased economy-wide demand for goods occasioned by stimulus payments, mentioned above.

By 2022, prices were rising at an even higher rate (as seen in fig. 7.1), and central banks in rich countries began to worry that inflation was not merely a transitory phenomenon. As its Latin American counterparts had done almost a year earlier, the Federal Reserve began raising interest rates and slowing the growth of the money supply to slow the rate of economic growth in the United States, and the European Central Bank, the Bank of England, and the Bank of Canada, among others, followed suit. Tighter monetary policy at the Center raised the cost to governments and firms in Latin America of borrowing and servicing their debts, which added an additional recessionary risk to the region (Acosta-Ormaechea et al. 2022; IMF 2022). By early 2023, sustained restrictive monetary policy among Latin American central banks had not yet eliminated inflation: Even taking out energy and food prices, other prices continued to increase (Adler et al. 2023).

But just as Latin American monetary authorities had tightened monetary policy before their rich-country peers, so too were they the first to begin loosening monetary policy by mid-2023 (Dubé and Harrup 2023; IMF 2023b). In late 2023, the Federal Reserve opted not to raise interest rates and signaled it might cut them in the following year. The United States, like many Latin American countries had achieved a "soft landing"—that is, they had used tight monetary policy to slow inflation without causing an economic recession (fig. 7.2a).

Former IMF chief economist Olivier Blanchard and former Federal Reserve chair Ben Bernanke sought to settle the "transitory versus permanent" inflation debate in early 2023 with an economic model that received the wide attention one would expect given the authors' high-profile policy-making pedigrees (Blanchard and Bernanke 2023). Their conclusion was that early on, the post-pandemic inflation was in fact driven by supply shocks that the transitory camp pointed to, but

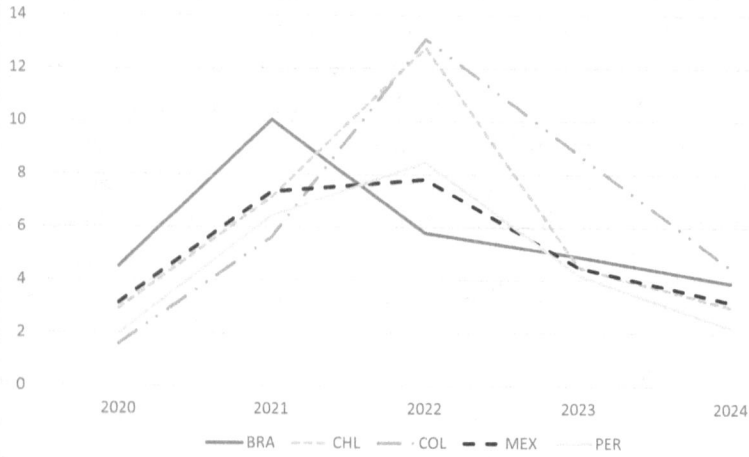

Figure 7.2a. Rates of inflation, LAC-5 countries, 2020–2024. *Source*: WEO database October 2023, IMF.

that with time, pressure in the labor market led to higher labor costs and more persistent inflation. At the same time, there were signs that the supply-chain shocks might *still* be causing slowdowns as late as the second half of 2022 (Bai et al. 2023; Lahart 2024).

The Causes of Latin American Inflation and the Cases of Argentina and Venezuela

Argentina's and Venezuela's inflationary experience during the pandemic did not follow that of their LAC-7 peers (fig. 7.2b). While Argentina's inflation rate traced the same up-then-down pattern of other countries in the region, it did so at far higher rates of inflation, rising from 51 percent in 2021 to 136 percent in 2023. Venezuela's inflation, meanwhile, steadily declined throughout the pandemic, but started from a hyperinflationary high of nearly 3,000 percent per year in 2020 and fell to the still very high rate of 250 percent in 2023.

High inflation in Argentina and Venezuela in the twenty-first century was driven by many factors, internal and external to the countries in question. What set these two cases apart from most other countries' inflationary experiences was that the relative contribution of internal factors was much higher in Argentina

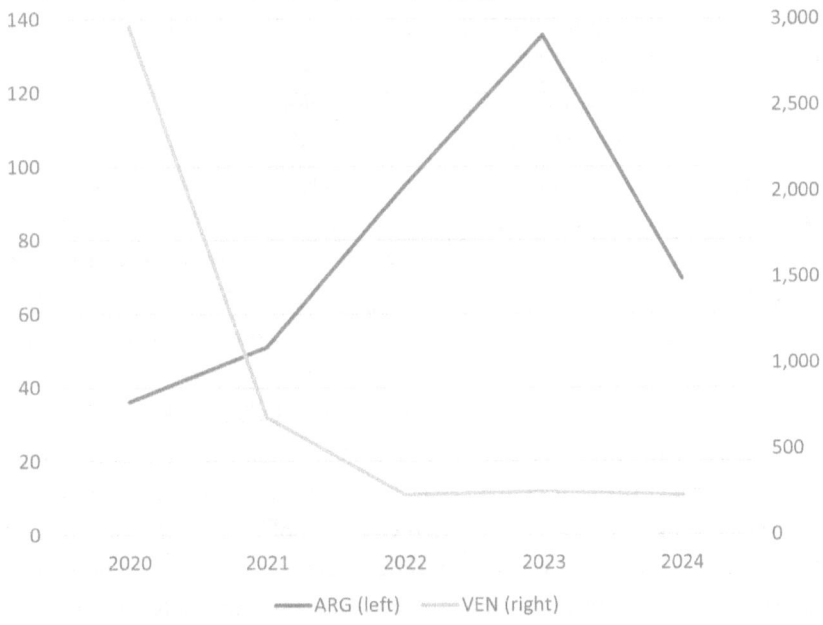

Figure 7.2b. Rates of Inflation, Argentina and Venezuela, 2020–2024. *Source*: WEO database October 2023, IMF.

and Venezuela than elsewhere in Latin America during this century. The orthodox interpretation of internal factors, in turn—that subscribed to by the IMF or mainstream economics textbooks—points to the importance of fiscal deficits and excessive money supply growth.

It turns out there is a long-standing debate in Latin America about these inflationary dynamics, which were a major chapter in the annals of High Developmentalism (see chapter 2), particularly of the cepalino variety. High Developmentalist economists argued that there were *structural* reasons for the higher rates of inflation observed in Latin America compared to the Center economies in the 1940s through the 1960s. Cepalino economist Juan Noyola outlined a theory in which (1) the falling terms of trade for commodity exports limited export earnings, while (2) inefficient and backward agrarian sectors limited the responsiveness of food production to increasing demand; as populations and economies in Latin America grew, these demand pressures drove prices up.[3] The "structuralist" analysis of

Latin American inflation positioned itself as opposed to what the CEPAL called the "monetarist" school of the IMF and orthodox economics.

The monetarist view attributed inflation to inappropriately large expansions of the money supply—not structural factors like Center-Periphery relations or backward agriculture. The money supply is determined, at least in part, by central banks, who have a few levers at their disposal. They can engage in *open market operations*, by purchasing securities from banks and households; the money that central banks use to pay for securities goes into the hands of private actors in the economy, increasing the supply of money. In the twenty-first century, open market operations in rich economies of the Center were vastly expanded under the banner of *quantitative easing*, which broadened the scope of financial assets, public and private, that central banks might buy or sell, and on a much larger scale (quantitative easing was an innovation in monetary policy developed to help economies recover from the global financial crisis of 2008). Central banks can also reduce *reserve requirements* for private banks, the share of banks' deposits that they are required to have on hand. This increases the loanable funds that banks have available to lend, thereby increasing the money supply. Central banks can also reduce the *interest rates* they charge to private banks, in an effort to lower interest rates in the economy more generally; this increases the demand for credit, leads banks to lend more, and thereby increases the money supply. All of these tools of monetary policy are sometimes called, often pejoratively, "printing money," though it is increasingly not literally the case that someone is burning the midnight oil in the basement of the central bank, running the printing press to increase the amount of legal tender in the economy.

What is meant by "inappropriate" increases in the money supply? We have seen a version of this argument already in this chapter. Influential economists in the rich countries worried that generous government stimulus payments would lead to too much additional income chasing too few goods, in economies where there were conditions of little slack in labor markets or capacity utilization. This would, the critics averred, create persistent inflation.

The issue of increased government spending, like that which occurred during the Covid-19 era, raises an important wrinkle in the monetarist analysis of Latin American inflation, past and present: It is not an indictment of Latin American central banks per se, despite the critical role of the latter in controlling the money supply. The culprit is instead fiscal policy—public finances controlled by the executive and legislative branches of government. In this critique, too few Latin American central banks are independent—whether or not de jure, certainly not de facto—of the government authorities. When governments in such situations expand their spending without new revenues (from taxes or the issuance of government debt), they can lean on non-independent central banks to expand the money supply, creating the resources needed to pay for the increased government expenditures.[4] When central banks accommodate fiscal deficits in this way, economists call that *fiscal dominance*; when, in contrast, independent central banks are able to counteract inflationary fiscal policy, it is termed *monetary dominance*. Many historic cases of Latin American inflation—and Argentina and Venezuela this century—are expressions of fiscal dominance.

The monetarist view has largely won the day in Latin American macroeconomic policy since the inflationary days of the last century. This can be deduced from the fact that even Neo-Developmentalist presidents like Lula in Brazil and Ollanta Humala in Peru appointed monetarist central bank governors (Henrique Mirelles and Julio Velarde, respectively). In between the 1990s and today, painful agreements between Latin American governments and the IMF have helped ensure more conservative fiscal policy, thereby reducing the pressure on central banks to increase the money supply and with it, inflation. (We will look more closely at the question of fiscal policy as an indicator of the quality of governance in chapter 10.)

That is, except in Argentina and Venezuela, countries that are seen as largely exceptional in the context of this century. There is little doubt that textbook monetarist factors contribute to their inflationary experiences in an important way. And both cases are distinguished by restrictions on access to foreign capital markets that complicate the story. In Argentina's case, frequent defaults by the government on servicing public debt led private lenders to refuse to lend to the government. In Venezuela's case, diplomatic action, including sanctions, by governments in the Center seeking to punish the Chávez and Maduro governments for human rights abuses and other sins, similarly closed off access to international credit markets. This had the effect of eliminating one of the levers for paying for government spending—external debt—and increasing the appeal of paying for deficits by increasing the money supply. In both Argentina and Venezuela, furthermore, inflation has been conditioned by an interplay between economic factors—notably, the government deficit—and political ones: in Argentina, a toxic kind of interparty and intraparty politics; in Venezuela, the increasing ineptitude of the authoritarian government of Nicolás Maduro after 2013.

Argentina suffered hyperinflationary[5] episodes in 1975, 1985, and 1989. It first skirted into hyperinflationary territory in the twenty-first century during the lead-up to the 2023 presidential election, and inflation was exacerbated by the early measures enacted by "anarcho-capitalist" president Javier Milei, including a sharp devaluation (which raised the price of imports for Argentinians) and an elimination of some price controls put in place by his predecessors. In contrast to the IMF's October 2023 forecast for end-of-year 2023 inflation of 136 percent annually (used in fig. 7.2b), official data suggested that the 2023 rate was in fact 211 percent (Nessi 2024; Criales 2024). Even before the 2023–2024 acceleration, Argentina's inflation had been higher than in most other countries of the region.

Luis Caputo, Milei's newly named minister of the economy, laid the blame for Argentina's inflation upon the country's "addiction to fiscal deficits" squarely in line with the monetarist analysis of fiscal dominance (Cabot 2023). It is hard to dispute that the country has had persistent fiscal deficits; these were accentuated by the government's inability to access foreign capital markets for many years of this century following its 2001 sovereign default (refer to the news dispatch in the introduction). But the causal link between deficits and inflations and hyperinflations is not straightforward. As the noted Argentinian macroeconomist Guillermo Calvo pointed out[6], Argentina's late-1980s hyperinflation followed years of steadily declining, not increasing, fiscal deficits, considered as a share of GDP. Some additional factors must have surfaced to trigger what he calls an inflation explosion. Calvo suggests that in this case it was the sharp increase in global interest rates occasioned by the Paul Volcker-led Federal Reserve System's tight monetary policy, and the financial measures undertaken by the Argentinian government to address the consequent increase in its debt-servicing costs.

Political factors, too, interacted with persistent deficits in Argentina to trigger and prolong inflationary episodes. More basic to this interaction are the political factors that led Argentina to maintain government deficits more often than in other countries. A couple of Argentinian economists have offered some insights into these political phenomena. Though many in the international business press point to social transfers made under Peronist governments, Martín Schorr (2023) of the University of Buenos Aires emphasizes that these pro-poor government expenditures are accompanied by a host of transfers and benefits to powerful business, financial, and export interests in the country; Schorr describes this as a "capture of the State" by these interests after the end of the military dictatorship in 1983. Many of the government expenditures in favor of economic interests took the form of complicated, inefficient, and counterproductive means of access to foreign exchange.

Eduardo Levy Yeyati, onetime chief economist of Argentina's central bank, and professor at the Torcuato di Tella University, like Schorr, decries this "dense web of privileges," which is by no means limited to support for the poorest Argentinians (Levy Yeyati 2022). Levy Yeyati emphasizes the toxic interaction between outgoing and incoming presidential administrations in the area of fiscal deficits (Levy Yeyati, 2023). Drawing on late twentieth-century contributions to political economy analysis (Persson and Svenson 1989; Alesina and Tabellini 1990), he argues that both left- and right-leaning governments faced incentives to leave successor governments with deficits. Left-leaning governments might enact permanent social-assistance programs that are hard to dismantle; right-leaning governments, stranger still, might cut taxes to leave a deficit that will force the next government to adopt austerity measures.

Arguably, this kind of "poison pill" politics can be detected in the transfer from Peronist (neoliberal, yes, but also Peronist) president Carlos Menem to Radical Fernando de la Rúa in 1999, who inherited a historically high 5 percent budget deficit. In the twenty-first century, an important chapter in the history of poison pill politics can be seen during and after the presidency of Mauricio Macri (2015–2019). The right-leaning Macri took the reins of power from the Peronist president Cristina Fernández de Kirchner (she of the "Jazz Effect" in chapter 4), and inherited precarious government accounts. Macri campaigned on the promise of economic revitalization but by the time he ran for reelection in 2019, conditions had gotten worse. Peronist Alberto Fernández—with Cristina as vice presidential candidate—succeeded Macri. Murillo and Zarazaga (2020) analyze the 2015 and 2019 transfers of power in Argentina and point out that Macri ran against pro-poor social transfers in 2019, transfers with origins in previous Peronist governments; but Macri in fact expanded the social transfers during his term in office. The worsening of government accounts at each transfer of power may reflect the poison pill dynamics highlighted by Levy Yeyati, or more generally the overall deterioration of the macroeconomy for independent reasons—perhaps both.

Tendencies like those underscored by Schorr and Levy Yeyati help explain the cumulative pressure on government spending that contributed to nagging deficits. They do not, necessarily, explain why government revenues are insufficient to cover expenditures. Part of the answer is that many of the benefits of the "dense web of privileges" were themselves tax exemptions, corroding tax revenues. Another part was a systematic weakness in tax administration and in the design of tax systems in Latin America generally. A long-standing phenomenon, this was the subject of the OECD's *Latin American Economic Outlook* in 2009, which highlighted several dimensions of the problem: a reliance on indirect taxes (e.g., value-added taxes) rather than direct corporate or personal income taxes; exemptions from personal income taxes for a majority of the population; a large informal sector at the margin of legality; and weak administrative capacity to enforce tax compliance. In the absence of a fundamental reform of tax systems like Argentina's, it is unlikely that tax revenues can be readily increased to keep up with the underlying pressure on government expenditures of the Schorr–Levy Yeyati type.

In Venezuela, the genuine hyperinflationary episode that began in 2017 was only one aspect of uniquely poor economic performance, with grave consequences for people's well-being.[7] Gross domestic product shrank over seven years by something like 75 percent (IMF 2022, 30), and resulting hardships contributed to the emigration of as much of one fifth of the country's population. Economic policy making by the regime of Nicolás Maduro, who assumed the presidency in 2013 at the time of Hugo Chávez's death, was erratic, unorthodox, and at times violent (as in the enforcement of price controls by having the armed forces occupy factories and stores).

Venezuela's inflation stemmed from a large increase in the money supply to cover growing government deficits. The yawning gap between revenues and expenditures was made worse by declining oil prices starting in 2014 (refer to fig. 3.5), and the losses at Venezuela's national oil company, PDVSA, contributed to the deficit that was covered via money supply expansion. For example, though prohibited by Venezuelan laws establishing the independence of the central bank, the latter purchased debt (bonds) from the PDVSA, expanding the money supply in so doing, a straightforward example of fiscal dominance.

Venezuelan inflation was made worse by exchange rate factors. The government attempted to defend a fixed exchange rate of the bolívar to the dollar that was far from the black-market rate. For example, in 2013, the official rate of exchange was 4.3 bolívares fuertes (VEF) to the dollar, while the black-market rate was 27 VEF to the dollar. This created the incentive to purchase dollars from the central bank and then sell them on the black market, thereby depleting the central bank's dollar holdings and putting pressure on the central bank to devalue the currency. And the disparity between the official rate and the black-market rate would widen precipitously after 2013, amplifying this drain on the central bank's international reserves. Sanctions imposed by the Trump administration in the United States further crimped the central bank's ability to hold dollars.

Thus inflation engendered by extreme fiscal dominance gave way to hyperinflation, under the combined pressure of mismanaged exchange rates, falling oil prices, and international sanctions in 2017. As the value of the currency (renamed the bolívar soberano in 2018) plummeted, the willingness of people to use the bolívar plummeted as well, leading to a de facto dollarization of the economy. (In the meantime, Maduro had also introduced a cryptocurrency called the Petro as an alternative medium of exchange.)

Despite the unraveling situation, hyperinflation was eliminated by the Maduro regime—though triple-digit inflation persisted. The means for combating hyperinflation were surprisingly orthodox (Moleiro 2024). First, following years of frequent and rapid increases in the minimum wage, a de facto wage freeze was held in place for years. Second, the government raised the reserve requirement for banks—a classic tool of monetary policy, though the 73 percent requirement in Venezuela was astronomical compared to other countries, where the ratio often varies between zero and 5 percent. The high reserve ratio drastically curtailed private bank lending, and with it, growth of the money supply. Third, the government engaged in more sustainable exchange rate management. Ongoing dollarization—the preference of people to use dollars for transactions rather than bolívares—contributed to price stabilization. Though the economy began to grow again amidst the fight against inflation, the social costs of the adjustment were high.

The historical roots and social costs of high inflation, and of efforts to combat it, in Argentina and Venezuela serve to underscore the reasonably capable management of twenty-first-century inflation elsewhere in Latin America and the Caribbean. The social cleavages revealed by the pandemic, however, reversed gains in poverty reduction in nearly all countries, and could continue to cast a long shadow over the region for decades to come.

Part Three

DEVELOPMENT

CHAPTER EIGHT

Structural Transformation Delayed

"COMMODITIES ARE ASSETS THAT can be extracted, drilled, harvested, melted, hammered, stretched, burned, boiled, baked, pounded, fried or eaten; so can the people who think they are investing in them" (Zweig 2019); thus did an investment columnist wryly define "commodities" in the pages of the *Wall Street Journal*. Investing in commodities is not advisable for those with a low tolerance for risk and volatility. On the other side of all those risky investment transactions, of course, are agricultural, mining, and energy concerns, equally subject to wild price swings, and national governments of commodity-exporting economies, reliant on revenues from commodity exports. Perhaps most economically vulnerable of all are the farmworkers, miners, oil workers, and all the other laborers in the varied commodity sectors of the world economy.

The preceding chapters of this book focused on economic growth, and growth of per capita income in particular, as the primary measure of economic performance. A great deal can be discerned about an economy by paying close attention to growth. But it is at best a partial and imperfect indicator of expanded well-being or freedoms or whatever fundamental underlying value society seeks to promote. In this final part of the book, we will turn our attention to other dimensions of economic development complementary to growth. Accordingly, this chapter focuses on the question of *structural transformation of the economy* in Latin America in the twenty-first century. The classic view of structural transformation during economic development suggests that economies will witness first a rising and then a declining share of industry in national output; this is the pattern that the rich economies of Prebisch's Center have largely experienced as they moved from being primarily agricultural economies, through industrial revolutions, and then to a predominance of services (notably including financial services). High Developmentalists sought to accelerate the transformation away from agriculture and the commodities dependence that "melts, hammers, stretches, burns, boils, bakes, pounds" economies and people in the Periphery.

In this chapter, we will

1. measure and assess "reprimarization," the economic and political evolution from Commodity Pessimism to a "Commodity Consensus" in many Latin American countries in this century;
2. explore the parallel process of premature deindustrialization in the region;
3. survey microeconomic and qualitative evidence of innovation by firms—the so-called *multilatinas* among them—and governments;
4. close with a consideration of total factor productivity, and of the discouraging quantitative evidence it provides of lagging efficiency and effectiveness of Latin American economies.

From Commodity Pessimism to the Commodity Consensus

In this century, the explosion in demand for many of the commodities that Latin American countries produce and export, an explosion driven principally by Chinese industrialization, raised the share of primary products in both national output and export baskets for many countries. As such, it appeared that countries in the region were moving backward (at least compared to the paradigmatic timeline of structural transformation), away from the secondary and back toward the primary sector (key #3, chapter 1).

Is this a bad thing? There are two parts to the answer: an argument opposed to a specialization in commodities and another in favor of specialization in manufacturing, to which we will turn later in this chapter. The anti-commodity argument is Commodity Pessimism, and it forms a central tenet of the High Developmentalist economic philosophy developed in Latin America starting in 1949 (refer to chapter 2). CEPAL economists and others were skeptical of commodity specialization because of the volatility of global commodity prices, because of the declining terms of trade faced by commodity exporters (which meant that every year the income gap between Central and Peripheral economies would widen), and because of the Dutch Disease, the negative impacts of commodity exports on non-commodity sectors of the economy. The twenty-first-century shift (back) to primary products has been dubbed "reprimarization" (Quenan and Vélut, 2014); a part of the critique of reprimarization is the extent to which Latin America, though it may have benefited from high commodity prices during the last twenty years, has merely postponed the hard but necessary work of transforming the structure of their economies (key #4, the market versus state debate, chapter 1).

The Argentinian sociologist Maristella Svampa (2013) argued that a new development paradigm emerged around the turn of the twenty-first century, a "Commodities Consensus," consciously echoing the "Washington Consensus" of the 1990s. And while, paradoxically, neither the Washington Consensus nor the Commodities Consensus represented a genuine consensus among all the relevant parties, there's a case to be made that the latter comes closer to a consensus, in an important sense compellingly assessed by Svampa. First, it's not surprising that the usual suspects who would support a commodities-led growth model—economic liberals in the nineteenth-century sense of the word, who would be persuaded by the argument that Latin America's comparative advantage should lead the region to export primary products and import manufactures—lined up behind reprimarization. Right-leaning and center-right political parties, as well as many rich-country governments, banks, and multilateral organizations, together with media friendly to these actors, thus welcomed the commodity focus. The consensus emerged when center-left and more radically left-leaning governments embraced the commodity-led growth strategy. Svampa argues that "in the heat of the Commodities Consensus, progressivism began to constitute a kind of lingua franca," including notably "the questioning of neoliberalism, heterodox economic policies, the expansion of social spending and the expansion of consumption," all of which "was linked to the rise in international prices of raw materials" (Svampa 2019, 95–6). Perhaps the most paradoxical cases, for Svampa, were Bolivia and Ecuador, whose governments had adopted innovative constitutional protections for the Earth and the environment.

The Commodities Consensus not only turned its back on the High Developmentalist terms of trade argument—after all, terms of trade were improving for many Latin American countries during the Milagrinho years—but on other aspects of Commodity Pessimism, as well. These include the Dutch Disease (see chapter 2), the threat that a booming commodity-export sector would diminish the prospects for other sectors of the economy. By the time of the first peak of the commodity price boom, economists Mauricio Cárdenas and Eduardo Levy Yeyati (2013) worried that exchange rate appreciation threatened to cause Dutch Disease effects for non-commodity producers in those countries with the most vigorous commodity exports, including Argentina, Brazil, Chile, and Colombia.

Reprimarization in Latin America can be seen in export data presented in the OECD's 2019 *Latin American Economic Outlook* (fig. 8.1), which illustrates how Latin America's experience differed from that of other regions of the developing world. Commodity-related exports—the share of goods exports made up of commodities and natural resource-based manufactures—fell since 1990 in Africa and Asia. In Latin America and the Caribbean, in contrast, the share of those exports in the total, which fell between 1990 and 2000, rose between 2000 and 2016.

Indeed, Latin America's reprimarization looks even more marked if we take Mexico—a large exporter of manufactured goods—out of the regional total. Without Mexico, the commodity and commodity-based-manufactures share of

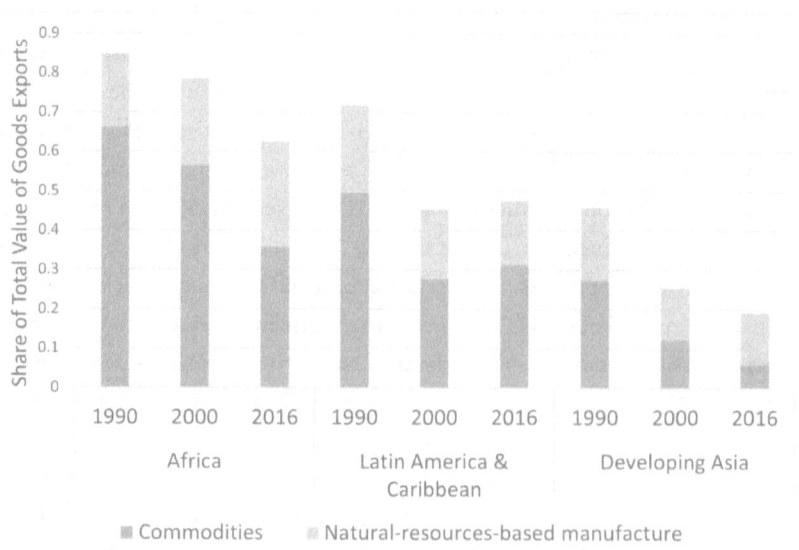

Figure 8.1. Commodity and natural-resources–based manufactured exports (% of goods exports), developing regions, 1990–2016. *Source*: Data from OECD/CEPAL/CAF/EU (2019, fig. 3.4).

exports was virtually identical in 2016 (74 percent) to its 1990 value (75 percent). Africa's export basket has shifted away from commodity-related exports, and within the latter, it has shifted from commodities to natural resource-based manufactured goods, typically marked by higher value added than raw materials themselves. Asia, meanwhile, progressed much further along a continuum that starts with commodities and ends with high-value manufactures, compared with either Africa or Latin America and the Caribbean, and was further along that process at every date in the figure. As measured by the two aggregate export quantities included in the figure, Latin America in 2016 roughly resembled developing Asia in 1990.

The explosion of soybean production in Argentina, Bolivia, Brazil, Paraguay, and Uruguay stands out among more striking reprimarization episodes. The principal export market was China, where soybeans were used to produce oil for cooking and meal for livestock. The amount of land under soybean cultivation increased from under 25 million hectares in these five countries in 2000 to nearly 55 million at the end of the first commodity boom in 2014. Each of these five soybean producers had converted large shares of cultivated land to the crop, ranging from 30 percent of the total in Bolivia to 68 percent in Paraguay. Brazil emerged as the quantitative leader in the soybean economy: Brazilian soybean exports surged to 40 percent of the global total, displacing the United States as the world's top exporter; Brazilian producers were furthermore key investors in soybean production in Bolivia and Paraguay.[1]

A parallel strain of Commodity Pessimism attracted attention among observers of Latin America's economic performance in the last half century: namely, the so-called natural resource curse, which posits a relationship between dependence upon natural resources (particularly minerals and oil) and authoritarianism. Where oil revenues are easily captured, elites need not develop representative politics in order to generate tax revenues; indeed, they can furthermore bribe or coerce potential opponents more readily than democratic leaders. The logic is derived from the experience of Middle Eastern economies, which makes the theory worth considering for students of Argentina, Brazil, Ecuador, Mexico, Venezuela, and other oil-exporting economies of Latin America. Furthermore, oil dependency might be substituted by concentrated production of soybeans or copper or palm oil, and the argument would be similar.

Stephen Haber and Victor Menaldo (2012) undertake a careful statistical analysis of the natural resource curse that improves upon earlier, less quantitatively defensible studies. For Latin American countries, they find no statistically significant effect of oil dependence (measured by oil revenue per capita, or total oil revenue, or total revenue from oil, gas, coal, and metal) on a widely used measure of the quality of democratic governance. Oil (or a broader measure of oil plus minerals) is neither a curse nor a blessing for democracy in the region. Their result is convincing in the aggregate (across the full set of countries studied) and at the national level.

Arguably, the qualitative nucleus of the discredited resource curse hypothesis—that in the presence of concentrated control of raw materials-based production, violence is more readily used as a political tool—is a feature of new critiques of the Commodities Consensus. Svampa (2019, ch. 4) and others document, quantitatively and qualitatively, new cycles of violence related to natural resource exploitation—what they call "neoextractivismo" (neo-extractivism)—which may be exercised by governments directly, or by private actors with or without the tacit approval of governments. Thus, a report by the NGO Global Witness tallied 908 murders of environmental activists globally between 2002 and 2013, 760 of whom were killed in Latin America; Brazil and Colombia led in the region. These authors point also to the violence to be found in natural resource enclaves, isolated from larger societies but subject to many of the same social problems, only exaggerated and exacerbated by the presence of criminal networks. Especially toxic is the relationship between illegal mining enclaves and human trafficking in Bolivia, Peru, Colombia, and Mexico.

Premature Deindustrialization

The influential Harvard economist Dani Rodrik (2015) found that manufacturing was shrinking in importance—both in terms of its share of employment and its share of output—in many peripheral economies. This happened at a lower level of manufacturing share of output or employment, and at a lower level of average income, than was the case in the history of the central economies. It is striking that Asian countries largely avoided premature deindustrialization, while Latin American countries (where average income is higher than in Asia) and African countries (where average income is lower than in Asia and where industrialization was much less advanced) succumbed to the phenomenon.

Premature deindustrialization differed from its counterpart in Center economies like the United States or France. In the Periphery, both industrial employment and industrial output fell as shares of total employment and output, whereas in the Center, only industrial employment was falling, as Center industry became more productive. Rodrik attributes the trend in the Periphery to globalization, by which he means the effects of trade liberalization. In decades past, countries might have had an incipient industrial sector nurtured by tariff protection and other measures from the CEPAL policy tool kit. But once they turned toward the Washington Consensus policy package, they found that they could not compete with their more industrially successful trading partners. That is, the cost per unit of industrial goods was lower (and falling, with technological progress) in the Center than in the Periphery, and the latter began to import manufactured goods to a greater degree than during High Developmentalism.

This notion of premature deindustrialization, as it happens, has a longer intellectual (as well as economic) history in Latin America; a quick review will take us back into the twentieth century, and will help us better understand the features of the phenomenon in Latin America and the Caribbean. But first we will look at some data on deindustrialization in Latin America.

Documenting Latin America's deindustrialization requires us to look carefully at detailed statistics describing the changing structure of output over time, using the exhaustive framework developed by the United Nations Statistical Commission over the years, the International Standard Industrial Classification of All Economic Activities; the latest version of which (2002) is known as ISIC Rev 3.1.[2] Commonly used measures based on ISIC give us a couple of ways to conceptualize industrialization: manufacturing and industry. Manufacturing (divisions 15 through 37) includes machinery and equipment.[3] Industry (divisions 10 through 45), meanwhile, includes all of manufacturing, and also includes all mining activity, including petroleum extraction, as well as electricity generation and construction.

One might think of industry as the mirror image of primary production, and deindustrialization as the reflection of reprimarization. But "industry," in the ISIC conception, is too broad a category to stand in as the converse of reprimarization, notably because industry includes significant commodity-based economic activity. For example, Division 11, a part of industry but not manufacturing, includes "extraction of crude petroleum and natural gas"; manufacturing only includes "manufacturing of refined petroleum products," under Division 23. That is, a rise in petroleum extraction—a sign of reprimarization—would be associated with a rise in industrial activity by this measure. At the same time, however, "manufacturing" might be too narrow a metric, as some of the activities related to utilities and construction in industry, are left out of manufacturing.

For now, let us look at both manufacturing and industry for four Latin American countries for which there are continuous data on both in the World Development Indicators going back to 1960: Brazil, Chile, Ecuador, and Honduras (fig. 8.2). The figure illustrates the difference between industrial and manufacturing value-added, as a share of gross domestic product, from 1960 until 2022. "Value-added" of an economic sector is defined as the value of the net output of that sector, after having subtracted the value of the intermediate inputs used to produce the output. Thus, manufacturing value-added takes the value of manufacturing output, and subtracts the value of the intermediate inputs used, such as energy and raw materials (but not labor). In the figure, this value-added is

Figure 8.2. Industry and manufacturing value added, as a share of GDP, four Latin American countries 1960–2022. Industry corresponds to ISIC divisions 10-45 and includes manufacturing (ISIC divisions 15-37). It comprises value added in mining, manufacturing (also reported as a separate subgroup), construction, electricity, water, and gas. Value added is the net output of a sector after adding up all outputs and subtracting intermediate inputs. It is calculated without making deductions for depreciation of fabricated assets or depletion and degradation of natural resources. *Source:* WDI database, World Bank.

expressed as a share of total GDP; GDP, as it happens, also excludes the value of intermediate inputs, and includes the sum of all finished production.

Several observations emerge. First, the difference between industry and manufacturing value-added is always greater than zero for these four countries. As the ISIC definitions dictate, the industry's value-added must be at least as large as manufacturing. Second, there is considerable variation among countries. The average difference between the two data series ranges from just over eight percentage points of GDP in Honduras to seventeen and a half percentage points in Chile. Third, jumps in industry's value-added relative to manufacturing value-added reflect the commodity boom of the Milagrinho: The sharp increase starting in 2004 in Chile and Ecuador represents the jump in prices, and therefore in value, of copper (Chile) and petroleum (Ecuador). Copper mining and petroleum production count, after all, as industrial activity. Brazil and Honduras, meanwhile, witnessed no Milagrinho bump in industrial value-added relative to manufacturing.

There was a long-term decline in both manufacturing and industry over the decades. The simple arithmetic average of industrial value-added as a share of GDP fell from just under a third in the twentieth century to about a quarter in the 2020s. Manufacturing value-added as a share of GDP, meanwhile, fell from about 20 percent in the 1960s and 1970s to about 13 percent in the 2020s. On the face of it, Latin America has been deindustrializing since the 1980s, and the Milagrinho commodity boom accelerated a trend already underway in most of these countries.

Deindustrialization, of course, has not proceeded at the same pace everywhere in the region (fig. 8.3). Among the seven largest Latin American economies, the experience is quite varied. The countries in fig. 8.3 are arrayed alphabetically, but it just so happens that alphabetical order closely matches the ranking of average manufacturing value-added in the 1960s. Thus, Argentina's manufacturing value-added was highest of these seven countries in that decade, at 38.6 percent of GDP, far above the rest and more than twice as large as last-ranked Venezuela (16.8 percent). Mexico, meanwhile, was fifth-ranked in the 1960s, but was the most manufacturing-intensive LAC-7 economy in the 2020s (20.8 percent).

Widening the aperture beyond the LAC-7 countries, fig. 8.4 compares manufacturing value-added in the 1970s and in the 2010s for all Latin American countries for which there are available data. Here, too, Argentina's drop was remarkable for its scale, and Mexico's was small, when compared to this broader set of

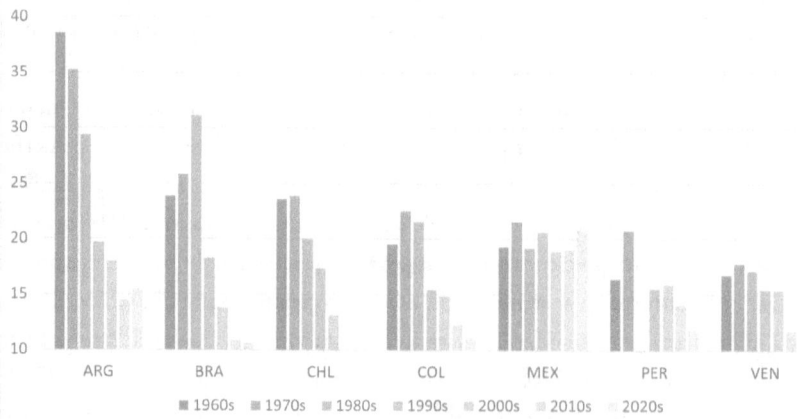

Figure 8.3. Manufacturing value-added as a share of GDP, LAC-7 countries, 1960s–2020s. See note to fig. 8.2 for definitions of manufacturing and value added. There are no data for Peruvian manufacturing for the 1980s and none for Venezuela in the 2020s in the WDI. *Source*: Decadal averages computed from WDI database, World Bank.

countries. Only Honduras, Paraguay, and Cuba saw their manufacturing intensity increase between the two decades. Cuba's trend in manufacturing intensity over the decades was the reverse of that observed continent-wide, rising steadily, with a big jump in the 1990s. Honduras and Paraguay had small variations in manufacturing intensity over the decades, but not a sustained rise.

Manufacturing is not declining to the benefit of agriculture, mainly; agricultural value-added is declining over the twentieth century as well. The drop in manufacturing value-added is picked up in part by an increase in the nonmanufacturing divisions of industry and by an increase in services (from just under half to about 60 percent of GDP).

Having confirmed Rodrik's deindustrialization (whether premature or not) in Latin America, and having reviewed differences across Latin American countries, let us turn our attention to the Latin American critiques of industrial performance for further insights into this history and its variations. As far back as 1983, Fernando Fajnzylber, a Chilean economist and former trade official in the Allende government, decried, in an exhaustive, constructive and influential study, the "truncated industrialization" of Latin America. To understand Fajnzylber's critique, it helps to add more refined detail to the agriculture/industry/

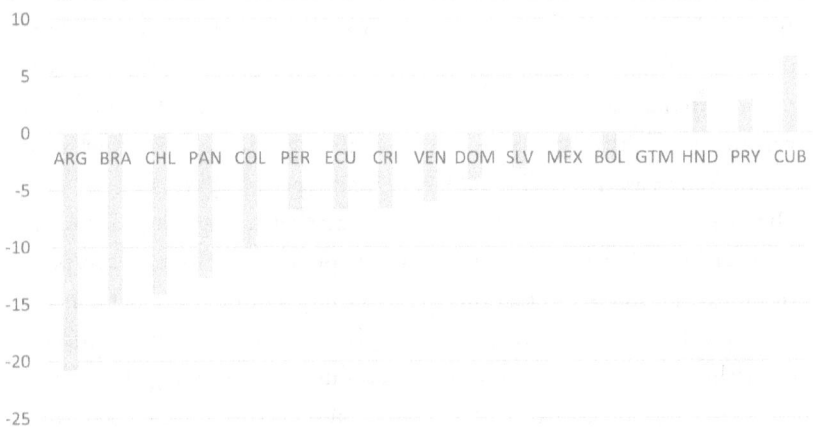

Figure 8.4. Changes in manufacturing value-added (% of GDP) 1970s vs. 2010s. Decadal average for the 1970s is subtracted from decadal average for the 2010s. See note to fig. 8.2 for definitions of manufacturing and value-added. 1970s data are missing for Nicaragua and Uruguay. *Source*: WDI database, World Bank.

services (or primary/secondary/tertiary) timeline for structural transformation. Industrialization might typically begin with the production of consumer goods, marked by plentiful demand at home and abroad. In most countries, this phase is exemplified by clothing, footwear, and textiles. In a second phase, industry will produce intermediate goods—manufactured goods that are used as inputs by manufacturers in the production of consumer goods. Thus, in the early industrialization experience of Monterrey, Mexico, in the 1890s, the Cuauhtémoc brewery began producing Carta Blanca beer (a consumer good); other Monterrey investors followed by establishing iron and glassworks to produce bottles and bottle caps for the beer. In a third phase of industrialization, capital goods are produced: These are goods used to produce goods, including machinery, tools, factories themselves, and various types of information technology.

Fajnzylber judged Latin America's industrial processes to have stagnated by the late 1970s, marked by their failure to adequately move on to the production of capital goods. He attributed this failure to a "fragile industrial vocation" on the part of local investors, driven in part by the elevated share of foreign firms in most countries, and to inadequate public policies, which created weak or distorted incentives (Fajnzylber characterized Latin American tariffs, for example, as "frivolous" rather than strategic.) Fajnzylber contrasted Latin America's experience with that of South Korea, Singapore, Hong Kong, and Taiwan, economies that were often suggested as a model for Latin America; he detects political, geographic, and cultural characteristics that distinguish the Asian context from the Latin American (Fajnzylber 1983, ch. 2, and especially p. 147).

The interaction between the state and industrialists implicit in Fajnzylber's account can be understood as a simple game theory model. There are two players, Government and Industry.[4] Before the start of the game, Government announces that it will raise tariffs to allow Industry to begin production of manufactured goods without competition from foreign producers; imported goods would be too expensive for domestic consumers who would have to pay the tariff. But the tariff protection is time-limited and will be lifted in the second period of the game. In the first period of the game, Industry moves: Its choices are to invest in productivity enhancement (which will lower future costs of production), or not. In the second period of the game, Government moves: Its choices are to drop the tariff (as it has announced it would do) or not. A fully articulated *strategy* for Government must specify what it will do in two states of the world: when Industry has invested in productivity, and when Industry has not invested (thus one of Government's four strategic choices could be described as "LIFT tariff if Industry invests, LEAVE tariff in place if Industry does not invest"; another is "LEAVE tariff if Industry invests, LIFT tariff if Industry does not invest," and so on). After Government has moved, the game ends and each player earns a payoff, which depends on the combination of strategies chosen by the two players.

Both Asian countries, like South Korea, and Latin American countries, like Brazil, implemented import-substituting industrialization policies. The key to the difference between the two, in the setting of the simple model described above, has to do with the *credibility* of Government's threat to lift tariffs even in the state of the world in which Industry has not invested in productivity. This credibility can be detected in the structure of the model in the payoffs accruing to each player in the case where Industry does not invest and Government lifts the tariff as threatened. Clearly, if Industry has not invested in productivity, it would prefer that the State leaves the tariff in place. But what would Government prefer? In some settings, lifting the tariff would cause Industry to shut down, leading to unemployment and protests against Government—a bad payoff for Government. Or Industry might lend support to opposition candidates, leading to loss of control by Government—another bad payoff to Government. In other settings, however, Government may not face adverse payoffs if it lifts the tariff as threatened, perhaps because it is autonomous of Industry influence in politics or does not fear workers' protests. The former setting, arguably, more resembles a country like Brazil in the 1970s or 1980s. The latter, a country like South Korea, where President Park Chung Hee began his rule in 1961 by imprisoning leading businesspeople and threatening to confiscate their assets, and subsequently rewarded *chaebols* (large family-owned business conglomerates) that met their production and export targets.[5] Brazil's threat to lift tariffs if Industry does not invest, however, is not credible, because such an option would be harmful to the State.[6] This is the crux of Fajnzylber's notion that Latin American governments' tariff policy was "frivolous," while Asian governments' policy constituted protection of learning by national industry (*protección al aprendizaje de la industria nacional*).

Not long after Fajnzylber's critique, the English economist Robert Gwynne (1986) would look at Chile and decree it not merely a case of truncated industrialization, but rather veritable deindustrialization (as can be seen in fig. 8.4). Gwynne's study makes for a compact history capsule of a process of structural change, as well as a preview of the changes that would sweep the remainder of the LAC-7 during the decades to come. Gwynne reviews the efforts of the presidential administrations of Jorge Alessandri (1958–1964) and Eduardo Frei (1964–1970) to follow Prebisch's import-substituting industrialization model, with elevated rates of tariff protection and (under Frei) the encouragement of foreign direct investment in manufacturing. Salvador Allende, elected president in 1970, nationalized important industries in an unsuccessful attempt to maintain rates of industrial investment.

Allende, of course, was overthrown in a brutal military coup led by General Augusto Pinochet (Allende committed suicide during the assault on the presidential palace). The military government had a very different economic philosophy than did the elected presidents who preceded the junta, effectively a Washington Consensus avant la lettre. Pinochet's economics borrowed heavily from the liberal perspective of the economics department at the Pontificia Universidad Católica, where many of the regime's economists were trained, and even more so from the free-market economics of the University of Chicago, whose most well-known evangelist, Milton Friedman, made trips to Chile to advise the junta. These men (yes, men) became known collectively as the "Chicago Boys." In post-coup Chile, years of budgetary austerity meant to reduce Allende-era inflation were accompanied by sharp reductions in trade protection and privatization of government-owned enterprises. The effect on Chilean industry was swift and thorough. Industrial output as a share of total output, and industrial employment as a share of total employment, fell precipitously: Gwynne estimates the drop in industrial output at 11 percent, and the drop in industrial employment at 33 percent, over the first decade of the military dictatorship. The drop in output and employment in textiles, leather, footwear, and ceramics, among other industrial subsectors, was partly offset by growth in subsectors more closely linked to raw materials: copper and oil refining, steel and cement production, and paper manufacturing. Gwynne notes that paradoxically, the growing natural resource-based industries were less labor-intensive than the declining import-substituting industries, as reflected in the steeper drop in industrial employment than industrial output. At the onset of the debt crisis of the early 1980s, a heavily indebted Chile found itself unable to expand high-value exports to generate the dollar revenues needed to service debt.

The policy adjustments implemented by Latin American governments in the wake of that debt crisis would follow a similar trajectory in the 1990s and 2000s: liberalization of trade and a privatization of state-owned enterprises, followed by a drop in the relative share of industry and manufacturing in the economy (figs. 8.1–8.4).

Which brings us to the examples of twenty-first-century deindustrialization. The best way to characterize the many decades of Latin American industrial decline—stagnating, then precociously deindustrializing—is to let the late Fernando Fajnzylber address Dani Rodrik's observation that Asia has escaped this fate. Rodrik illustrates, without saying as much, that High Developmentalist concepts like the Center and Periphery matter. Industrialization in Chile or Brazil does not happen in a vacuum and proceed always and everywhere along exactly the same path trodden by industrialization in England or the United States. Late industrialization happens in a world transformed by the early industrializers, which changes the context. That does not preclude successful late industrialization, but the latter will require a combination of characteristics and actions—adduced by Fajnzylber from his reading of the Asian success stories—that may not be transferable to all settings. Those conditions have to do with politics and economics; with the capacity of states to design and implement transformative economic strategies, questions to which we will turn in chapter 11.

Multilatinas and Latin Innovation

Though deindustrialization proceeded apace during the Milagrinho/Commodities Consensus years in most Latin American economies, some observers were nevertheless optimistic about structural transformation. They looked with hope to growth and innovation among a growing number of multinational corporations based in Latin America, *multinacionales latinas*, which was abbreviated as "multilatinas." The enthusiasts' research took them as often to the pages of the business press as to datasets of international economics statistics. In 2008, the year of the height of the Jazz Effect, ten Latin American companies placed in *Fortune* magazine's Global 500 (table 8.1).

These ten firms had total annual revenues of over four hundred billion dollars. To put that figure in context, the twenty-nine Chinese firms in the same list had total revenues just over one trillion dollars. While Latin America might not have been leading in the emergence of multinationals from developing economies

TABLE 8.1. Latin American firms in the Fortune Global 500, 2008

Firm	Country	Sector
Pemex	Mexico	Oil
Petrobras	Brazil	Oil
Bradesco	Brazil	Finance
Vale	Brazil	Mining
Itaúsa Investimentos	Brazil	Finance
Banco do Brasil	Brazil	Finance
América Móvil	Mexico	Telecommunications
Cemex	Mexico	Construction
Comisión Federal de Electricidad	Mexico	Electric utility
Carso Global Telecom	Mexico	Telecommunications

Source: Casanova and Fraser, n.d.

(China and India were), it was nevertheless visibly part of the phenomenon. The multilatinas in the Fortune Global 500, as a group, exhibit interesting characteristics. First, all were based in Brazil or Mexico, the two largest economies in the region, pointing to the importance that large domestic markets played in the initial growth of these firms—though as we shall see in a moment, some were investing and selling beyond their national borders, and even outside of Latin America. Second, there were three state-owned enterprises (the national oil companies, and the Mexican electric company) and three private firms whose origins lay in the privatization of formerly state-owned firms (Vale, América Móvil, and Carso[7]). Third, there were three huge Brazilian banks (further evidence of the importance of a large domestic market). Fourth, and finally, there were no manufacturing firms (though Vale and Cemex are industrial firms by the definitions considered earlier).

Javier Santiso, who was at the time a high-ranking economist in the OECD, argued that the roots of the multilatinas lie in the activity of dynamic Spanish firms: to begin with, two banks (BBVA and Santander) and a telecoms giant (Telefónica); subsequently, Spanish multinational firms in the energy sector (Endesa, Iberdrola, and Repsol among them). For Santiso, these Spanish firms had three important characteristics. First, they were examples of emerging country multinationals themselves (as they were founded at a time when Spain was among the poorest countries in Europe). Second, they led in regional concentration of industries, at the European level. Third, they parlayed their regional integration experience into investments beyond their region of origin. In each of these respects, they not only made sizeable investments in many multilatinas, but they also provided a blueprint for the business strategies of the Latin American firms (Santiso 2008; Santiso 2013).

Santiso provided a complement to the *Fortune* list, also tabulated at the high point of the Milagrinho years, taking out the banks and ranking in terms of the value of the firms' overseas assets (table 8.2). This made room for Venezuela's state-owned oil company, and for some more Brazilian and Mexican firms. What stood out among Santiso's multilatinas was their investment outside of their countries of origin. Cemex purchased cement and building materials companies in Spain, the United States, and beyond.[8] Brazilian steel producer Gerdau purchased Spanish Sidenor in 2005 (and sold it back at a loss in 2016). Mexican FEMSA—the modern-day incarnation of the Cervecería Cuauhtémoc, whose

TABLE 8.2. Top ten non-financial Latin American firms

Firm	Country	Sector	Overseas Assets, End 2006 (Billions $)	Total Assets, End 2006 (Billions $)
Cemex	Mexico	Construction	24.9	30.0
Vale	Brazil	Mining	24.4	61.0
América Móvil	Mexico	Telecommunications	10.7	29.5
Telmex	Mexico	Telecommunications	10.6	44.5
Petrobras	Brazil	Oil	10.0	98.7
PDVSA	Venezuela	Oil	8.9	55.4
Gerdau	Brazil	Steel	4.9	12.6
FEMSA	Mexico	Food and beverage	3.5	13.5
Gruma	Mexico	Food and beverage	1.5	2.8
Grupo Bimbo	Mexico	Food and beverage	1.4	3.9

Note: Ranked by value of firms' overseas assets. Based on data sources from the OECD and UNCTAD.
Source: Santiso (2008, cuadro 2).

example helped explain the concept of intermediate goods earlier in this chapter—became the world's largest bottler of Coca-Cola products in several countries. Mexican Gruma, which began as a regional producer of corn tortillas, expanded to become a major producer of tortillas in the United States. It is this practice of purchasing or starting companies beyond their region of origin, mimicking the Spanish multinationals, that led Cornell University business school professor Lourdes Casanova to speak of "Global Latinas" graduating from the ranks of the multilatinas, including most of the firms identified by Santiso (Casanova and Fraser n.d.; Casanova 2009).

Casanova highlighted innovative aspects of Latin American firms, multilatinas, and otherwise, in addition to overseas expansion. Notable among these are firms that found ways to serve the burgeoning middle classes of Latin America; in practice, these strategies included displacement of informal economy sellers, as well as the combination of retail sales with the provision of consumer credit. Examples include Costa Rican Grupo Monge, a retailer of consumer electronics and household appliances that also offers consumer credit for in-store purchases;

Monge operations spread to all the countries of Central America. Mexican OXXO, established as storefronts to sell beverages produced by FEMSA (again), expanded to become the largest chain of convenience stores in Latin America, with thousands of locations in Mexico, as well as in Brazil, Colombia, Chile, and Peru (Casanova and Renck 2015). Examples like these highlight the competitive advantage that Peripheral country firms might have in serving low-income customers on a large scale, advantages that Center country firms might not have (although the latter are likely to have considerable advantages in terms of access to lower-cost credit, and to marketing and distribution resources).

Celebrating expansion and innovation among Latin American firms—large and small, state-owned and in the private sector—probably served as a necessary corrective to bemoaning the low productivity of Latin American business, a perception that Santiso, Casanova, and other authors correctly pointed out was becoming outdated. InnovaLatino, a research project carried out by the OECD and the INSEAD business school in France, questioned whether conventional measures of innovation were in fact appropriate to peripheral economies (INSEAD/OECD 2011; Casanova et al. 2016). By those conventional measures, Latin America did not look strong in the 2010s. Research and development (R&D) expenditures as a share of GDP averaged 2.4 percent in OECD countries (and fully 4 percent in South Korea), but only 0.3 percent in Latin America (where Brazil led, at 1.2 percent). The gap in patent applications between the OECD and Latin America was yawning: over 24,000 annually for the OECD versus 400 or so for Latin America. High technology exports as a share of total exports cast Latin America in an apparently more favorable light: The regional high-tech export share was 10 percent, versus 13.6 for OECD countries. The Latin American number, however, was skewed upward by unusually high high-tech export values for Costa Rica, Panama, and Mexico, which reflect the effect of transshipment of high-tech goods, and the assembly of high-tech goods in twin plants or maquiladoras (generally foreign-owned factories where imported parts are assembled for export).

The InnovaLatino research argued that forms of innovation not detected by statistics related to R&D expenditures, patent applications, and high-tech exports were quite prevalent in Latin America, and more relevant to the developing-economy context. These include process and marketing innovations (like the Monge and OXXO examples, and there are many others) rather than product innovations that are captured by the indicators in the previous paragraph. Latin American innovation included public sector nonprofit initiatives to increase productivity in the natural resource sector, including Embrapa in Brazil, focused on agriculture; CORFO in Chile, which has innovated in mining and aquaculture; and FONTAR in Argentina, which has funded dynamic clusters, including in agricultural machinery. These public sector innovation entities, it should be noted, pragmatically leverage the natural resource abundance of the countries where they were founded; they also promoted and extended the commodities focus of their home economies for good and for ill.

Process and marketing innovations, as well as the important role of coordination provided by public sector entities, were likewise features of successful agribusiness enterprises analyzed in a comprehensive Inter-American Development Bank report on the sector (Ghezzi et al. 2022). For example, the small US-Nicaraguan firm Sol Orgánica, which produced dried mango, dragon fruit, and other fruits, connected very small-scale growers and suppliers to global value chains by providing marketing and quality-assurance inputs, among other contributions (Ghezzi et al. 2022, 76–81 and passim). The IDB report included other, equally encouraging examples, including Peruvian coastal blueberry and avocado exporters and a beekeeping cooperative in the Gran Charco region of Argentina. All of the cases studied by the IDB embodied process and marketing innovations to varying degrees—but also an optimism regarding the prospects for productive initiatives in the primary sector. Firms and networks like those described in the IDB study held the promise of generating greater value-added, enhancing productivity, while pursuing social and environmental objectives alongside profitability. Sol Orgánica and the other firms like it may yet prove the High Developmentalist Commodity Pessimism of yesteryear to be outdated and inaccurately Manichean.

Total Factor Productivity Growth

Innovative practices by Latin American firms may have contributed to, and been encouraged by, higher growth during the Milagrinho years; at the same time, such practices were insufficient to maintain those growth rates during the Hurricane Season years. One suspects nevertheless that these qualitatively important experiments were not quantitatively important to long-term economic growth rates. This suspicion is lent empirical support by the exhaustive "growth accounting" work of Uruguayan economists Christian Daude and Eduardo Fernández Arias (Daude 2010; Daude and Fernández Arias 2010). Daude and Fernández Arias focused on the concept of *total factor productivity* (TFP), which is defined as the efficiency with which an economy combines the factors of production to produce gross domestic product. TFP is thus distinct from the concept of labor productivity, which measures the output an economy produces per worker. TFP is furthermore contrasted with *factor accumulation*, which measures the net increase in factors of production in the economy: human capital and physical capital. An economy can grow because there is more labor and more capital, or it can grow because it gets better at combining a given amount of labor and capital; in fact, growth is attributable to both factor accumulation and improvements in TFP. Growth accounting of this kind seeks to estimate the relative contribution of factor accumulation and TFP improvements to growth for many countries over many years. Daude and Fernández Arias's work compares the pattern of these relative contributions in Latin American countries to many other economies over the period 1960–2005. Daude and Fernández Arias's findings are three. First, average income has grown more slowly in Latin American countries than elsewhere, and lower-, and slower-growing TFP—not factor accumulation—is the reason. Second, and contrary to expectations, Latin American TFP is not catching up with TFP elsewhere; it is falling further behind over time. Third, Latin America's TFP is about half its potential level; that is, given levels of human and physical capital available in most Latin American economies, average income could be as high as it is in economies at the Center.

Daude and Fernández Arias's analysis ends in 2005, but more recent analyses along these lines suggest that the patterns of productivity shortfalls endured further into the twenty-first century. A research paper prepared for the UNDP found that Latin America's average-income growth performance improved after 1990, but its productivity growth did not (E. Fernández Arias and N. Fernández Arias 2021). The UNDP study asked whether higher inequality in Latin America contributed to the TFP shortfall, and found that it did; higher inequality, however, was also associated with higher factor accumulation (presumably, investment in the capital stock), which offset the lower TFP effect upon growth.

A 2022 study by IMF economists included "informality, burdensome regulation, tax design problems, poor governance and outdated insolvency frameworks that do not facilitate firms' entry and exit" among the factors that keep Latin American TFP low and slow growing. They furthermore argued that those same factors make the region more vulnerable to economic shocks, and forecasted that Covid-19 would leave a long-lasting "scar" on the region's productivity (Acosta-Ormaechea et al. 2022).

What does it mean for one economy to combine factors of production less efficiently than another? The first answer that comes to mind is that some economies lack access to the best technologies. While it is true that some technologies are patent-protected or otherwise inaccessible, this is unlikely to account for the TFP shortfall Daude and Fernández Arias measured. The history of economic growth globally over two or three centuries is in large part the story of new technologies diffusing around the world. It is more probable that Latin America's TFP shortfall is a matter of economies' being less capable of using leading-edge technologies as well.

Many of the innovations that the InnovaLatino project celebrated in Latin America and the Caribbean could have made TFP higher than it would have been in their absence. At the same time, however, it could well be that these innovations—a rangy, agile informal economy; new forms of providing credit to poor households; and government agencies to promote natural resource exploitation—were workarounds to address larger inefficiencies. Those more consequential inefficiencies included the failure to deepen industrialization; profound income and wealth inequality, and the conflicts to which those inequalities gave rise; and states that fail to consistently enact effective public policies. Accordingly, we turn our attention in the next chapter to inequality, and in the following chapters, to statecraft.

CHAPTER NINE

Declining Inequality

IN EARLY 2004, THE World Bank released an exhaustive analysis that suggested that inequality was on the decline in Latin America. The publication bore the suggestive subtitle, "Breaking with History?" (De Ferranti et al. 2004). Indeed, Latin American economic inequality has a long history (key #2 from chapter 1). Oxford University historian Rosemary Thorp has traced its roots to the concentration of landed wealth in the hands of conquistadores, as well as repressive regimes of labor mobilization, during the four centuries of the colonial era; she shows furthermore that these processes were not ended with independence from the Spanish, Portuguese, and other colonial powers (Thorp 2012).[1] If the evidence of a change presented by the World Bank and others in the twenty-first century proves robust, and if the factors driving this change prove enduring, we are witnessing a historic transformation. But note that the title of the World Bank report ends in a question mark, and more than twenty years following its publication, the question mark remains.

In this chapter, we will

1. define economic inequality (in terms of income and wealth) and introduce measures of inequality (focusing on the Gini coefficient and income shares);
2. trace the time path of these measures since the 1990s;
3. consider hypotheses to explain the observed decline in some of these measures;
4. broaden the focus to consider general economic models linking inequality and economic development (both the effect of development on inequality, as well as the effect of inequality on economic growth).

Measuring Inequality

Inequality takes many forms: social, political, regional, cultural, racial, ethnic, gender-based, and economic (Sen 1995). The concept of intersectionality posits that those dimensions of inequality furthermore overlap, though imperfectly (Crenshaw 2014). *Economic* inequality, to which we will restrict ourselves here, is just one dimension of the larger phenomenon. And economic inequality, in turn, itself has many dimensions; this multidimensionality will be reduced in this chapter largely to a discussion of inequality of *incomes* and *wealth*.

The historical roots of Latin American inequality spring from wealth inequality, as the concentration of landholding in the colonial era laid the groundwork for what Rosemary Thorp calls the "embeddedness" of inequality in Latin America. Wealth—a household's stock of land and capital of various forms—is a source of income (labor is another). Households earn rent from land and capital; they earn wages from selling their labor in the labor market. Note that income is a *flow* variable: lempiras or pesos or reais per week or month or year. Wealth is a *stock* variable, though it produces income flows as described above.

The distribution of wealth is always more unequal than the distribution of income; almost every household has labor income, but many households do *not* own capital or wealth. Income inequality derives in large part from wealth inequality, as capital owners' income is concentrated in relatively few hands. Increasingly, labor income too is becoming more dispersed, at least in richer economies; inflation of executive pay contributes to labor income inequality alongside the disparities between capital and labor income.

For many years, cross-country information on the distribution of incomes and wealth was hard to obtain on a systematic, consistent, comparative basis. That is because, unlike estimates of average income—which can be computed from two numbers, gross domestic product and the size of the population—inequality measures require quite granular information on individual household incomes and wealth levels. Such data come from surveys of households that are designed to be representative of the entire population. The increased quality and frequency of household surveys of economic variables beginning in the 1980s has increased the precision and coverage of inequality measures in recent decades, but data gets spottier as one goes backward into the historical record. There are still good reasons to suspect that even recent income data from household surveys underreport the highest incomes. Moreover, wealth is not as consistently reported as income. In fact, problems with the data on wealth dispersion mean that wealth inequality has not been a subject of consistent study for as long as income. For all of these reasons, comparative measures of economic inequality must be interpreted with caution. We will return to these data complications throughout the chapter.

How then do we measure *income* inequality? Economists frequently use the Gini coefficient to measure an economy's level of income inequality.[2] The Gini coefficient is computed according to a somewhat complicated formula and is not always easy to interpret. An example gives an idea of what the measure represents. Consider the annual income of all households in a given economy—say, Argentina—over the course of a year—say, 2021. Roughly speaking, the Gini coefficient can be understood as measuring the average difference between all households' incomes. That is, start with one household, perhaps a retired couple in Mendoza, and add up the difference between that household's income and the income of each other household in all of Argentina. Then do the same exercise for every other Argentinian household. Of course, actual computation of Argentina's—or any other country's—Gini coefficient is not based on *all* households' incomes, but on the incomes of a representative sample of all households.

The sum of all these pairwise differences is converted into a number that lies somewhere between zero and one hundred. A zero Gini indicates perfect equality, in which every household's income is identical and therefore there are no differences in income to add up. A Gini equal to one hundred indicates that a single household earns the entirety of national income. As we will see in a moment, the Gini coefficient for Argentina in 2021 was in fact 42. (Note that some analysts scale the Gini coefficient to lie between zero and one, so that Argentina's in 2021 would be 0.42; others express Ginis with a "%" afterward—thus, 42%—though there is no real sense in which this number represents a percentage of anything.[3])

One of the primary benefits of using the Gini coefficient to measure income inequality (and there are downsides as well) is that, unlike the statistical variance of income in an economy, a rise in the Gini means that inequality has increased and a decline in the Gini means that inequality has fallen. This is true in a very specific sense, denoted by the "principle of transfers." If, say, you take some income from the retired Mendoza couple and transfer it to a poorer household in Rosario—without transferring so much that the *mendocinos* in question become poorer than the *rosarinos* in question, and without any other changes to the income distribution—then the measured Gini coefficient for all Argentina will decline. Note that there is no change to Argentina's GDP, or to average income in Argentina, as a result of this transfer. This can be called an *equalizing transfer* and could be carried out by governments in the real world by taxing income from relatively higher-income households (like the mendocinos) and making transfer payments to relatively lower-income ones (like the rosarinos). Putting it another way, given any two potential values of the Argentinian Gini coefficient—say, 42 and 51.1—there exists series of such equalizing transfers among households that could reduce the Gini from 51.1 to 42.

As it happens, Argentina's Gini coefficient in 2000 was 51.1, which means that income inequality has fallen since that time; this is the central finding of the World Bank study cited at the start of this chapter. Moreover, Brazil's Gini coefficient in 2021 was 52.9, suggesting that its income inequality was higher than that of its neighbor to the south. Interregional comparisons of Ginis routinely rank Latin America and the Caribbean as the most unequal part of the world economy. A tabulation of regional Ginis near the beginning of the twenty-first century (in 2004) by economists Luis Felipe López-Calva and Nora Lustig reports the following worldwide distribution of Ginis: high-income economies in Europe and North America, in the mid 30s; Eastern European and Central Asian countries, just above 30; South Asia, Middle East and North Africa, East Asia and the Pacific, just under 40; sub-Saharan Africa, just over 40; and Latin America and the Caribbean, well over 50 (López-Calva and Lustig 2010, fig. 1–1; see also CAF 2022, gráficos 1.1 and 1.3).

More recent data, with less global coverage, illustrates what has changed and what has remained the same since the beginning of the twenty-first century (fig. 9.1). Fifteen Latin American economies are depicted in fig. 9.1, together with three additional comparative cases: China, the United States (emblematic of the "Anglo-American economies" typically the most unequal among the rich countries), and France (emblematic of the comparatively egalitarian Western European countries).

Three findings are worth underscoring in fig. 9.1. First, as always (key #5 from chapter 1), there is substantial variation among Latin American economies in terms of income inequality, ranging from a high of 52.9 in Brazil to a low of 38.5

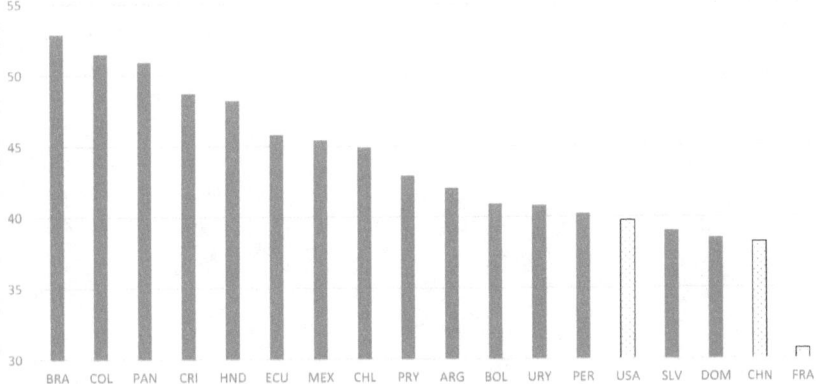

Figure 9.1. Gini coefficients for Latin American and selected economies, 2021. *Source*: WDI database, World Bank.

in the Dominican Republic. Second, Latin American Ginis have fallen since the 2004 summary evidence cited above; only three are higher than 50, while the regional average for all countries exceeded 50 at the start of the century. Third, Latin American Ginis are nevertheless higher than most of the outside economies included in the figure.

Fig. 9.2 depicts the evolution of Gini coefficients for the LAC-7 countries and the same three comparator economies outside the region. For each of the last five decades, the available Gini coefficients are averaged for each of these countries. Note that there are missing values for some countries and some decades; note also that "the 2020s" denotes the average of just two years (2020 and 2021) for each country. In every decade, the LAC-7 Gini coefficients lie above those from China, France, and the United States. By and large, LAC-7 economies' Gini coefficients are declining over this time span, however, while the non-Latin economies' Gini coefficients have generally been rising since the 1980s. There are slight variations on these patterns, of course. Brazil, Colombia, Chile, Mexico, and Peru have mostly observed sustained declines in their Gini coefficients since the 1980s, while Argentina's recent decline appears to return the country to its 1980s level, following an increase in the 1990s. Venezuela's Gini, meanwhile, was rising before the data availability stopped in the 2000s.

The measured decline in Gini coefficients in Latin America was not limited to the LAC-7 economies. Fig. 9.3 depicts the change in the average Gini for each

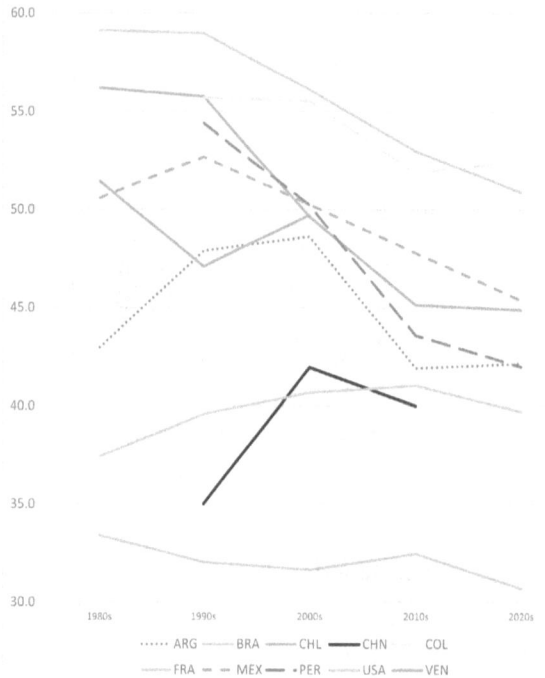

Figure 9.2. Gini coefficients over time. LAC-7 and comparator economies, 1980s–2020s. Source: Decadal averages computed from available data in the WDI database, World Bank.

decade between the 1990s and the 2010s, for all Latin American countries with available data. The largest drop was witnessed in Bolivia, where the decadal average for the Gini coefficient fell from 58.2 in the 1990s to 45.4 in the 2010s, a decline of 12.7; the numbers for the other economies in the figure are computed in the same way. Bolivia's Andean neighbors Peru and Ecuador also registered significant declines in their measured Gini coefficients, as did El Salvador, Chile, and Nicaragua. Only Costa Rica, among the Latin American countries in the figure had a (small) increase. The units in which the Gini coefficient is denominated make it hard to interpret exactly what is meant by a drop in the Gini coefficient of 12.7 points (Bolivia), except that it represents a proportionately larger drop in the average income difference between households than a drop of six points (Argentina).

Explaining the Drop in Gini Coefficients in Latin America

What accounts for the decline in the Gini coefficients since the 1990s?

Figure 9.3. Changes in Gini coefficients between the 1990s and the 2020s, selected economies. *Source*: Decadal averages computed from available data in the WDI database, World Bank.

Economists Nora Lustig of Tulane University and Luis Felipe López-Calva of the World Bank (and previously, the United Nations Development Programme), led an important research team project to analyze the factors that accounted for the equalizing growth of the twenty-first century in Latin America: Their 2010 Brookings Institution publication *Declining Inequality in Latin America: A Decade of Progress?* summarizes much of the initial phase of their project. According to these researchers, there are two factors at work: One has to do with the gap between wages earned by higher-skilled workers and those earned by less-skilled workers; the other has to do with historically generous and effective social-assistance programs that reduced poverty.

The wages of skilled, or more educated, workers are higher than those of their less-educated compatriots; the difference is called the *skill premium*. But labor income has become less unequally distributed over time in Latin American countries as the skill premium has declined. That is, the gap in wages between relatively skilled workers (those with more experience, or education, or both) and less skilled workers, has shrunk, bringing earnings of the two groups closer together and overall income inequality lower. The declining skill premium arises from the interaction of supply and demand for skilled labor, and ultimately, from the mechanisms that affect the supply and demand curves for skilled labor. Let us start with a critical supply-side factor. Over the last several decades, Latin

America has witnessed increasing enrollment rates at the secondary (high school) level. Higher high-school enrollment rates, in turn, raise the supply of more skilled workers relative to the supply of their less-skilled compatriots; and this in turn slows the rate of growth of the skill premium.

The demand-side factors driving changes in the skill premium largely have to do with technology. In general, when businesses accelerate their investments in technological upgrading, that increases the relative demand for the skilled labor needed to work with more advanced technology—and that, in turn, increases the skill premium, all else remaining equal. The declining skill premium witnessed in Latin America in the last few decades, thus, could be driven by a slowing-down of technological upgrading, or a relatively less technology-intensive capital stock. There is evidence from some Latin American countries that greater integration in global trade networks was associated with less technology-intensive investment; this would be the case if more trade meant more specialization in commodity-related export sectors, for example. Indeed, this is the pattern of Milagrinho growth recounted in chapter 3 (consider anew the case of Peru, Ecuador, Bolivia, and Chile—important commodity exporters—in fig. 9.3).

In sum, Latin America has seen an expansion in the supply of skilled workers and a slowing in the demand for skilled workers, reducing the wage difference between skilled and less skilled laborers, and reducing income inequality in the aggregate. The balance of demand and supply factors in reducing the skill premium vary from country to country. Lustig, López-Calva, and Ortiz-Juárez (2013), for example, summarize evidence pointing to a substantial role for increased supply of skilled labor in Brazil; in Argentina, a relatively low-skill bias in investment acted to reduce the skill premium there via demand.

This equalizing pattern detected by Lustig and López-Calva over the last few decades is the reverse of one of the more persuasive explanations for *increasing* inequality in the United States, as explored by the well-known research of Harvard economists Claudia Goldin (winner of the 2023 Nobel Prize in economics) and Lawrence Katz (2007*a*, 2007*b*, 2008). Their analysis of increasing income inequality in the United States since 1980 emphasizes the "race between education and technology." Simplifying only slightly, Goldin and Katz characterize trends in US income inequality according to which of these factors is winning the race; educational expansion before 1980, technological advancements thereafter. Accordingly, inequality was stable before 1980, and increasing thereafter in the United States. The Lustig/López-Calva results suggest that in recent decades, educational expansion has been winning the race in Latin America, and inequality of labor incomes has fallen as a result.

At the same time as education has been "winning the race" in Latin America in the Goldin and Katz sense, pro-poor government transfer programs raised household incomes at the lower end of the income distribution. The most widely commented upon among these are conditional cash transfer (CCT) programs, which flourished in the early years of the new millennium, many of them modeled on the earlier success of Mexico's Progresa program, subsequently renamed Oportunidades and, later, Prospera. These include Jefes y Jefas de Hogar (Argentina), various programs in Bolivia, Bolsa Família (Brazil), Chile Solidario, Familias en Acción (Colombia), Bonos de Desarrollo Humano (Ecuador), and Juntos (Peru).

The key characteristics of CCTs are right there in their name. They are generous *transfers* to low-income households, more generous than social policies in the constrained final decades of the twentieth century allowed; this is the fundamental equalizing feature of CCTs. They are *cash*; increasing the spending power of households at their discretion (and not restricted in the way that in-kind transfers of food or farm equipment, say, would be). And they are *conditional*; in order to receive the transfers, a household needs to exhibit certain behaviors—usually, that their children attend school, or that expectant mothers attend neonatal health workshops. In this way, the programs are designed to have long-lasting effects on poverty reduction by increasing schooling and health levels of poor households both today and in the future. Thus, for example, substantially higher high-school attendance by girls in the poorest states of Mexico is attributed to the effect of the Progresa-Oportunidades-Prospera programs (a full assessment of the literature on these Mexican programs is provided by Susan Parker and Petra Todd, 2018). In the absence of income from the programs, households would have opted to keep those girls working at home. CCTs' effectiveness in achieving longer-term goals has been debated, but the programs' impact on lower inequality levels is amply borne out by analysis (Stampini and Tornarolli 2012; Adato and Hoddinott 2010).

Increases in the minimum wage, at least in Brazil, had an effect on reducing poverty and inequality that could rival the effects of CCTs. Engbom and Moser (2022) estimate that increases in the Brazilian minimum wage between 1995 and

2018 accounted for 45 percent of the reduction in earnings inequality over that time frame. The minimum wage increase was large: 128 percent over two decades. But the effect of the increase extended upward beyond those workers earning the minimum wage: Firms were induced to raise wages for those workers already earning more than the minimum wage, to retain their rank in the wage distribution. In practice, it is possible that some workers' pay, even those earning above the minimum, was explicitly linked to the minimum wage. At the same time, the sustained increase in the minimum wage encouraged a reallocation of workers from less productive to more productive firms, leading to an increase in output that outweighed any negative employment or output effects from increased labor costs. A significant increase in the Mexican minimum wage in 2019, meanwhile, could portend similarly large impacts on inequality; Campos-Vázquez and Esquivel (2022) estimate significant effects upon poverty reduction in municipalities near the US border where the increase was larger.[4]

All of the figures presented in this chapter so far—and more important, most of the analysis cited herein of declining inequality in Latin America—come from our much-consulted World Development Indicators (WDI), maintained by the World Bank. Gini coefficients in the WDI are estimated on the basis of representative household data, typically gathered from national surveys. While such survey data have steadily increased both in terms of quality and quantity, even the best such data collection exercises may provide insufficient information about the top incomes in an economy. If so, then income inequality is likely to be underestimated.

Top-income earners are likely to be underrepresented in household surveys for two reasons. First, top income earners—like the "1 percent" decried by the Occupy protestors around the world during the present century—are by definition a small share of an economy's population, and the number of "1-percenters" in a survey sample might be very small indeed, or even zero. Second, top income earners, even if they make it into a survey sample, may be less likely to respond to the survey than lower-income people, perhaps because of their unwillingness to divulge their income level.

For these reasons, Thomas Piketty and his collaborators at the World Inequality Lab have turned their attention to alternative sources of data in pursuit of information about top incomes: notably tax returns, but also social security records and data from national accounts. Systematic inclusion of tax data for high-income households, often combined with survey data, reveals a much greater concentration of income at the upper end of the income distribution than was previously acknowledged (De Rosa, Flores, and Morgan 2020*a*; De Rosa, Flores, and Morgan 2020*b*).[5]

In addition to drawing from a different mix of data sources, the World Inequality Lab researchers favor an alternative measure of income (and wealth) inequality to the Gini coefficient: namely, income shares. Income share measures are best understood by imagining that the population is lined up, left to right, ranked by income, so that the people with the lowest incomes are at the left end of the lineup, and the highest incomes are earned by those at the right-hand extreme. We can then ask, for example, what share of national income (or, roughly, gross domestic product) flows to the 10 percent (decile) of the population at the right-hand side of the lineup. There are trade-offs in using Gini coefficients and income concentration data. The top ten data tell us a lot about the top end of the income distribution, but little about the remainder; the Gini coefficient, meanwhile, is based on the entire income distribution. In this way, the top ten income share is akin to the head count poverty rate, which is similarly focused on just a portion of the income distribution (the bottom end, in the case of the poverty rate). At the same time, the top ten income share is arguably more transparent to interpret than the Gini coefficient.

To understand the interpretation of the top ten measure, consider one of the more unequal economies among the LAC-7: Brazil. During the 2020s, the average share of national income accruing to the 10 percent of highest-income households was 58.3 percent, according to the World Inequality Lab data (down from 60.9 percent in the 1980s). Put another way, the bottom 90 percent of Brazilian households earned roughly two-fifths of national income (41.7 percent), up from 39.1 percent in the 1980s, a fairly stark and straightforward statistic. The income shares of the bottom 90 percent in the 1980s in France and the United States were separated by five percentage points, at 68.7 percent and 63.7 percent, respectively; by the 2020s, that share remained the same in France, but had fallen to 55 percent in the United States, widening the gap between the two rich countries to almost fourteen percentage points of national income. Again: stark and straightforward.

Data on top income earners from the World Inequality Lab paint a slightly different picture of recent changes in income inequality in Latin America than the Gini coefficient data from the World Development Indicators. Many of the Gini time trends (fig. 8.3) are mirrored by the top ten share trends. Top ten inequality was falling, if slightly, in many of the LAC-7 countries, including Brazil, Colombia, Venezuela, and Argentina. But the evolution of top ten income shares in Chile and Mexico displays a very different pattern from the evolution of their Gini coefficients. The share of national income flowing to the top 10 percent of the Mexican income distribution, for example, rose from 54 percent in the 1980s and 1990s, to 64 percent in the 2010s and 2020s; that is, the increased income of the top decile is equivalent to fully 10 percent of the size of the Mexican economy. While Chile's top ten share fell in the 2020s, it had risen to 65 percent in the preceding decade. Even for the countries that saw a decline in the share of income flowing to the top decile, these statistics bespeak extraordinary income concentration at the top of the distribution.

The World Inequality Lab summarizes its findings for Latin America based on multiple data sources and indicators as follows. Income inequality genuinely decreased since 2000 in Argentina, Colombia, Ecuador, and Uruguay. Income inequality remained high and stable in Peru during that time frame, and increased even further in Brazil, Chile, and Mexico (De Rosa, Flores, and Morgan 2020a). So which is it? Is the race between education and technology being won by education in Latin America, reducing income inequality across the board? Or is income being increasingly concentrated at the high end of the income distribution? The first story is supported by the trend in Gini coefficients in the World Development Indicators, calculated on the basis of national survey data. The second story is supported by granular data from multiple sources, including tax returns, on top incomes.

The two stories are not entirely mutually exclusive. The education versus technology mechanism analyzed by Goldin and Katz is based on inequality in *labor* incomes; labor incomes could be growing more equal but income from *capital* might be growing disproportionately among top income earners, widening the gap *between* labor income and capital income. In this way, the Gini coefficients and the top incomes data may be moving in opposite directions. (Similarly, targeted transfers to poorer households may be reducing poverty at the lower end of the income distribution, even as incomes rise at the top.) It is a mathematical possibility that the two inequality indicators we have been looking at are diverging for some countries in some time periods. Income gains to sufficiently many households at the bottom and middle of the income distribution could reduce the Gini coefficient by a greater amount than the ultrahigh income gains at the top tend to increase the Gini coefficient. Even if this is so, the concentration of income at the top would be of concern, Piketty would argue: He worries that such concentration threatens the effective exercise of democracy.

Before turning to a broad overview of the economic analysis of inequality and development, let us consider *wealth*, rather than income, inequality. Recall two points about wealth inequality: It will always and everywhere be higher than income inequality, and, despite recent and ongoing improvements, the database available for analyzing wealth inequality is less extensive than data for looking at income inequality.

The Commodities Consensus-driven expansion of primary production and exports highlighted the degree of inequality of wealth in one of its oldest forms: landholding. A 2016 Oxfam study on landholding and inequality in the context of the commodities boom compiled information from agricultural and livestock censuses (*censos agropecuarios*) for as many countries as possible. They computed the share of total agricultural/livestock-raising land controlled by the 1 percent of operations with the largest landholding. For the region as a whole, this number is 51 percent; the largest 1 percent of farms and ranches control over half of the farming and ranching land. The concentration is higher in Peru (77 percent), Chile (75 percent), and Paraguay (71 percent); and notably lower in Uruguay (19 percent), Ecuador (23 percent), Nicaragua (25 percent), and El Salvador (29 percent) (Oxfam 2016, gráfico 2). At the other end of the landholding distribution, Oxfam found that the bottom 80 percent of farms and ranches, again ranked by size, control about 12 percent of farming and ranching land (the share of the bottom 80 percent was below 4 percent in Chile and Colombia, and above 20 percent in Brazil, El Salvador, and Uruguay) (Oxfam 2016, tabla 1). Note that these disparities are calculated on the basis of all landholdings, not for all rural people, much less all people, in any of these economies. The shares of landed wealth computed for all people would reflect even more inequality, as many agricultural workers in the spot labor market, or people who live in cities, control no land at all. The Oxfam study argues further that the rate of landholding concentration has been increasing since 1960s, despite land redistribution efforts (including the ambitious Brazilian agrarian reform carried out between 1995 and 2010), and that concentration has been exacerbated by the commodities boom.

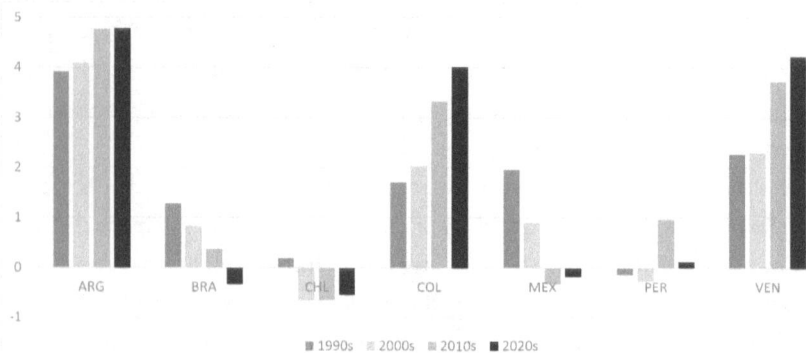

Figure 9.4. Share of total net personal wealth held by bottom half of national wealth distribution, LAC-7 countries, 1990s–2020s. Observations for Argentina from 2006 to 2011 inclusive were removed because of extreme volatility. *Source*: World Inequality Database, World Inequality Lab.

With the help of the World Inequality Database, we can expand our focus to inequality in the holding of all forms of wealth. The share of total net personal wealth in the LAC-7 countries in the hands of the poorest half of the population varies between 4.9 percent (Argentina, 2012) and −1.3 percent (Peru, 2001) (fig. 9.4). Your net personal wealth can be negative if your debt exceeds your assets; what is striking is that the *total* personal wealth of the poorest half of the population is negative for years at a time, in Brazil, Chile, Mexico, and Peru. This personal indebtedness—driven in part by high interest rate credit card debt—points to widespread precariousness of the economic circumstances of many people, even if their *incomes* are rising. Increases in the wealth share of the bottom 50 percent can be seen in Argentina, Colombia, and Venezuela—a heterogeneous mix of countries in terms of economic policy making during this century, to be sure. By way of comparison, the average wealth share of the bottom half of the population over the period 2018–2022, according to the World Inequality Lab data, for China was 6.3 percent; for France, 5.1 percent; and for the United States, 1.5 percent.

The share of wealth held by the top 1 percent of the population in LAC-7 countries was several times that held by the bottom 50 percent (fig. 9.5), ranging from 24.6 percent (Argentina, 2012) to 55.8 percent (Chile, 2011). This extreme measure of wealth concentration declined over the period in the figure in

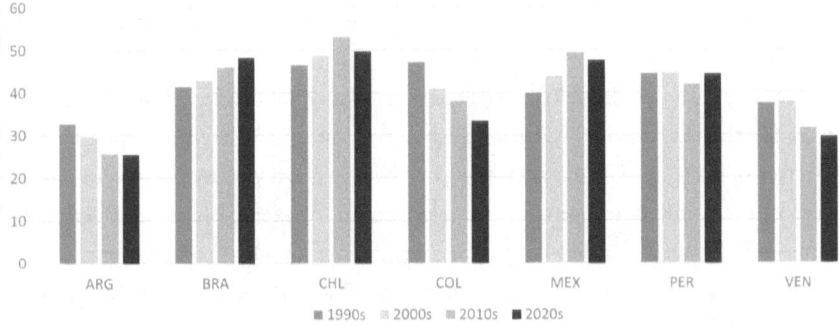

Figure 9.5. Share of total net personal wealth held by top 1% of national wealth distribution, LAC-7 countries, 1990s–2020s. Observations for Argentina from 2006 to 2011 inclusive were removed because of extreme volatility. *Source*: World Inequality Database, World Inequality Lab.

Colombia, Venezuela, and Argentina—the same three countries for which the bottom-half share of wealth was rising—as well as Peru. Wealth concentration among the top 1 percent increased for Brazil, Chile, and Mexico. (All of these statements are based on a simple linear best-fit line for the trend in each country.) For comparison's sake, the top 1 percent's wealth share over the period 2018–2022 was 24 percent in France, 31.9 percent in China, and 34.9 percent in the United States. This indicates that, with the arguable exception of Argentina, wealth concentration in the LAC-7 countries remains extraordinarily high on a comparative basis.

The wealth data compiled by the World Inequality Lab, even taking into consideration the caveats regarding the quality, consistency, and comparability of data, if anything, casts further doubt on the hopeful question mark posed by the World Bank and cited at the start of this chapter.

The Two-Way Relationship Between Economic Inequality on Economic Growth: Implications for the Latin American Experience

I take it as given that the reduction in economic inequality is an appropriate political goal, and among the objectives of any reasonable economic development philosophy; that is, the reduction of inequality has *intrinsic* value. Certainly, this is the case if we subscribe to Sen's notion of development as the enlargement of freedoms enjoyed by members of society.

An alternative perspective on the question of inequality and development advocates for the *instrumental* value of inequality reduction. That is, inequality, irrespective of its intrinsic harm, might be harmful to the achievement of other objectives of economic development: notably, growth of average income. Such questions—that is, is inequality neutral to, harmful for, or a by-product of growth?—naturally take on particular importance in the Latin American context, given its historically high levels of income inequality. The question is further complicated by the history of inequality in the region, as summarized by Rosemary Thorp's assertion that throughout much of the continent's history, inequality has been "functional" to economic growth, "in the sense of supportive of the particular growth path, even constructive at times to facilitate the growth path" (Thorp 2012, 149). That is, in the colonial and nineteenth-century contexts, and perhaps more recently, powerful interest groups have viewed inequality as being *good* for growth: The violent expropriation of peasant landholdings in the latter part of the nineteenth century during the long presidency of Porfirio Díaz in Mexico, for example, increased inequality, de facto, and was deemed favorable to growth by the *científicos*, Díaz's technocratic and positivist advisors, who argued that concentration of landholding contributed to higher agricultural output for export.

For all these reasons, Latin American social theorists have had a long and sophisticated fascination with, and talent for, theories of economic inequality and growth, including but not limited to Marxian-inspired models from the High Developmentalist era. An excellent example, in which inequality is *not* functional to growth: a model developed by Brazilian economists Maria da Conceição Tavares and José Serra in a 1971 paper, for example, who probed the stagnation of Brazilian industrialization and growth at the close of the High Developmentalist miracle. Brazilian growth, they observed, was accompanied by a growing concentration of income, on the one hand. The composition of industrial output, in the meantime, was evolving toward goods—like automobiles—demanded by the ever-richer though less and less numerous economic elite.[6] The combination of these forces led to a strangulation of the dynamism of Brazilian growth. Mainstream economics in the North would catch up with these long-standing concerns of Latin American High Developmentalist economists beginning in the 1990s.

The 1990s witnessed the proliferation of a rich neoclassical vein of political economy models that run from inequality to lower growth, beginning with the work of the late Harvard University economist Alberto Alesina. These studies seek to explain an empirical finding that emerged with the advent of more robust cross-country datasets that showed that more unequal economies, all other things remaining equal, tend to experience slower economic growth. That is, countries with higher Gini coefficients in 1960 or so (like the Philippines), controlling for other factors, grew more slowly over the subsequent quarter century than those with lower Gini coefficients (like South Korea).

There are arguably three variants of these models. All three work through investment as a driver of economic growth: Higher inequality is associated in all of these models with depressed investment, which reduces economic growth in turn.[7]

The first of these mechanisms is based on *capital-market imperfections* (Banerjee and Newman 1993; Galor and Zeira 1993). Suppose that good investment ideas occur randomly throughout the population. However, because of the risk of default, banks are only willing to lend to potential entrepreneurs who have sufficient wealth to post as collateral. This is the "capital-market imperfection" in question: "Perfect" capital markets would lend to *all* entrepreneurs with good prospects for loan repayment. Not all good business projects will receive funding where wealth is unequally distributed: Some poor entrepreneurs will not make investments because they cannot post collateral for loans. An economy with the same average level of wealth, more equitably distributed, will have higher rates of investment and economic growth than one that is more unequal. Note that this explanation relies on wealth inequality rather than income inequality. It is wealth—land, a house, durable goods like cars or tractors, financial instruments—that would-be entrepreneurs can use as collateral to secure borrowing.

A second variant of this literature argues that more unequal economies are marked by higher levels of *social conflict*: This could take the form of dispersed violence like crime and delinquency, or more generalized violence like civil war (Alesina and Perotti 1996; Benhabib and Rustichini 1996; Easterly 2001). Consider a simple example that illustrates how this mechanism works to depress growth. Suppose a potential investor is considering building five factories in an unequal society like this. She might decide it is smarter to build only four factories and divert the resources that might have paid for a fifth factory to building a fence around the other four and hiring security guards. More generally, in the presence of inequality, resources are diverted away from productive investment, lowering economic growth in the process. A more equal economy would see more such factories built, and less spent on private security. More extreme versions of the social-conflict mechanism focus on more widespread violence, up to and including civil war, the depressive effects of which upon investment are clear.

A third variant of this research is based on the notion of *redistributive public finance* (Alesina and Rodrik 1994; Persson and Tabellini 1994). This mechanism relies on democratic governance; that is, it presupposes that voters support politicians and political parties based in part upon their proposals for economic policies, and especially economic policies related to taxation and government spending. Where there is greater inequality, there will be greater electoral support for candidates whose platform includes more redistributive public finance: higher income taxes to finance higher spending on schools and clinics and other publicly provided goods and services. This, in turn, reduces investment through a time-honored neoclassical argument: higher income tax reduces an investor's incentive to invest, since she will pocket a smaller share of the earnings.

This last redistributive-public-finance variant received surprising attention from an IMF study (Ostry et al. 2014) which statistically analyzed the relationship between inequality, redistributive public finance (roughly, the magnitude of tax-funded government spending), and growth. The IMF economists confirmed that more unequal economies tend to redistribute more income. Roughly speaking, Bernie Sanders– or Jean-Luc Mélenchon–style politicians will find greater support among voters in unequal societies. The IMF's focus on the effects of inequality is surprising in itself, as the Fund was a latecomer to worrying about the instrumental harm done by inequality. But the findings of this study are, arguably, more surprising still. The authors conclude that more redistribution is *not* associated with slower growth: Sanders/Mélenchon–style redistributions do not slow growth. Christine Lagarde (2015), IMF managing director at the time, argued forcefully in favor of measures that would reduce inequality.

There is a sense in which the Pink Tide of elected leftist governments is surprising only in that it did not occur earlier. In light of the Persson/Tabellini and Alesina/Rodrik models, you may well wonder what took the Pink Tide so long. The Pink Tide governments are in fact quite heterogeneous (which should not surprise us as this heterogeneity is a manifestation of key #5 from chapter 1). But one characteristic they share is that they all ran for office on a platform that emphasized redistributive public finance, especially the creation of new and better ways to channel resources to the least fortunate people in society. In a setting of still-high income inequality, one would expect, along with Alesina, Rodrik, Persson, and Tabellini, that such candidates would be awarded with electoral victory.

And redistribute they did; the Concertación governments oversaw a reduction of the Chilean poverty rate from 45 percent in 1987 at the end of the Pinochet dictatorship to 13.7 percent in 2006, on the eve of the global financial crisis (Ffrench-Davis 2016). More generally, leftist governments contributed to the reduction in inequality explored earlier in this chapter. An econometric analysis of reductions in the Gini coefficient for Latin American countries over the period 1992–2017 found that countries with leftist governments saw their Gini coefficients decline significantly more—what the authors call a "leftist premium"—than those with non-leftist governments, even taking into account terms of trade and export growth (which should capture the contribution of the commodity boom). What did leftist governments do that contributed to the steeper-than-average decline in Gini coefficients? The authors provide an inventory: increased cash transfers, both conditional and unconditional, as well as social pensions, which are not linked to contributions; increases in the minimum wage; and increased tax collection to pay for these and other programs—in short, redistributive public finance (Feierherd et al. 2023). Stein and Caro (2017), meanwhile, find that between 1990 and 2010, the shift to a leftist government in Latin America led to a rise in income-tax revenue of about 1 percent of GDP. In a region where income taxes constituted about 3.6 percent of GDP, that was a sizeable increase. As we will see in chapter 10, on fiscal policy, income taxes are more likely to be progressive than value-added taxes, and an increase in income taxation is more likely to contribute to lower levels of income inequality.

In sum, most of these economic models provide support for policies to reduce income inequality in Latin America for instrumental as well as intrinsic reasons; that is, because inequality likely retards growth in the region. And, moreover, the IMF findings suggest that redistributive public finance as a means of reducing inequality need not prejudice economic growth. Taken together, this body of quantitative political economy research from the 1990s suggests that comparatively high levels of economic inequality constrain the growth possibilities of Latin American economies. That is, the Milagrinho might have been a full-blown Milagro in the presence of lower inequality levels; and growth during the Hurricane Season might not have been so stormy.

New Perspectives on the Long-run Pattern of Inequality

The 1990s theoretical and empirical research on the relationship between inequality and economic growth explored the effects of inequality upon growth and development. More recent research has explored the reverse direction of causality; namely, how does the level of inequality evolve over time as an economy grows and develops? And this new research has upended a long-held consensus about this relationship.

The twentieth-century consensus view derives from an ingenious model developed by W. Arthur Lewis in 1954. Like Raúl Prebisch (see chapter 2), Lewis was an economist from the Periphery who adapted orthodox economic tools to better reflect the structure of the economy close at hand: in Lewis's case, the Caribbean island of Saint Lucia. Lewis modeled a two-sector economy, including an agricultural and an industrial sector. Lewis's insight was to assume that there is "excess" labor in agriculture. That means that if agricultural workers migrate to the city, total food production could be maintained even by the smaller agricultural labor force left behind. It also means that industrial capitalists could pay pretty low wages, not much higher than the meager earnings agricultural workers could command back on the farm. At some point, however, rural-to-urban migration will reach a point where there is no longer excess labor in agriculture. At that point, food supplies will fall with further out-migration, food prices will increase, and industrialists will have to pay higher wages than they did before to lure rural workers to the factory. The Lewis model, further formalized by Ranis and Fei (1961), provided a reasonably good schematic for analyzing the process of economic development, and especially the transformation of a fundamentally agrarian economy into a predominantly manufacturing one—transformation very much on the minds of many in the Periphery during the postcolonial era in which Lewis was working.

The Lewis model makes clear predictions for the path of inequality over time. Think of the Lewis world as having three historical phases. In the first, the economy is largely agrarian, and most people have incomes very near the subsistence minimum. Inequality of incomes is therefore relatively low. In a second, transitional, phase, rural-to-urban migration takes off. In this phase, wages are low for agricultural and industrial workers alike, but there are quite elevated profits for a small group of industrial capitalists (even accounting for the share of industrial revenues that are reinvested in new manufacturing capacity). As such, inequality is high and increasing. In the third and final phase, workers have migrated from agriculture to industry in sufficient numbers that productivity and wages are increasing in both sectors, and capitalists' incomes decline as the super-profits of the second phase disappear. In this final phase, inequality is lower than in the second phase. Over time, then, inequality in an economy will trace an inverted-U shape.

The inverted-U time path of inequality in the Lewis model enjoyed the empirical support of work by economist Simon Kuznets (1955). Kuznets compared measured levels of inequality in low-, middle-, and high-income countries, and detected an inverted-U curve pattern. That is, inequality was relatively low in low- and high-income economies, and higher in the middle-income economies—if plotted against average income on the horizontal axis, the observed levels of inequality would trace an upside-down U (CAF 2022, gráfico 1.2 provides an updated version of this graphic). What Kuznets found was consistent with the theoretical predictions of Lewis. A consensus was consolidated; both men would later be rewarded with Nobel Prizes in economics. This consensus was furthermore a reassuring one for places like Latin America, where people worried about high levels of income inequality: The workings of capitalist development, Lewis and Kuznets averred, would naturally lead to falling levels of inequality over time.

That consensus would be shattered by new research in the twenty-first century. Thomas Piketty's *Le capital au XXIe siècle* (2013) marked a turning point in the study of economic inequality. The contribution of Piketty and his contributors is twofold. First, Piketty and his collaborators compiled an enormous cross-country, historical database, especially for the rich capitalist countries, based on the finer-grained data needed to analyze inter-household inequality. Second, using that database, Piketty argued that the Kuznets inverted-U hypothesis is not borne out: In several mature capitalist economies, inequality has been rising, not falling, in recent decades. It's not so much that Lewis and Kuznets were wrong; their work matched reasonably well the world they were describing in the middle of the last century. But their frameworks performed less well in the context of the world after 1980 or so.

Piketty argues that if left unchecked, income and wealth inequality will tend to increase, not decline over time. There are no "self-regulating" forces of the capitalist economy—such as the upward pressure on rural and urban wages in the Lewis model—to counteract increasing inequality. This follows from the tendency of the rate of return to capital r to exceed the economic growth rate (g). The rate of return, r, is the going rate of income to owners of capital, analogous to the wage rate for laborers ("owners" of labor). Those whose incomes derive from the capital (owners of capital and inherited fortunes), will see their incomes rise more quickly than those whose incomes tend to track the rate of economic growth (laborers). Piketty's mechanism has been widely summarized as $r > g$.

A corollary of Piketty's findings of particular importance to the study of governance is that where public policy (and the balance of political forces that underlies policy) is different, so too is the level of inequality. Thus, the rich Anglo-American economies—Australia, Canada, the United Kingdom, and the United States—had a U-shaped (not inverted-U-shaped) path of inequality over the twentieth century: falling in the wake of the global Great Depression; stable in the postwar period; and rising again to Gilded Age/Belle Époque levels in the decades since 1980. But other rich economies—France, Germany, Japan—had "L-shaped" patterns of inequality, falling with their Anglo-American counterparts during the 1930s, but remaining lower thereafter. The difference is due to political economy: redistributive public finances and different norms of corporate governance between the two sets of rich countries. The first is reflected in higher personal and corporate income taxes, and higher spending on goods like public education and health care. The second is reflected in norms governing the pay of corporate executives, which have exploded in the first group of countries relative to the second. These political economy distinctions usefully orient our analysis of Latin America's experience with inequality in recent decades.

Prospects for the Future Path of Inequality

The success story told in this chapter—however truncated or qualified—provides broad support for Piketty's overarching thesis that politics and policies matter in the evolution of inequality. The centuries-long tenacity of Latin

American inequality yielded, to the extent that it yielded at all, to deliberate public policies. The expansion of secondary schooling over several decades, for example, reduced the earnings gap between those with only primary and those with secondary schooling. Conditional cash transfers and other social policies launched by possibilist governments of various ideological hues were more explicitly and directly targeted at the reduction of poverty and inequality.

But the question mark remains, for at least two reasons. First, both the successes and failures of the first twenty-five years of the twenty-first century in Latin America have been driven, broadly speaking, by the vicissitudes of the extractive commodity economy. To the extent that the region's economic fortunes are tied to commodity exports, governments' aspirations to long-term macroeconomic resilience will be hamstrung. Second, egalitarian political coalitions are precarious; civil and social unrest in the Hurricane Season has weakened and divided support for the incipient anti-inequality policy package.

CHAPTER TEN

Improved Fiscal Policy

IN THIS AND THE following chapter, we turn our attention to the Latin American state, and argue that the twenty-first century has witnessed better economic governance in the region. We begin with fiscal policy: the use of taxes, public spending, and public debt to finance government operations, stabilize the macroeconomy in times of recession or inflation, and pursue the aims of economic development.

In this chapter, we will

1. introduce the components of fiscal policy, and review trends in fiscal deficits as well as the level and composition of tax revenues;
2. explain the factors that have led fiscal policy to be procyclical in Latin America and why that is so injurious, and discuss institutional improvements such as fiscal rules that promise to reduce procyclicality;
3. trace the improvements in public indebtedness during the Milagrinho, followed by deterioration during the Hurricane Season;
4. argue that fiscal policy is a sort of social contract linking a government and the citizens it serves, and that Latin America's fiscal inadequacy, despite improvements, indicates a tattered, if not broken, social contract.

A Legacy of Fiscal Inadequacy

Latin American governments and states have been much maligned for decades: for poor performance, poor policies, and poor strategies; for ineffectiveness, corruption, and graft; for authoritarian violence and populist indulgence; for obeisance to global powers at the expense of their citizens; and for quixotic crusades ineffectually swimming against global alliances and movements. They have been criticized by political scientists and investment bankers; by the humblest of their citizens and the business and media magnates in their midst; by their neighbors on the continent; and in an especially pointed rebuke, by US residents of every social class and ideological stripe, in every century of US history. In the face of such relentlessly negative assessments over such long period of time, clearly there is an exaggerated stereotype at work. And as is so often the case with injurious stereotypes, there are glaring inconsistencies among these caricatures. One wonders, nevertheless, whether there is a kernel of truth behind the exaggeration. Behind the stereotype is a precariousness, an instability of the Latin American state, rooted, perhaps, in the state's emergence from colonial regimes (key #1, chapter 1), fed by a century of post-independence violence and buffeted by the local vicissitudes of global conflicts, including during the eras of High Developmentalism and the debt crisis of the 1980s, as well as the Cold War.

The relentless criticism of the Latin American state extends to virtually all aspects of its activity, but I want to focus on the half century or more of denunciation of Latin American governments' *economic* management. It was into this noisy thicket that Albert Fishlow, an American development economist with a long experience in Latin America, waded at the nadir of the no-growth debt crisis of the 1980s.[1] Fishlow read the prevailing criticisms of the Latin American state in 1990 as focused on excessive and harmful intervention by the state into the workings of the market mechanism. This was after all, you will recall, the time of the emergence of the Washington Consensus, which exhorted governments to pursue market-friendly approaches to markets for trade, foreign exchange, credit, and labor, and to sell off state-owned enterprises. This bundle of recommendations formed the economic policy latticework of what would become universally called (and equally universally deplored as) neoliberalism.

Fishlow argued that intervention in the economy by Latin American states was not a matter of overreach or predation but rather the logical consequence of the High Developmentalist analysis of the principal problems of Latin American economic development. That is, state intervention represented rather the deliberate and principled application of Raúl Prebisch's CEPAL recommendations to foster import-substituting industrialization; this in turn was meant to escape the long-term stagnation of commodity dependence (key #3, chapter 1). Fishlow pointed out that the market optimism of the Washington Consensus package neither addressed nor refuted the premises of Prebisch's diagnosis (this point was also made by Barry Lesser 1991) nor did it attempt to address the pitfalls of commodity dependence.

Instead, Fishlow argued, the real sin of Latin American states was what he called "fiscal inadequacy," and especially, high levels of public debt. This, too, was a foreseeable consequence of governments' industrialization strategies if not carefully managed. East Asian Developmentalist states had better managed the fiscal effects of import substitution than their Latin American counterparts, to be sure. But pinning the debt crisis of the 1980s on governments' intervention in the economy missed the mark.[2] Many decades later, we can read Fishlow's argument as an observation that critiques of Latin American economic management were distorted by ideological blinders; at the time, such questions were viewed through the prism of "market versus state" (key #4, chapter 1) binaries.

Two strands in Fishlow's argument shed light on discussions of Latin American economic statecraft in the twenty-first century: the primacy of fiscal policy, and the market versus state ideological divide. The first, because the importance of fiscal policy both as a tool to promote economic development and as a set of indicators for good economic management rose in prominence in the new century—this is the subject of this chapter. The second, because Latin American political leaders, policy makers, and bureaucrats appeared, in the twenty-first century, to abandon the tired market/state binary in favor of a non-ideological pragmatism—this second element is at the heart of chapter 11.

An Introduction to Fiscal Policy

Fiscal policy has three components: taxes, public spending, and public debt. Government expenditures range from wages and salaries for public sector workers, from the president to schoolteachers to soldiers, to investment in highways and railroads and electricity generation, to payments on the public debt. Governments can pay for those expenditures with tax revenues, which depend on tax rates, the tax base (those households and companies whose incomes are taxed, or transactions that are subject to taxes), the efficiency of the tax administration, and the prevalence of tax evasion. Non-tax revenues, notably including revenues from natural resource exploitation under government control, can be quantitatively important to some governments, as is the case in much of Latin America and the Caribbean. Governments can also finance expenditures by issuing debt—borrowing money directly from banks at home and abroad or issuing bonds to buyers in financial markets. Of course, debt adds to expenditure needs as governments must make interest and principal payments in the future.

The time path of fiscal policy in Latin America during this century can be traced with attention to two indicators. The first is the fiscal deficit or surplus, expressed as a share of total government revenues,[3] and the level of government debt, expressed as a share of GDP. Budget balances among the LAC-7 countries varied considerably (fig. 10.1a). Brazil's budget deficit closely resembled the regional average, as is expected given its size: Both Brazil and the Latin American average remained in deficit territory throughout the century and were closest to zero during the Milagrinho boom. Sizable Milagrinho surpluses were observed in Chile (especially), Venezuela, Argentina, and Peru. During the smaller and shorter commodity boom of the Hurricane Season, Chile and Peru once again had surpluses, smaller this time. Venezuela, meanwhile, experienced large and persistent deficits after the oil-fueled surpluses of the early century (fig. 10.1b), reaching huge magnitudes unmatched in any other countries of the region (the Venezuelan fiscal deficit reached almost five times the size of government revenues in 2018).

Keeping debt within sustainable bounds depends in part upon a government's capacity to collect tax revenues to finance current expenditures, rather than borrowing. A comparison of Latin American government revenues with those of OECD countries illustrates that tax revenues were proportionally lower in the former set of countries (fig. 10.2a) and had a different composition (fig. 10.2b).

In Latin America, tax revenues were substantially lower, as a share of GDP, than in OECD countries, and had been for many decades. On average, tax revenues were 20 percent of GDP in Latin America this century, compared to 32.7 percent in the OECD over the period 1990–2021. But Latin America's tax-to-GDP ratio has been growing, thus shrinking the gap between the two sets of countries from sixteen and one tenth percentage points of GDP in 1991 to twelve and a half percentage points in 2021, with somewhat higher and lower values in between. The gap nevertheless remained large throughout this period: In 1991, tax revenues in the OECD were more than twice as large as in Latin America, proportionally speaking, and fell to just over one and a half times as large in 2015. Lower tax capacity

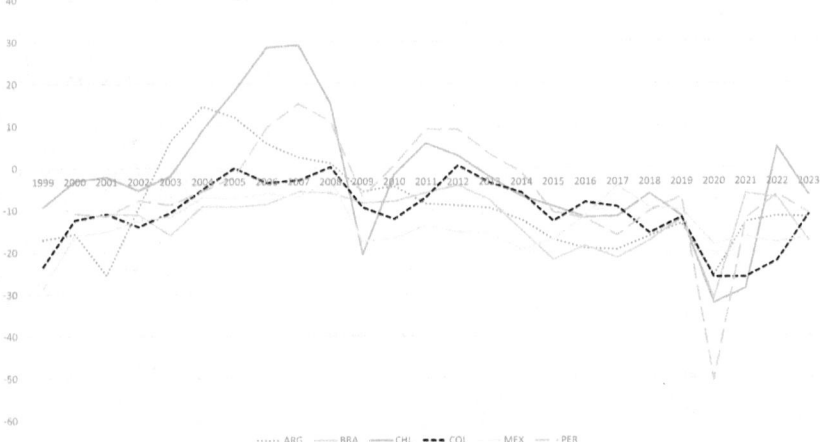

Figure 10.1a. Fiscal deficit/surplus (% of total government revenue), LAC-7 countries (exc. Venezuela), 1999–2023. 2023 data represent IMF estimates. *Source*: Calculated from data on total expenditure and total revenue as a share of GDP, extracted from the October 2023 WEO database, IMF.

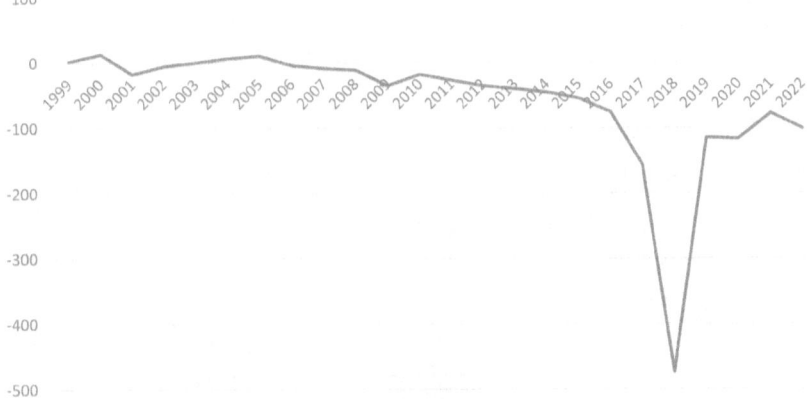

Figure 10.1b. Fiscal deficit/surplus (% of total government revenue), Venezuela, 1999–2022. *Source*: Calculated from data on total expenditure and total revenue as a share of GDP, extracted from the October 2023 WEO database, IMF.

constrains governments' ability to finance current expenditures; address economic crises; or invest in infrastructure, health care, and education. Lower taxation capacity also predisposes a government to turn to borrowing when it can, with consequences for long-lasting debt overhang.

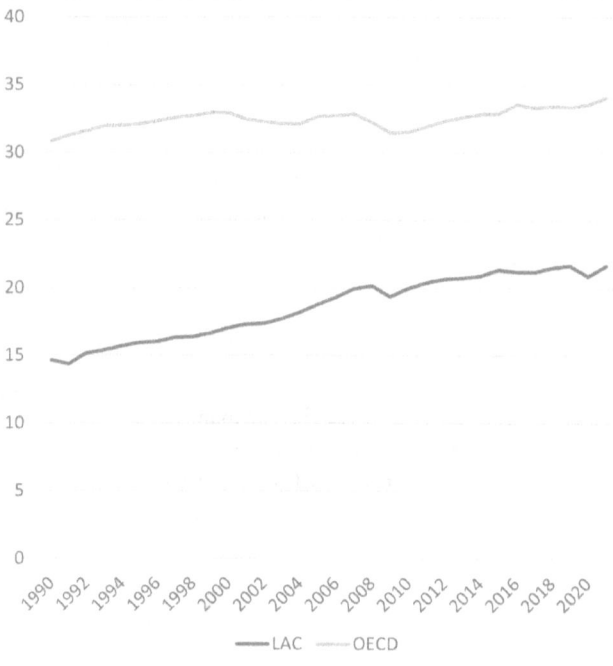

Figure 10.2a. Tax revenues (% of GDP), Latin America and OECD, 1990–2021. The LAC average represents the unweighted average of twenty-five countries and excludes Cuba and Venezuela due to data availability issues. The OECD average represents the unweighted average of the thirty-eight OECD member countries. Chile, Colombia, Costa Rica, and Mexico are members of both groups. *Source*: From data included in OECD Revenue Statistics in Latin America and the Caribbean 2023, fig. 1.6 (a); fig. 1.13 (b).

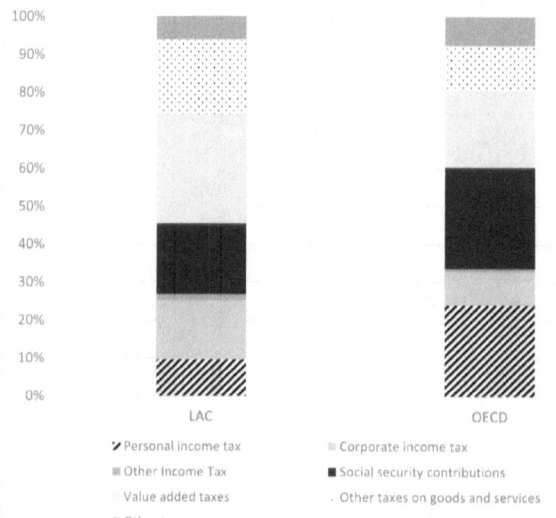

Figure 10.2b. Structure of tax revenues, Latin America and OECD, 2020. The LAC average represents the unweighted average of twenty-five countries and excludes Cuba and Venezuela due to data availability issues. The OECD average represents the unweighted average of the thirty-eight OECD member countries. Chile, Colombia, Costa Rica, and Mexico are members of both groups. *Source*: From data included in OECD Revenue Statistics in Latin America and the Caribbean 2023, fig. 1.6 (a); fig. 1.13 (b).

Not only was the *level* of taxation different between the OECD and Latin America, so was the *composition* of tax revenues (fig. 10.2b). Comparing a snapshot of average tax structures in 2020, four important differences emerge. Keep in mind that the OECD tax revenues summed to much larger shares of GDP than the Latin American revenues; these comparisons thus compare the breakdown of a smaller share of GDP (Latin America) to a larger share of GDP (OECD) across the different types of tax. First, OECD countries collected a much larger share of taxes in form of personal and corporate income taxes: 33.7 percent of taxation in the OECD, versus 27 percent in Latin America and the Caribbean. Second, within the category of income taxes, Latin America relied far less on personal income taxes: personal income taxes accounted for 36 percent of income tax revenue in Latin America, versus 71.3 percent in the OECD. Indeed, most households in most Latin American countries were exempted from any personal income tax liability. Third, Latin American countries relied to a far greater degree on taxes on goods and services, including value-added taxes (VATs): 48.5 percent of Latin American tax revenue, versus 32.1 percent of OECD tax revenues. Fourth and finally, social security contributions were a relatively larger share of OECD (26.6 percent) than of Latin American (18.5 percent) tax revenues.

Economists refer to income taxes (whether levied on individuals or companies) as direct taxes; taxes on transactions are called indirect taxes. The evidence summarized in fig. 10.2b illustrates that, in general, Latin America relied more on indirect taxes to finance government and OECD countries relied more upon direct taxes. There are important differences between direct and indirect taxes. The most important, perhaps, is that direct tax systems can be designed to be progressive; that is, the tax burden is proportionally higher on higher-income individuals or companies. Income-tax systems with rising marginal tax rates for higher-income tax brackets make the system progressive. Indirect taxes, meanwhile, are more likely to be regressive: The tax burden is proportionally larger on lower-income contributors. This happens because taxes on transactions are, roughly speaking, taxes on consumption, and lower-income people allocate a larger share of their income (often 100 percent) to consumption than do higher-income people. Given their reliance on regressive taxes, Latin American tax systems were more likely to increase income inequality than were OECD tax systems, which are more reliant on progressive taxes. Of course, the effect of fiscal policy as a whole on income inequality also includes the potentially equalizing effect of transfers, like the conditional cash transfers considered in chapter 9. Social security contributions are in general neutral or regressive (households do not contribute beyond a given income threshold in many countries), but the net impact of social security upon income inequality must also consider the pattern of benefits paid out, which are progressive.[4]

An additional difference between Latin America and OECD countries is that non-tax revenues comprised a much larger share of total government revenues in the former than in the latter set of countries. Over the period 1990–2006, non-tax revenues, which include fees and royalties from natural resource extraction and exports, made up 28 percent of government revenues in Latin America on average, and exceeded 40 percent in Bolivia, Colombia, Panama, and Venezuela; in OECD countries, in contrast, non-tax revenues contributed only 15 percent of government revenues (OECD 2008, 60). For ten oil-producing countries in the region, general government revenues from oil and gas exploration and production ranged between 2 and nearly 6 percent of GDP (not just of government revenues) over the period 2013–2022; the contribution was particularly high in Guyana (9.5 percent of GDP in 2022), Ecuador (9.7 percent), and Trinidad and Tobago (10.8 percent) (OECD/CIAT/IDB/CEPAL 2023, fig. 2.2). Government revenues from mining, meanwhile, in twelve countries in the region with significant mining operations, contributed amounts smaller with respect to GDP, between two tenths of 1 percent and nearly 1 percent of GDP between 2013–2022. Mining's contributions to government revenue came to 1.7 percent of Peruvian GDP and 3.2 percent of Chilean GDP in 2022 (OECD/CIAT/IDB/CEPAL 2023, fig. 2.3).

Changing Perspectives on the Aims of Fiscal Policies

Any state must engage in fiscal policy as a matter of financing its operations, but the aims and scope differ over time and across countries. To the market-oriented "Chicago Boys," whom we encountered in our discussion of Chile's premature deindustrialization in chapter 8, "less is more": Fiscal policy is a necessary evil that should be kept as small as possible, especially on the revenue side. On this view, taxes reduce incentives to work and invest, because owners of capital and labor do not get to keep all of the returns of their work and investment; taxes, therefore, are to be used sparingly if at all. Government borrowing, meanwhile, "crowds out" borrowing by private businesses, reducing the availability of credit, or raising the cost of borrowing, for the private sector; public debt, therefore, is to be used sparingly if at all. Public spending, finally, must be kept small so as not to require expansion of taxes and public debt. The Keynesian revolution of the 1930s (more in a couple paragraphs' time), however, introduced a positive role for fiscal policy; namely, the stabilization of macroeconomies subject to the potentially harmful swings of the business cycle.[5]

Latin American debates on fiscal policy in the twenty-first century moved beyond the less-is-more and stabilization conceptions and began to recognize fiscal policy's potential to pursue longer-term development goals. In part, this reflected a renewed focus upon fiscal policy in policy-making debates in the aftermath of the global financial crisis, in which massive bailouts—fiscal bailouts—were the first response of governments, including the United States ($700 billion) and China ($500 billion) (Dayton-Johnson 2008/2009). Fiscal policy for development acted through the types of expenditures pursued—notably, health care, education, and infrastructure—and through its capacity to reduce poverty and inequality (Dayton-Johnson 2008b). Fiscal legitimacy springs from the proper use of these policy tools to promote development and is therefore intimately linked to the consolidation of democracies (Elizondo and Santiso 2012).

Import-substituting industrialization created pressures on government deficits but the chronic deficits of many Latin American governments over the last half century were exacerbated by political pressures not related to ISI. Chronic fiscal deficits weaken governments' capacity to address economic crises in the short run, and development priorities requiring government expenditures and investment, in the long run. Moreover, as we saw during our review of inflation in chapter 7, chronic fiscal deficits can have knock-on effects on monetary policy, leading to inflation, and sometimes hyperinflation.

The most straightforward of the politically pressured fiscal deficit drivers, and arguably the most widespread, is *procyclical government spending*.[6] The "cycle" in "procyclical" refers to the business cycle, the quarter-to-quarter variation of GDP above or below its long-term trend rate of growth. In boom times, GDP is above that long-term trend; in recessions, it is below. Procyclical government spending therefore refers to a pattern in which governments spend more when economic conditions are good and spend less during recessions and crises.

This pattern flies in the face of textbook policy recommendations extending back to John Maynard Keynes[7]; his *General Theory of Employment, Interest and Money* (1936) encouraged governments mired in the Great Depression to expand government spending, thereby stimulating aggregate demand in their economies and lifting them out of a recession. Though US President Franklin Delano Roosevelt claimed to understand nothing the British economist said to him during their conversation on the subject, the US and other Center economies increased government spending, which helped end the global depression. Keynes also recommended that governments cool their spending when their economies were booming; too much government spending risked stoking inflation of the price level, with its attendant economic harms. To end slumps, governments could reduce taxation instead of raising government spending—the stimulus is roughly the same. In this way, Keynes invented the notion of macroeconomic stabilization, and the principal lever for attaining stability was countercyclical fiscal policy. Note that Keynesian macroeconomic management could lead to government deficits during economic downturns, from increased spending or reduced tax revenue, or both—and government budget surpluses during boom times.

Procyclical government spending, in contrast, is destabilizing. During recessions, reductions in government spending exacerbate the economic downturn; expanding spending in boom times can trigger inflationary episodes. Yet this is precisely the pattern that many Latin American governments have followed. Why?

The simple answer is that in imperfect democracies—that is, in pretty much all democracies in the world—government spending is subject to political pressures. Consider an archetypal example. Suppose that, like Chile, your government is especially reliant on revenues from natural resource exports (copper, in Chile's case) for government revenues. When the world copper price is high, copper export revenues surge, and government revenues with them (this could be because governments tax copper producers, or because copper mining is carried out by a state-owned enterprise, whose income is by definition government revenue). The government, buoyed by this good fortune, undertakes long-postponed projects, probably starting with investments in new copper mining capacity. Roads and schools and hospitals are built and improved. Of course, everyone in Chile can observe that the world copper price is high, and they put pressure on the government to increase certain kinds of spending. The prospect of higher government revenues encourages various government departments to propose higher budgets, without consideration of the aggregate increase in spending this will encourage. UCLA economist Aaron Tornell has written extensively of this tendency for uncoordinated interest groups to arrive at unsustainable spending, what he terms the "voracity effect."[8] Maybe copper miners seek higher wages; other public sectors, emboldened by their copper-mining counterparts' efforts, likewise strike for higher pay. All manner of influence seeking and peddling are possible; not all or even most of this boom-time spending is productive or useful. If the economy is close to full employment—people seeking work can find work, and factories are running at full capacity—this increased government spending will put upward pressure on prices, and, in the absence of efforts by the Banco Central de Chile to forestall it, inflation and even hyperinflation may ensue.

Suppose now that sometime later, world copper prices decline for reasons having nothing to do with the Chilean economy. Government revenues plummet: Government stops spending wherever it can. Bosses order tools down at half-finished hospitals and schools and roads projects. Workers at those sites are out of work and reduce their own spending. Corner stores sell less and cut orders. A negative multiplier effect rebounds throughout the Chilean economy, amplifying the effect of the downturn in the copper sector. Out-of-work people and struggling corner stores beseech the government for help, and for payments to ease their descent (further) into poverty. The government, however, has no resources—no "fiscal space"—to respond to such demands. In fact, the government finds that it is unable to meet regular payments on its debt, which leads lenders and bond buyers to threaten to stop lending and buying bonds, further reducing government revenues. This leads the government to seek an emergency arrangement with the International Monetary Fund, who agree to extend short-term financing to the Chilean government, on the condition that it use the funds to service its debt—and that it makes further cuts in its expenditures, to ensure that it will be able to repay the IMF in due time. Indeed, some economists argue that it is the sudden stop in credit availability more than the voracity effect that leads governments to reduce spending during bad economic times.

That is a stylized account of what procyclical fiscal policy looks like. One can imagine that, when the copper price booms again, as it likely will, the pressure to expand government spending will be even more accentuated than it was in the previous round, so that procyclicality can become more entrenched, and variations in spending wider, over time. The institutional features of this stylized version of the Chilean economy that make it more susceptible to destabilizing procyclical fiscal policy are at least three: first, the disproportionate influence of a volatile commodity price upon the government's revenues; second, the inability of the government in power to resist calls for increased discretionary spending (or tax cuts); and third, the failure of the central bank to counter inflationary pressures (i.e., the central bank is not independent of the executive branch).[9]

Qualitative Improvements in Fiscal Policy in the Twenty-First Century

This context makes what Chile actually accomplished in the early twenty-first century even more remarkable. Chile was among the governments around the world that designed and put in place a fiscal rule, adopted during the administration of Ricardo Lagos (2000–2006) and substantially strengthened under the Fiscal Responsibility Law of 2006 championed by finance minister Andrés Velasco during the following presidential administration, that of Michelle Bachelet (2006–2010). A fiscal rule commits and constrains the government to a particular target—which may be the size of the deficit or surplus, or of government spending (all of these usually expressed as a percentage of GDP). In some countries, these commitments are more binding than others, though even where they are notional, they signal fiscal discipline to observers in the country and beyond. Chile's rule committed to a fiscal surplus equal to 1 percent of GDP, but with an ingenious wrinkle linked to copper prices.[10]

The Chilean fiscal rule addressed two of the institutional susceptibilities listed above: the vulnerability of fiscal policy to copper-price gyrations, and the incentives for Tornell's voracity effect. The third vulnerability was addressed with the formal declaration of the independence of the Banco Central de Chile in 1989 as part of the return to democracy and civilian rule. In simple terms, under the fiscal rule regime, a team of independent experts forecasts the long-term price of copper, smoothing out the short-term ups and downs. Government revenue is then recalculated as though copper revenue was valued at the long-term price—not its actual market price. Thus, if, as in the Milagrinho years, world copper prices were historically high, the fiscal rule system would compute Chile's available government revenue to be substantially below its actual level.

What's more, under the fiscal rule, the Chilean government cannot expend more than this long-term revenue amount. Whatever pressures might arise, expenditures approved by the legislature and the executive cannot exceed the recalculated revenues, and this legal injunction provides credibility to the government in the face of these demands. The unspent surplus—proportional to the difference between the temporarily high price and its long-term level—is saved by the government and invested in a pair of sovereign wealth funds. When copper prices are low, meanwhile, the fiscal rule authorizes expenditures above actual revenues; savings from the boom times can be drawn down.

The incorporation of the long-term copper price provided fiscal space to the Chilean government to address recessions—as indeed happened in the wake of the Jazz Effect beginning in 2007 (refer to fig. 10.1a, which illustrates Chile's Milagrinho-era surplus and Jazz Effect deficit). Chile's countercyclical fiscal spending to combat the effects of the global financial crisis far outstripped those of its Latin American neighbors, and indeed exceeded efforts of more than a few rich countries, as a proportion of the size of the economies in question. Chile's "effective" fiscal balance in 2007—the difference between its revenues, swollen by high copper prices, and its expenditures—exceeded 8 percent of GDP; its "structural" surplus that year, computed with the long-term copper price, was only 1 percent of GDP, as required by the law. In 2009, Chile's deficit was over 4 percent of GDP, but its structural deficit was less than 1 percent (Velasco and Parrado 2012, fig. 3.4).

Fiscal rules of various forms were adopted during the twenty-first century by Argentina, the Bahamas, Brazil, Chile, Colombia, Costa Rica, Ecuador, Jamaica, Mexico, Panama, Paraguay, Peru, and Uruguay. Many small Caribbean economies were subject to supranational fiscal rules as part of the CARICOM, or Caribbean Community.[11] Not all of these are equally effective or binding, and compliance dips during crises. A study by the Inter-American Development Bank computed an index of compliance for Latin American and Caribbean countries, ranging from zero to one; the measured index varied mostly between 0.5 and 0.7 during the twenty-first century, but dipped to below 0.3 at the time of the Jazz Effect, and just below 0.5 during the Covid-19 pandemic (Valencia and Ulloa-Suárez 2022; see Davoodi et al. 2022b, for a worldwide look at fiscal rules during the Covid-19 crisis).

Procyclicality has diminished in the twenty-first century compared to the twentieth but is still quite common. A joint study by economists at the OECD and the Bank for International Settlements of eight large Latin American economies with fiscal rules confirmed the important countercyclical response of fiscal policy in 2009, as we have already seen in the case of Chile. And there have been more episodes of increased fiscal surpluses when GDP is above normal, and increased deficits when GDP is below normal (one way of identifying countercyclicality). But the evidence that fiscal policy has become more countercyclical for any of the eight countries between the 1991–2001 and 2002–14 periods is weak (in part because of small sample sizes at the country level); meanwhile, there is statistically significant evidence that Argentina and Uruguay became more procyclical with time. The path to fiscal discipline is not yet fully traversed for these countries (Alberola et al. 2017).

A further indicator of politically driven fiscal inadequacy has to do with so-called electoral business cycles, and here too there is emerging evidence that performance improved during this century. Electoral business cycles emerge when an incumbent government expands fiscal spending in the lead-up to an election to build (or more bluntly, to buy) support among voters for reelection. Economists Sebastián Nieto-Parra and Javier Santiso (2012) compare fiscal policy in election years (legislative elections for countries with parliamentary systems and executive elections for countries with presidential systems) and non-election years over the period 1990–2006. The primary fiscal balance (which does not include interest payments on government debt) fell by almost 1 percent of GDP in election years in Latin America; that was almost entirely accounted for by increases in government expenditure. The difference was largest by far in Brazil, where expenditure increased by nearly 4 percent of GDP in election years; increases in excess of 1 percent were also observed in Bolivia and Nicaragua. In OECD countries, meanwhile, the difference in fiscal policy between election and non-election years was essentially zero. In a multivariate statistical model, the estimated election-year effects in Latin America were a little more than half as large, but still significantly different from zero (and the effects in OECD countries were not statistically significantly different from zero). Nieto-Parra and Santiso exploited the unusually large number of elections in 2005–2006 to compare the fiscal impact of elections to earlier effects and find that the increase in spending (or the decline in the surplus) was substantially smaller in the later episode. This may be thanks in part to the proliferation of fiscal rules and more disciplined fiscal policy generally. It may also be attributable to the booming commodity revenues of the Milagrinho years. Higher government revenues might have meant that incumbents did not need to spend quite as much to drum up votes—and even if they did, the increases were smaller as a share of GDP, given that the latter was growing quickly. But even if the tentative improvement in electoral budget cycles was ameliorated by the commodity boom, that is preferable to an alternative scenario in which incumbents used commodity windfalls to exacerbate electoral budget cycles.

Falling, Then Rising, Public Indebtedness

What of public debt, a long-term headache in Latin America, and the source of repeated economic crises (e.g., continent-wide in the 1980s, in Argentina and Uruguay in 2001)? Recurring and persistent fiscal deficits are reflected in public indebtedness. Government debt at any point in time is not an instantaneous indicator of fiscal performance, as it represents the cumulative consequences of past borrowing. Debt is nevertheless an important instantaneous indicator of constraints facing a government, as current debt dictates the amount of debt service to be paid this year, and current debt levels might condition the terms under which a government can borrow further this year. The general pattern of indebtedness over the century for the LAC-7 economies traced a U shape, though the trough level differed across countries, as did the asymmetry between the left- and right-hand peaks of the U. The measure of debt in figs. 10.3a and 10.3b includes all central government indebtedness, whether to domestic or foreign creditors, in whatever currency, both short term and long term.

Lower deficits and even surpluses along with economic growth allowed governments to reduce the size of their debt as a share of GDP during the Milagrinho years. The trough of the U corresponded either to the Jazz Effect crisis (Chile, Colombia, Mexico, and Venezuela) or to the commodity price drop midway through the Hurricane Season (Argentina, Brazil, and Peru). As of 2023, the debt-to-GDP ratio exceeded its level at the start of the century, spurring concern about the sustainability of the debt in many countries.

Better discipline with the fiscal surplus led debtor countries to improve their debt position. As it implemented its fiscal rule, Chile reduced public debt from more than a third of GDP in the early 1990s to around 5 percent of GDP at the

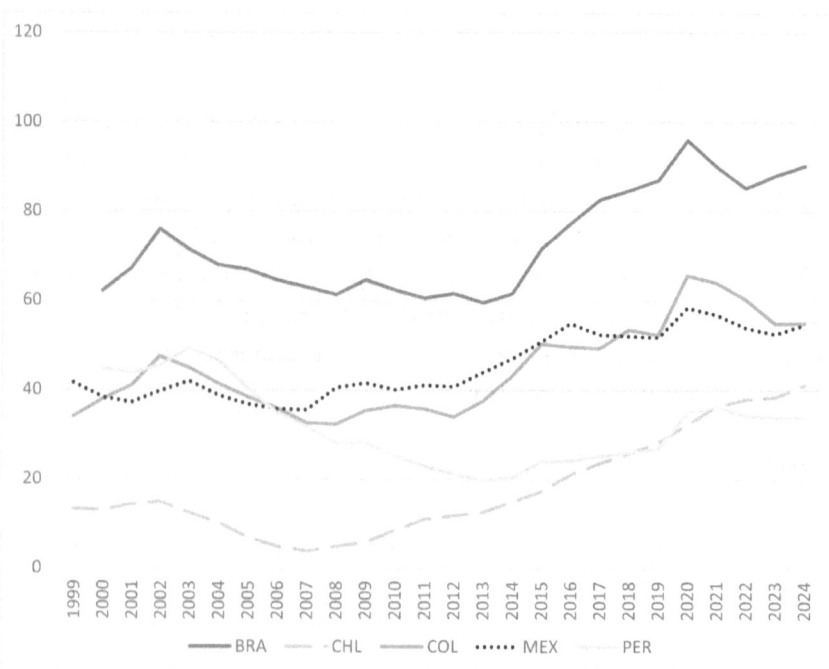

Figure 10.3a. Government debt (% of GDP), LAC-5 countries, 2001–2023. Gross government debt. 2023 data represent IMF estimates. *Source*: Calculated from data extracted from the October 2023 WEO database, IMF.

Figure 10.3b. Government debt (% of GDP), Argentina and Venezuela, 2001–2023. Gross government debt. 2023 data represent IMF estimates. The left scale corresponds to Argentina, the right scale to Venezuela. *Source*: Calculated from data extracted from the October 2023 WEO database, IMF.

height of the Milagrinho. More evocatively, the government shifted its net position (government assets minus liabilities as a share of GDP) from −31 percent to + 6.6 percent; that is, Chile passed from the status of net debtor to that of a net creditor.

An illustrative example of improvement of the debt outlook—the downward-sloping side of the U curve traced in fig. 10.3a—is provided by the efforts led by finance minister Luis Carranza in the second presidential administration of Alan García (2006–2011) to reduce and restructure Peru's public debt. Public debt stood at 45 percent of GDP in 2000 and fell to a low of 20 percent in 2013; it climbed back over 30 percent by 2023. Equally important are the changes in the composition of Peruvian public debt. In 2001, 91.7 percent of the debt was denominated in foreign currency (primarily US dollars), which meant that in order to make interest payments, the Peruvian treasury needed to purchase dollars, making debt repayment vulnerable to fluctuations in the exchange rate. Furthermore, in 2001, 65.1 percent of Peruvian debt had a flexible interest rate, making the total amount vulnerable to increases in international interest rates—this is precisely the factor that led to the detonation of the debt crisis of the 1980s. The Peruvian authorities issued bonds in local currency and used the proceeds to purchase dollars and accelerate the paydown of foreign currency-denominated debt. The interest to be paid on the local currency bonds was more likely to be fixed. By 2009, foreign currency-denominated debt had fallen to 64.9 percent of the total, and only 24.6 percent was exposed to flexible interest rates.[12] All of this while reducing the overall level of indebtedness; the trough of Peru's debt U-curve is lower and later than other countries' (fig. 10.3a), and even when debt-to-GDP ratios started climbing again, Peru found itself with lower debt than even superstar Chile. These improvements in the administration of its public debt led ratings agencies to classify Peruvian debt as investment grade (see the news dispatch in the introduction). By way of contrast, during García's first presidency (1985–1990) inflation peaked at 2,775 percent. The divergence between economic management under García's first and second presidencies is one of the most potent illustrations of the sense that the Latin American economy, with all the nuances that need to be borne in mind when making a statement like this, was in better condition in the first quarter of the twenty-first century than it was during the last quarter of the twentieth.

Those who persist in viewing the Latin American economy as condemned to poor performance could nevertheless find support for their view in the levels of indebtedness suffered by Argentina and Venezuela (fig. 10.3b). The shape of Argentinian debt's time path at least resembled that of other LAC-7 countries: Its debt-to-GDP ratio was U-shaped, falling steeply in the wake of the country's 2001 default, and rising again beginning in 2011. In contrast to the other large Latin American economies, the scale of Argentina's debt was much greater, peaking at nearly 150 percent of GDP, falling to 40 percent, and rising again to about 100 percent in 2020. Like other LAC-7 countries, Venezuela experienced declining debt-to-GDP ratios during the Milagrinho, but debt rose vigorously (and GDP declined) beginning with the Jazz Effect. Debt stood at over three times the size of the Venezuelan economy by 2020.

Fiscal Policy and the Social Contract

Fishlow's verdict of "fiscal inadequacy" refers to Latin American states' historical lack of consistent capability to balance tax revenues and expenditures. Such an imbalance can be bridged either by expanding the money supply, or by taking on public debt. Where central banks are insufficiently independent of the executive branch, a monetary expansion is possible but risks being inflationary (as described in the discussion of post-Covid inflation in chapter 7). Where debt is contracted from external sources, and in foreign currency, as was the case for countries in the region in the late 1970s, a risk emerges of debt default and the "sudden stop" of capital inflows. It is the debt default risk with which Fishlow was primarily concerned. This kind of fiscal inadequacy is therefore an inability of governments to use fiscal policy to finance public sector activities.

More than that, however, this inadequacy bespoke an incapacity to use fiscal policy according to its basic Keynesian dictates: to smooth the volatility of the business cycle, buoying economic activity during crises (as during the Jazz Effect and in response to Covid-19), and restraining inflationary pressure. In this chapter we have seen tentative evidence that Latin American states have gotten better at implementing this kind of countercyclical fiscal policy (or at least, that governments are less procyclical than in previous decades).

In addition to paying for government activities and initiatives and smoothing volatility countercyclically, a third objective of fiscal policy emerged as a topic of discussion during the twenty-first century in Latin America and elsewhere:

using fiscal policy to promote development. The OECD's 2009 *Latin American Economic Outlook* made the case for fiscal policy as a tool for development (OECD 2008). Such a perspective takes a longer-horizon view of public finances and leans more toward what we will call "state policies" (rather than "government policies") in the next chapter. Fiscal policy is relevant to development outcomes because the structure of taxes, for example, can be used to guide the structural transformation of the economy: This is, after all, the objective of High Developmentalist policy of imposing import tariffs (a tax) to promote import-substituting industrialization. Fiscal policy can contribute to development outcomes via the structure of expenditures: The innovative and successful conditional cash transfers discussed in chapter 9, for example, seek to reduce poverty today and sustainably reduce poverty in the future by encouraging families to keep their kids in school. And the tax and transfer system taken as a whole can serve to reduce income inequality: Progressive taxes (defined and discussed earlier in this chapter), together with poverty-reducing expenditures on CCTs or health and education, can reduce the Gini coefficient, in principle.

Seeing fiscal policy as a tool for development links the technical matters of public finances to the political concerns of the democratic functioning of societies. As the OECD's 2009 report argued, a development-inflected fiscal policy is a form of social contract between taxpayer-citizens and their government. In exchange for publicly provided goods and services—like schools and hospitals—of reasonably good quality and quantity, citizens are willing to support and pay reasonable taxes. Low rates of tax evasion and voters' support for political candidates who support robust taxes and redistributive public finance provide revenues to the state to finance high-quality services including health and education. High-quality services in turn encourage low rates of tax evasion. Public support for democracy is strengthened. A virtuous circle is enacted. Of course, there is another way of looking at this: *Poorly* functioning—what Fishlow might call inadequate—fiscal policy setups are a sign of (and a contributor to) a tattered or broken social contract. Citizens, unhappy with the low quality and quantity of publicly provided services, seek to evade taxes, exploiting loopholes in the tax code, perhaps, or by moving their economic activities to the informal sector; lower tax revenues, in turn, reduce the resources available to pay for high-quality public services. Citizens' enthusiasm for democracy wanes. A vicious circle.

Survey evidence from the early twenty-first century suggests that the state of the social contract was precarious, as reflected in citizens' attitudes toward tax evasion, on the one hand, and satisfaction with publicly provided services, on the other. Twenty percent of Latin American respondents, versus 7 percent of respondents in OECD countries, believed it was "justifiable" not to pay one's taxes. Moreover, there was a correlation within Latin American economies between tax morale (the proportion of survey respondents who say it important to pay one's taxes) and tax revenues as a share of GDP. Where governments mobilized more tax revenues, citizens looked less favorably upon tax evasion; where tax evasion was more widely accepted, tax revenues were lower (Daude and Melguizo 2015; Daude, Gutiérrez and Melguizo 2012).

If public finances are a reflection of the social contract linking citizens and their states, then an additional and complex layer of meaning is added to the notion of fiscal inadequacy: Fiscal systems can be inadequate insofar as they fail to promote economic development. Political economists Carlos Elizondo and Javier Santiso go so far as to talk of "fiscal violence," which they define as "the distortion and alteration of the entire lattice of the tax system, its rules, processes, and institutions, to favor a particular social sector, the business world or a well-organized political group." This includes "the legal appropriation of tax resources through wages, pensions, subsidies, exemptions, and redemptions" (Elizondo and Santiso 2012, 463–4). Fiscal violence prevents states from directing resources toward public goods to address broad-based development objectives. Elizondo and Santiso contrast fiscal "termites," who nibble away at public revenues (as in the case of tax breaks for corporations) and fiscal "gluttons," who devour disproportionate chunks of public spending (as in the case of comparatively generous pension payments for public sector employees). Termites and gluttons alike represent political constraints on the capacity of states to deploy fiscal policy as a tool for development.

The converse to fiscal violence, for Elizondo and Santiso, is "fiscal legitimacy." Evidence adduced by the OECD in the 2000s and 2010s suggested that Latin American states exhibited low levels of fiscal legitimacy. Consider the case of inequality reduction by means of the fiscal framework (fig. 10.4). The Gini coefficient of market incomes—before people pay taxes or receive government transfers—was 47.6 in European countries, and 51.6 in Latin American countries in the early 2000s. The Gini coefficient of disposable incomes, however, taking into account the effects of taxes and transfers, fell to 28.2 in Europe and barely at all

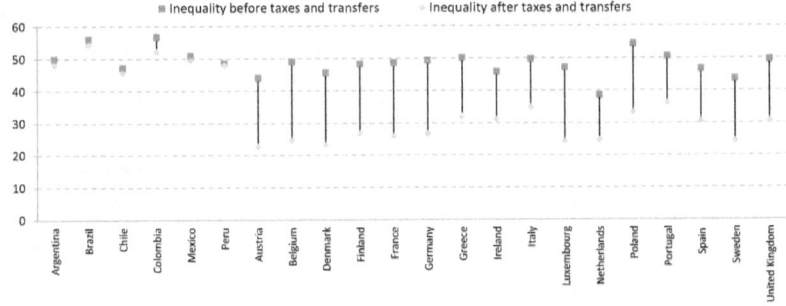

Figure 10.4. Gini coefficients of market and disposable income, selected Latin American and European countries, early 2000s. Disposable income is defined as market income plus transfers from the government and less taxes paid to the government. *Source*: Data from OECD (2008, fig. 4-1).

to 49.6 in Latin America (OECD 2008, 122). We can connect these statistics to the reasons provided for declining inequality in chapter 9. There we argued that the cumulative effect of education spending served to expand the supply of relatively skilled labor and to reduce the skill premium earned by the latter compared to their less-educated compatriots. This mechanism reduced *market* inequality. Conditional cash transfers and other transfers intended to reduce poverty led to a reduction in inequality in disposable income. Transfers and the like will over time improve the Europe–Latin America comparison in this graphic, though not altogether. To the extent that reduction of inequality is an indicator of economic development, Latin American states suffered from a deficit of fiscal legitimacy in comparison to their European counterparts circa 2008.

In summary, the design and execution of fiscal policy improved tentatively in most Latin American countries during the twenty-first century. The improvement was arguably as much qualitative—the adoption of new fiscal rules, for example—as it was quantitative. When Colombian president Juan Manuel Santos declared the inception of the Latin American Decade at the OECD in January 2011 (see the news dispatch in the introduction), there was reason to believe that the quantitative effect would be larger. Many countries in the region had successfully mobilized countercyclical fiscal policy to emerge from the Jazz Effect. And the ratio of the government budget balance to government revenues (the indicator depicted in fig. 9.1) fell from −10.6 percent during the period 1970–1995 (Gavin and Perotti 1997) to −5.4 percent during the Milagrinho years. But a quantitative improvement of this magnitude would not be sustained. The budget balance-to-revenues ratio ballooned to −13.2 percent during the Hurricane Season decade leading up to the pandemic and swelled to a further −16.9 percent between 2020 and 2023. For the full 2000–2023 period, the ratio was −11.6 percent, slightly higher than the late twentieth-century average.[13] Seen from the perspective of fiscal legitimacy, the qualitative improvement can be interpreted as a positive directional indicator of improved legitimacy; but the weak quantitative performance (in terms of budget balances or inequality reduction) a signal that such improvement in fiscal policy outcomes remains imperfect and incomplete.

CHAPTER ELEVEN

Better Economic Statecraft

THE QUALITY OF ECONOMIC governance improved in countries that together comprise much of the Latin American population during the first quarter of the twenty-first century. The quantitative and qualitative steps forward in the realm of fiscal policy outlined in chapter 10 provide clear examples: mixed successes, yes, but then again fiscal inadequacy had been only decades before the gravest shortcoming of governance in the region, with disastrous consequences during the debt crisis of the 1980s. In this chapter, inspired by the institutional advances made in the fiscal policy realm, we will widen our focus to consider the challenges of economic statecraft and the progress made—and unfinished business, too—during this century.

In this chapter, we will

1. review the contributions by institutional economists to our understanding of what makes a state effective for growth and development, focusing on the characteristics of centralization, pluralism, and autonomy;
2. outline the "welfare theorems" proposed by Kenneth Arrow and Gérard Debreu in the 1950s to "prove" Adam Smith's invisible hand logic, arguments that also make the case for state intervention to enhance the functioning of a market economy;
3. using sociologist Peter Evans's concept of "embedded autonomy," contrast the types of development pacts struck by pragmatic, "possibilist" governments, left and right leaning alike, with those pursued by left-populist governments.

States and Governments

In principle, the *state* refers to a complex of institutions: the structure of executive, legislative, and judicial power; the processes by which people are selected to play those roles; and laws, regulations, and procedures, and how those are proposed, adopted, and changed over time. For economic considerations the institutions of the state notably include those that govern public finances and monetary policy. *Government*, meanwhile, refers to the parties, coalitions, and individuals in power at a point in time: those charged with the responsibility for the institutions of the state. In practice, the distinction between states and governments can be muddied; no small part of the criticism of the Latin American state to which Fishlow was responding (we assessed Fishlow's response in chapter 10) was in fact criticism of the actions of given governments.

In the twenty-first century, this fuzziness of the state-versus-government distinction was reflected in debates that contrasted "state policies" with "government policies." Typically, the latter were considered inferior to the former, which largely meant that the former were longer-lasting and more immune to whimsical, corrupt, or otherwise inefficient meddling by ephemeral governments with impure motives. Political scientist Damien Larrouqué (2019) analyzes this idiosyncratic feature of Latin American policy debates in the twenty-first century, yielding insights into the nature of policy making, and especially of policy reform, to which we will return later in this chapter. Some of the pragmatism of what we will describe as "possibilist" states took the form of maintaining policies adopted by previous governments, even governments of opposing parties or hostile ideologies. Left-populist governments in the region, often contrasted with the possibilists, nevertheless also adopted policies meant to be enduring, like state policies.

At least some of the criticism of Latin American states in the era of the Washington Consensus masked a continuing debate between High Developmentalists and neoliberals, in which the latter putatively made non-ideological arguments, they claimed, seeking only to unobjectionably point out misguided, distortionary, and clumsy actions by overreaching governments. To this there was no easy retort by High Developmentalists (though Fishlow's piece could be read as a response). In chapter 12, I will propose a sketch of a Neo-Developmentalist State for this century.

Characteristics of Economically Effective States

What makes an effective state, that is, a state that is conducive to desirable economic development? A rich institutional economics literature—notably, including foundational contributions by Daron Acemoglu, James Robinson, Timothy Besley, Torsten Persson, Douglass North, and Barry Weingast[1]—underscores two characteristics of effective states. The twin themes are *centralization*, by which they mean effective central government control over the national territory and subnational jurisdictions, and *pluralism*, which helps guard against predatory behavior by executives. Centralization and pluralism are closely related in turn to the notion of state *autonomy*, that effective states cannot be mere pawns of one class or interest group but must be able to mediate and negotiate among diverse interests.[2] A hopeful research literature furthermore suggests that democratic states are especially likely to exhibit effective centralization of power and pluralism (Cason and Ramaswamy 2003), though democracy is likely neither necessary nor sufficient to ensure that the state promotes economic growth (China serves as the permanent counterexample to those who suggest that democracy is necessary for growth); the relationship between democracy and development is complex.

In short, autonomous states are capable of enforcing contracts and other institutional underpinnings of a market economy, while constraining the executive from seizing (too much) of the gains of market activity. Such a state, whether democratic or not, is compatible with a largely liberal economy. By a liberal economy, I mean a market-oriented one, in which the private sector plays a principal, maybe predominant, role in what economists call the allocation of resources: who works in what sector; how much is produced by each sector and by each firm; how much labor and capital each firm uses; what technologies are developed and adopted; and so on.

The Rationale for State Intervention in Liberal Economies

Even in a liberal economy, however, there is a well-established and long-standing rationale for state intervention to ensure the efficient functioning of the market mechanism. This goes beyond securing and protecting property rights as emphasized by the institutional economists. And it is worth reiterating that the rationale for state intervention comes from the same theoretical framework that leads economists to affirm with such conviction that the market mechanism is the most efficient means for economic coordination and organization.

Market-enhancing state intervention goes back to the heady days of the explosion of sophisticated mathematical methods in economic theory in the 1950s, and in particular to the parallel work of Kenneth Arrow (of Stanford University) and Gérard Debreu (of the University of California, Berkeley). Arrow and Debreu worked out the theoretical underpinnings of the "invisible hand" mechanism outlined by Adam Smith in the eighteenth century; namely, that the impersonal, decentralized workings of the market mechanism will ensure the most efficient allocation of resources in an economy. Arrow and Debreu approached this in the form of a series of mathematical theorems: defining with great precision what is meant by an economic equilibrium (a description of the allocation of resources, including the price of each) and by an efficient or optimal allocation of resources. They determined the assumptions under which (i) a general market equilibrium exists, (ii) a market equilibrium is efficient, by which they mean socially optimal, and (iii) any socially optimal allocation of resources can arise from the working of the market mechanism. The theorems underlying (ii) and (iii)—known as the first and second theorems of welfare economics—are the most important to the formalization of Smith's invisible hand mechanism (Arrow 1951; Debreu 1959, chs. 5–6).

The assumptions underlying the Arrow-Debreu theorems are not identical, but the principal ones to emphasize can be summarized (somewhat roughly) as follows. That is, the market mechanism is likely to allocate resources in an efficient and socially optimal way if:

1. Every good's market-determined price accurately reflects its value. In part, this means there are no negative or positive spillovers of the production or consumption of the good; alternatively, no good or bad side effects of the transaction are imposed on any party outside the transaction. (The classic example where this assumption is not met is environmental pollution generated by the production of a good like steel—a cost imposed on people outside the transaction and paid for neither by the producer or consumer of the steel.) An extreme case of positive spillovers is a public good, a good—like public safety or national security, and unlike food or clothing—that is no less available to you if I am consuming it.[3] Call this the *no-externalities* assumption.

2. Consumers and producers have excellent information about all relevant aspects of the production and consumption of all goods, including the quality of the good produced, and the future demand for the good. This is the assumption of *complete and perfect information*.
3. The technology for producing the good involves no significant start-up investment costs, and firms can therefore easily enter or exit the market for this good in response to increases or decreases in its demand. This assumption is known in economics as *constant returns to scale*.
4. Finally, the market for this good would be supplied by a large number of firms, each providing an identical good, none of which had any power to influence the price of the good. Call this assumption *perfect competition*.

When these assumptions are met, Arrow and Debreu demonstrated that the free play of market forces will lead to the allocation of resources that, conditional on the original distribution of wealth, is most efficient. Efficiency in this case means that no reallocation of society's economic resources could improve on the market outcome without making someone worse off.

Of course, no real-world economy exhibits all these characteristics, and the consequence, according to Arrow and Debreu, is that the real-world, imperfect market mechanism will not allocate resources efficiently. In such a situation, society will be better off if the state changes the incentives facing markets and firms to modify the allocation of resources. In the presence of positive externalities, for example, individual firms will undersupply the good in question, as they do not stand to benefit from the positive spillovers. The state can address this by offering subsidies for each unit of the good produced with positive spillovers (or taxing each unit of a good that creates negative spillovers, such as pollution). If there are increasing, rather than constant, returns to scale in some industry, it means that the start-up investment is huge and will tend to limit the number of firms in that industry. That, in turn, violates the assumption of perfect competition and could allow the small number of firms to charge monopoly prices (over and above the economic value of the good in question). In this case, the state might directly supply such a good, or regulate private producers to prevent monopoly prices. Thus, many states own and operate utilities like electricity generation or water supply, both of which feature increasing returns to scale. And so on.[4]

A robust menu of state interventions to influence the allocation of resources in the economy and thereby move closer to a more socially optimal or efficient allocation flows therefore ineluctably from the same logic that champions the efficiency of the market mechanism itself. What this means in practice: support for competition authorities; environmental legislation and regulation; subsidies (per unit of output, for credit and for wages) for producers of goods with positive externalities; taxes (like a carbon tax for goods that occasion pollution); and state-owned enterprises to manage natural monopolies like electricity generation and the creation and maintenance of transport infrastructure. One could be forgiven for concluding that this sometimes seems to have slipped the mind of neoliberal critics in expressing their distaste for High Developmentalism.[5]

High Developmentalists, of course, recommended state intervention above and beyond market-supporting activities like those mentioned above, as we have seen in chapter 2. These are based on the imperative to transform the structure of the economy from a fundamentally commodity-producing and exporting one to a diversified economy based on manufacturing of various forms. Prebisch and others argued that Peripheral economies could be efficient manufacturing economies—they could enjoy a comparative advantage over time in manufacturing—but they would not develop in that direction without state intervention to change the incentives facing firms and investors. In the context of Fishlow's 1990s assessment of the Latin American state, our review of the Arrow-Debreu social welfare theorems illustrates that it is disingenuous to criticize the state for intervention per se, though one could more usefully distinguish among effective or skillful and ineffective, inefficient, and unskillful forms and examples of intervention.

Possibilist and Left-Populist States and the Pacts They Crafted

The improvements in the design and practice of fiscal policies described in chapter 10—some striking, some only incipient—coincided with the Pink Tide phenomenon, the wave of left-leaning governments mentioned at various times in this book. Nora Lustig of Tulane University and Darryl McLeod of Fordham University analyzed the reduction in inequality through 2010 in two groups of left-leaning countries: first, what they call social democratic governments (Brazil, Chile, and Uruguay); and the second, left-populist (Argentina, Bolivia, and Venezuela). They found that both groups of countries took steps to reduce inequality, but that the social democratic governments had better outcomes in terms of reductions in the Gini coefficient (McLeod and Lustig 2010).

McLeod and Lustig's work raises a question: Were there camps within the Pink Tide movement—and specifically, were some of these governments and states more effective than others in reducing inequality? It was not unusual in the international press (especially the business press) to separate the left-leaning government into two subgroups: the "responsible," "moderate," "social democratic" camp (exemplified by Bachelet), and the "irresponsible," "populist," "socialist," or even "loony" camp (exemplified by Chávez). Just where all the other Pink Tide leaders were sorted in this typology was a matter of evolving debate. Morales and Correa were generally cast with the populist left; with time, Lula was placed alongside Bachelet among the "good" leftists. Such a dichotomy was reductive and poorly informed, and was contested by the Pink Tide leaders themselves. Chávez and Bachelet, though placed in opposing camps, maintained a cordial relationship, as did the countries they led. Bachelet eulogized Chávez as a "gran amigo" and a "gran colega" upon his death in 2013 (CNN Chile 2013). Moreover, more than a few of Lula's Workers Party allies would chafe at being lumped in with the moderates in the Concertación mold, though they clearly came to respect the Chileans. As Marco Aurélio Garcia, a founder of the PT, advisor to Lula, and promoter of the São Paulo Forum, told a French journalist in March 2005:

> Now that we are in power, we realize that we have unfairly scorned the Chilean socialists, who we treated as pale reformists subservient to the neoliberal model. Criticism is easy but, in reality, we will be very satisfied if, after two mandates, we have been able to implement policies as effective as those of the Chilean Concertación, particularly in terms of infrastructure, poverty reduction and broad-based health coverage (Saint-Upéry 2008, 18–9).

Then there was the problem of where to put Argentina under the Kirchners. While their economic rhetoric may have tended toward the realm of Chávez, they alternated in comparatively orderly electoral fashion with right-leaning governments just like the Concertación did in Chile.

Readers of this book will have noted that, at least among the LAC-7 countries, Argentina and Venezuela are often in a class by themselves, at least insofar as the values of some of their macroeconomic performance indicators are so different from the other five economies that I have often needed to put the Argentinian and Venezuelan data in separate graphics. For the purposes of our study, it is enough to acknowledge differences among the countries in terms of their economic outcomes—as McLeod and Lustig do with respect to success in reducing inequality. But this should not be extended to attributing ex ante characteristics to certain regimes based on ex post outcomes.

Javier Santiso (2005) argues that the Latin American governments of the twenty-first century are more usefully divided into those that are *possibilist* and those that are not. Santiso borrows the concept of "possibilism" from the brilliant and unorthodox political economist Albert O. Hirschman. According to one of Hirschman's biographers, possibilism for Hirschman was a characteristic not of the good leader, but of the effective researcher seeking to understand social reality, a "combination of doubt, intellectual openness, moral values and pragmatism" (Alacevich 2021). That Santiso attributes a trait of good social research to the Latin American leaders he admires is fortuitous, given that so many of those leaders led double lives as accomplished economists and social scientists in academia and think tanks. Fernando Henrique Cardoso, founding father of the sixties dependency theory turned pragmatic president of Brazil, is surely the most emblematic example. But there are many others, some of whom we have encountered in the pages of this book: Andrés Velasco (minister of finance) in Chile; Luis Carranza (minister of finance) in Peru; Martín Redrado (head of the central bank) in Argentina; Luciano Coutinho (head of the national development bank); Marco Aurélio Garcia (advisor to the president) in Brazil; Mauricio Cárdenas (minister of planning, mines, and finance), and Alejandro Gaviria (minister of health) in Colombia; among many others.[6] These policy makers are both the researchers that Hirschman was addressing, as well as public servants praised by Santiso.

That so many of the possibilist governments highlighted by Santiso were left leaning is not, according to him, their most noteworthy feature. What is noteworthy is their willingness simultaneously to embrace policies championed by left and right parties. The key to possibilism is pragmatism, and a willingness to leave behind twentieth-century ideological blinders—those of "free marketeers" and "revolutionaries."

On the one hand, before the advent of the possibilists, there was a savagely excessive free-market policy package, exemplified best by the so-called "Chicago Boys," the University of Chicago-trained economists who advised the Pinochet dictatorship in Chile. As pointed out elsewhere in this study, the Chicago Boys' development strategy coincided in many ways with the Washington Consensus of the 1990s: privatization of state-owned enterprises, liberalization of capital and labor markets, and liberalization of restrictions on trade and capital flows. At the other end of the pre-possibilist spectrum was romantic revolutionary change. The application of a truly revolutionary socialist development strategy was limited to Communist Cuba and, arguably (though only briefly), Sandinista Nicaragua. Even where there were more or less bona fide revolutionary insurrections—in the Dominican Republic in 1965, say, or Peru in 1968—revolutionary socialism did not follow. Elected left-wing governments in the twentieth century—like Salvador Allende in Chile, overthrown by Pinochet—meanwhile, followed what might be called an aggressively political approach to High Developmentalism. The Allende policy framework—like that of coterminous Peronist governments in Argentina—tended to be the object of pejorative assessment by writers like Santiso and many contemporary political leaders in the region.

The possibilist politicians, technocrats, and policy makers who arose during the Milagrinho years, in contrast, were pragmatic and post-ideological. This pragmatism took at least two forms. First, governments mixed elements of left- and right-leaning economic policy platforms. Second, they often maintained policies put in place by prior governments to whom they were ostensibly opposed.

The classic possibilist Latin American regime was anchored by orthodox fiscal and monetary policies that would not displease the IMF; this kept inflation under control and stabilized or even reduced public indebtedness. At the same time, the possibilist regime enacted ambitious social development policies; this leads to historically steep declines in poverty and inequality. For Santiso and many other observers, the emblematic case was that of Chile. With the return to civilian rule in 1990, a series of left or left-leaning Concertación governments pursued orthodox fiscal policy, as we saw earlier in this book, while Chile's central bank hewed to an orthodox monetary policy. Externally, this bet on orthodoxy reassured international capital markets, while internally, it contributed to macroeconomic stability. In Chile's case, however, this macroeconomic orthodoxy also represented an explicit continuity with the economic policies of the reviled military dictatorship that had killed more than 3,000 political opponents and tortured many thousands more. The macro stabilization policies were not all that was held over from the dictatorship; structural changes including the privatization of social security and abridgment of rights of labor effected by Pinochet's military regime were likewise maintained by the Concertación governments. At the same time, the left-leaning and socialist governments of Chile, more in line with their partisan ideological preferences, introduced important anti-poverty initiatives, notably the Chile Solidario program, enacted under the government of President Ricardo Lagos in 2004. Needless to say, social assistance initiatives this ambitious and effective were not a part of the military dictatorship's development strategy.

Certain constraints present in earlier decades were lifted in this century. The end of the Cold War, which was frequently a dirty war in Latin America, meant that ambitious social assistance and social insurance schemes intended to reduce poverty and inequality could be enjoined without fear of extrajudicial reprisal, violent or otherwise. And the revenues of the Milagrinho commodity boom meant that governments were flush with resources to entertain such social development programs.

But alongside the lifting of constraints, other constraints hardened and limited the scope of action of the would-be pragmatists. Alain Rouquié, a political scientist who served as France's ambassador in Brazil, El Salvador, and Mexico, characterizes possibilist governments like Chile's as existing in the "shadow of dictatorship":

> The proximity and connivance maintained by economic leaders with the dictatorship weighed on all the Concertación governments: if we want to ensure stability, we must be careful that employers, skeptical of democracy and fiercely opposed to the left, are not dissatisfied. The economic model put in place by the dictatorship will therefore not be called into question. [. . . .] Democracy is under watch . . . because the most powerful, the most influential part of the bourgeoisie, in particular the owners of the media, considers that the dictatorship was a success for its members, and therefore for Chile (Rouquié 2010, 145, 146).

The Chilean Concertación governments had not only to assuage powerful supporters of the dictatorship's development strategy, but also acted in the shadow of elements of the dictatorship itself (Black 2002). If Chile's case is particularly stark—both for the ruthless efficiency of its murderous military regime, but also for the successful development performance of its democratic governments—it is not unique. Brazil, Paraguay, and Uruguay also witnessed democratic transitions in the shadow of dictatorships. Argentina's post-military governments, after some false starts, went significantly further to dismantle the privileges of the military in government (Saint-Upéry 2008, ch. 3).

Another example of maintaining policies from the past: the successful conditional cash transfer programs pioneered by Mexico in the late twentieth century under governments led by the perennial PRI party. The PRI's conservative nemesis, the PAN, surprisingly continued the transfer program, changing only the name, when it took power in 2000. And so this would continue with the return of the PRI to power in 2012 (refer to the news dispatch in the introduction), and the new Morena party which came to power in 2018. Meanwhile, Santiso considers Mexico's earlier negotiation of NAFTA, a free-trade agreement with the United States and Canada in 1994 as an example of possibilism, and one which sought to tie the hands of successor governments (an example of a state policy which commentators favorably if imprecisely contrasted with government policies).

Those elements of the possibilist economic policy tool kit that might variously be described as orthodox, conservative, or neoliberal, were not only intended to placate powerful internal interests, as in Chile, but also external ones. Perhaps this is best exemplified by the first two terms of Luis Ignacio Lula da Silva. Lula, of course, was not the first post-military president in Brazil—much of the heavy possibilist lifting had been done by his predecessors, notably Fernando Henrique Cardoso, the erstwhile dependency theorist, who was also president for two terms, from 1995–2002. But Lula's Workers Party (PT) was substantially to the left of the post-dictatorship parties, in platform and in methods, and the prospect of a PT government frightened internal and external observers. Nevertheless, the relatively rapid way that Lula was able to ease capital markets between his first election in 2002 and his reelection in 2006 illustrates the impact of possibilism (see the news dispatch from the introduction).

What of those governments labeled left-populist by McLeod and Lustig? Santiso's taxonomy implicitly assigned them to the category of non-possibilist leftist experiments, having left them out of his analysis. Presumably this is because they did not transcend the old-school left-right dichotomy. But Morales, Correa, Chávez, and Maduro, and the governments they have led, cannot be said to have followed the twentieth-century path of revolutionary socialism forged by Cuba. (It's true that they have vocally supported Communist Cuba, but in this respect they are no different from the possibilist governments on the left.) They have neither come to power by means of guerrilla warfare, nor eliminated the trappings (or at times the substance) of democratic politics, nor nationalized the leading economic sectors. Most important to our argument here, their economies remained tightly linked via trade and investment flows to global markets for goods, services, and credits; and the role of the market mechanism in allocating resources remained potent in all three economies. These were not epigones of revolutionary Cuba, any more than Chile under the Concertación governments could be called Chicago Boys 2.0.

Of course, there are important differences between the left-populists—Bolivia, Ecuador, and Venezuela—on the one hand, and Brazil, Chile, and Uruguay, on the other. The most salient is that to varying degrees, the left-populist governments have tended toward the more hardened authoritarian end of the Latin American spectrum (where they are not alone); this is particularly the case in Venezuela, where President Maduro disqualified, exiled, or imprisoned virtually all of the likely opposition candidates he would face in the 2024 presidential elections, following years of the closing off of political alternatives through violent means. The populist three were more likely to pick political fights with private-sector interests, notably the media (a fight with which Lula in Brazil likely felt some sympathy given the relentless hostility he faced from the media conglomerates there). Of course, one of the fiercest foes faced by Chávez was the state-owned petroleum firm, a struggle that does not fit neatly into any habitual left/right matrix.

I do not mean to provide an apologia for the populist three. These were imperfect governments who achieved some of the audacious goals they sought to accomplish (in particular, all three were able to reduce income inequality and poverty significantly), but not all, and along the way engaged in corrupt and sometimes violent behavior (and the same could be said of some governments outside this group). What I do want to suggest is that the possibilist/non-possibilist, pragmatic/populist dichotomies provide poor conceptual frameworks for comparing the populist three to the other Pink Tide governments.

A more useful framework emerges from the work of political economists Patrick Clark and Antulio Rosales (2023), who compare the political outcomes of the Morales, Correa, and Chávez/Maduro governments. They revive a twentieth-century concept developed by the University of California, Berkeley sociologist Peter B. Evans, of *embedded autonomy* (Evans 1995). Evans's theory adds nuance to the concept of state autonomy considered above, to suggest that successful states need not only be free of the control of particular classes or interest groups in society, but that autonomy must be effectively "embedded" in the relationships among those classes and groups. That is, states that are successful in promoting economic development are able to strike effective pacts among particular groups, and between those groups and the state. The argument made by Fernando Fajnzylber in the 1980s regarding Latin America's "truncated" industrialization (reviewed in chapter 8), for example, is that South Korea's development success in the High Developmentalist era derived from the pact forged by the Korean state with the industrial chaebols. It's not that Mexico and Brazil or other Latin American states did not pursue development pacts. Rather, the local constraints and opportunities of their embedded autonomy led to different pacts and different expectations regarding private-sector actors, compared to what Korea, Taiwan, and others were able to achieve. To summarize crudely, the Latin American ISI experiment under High Developmentalism was led by states sufficiently embedded to rally their national private sectors, but insufficiently autonomous to impel those private sectors to realize the productivity gains that longer-term ISI required.[7]

In the twenty-first century, new development pacts emerged, sometimes deliberately, other times tentatively. Santiso's possibilist governments, whether in the Pink Tide, or center-right governments in Colombia or Mexico, forged pacts with domestic and international capital by means of macroeconomic stability, and with poorer regions and segments by means of social policies, including conditional cash transfers and higher minimum wages. For many countries, a comfort with reprimarization represented another dimension of the possibilist pact. Whether they did what they did because they were pragmatic (as erstwhile Tupamaro guerrilla José Mujica, a minister in Tabaré Vázquez's Frente Amplio government in Uruguay, told the *New York Times* they were), or because they feared the response of financial markets or the military if they did otherwise (as Alain Rouquié suggested), is important, and is subject to debate. Either way, however, their heterodox possibilism generated the economic results that we have surveyed throughout this book.

What kind of pacts did the Bolivian, Ecuadorian, and Venezuelan governments of the twenty-first century attempt to forge? Here the somewhat sloppy distinction earlier evoked between government and state policies has some usefulness: These governments sought, with the aid of political coalitions, to create state policies that would outlast their governments, as surely as, in 1994, the more or less neoliberal president Carlos Salinas de Gortari sought with Mexico's membership in NAFTA to tie the hands of his successors in Mexico. The key partner for the socialist-populist pacts were social movements, an alliance consistent with the form of socialist politics promoted by the parties in question. And each of the left-populist governments sought to establish what might be called a Neo-Developmentalist State, leaving behind the neoliberal Washington Consensus policy platform and reclaiming some elements of the High Developmentalist playbook (just which elements, it was not always clear).

The most politically successful of the three was arguably Bolivia under Morales, and the roots of that success lay in the profound and broad-based social movements which first carried Morales to the presidency in 2006. The Indigenous-led protest that became the so-called Cochabamba water war drew upon and strengthened long-standing social movements, including that of the coca growers led by Morales himself. The blockage of roads by the protestors forced the rejection of privatized control of municipal water services in the Bolivian highlands, dealing a blow to the neoliberal platform of the Washington Consensus as well as providing proof to the protestors of the efficacy of their joint action. Historian Sarah Hines (2022, 2024) illustrates the degree to which these struggles over control of water resources had deep historical roots, going back to pre-conquest times, and the mobilization of social groups was similarly long-standing. This set up a network of social groups and interests who supported Morales's presidency, but also acted as a quasi-independent check on the executive's power. In practice, the MAS governments were able to strike agreements, on some issues at least, with powerful political forces, including foreign firms and domestic business groups.

Correa's Ecuador and the Venezuela of Chávez and Maduro, by way of contrast, represented less successful examples of the Bolivian-style social pact. While Correa fostered political engagement by Indigenous groups, and oversaw the drafting of a new constitution that was, if anything, more radical than that of Bolivia, the social movements that supported him were less established than their Bolivian counterparts; Clark and Rosales argue that Correa's top-down style in engaging with the movements also contributed to weaker political support.[8] Hugo Chávez fostered the development of a broad array of social groups intended to support the government and spread the gospel of its development strategy. Clark and Rosales argue, however, that the oil windfall of the Milagrinho years weakened the incentive of the *chavista* state to seek meaningful political engagement with the network of groups (and weakened too the leverage of those groups to exert pressure independently upon the state). The strengthening of sanctions against the Maduro government in 2017, triggered by the deterioration of the human rights situation in Venezuela, led Maduro to adopt what Benedicte Bull and Antulio Rosales call "authoritarian capitalism"—based on private ownership accompanied by the denial of fundamental political and economic rights.[9]

Where the possibilist Pink Tide states privileged the interests and aims of financial markets (foreign and domestic banks, as well as foreign and domestic holders of government debt), the left-populists antagonized domestic and foreign banks and firms. Correa explicitly redirected external debt service toward social investments, broadly construed (Presidencia de la República del Ecuador n.d.). Maduro's antagonism of foreign capital was undoubtedly the most pugnacious of the three.

The possibilists' emphasis on social transfers and other anti-poverty measures revealed their commitment to poverty reduction. This commitment differed more in degree than in kind with that of the left-populist three; where the populists created or drew upon vigorous social movements, the possibilists' pact with the poor was more clientelist, intended to secure electoral support (this was glaringly obvious in the case of Lula's PT government, which drew reliably upon the votes of jurisdictions where Bolsa Família transfers were larger).[10]

As noted, many observers were uncertain whether to place Argentina among the possibilists or the left-populists. The examples of the left-populist three shed some light on this confusion. The Peronist political movement, historically, has resembled the social-movement based politics of Morales's MAS, Correa's Citizens' Revolution, or the early Chávez years. But the mass-movement version of Peronism, forged during the mid-twentieth century and surviving even the death of Juan Domingo Perón himself in 1974, was gravely, perhaps fatally, wounded by the introduction of Washington Consensus policies in the 1990s by President Carlos Menem (himself a Peronist, in one of history's ironies). As such, while the fervor of the Kirchner presidencies might have sounded like the socialist-populist three from a rhetorical standpoint, the Kirchners were not always as successful in terms of mobilization in the streets.[11]

The point I want to underscore from Clark and Rosales and Evans is that states make pacts; in fact, governments make pacts, but if they are even a little enduring, they are state pacts. Not all pacts are good, and not all are successful, either in terms of the states' own objectives, or in terms of criteria that might be brought to bear by outside observers—criteria such as economic growth, poverty reduction, or structural transformation of the economy. And the success of these pacts reflects the embedded autonomy of specific states.

Possibilist states crafted development pacts that assuaged foreign and domestic banks and financial institutions, the domestic private sector, by means of their relative macroeconomic orthodoxy; they sought the support of the poor and marginalized with their muscular anti-poverty programs. Left-populist states like Bolivia, Ecuador, and Venezuela, meanwhile, sought pacts that mobilized the poor less as clients but as the principal supporters of the regime in question. They antagonized foreign and domestic financial firms, partly to rally support domestically. They, too, made their peace with reprimarization despite the critical stance regarding commodity dependence and environmental degradation encoded in new constitutions in some of these countries.

Why and how well governments made the choices they did, has to do with the complicated process of policy reform. The sequence of reforms beginning with the stabilization packages of the 1980s, continuing with the adoption of Washington Consensus recommendations in the 1990s, and followed by heterodox possibilist platforms in the 2000s, led many observers to turn their attention to the question of how reforms happen. Researchers tended to fall into two camps. The first focused on what might be called the political economy of reforms, asking questions like: Does crisis make reforms more or less likely? How does the economic context affect the likelihood of reforms being approved? Is it better to introduce reforms in a "big bang" or "bitter pill," or to take the road of gradualism? The second school, led by researchers at the Inter-American Development Bank, focused on the policy-making process, the sequence of stages during which reforms were proposed, debated, adopted, implemented, and sustained (or not). Evans's concept of embedded autonomy is central to both schools of reform studies, as the state's degree and kind of embeddedness is a critical component of the political economy, but also to the functioning of the policy-making process.[12]

The country-level histories of reform are intricate, complex and difficult to generalize. But a few major themes merit mention here. The first is the enduring impact of *presidencialismo*, the tendency for the executive branch to be more powerful than the legislative or judicial branch in most Latin American countries. This means that the executive has far greater agency to put issues onto the policy agenda and to shepherd them through the policy-making process—or to suppress initiatives it does not support. In a related vein, presidencialismo contributes to imperfect democratic consolidation insofar as it is accompanied by incumbents' maneuvers to remain in power indefinitely. Second, external constraints like those emphasized by political economy students of reform have powerful explanatory power. Two such external constraints have recurred in our recounting of possibilist successes: the implicit effect of the military in the shadows of post-dictatorial states, and anxiety about how "the markets" might react to certain measures. Each of these contributed to the support for orthodox fiscal and monetary policy preferred by the former private-sector supporters of the military governments, and by international banks and institutions.

Finally, there are differences between the various waves of reforms in Latin America. The Washington Consensus wave included trade liberalization and privatization of state-owned enterprises. A subsequent wave included many of the measures undertaken by possibilist states. At the time—mostly during the Milagrinho period—governments conceptualized the possibilist wave of reforms as complementary to the first (and perhaps intended to unlock the promised benefits of the Washington Consensus, which were often slow to appear). These included fiscal reforms, among them fiscal responsibility reforms, like those considered in chapter 10, followed by pension reforms. The possibilist reforms were more complex than those of the Washington Consensus wave, involved a greater diversity of actors, and were arguably more reliant on the technical competence of governments who undertook them.

To the extent that they delivered results desired by the population—whether higher incomes, greater economic security, or participation in deliberative politics, among other possible goals—the outcomes of these pacts contributed to the process of democratic consolidation. Many observers celebrated the improvements in democratic governance in the region during the Milagrinho years. The OECD, for example, referred to the widely used "Polity IV" score of democratic quality, which ranges from −10 to 10, and sorts countries into democracies and autocracies at either end of the spectrum. In 2008, of the twenty-three Latin American and Caribbean countries in the Polity IV ranking, eighteen were ranked as democracies, and only Cuba was considered an autocracy. This was an improvement from 1980, at which date there were eight autocracies and seven democracies. The average Polity IV score for the region likewise improved, indicating both qualitative and quantitative strides forward in democratic consolidation. Costa Rica, Chile, and Uruguay all had Polity IV scores of 10 (OECD 2010, 148–9; see also IDB 2005 for related indicators).

During the protracted Hurricane Season, however, populations lost enthusiasm for their governments, possibilist and populist alike, and this disillusionment was accompanied by declining support for democracy per se. A powerful illustration of this was provided by Brazil-wide demonstrations against the Lula government in 2013, sparked initially by increases in public transport fares (see the associated news flash in chapter 1). And these demonstrations could be seen through the lens of fiscal legitimacy. "End Corruption," read the protestors' placards held up by thousands in the historic Maracanã Stadium in Rio de Janeiro—in English, sometimes: "We want security, health and education." Protestors rejected expensive projects to build new infrastructure to host the football World Cup and the Summer Olympic Games diverting resources from publicly provided services deemed of insufficient quality (Daude, Dayton-Johnson, and Melguizo 2013).

Latinobarómetro, a polling agency with many years of data collection on Latin Americans' attitudes regarding a number of social, economic, and political issues, documented the declining support for democracy across the region. The proportion of Latin Americans polled who agreed with the statement, "Democracy is preferable to any other form of government" fell from 63 percent in 2010 to 48 percent in 2023. In the short period from 2020 to 2023, support for democracy according to this survey question fell by more than five percentage points in Guatemala (−8), Mexico (−8), Costa Rica (−11), and Venezuela (−12). In the meantime, support *grew* by more than five percentage points over the same time span in Brazil (6), Argentina (7), and Panama (11). Another survey question, which asked whether respondents agreed with the statement "In some circumstances, an authoritarian government may be preferable to a democratic one" has had relatively stable support (between 13 and 19 percent over the years for all of Latin America), but with an uptick since 2020 in all countries save one. The study found that support for authoritarianism was higher—and that for democracy lower—among younger members of the population (Latinobarómetro 2024).

The souring on democracy among broad swathes of the Latin American citizenry is a component of the sharpening of insecurity, economic and otherwise. Development economist Pranab Bardhan analyzed the twin degradations of economic security and enthusiasm for democracy, and the consequent slowing or reversing of democratic consolidation, in large democracies including the United States, India, and Brazil (Bardhan 2022). In these and other cases, the concept of insecurity overlapped with income inequality, as low income reduces one's capacity to weather life's—and the economy's—vicissitudes. This increased insecurity was accompanied by growing bitterness among many people that democracy had not resolved more of their problems (including, in some cases, the problem of authoritarian excess). This raised the specter of right-wing populism, up to and including the elections of Donald Trump in the United States, Narendra Modi in India, and Jair Bolsonaro in Brazil, politicians able to convince voters that their problems stemmed from an entrenched political class, and perhaps even from the functioning of the democratic process itself.

An extreme case of the phenomenon was the rise of Nayib Bukele, onetime mayor of San Salvador, elected president of El Salvador in 2019. Starting in 2022, Bukele confronted the extension of the *maras*, extraordinarily violent gangs in the country, with a "state of exception," continuously renewed, that suspended a number of constitutional rights and loosened restrictions on police (including the need for warrants for some kinds of surveillance or the time detainees could be held without charges). The authorities rapidly and aggressively imprisoned more than 70,000 putative gang members. Even amidst the draconian encroachment the public reaction was overwhelmingly supportive—and indeed, murders, violence, and extortion declined sharply (Martínez, Lemus, and Martínez 2023). The generalized violence faced by Salvadorans tested their adherence to democratic norms. A sudden upswelling of gang-related violence in Ecuador led its president, Daniel Noboa, to seek state-of-exception-like powers there, in an

April 2024 referendum, in which he was mostly but not entirely granted the extraordinary powers he sought (Mella 2024).

Leaders like Bukele and Noboa did not fit well into either the possibilist or the socialist-populist molds. Like "anarcho-capitalist" Javier Milei in Argentina (see the news dispatch in the introduction), they represented new, more extreme presidential models, in response to the rise in physical, economic, social, and cultural insecurity. The social pressures that contributed to the rise of these leaders, as well as the extreme measures they undertook, point to the need for new models of social cohesion in Latin America and the Caribbean, a theme to which we will return in the following chapter. And though the account given herein emphasizes local conditions that contribute to democratic backsliding, the phenomenon was not limited to Latin America and the Caribbean.[13]

CHAPTER TWELVE

Lessons from This Century

A Quantitative Summary: Two Growth Episodes, Two Global Crises

This book's argument can be summarized in terms of a small number of quantitative and qualitative trends in Latin America and the Caribbean. On the quantitative side, this century has been marked by two episodes of economic growth: one quite rapid by historical standards (2003–2008), the other more volatile and less spectacular (2011–2019). Both episodes ended in global crises. The first—the Jazz Effect, the global financial crisis—was shorter and shallower in Latin America than it was elsewhere, notably in the rich countries of the OECD. The second—Covid-19—was sharper, deeper, and more deadly in Latin America than most other parts of the world.

That most countries in the region were better poised to withstand the Jazz Effect than the debt crisis of the 1980s is a major marker of progress in the quality of economic governance. But it did not prevent those same countries from being poorly situated to confront the pandemic. Each of these crises—the debt crisis, the Jazz Effect, and Covid-19—was transmitted to Latin American economies by means of the balance of payments, as we illustrated in chapters 4 through 6. The crises were accompanied by sudden stops in capital inflows of varying duration, as well as declining demand for Latin American exports. But just because the channels of international transmission of shocks were the same, that does not mean that the underlying causes of the crises were identical. The debt crisis was detonated by a global hike in interest rates, which rendered Latin American governments unable to meet the increased cost of servicing their debts. But the underlying cause of the debt crisis, as Albert Fishlow pointed out, was fiscal inadequacy. By the time the Jazz Effect struck in late 2007, most Latin

American countries had made substantial steps to put their fiscal houses in order, thereby positioning them to withstand the new crisis. And while they maintained their fiscal resistance throughout the Hurricane Season, the pandemic was another type of crisis altogether, the impact of which was magnified by other vulnerabilities of economies in the region: inadequate and uneven health care, and high levels of inequality and informality.

A Qualitative Summary: Steps Forward, Steps Back

Three qualitative trends emerge as well from the preceding pages. Each involves steps forward and steps backward in pursuit of the multidimensional goals of development. First, the *reprimarization/deindustrialization binary*: Primary products—commodities—came to occupy a larger share of the export basket for many countries, driven primarily by booming Chinese demand. A half step forward, let us say: surging commodity exports encouraged higher rates of growth and commodity revenues made possible effective social policy experiments. A full step back: these gains came at the cost of delaying, if not abandoning outright, the High Developmentalist dream of structural transformation, import-substituting industrialization, and longer-term productivity gains.

Second, there was a marked *decline in economic inequality*. This was in turn driven by decades of public investment in secondary education—and by the decisions of millions of parents to keep their children in school—which had the effect of reducing the wage gap between skilled and unskilled workers, thereby reducing earnings inequality. The inequality decline was also aided by ambitious social programs—such as the Brazilian Bolsa Família, Chile's Solidario, and Mexico's Progresa/Oportunidades/Prospera sequence of programs—pursued by pragmatic left-leaning and center-right governments alike. Given the historic persistence of high levels of economic inequality, this reversal, sustained over the course of a couple decades in many countries, represents a step forward, a striking turning point in the history of a centuries-old problem. But also a half step back: The reduction in salary inequalities was driven in part by slower growth in technological investments (and the demand for higher-skilled workers that such investments occasion), which was not in itself a positive thing. What's more, the picture of declining income inequality is muddied a bit by the emergence of more complete evidence of comparatively high and persistent *wealth* inequality.

Third, many governments across the region improved the quality of their *economic governance*, particularly in the domain of public finances. The design and implementation of a fiscal rule by Chilean finance minister Andrés Velasco in 2006 represents perhaps the most emblematic example: In a stark break with the past, the Chilean rule led to fiscal policy cycles that diminished, rather than amplified, business cycles. Peru's efforts, led by finance minister Luis Carranza, to restructure and reduce the size and the dollar-denominated share of its public debt is another. Chile and Peru and other countries in the region thereby found themselves with more fiscal resources to address the effects of the 2008 global financial crisis than did many OECD economies. "Possibilist" economic regimes (predominantly though not entirely left leaning) pragmatically mixed rather orthodox monetary policies—as ostensibly firebrand leaders like Lula and Ollanta Humala recruited conservative central bank presidents—while pursuing ambitious social programs and anti-poverty measures.

A quarter century into the twenty-first century, the contention that economic governance represents an unequivocal step or two forward is likely to strike many Latin American readers as misguided. The Latinobarómetro survey evidence reviewed in chapter 11, for example, illustrates a deterioration in support for democracy, and declining satisfaction with the functioning of democracy in respondents' home countries. Such disillusionment is difficult to square with better governance. Let me point out that steps forward in the quality of economic governance represent historic, important, and inspiring progress; but also, only a few steps along what will be a long and difficult path. Along the way, some governments' and states' improvements are clouded by allegations of corruption or illegal behavior by some leaders and bureaucrats—such as the Odebrecht scandal, in which managers at the Brazilian construction multilatina bribed officials in Argentina, Colombia, the Dominican Republic, Mexico, Peru, Venezuela, and beyond to secure lucrative public contracts (Dubé 2016)—or by attempts by presidents to consolidate self-serving *presidencialismo* rather than democracy per se. Securing and expanding the reach of better governance will need to be accompanied by sustained and principled pressure by political parties, social movements, and public institutions.

Taken together, these qualitative and quantitative tendencies necessarily represent a mixed record of success and failure alike. This summary masks the ever-present diversity of experiences that must be acknowledged in any overview of

Latin American history (key #5, chapter 1). And the Covid-19 crisis may have undone much of the good that occurred, it is true. Nevertheless, the combination of the windfall benefits of the commodity boom (an exogenous boon) and the move toward more pragmatic public finances and social policy (an endogenous improvement) among other elements of this story, represent historically important changes. It is this book's realistic but guardedly optimistic claim that the twenty-first century ought to give pause to pundits' reflexive pessimism about Latin America's economy—as exemplified by the 2019 *Wall Street Journal* headline cited in the introductory chapter: "Latin America's Prospects Dim, Again." To the extent that political, social, and business actors in the region and beyond can build upon this incomplete progress, there is a greater likelihood that an improvement in the region's prospects gains momentum and sustainability.

Challenges for the Next Seventy-Five Years

At the time this book is being written a number of relatively new trends are being bandied about everywhere in the world as being likely to affect the future of the global economy in fundamental ways: artificial intelligence, notably; the transformation of the rules-based international trading order into a set of overlapping blocs; the revival of industrial policy by US President Joseph R. Biden, and of mercantilism by his successor, Donald J. Trump; an apparently novel kind of inflation; and the shifting geometry of multipolar international relations. Some of these trends will look like a flash in the pan to the unlikely reader who picks up this book in the year 2100; others may prove enduring in their impact.

I will focus on longer-term phenomena in Latin American economic history and will consider three such ostinato themes in the twenty-first century that could, if properly understood, support a better future for the region. First, Raúl Prebisch's Center-Periphery framework remains a valid and useful way to interpret the global economy. Second, and as a consequence, Latin American countries require Neo-Developmentalist States to confront their development challenges. Third, new models of social cohesion must be jointly crafted by states and citizens to ensure the durability of development objectives, including the UN's Sustainable Development Goals for 2030, adopted by UN member countries in 2015.

The epiphanic nature of many Latin American economists' reactions when

Prebisch's Center-Periphery framework laid bare the structure of the world economy—and the role to which Latin America had been consigned as a raw materials exporter—faded a long time ago. Mixed levels of enthusiasm for what most observers call neoliberalism have replaced that sense of wonder. Neoliberal policy reforms in the 1990s rejected the notion that the structure of the global economy might mean that optimal economic strategies differ from place to place: The ten commandments of the Washington Consensus were adjudged universally applicable in all latitudes.

Of course, the experience of the twenty-first century calls for modifications to twentieth-century Center-Periphery thinking in order to ensure its continued analytical usefulness. China engineered, mightily, a transformation from what would have been part—a particularly remote part—of Prebisch's Periphery into the source of economic impulses (via trade and investment flows) in Latin America that rivalled those of the traditional Euro-American Center. The historical sequencing of Chinese industrialization two centuries after that of the North Atlantic and Japan meant that Latin America found itself once again subject to a demand for its raw material exports; Center-Periphery logic underlay the prolongation of Latin America's role as a commodity producer. But China's economic power only rivalled, and did not surpass, that of Europe and North America during this period. The economic Center had become multipolar. China did not displace Europe and the United States: It competed with the traditional Center at times, giving Latin American governments and firms some leverage to choose among lenders or trading partners. Elsewhere, China occupied spaces abandoned by the traditional Center, as in Ecuador and Venezuela, where the absence of lending by international financial institutions or the United States created a vacuum that Chinese state banks exploited.

A multipolar Center is not the only necessary update to Center-Periphery thinking. We can safely move beyond some of the conclusions that some derived from such thinking in the 1950s and 1960s. This leads to the second recurring theme that I want to highlight from previous chapters: the need for a new Developmentalism, a *Neo-Developmentalist State* that is not beholden to your grandparents' dependency theory. Neo-Developmentalism will marry a brand of macroeconomic orthodoxy, for lack of a better word, with policies intended to transform the structure of economies.

Beyond the quite conventional arguments for an active market-supporting state reviewed in chapter 11, the Center-Periphery logic continues to provide additional arguments for state action. This goes considerably beyond the fundamental work of ensuring a favorable environment for businesses large and small, private and public. Perhaps ironically, the most salient real-world example of a Neo-Developmentalist State in the twenty-first century is that of the People's Republic of China, with all the consequences for Latin America and the Caribbean analyzed in previous chapters. But the Chinese model is neither the most likely nor the best suited to the challenges faced in Latin America.

Four characteristics must infuse the Neo-Developmentalist State in Latin America. The first is *possibilism*, the pragmatic mix of orthodox macroeconomic management with heterodox policies. Luiz Carlos Bresser Pereira, finance minister during the consequential Brazilian presidency of Fernando Henrique Cardoso, argues (together with economist Éric Berr) for a Neo-Developmentalist State that is decidedly more liberal than its antecedents in the mid-twentieth century—and more liberal, by the way, than China. Berr and Bresser Pereira emphasize the cautious management of key macroeconomic variables including the exchange rate, interest rates, and the public debt, and they argue that the latter should largely be composed of domestic debt denominated in the local currency (Berr and Bresser Pereira 2018). This brand of liberal macro policy is largely congruent with the possibilism celebrated by Javier Santiso (2005) and studied in chapters 10 and 11.

The remaining characteristics of the Neo-Developmentalist State go beyond conventional static solutions to market failures discussed in chapter 11. The second characteristic is that it pursues an intelligent industrial policy. Of course, mainstream economists and US policy makers have roundly condemned industrial policy for many decades (which did not, of course, prevent the United States from pursuing industrial policies). That opprobrium has substantially diminished, and US President Joseph Biden explicitly embraced elements of industrial policy in the massive Inflation Reduction Act of 2022, ostensibly inspired by national security concerns in the context of growing acrimony between the United States and China. Latin American Neo-Developmentalist policy will do well to follow the proposal of Harvard economists Ricardo Hausmann and Dani Rodrik: They characterize successful economic development as a process of "self-discovery," during which economies learn about what they're good at producing and exporting. This self-discovery must overcome a market failure:

Self-interested profit-seeking firms and investors will devote inefficiently small resources to the discovery of information that will benefit many other agents. Self-discovery in this sense is a sort of semi-public good, with potentially powerful positive externalities. There is therefore a powerful justification for the State to channel resources, including capital and expertise, to the process of self-discovery (Hausmann and Rodrik 2003). This blueprint served as the basis for the pathbreaking research of the Harvard Growth Lab (Mazzucato and Rodrik 2024), whose influence extended throughout many Latin American countries during the last quarter century.

Self-discovery may be in pursuit of a twenty-first century brand of industrialization, one that avoids the prematurely abandoned, truncated industrialization decried by Dani Rodrik and Fernando Fajnzylber, with the lower growth of average incomes and productivity that implies. The audacious objectives of the Brazilian national development bank, BNDES, during the first two Lula administrations under the leadership of Luciano Coutinho, are the most striking example of Neo-Developmentalist industrial policy, and ought to be studied carefully in Brazil in the decades ahead (Coutinho et al. 2012).

Neo-Developmentalist industrial policy need not turn its back on commodity abundance. Argentinian economist Lucio Castro (2012) wonders why more Latin American countries, unlike Australia, New Zealand, Canada, Malaysia, Thailand, and other countries, do not export more differentiated natural resource-intensive goods. Such goods incorporate more capital and generate higher added value than raw material exports, but they also require more investment in research and development, transport and logistics infrastructure, and credit for local producers than most Latin American countries provide. Indeed, the growing number of incipient success stories of exporters studied by the Inter-American Development Bank feature agriculturally based exports of this type (Sabel et al. 2012; Ghezzi et al. 2022); these successes also provide concrete examples of the coordinating action of the Neo-Developmentalist State of the kind I am promoting here.

Indeed, the third characteristic of Neo-Developmentalist States is that they effectively promote coordination among agents: Economists would say that they are helping to solve *coordination failures*. Coordination failures are at the heart of development economist Pranab Bardhan's conception of the state and development. In this connection, Bardhan writes that economic development in successful East Asian countries was not founded just on institutions that secure property rights and enforce contracts—no doubt very important for long-term investment—but on a state that helped to foster coordination (particularly in financial markets in early stages of industrialization), facilitate interdependent investment decisions in orchestrated networks of producers and suppliers, establish public development banks and other institutions for long-term industrial finance, and nudge firms to upgrade their technology and move into sectors that fit with a national vision of development goals. Enabling and encouraging such coordination is fundamentally different from protecting property rights (Bardhan 2016, 881).[1]

States' attempts to resolve such coordination failures are entirely in line with the Hausmann-Rodrik conception of self-discovery, as without such coordination, the fruits of self-discovery are unlikely to be realized (though some observers are likely to endorse a more limited view of the State's responsibilities to self-discovery). Neo-Developmentalist coordination is moreover closely related to the discussion of embedded autonomy and the crafting of development pacts in chapter 11.

But the possibilities for exploiting commodity abundance in a Neo-Developmentalist framework like that being described here are complicated if the commodities in question are oil and gas. Faced with the need to transform the global energy economy, industrial policy emerged, or re-emerged, as a way to mobilize the massive investment flows required for the task. China's dizzying development of green technologies and investment in energy transformation is arguably the prototypical example. US President Biden's massive experiments in industrial policy—legislation providing between $500 billion and $1.2 trillion in climate spending—were likewise correctly interpreted as a means to accelerate an energy transformation of the US economy (Carey 2023). Of course, much of Biden's economic legislation was motivated by strategic concerns, particularly to compete with China in strategic sectors, but the effect of this geopolitical driver was to increase investment in greener energy production and use.

Latin American states will need to deploy green Neo-Developmentalist industrial policies to meet the challenge of energy transformation. The investment requirements are massive, and amply exceeded annual clean-energy investments actually made during the twenty-first century. A study by the

International Energy Agency (IEA) and the World Bank's International Finance Corporation (IFC) estimated that annual investment in Latin America and the Caribbean would need to total at least $150 billion in the latter half of the 2020s to meet the Sustainable Development Goals associated with climate change (namely, net zero emissions by the 2060s). The IEA and IFC further estimate that the required total in the region would climb to $243 billion annually to meet the goals of the Paris Agreement (net zero emissions by 2050 and global warming limited to 1.5 degrees Celsius) (IEA/IFC 2023). Contrast this with planned expenditures of some twenty billion dollars annually in the region (or with McKinsey estimates of the required investment closer to $700 billion annually in Latin America).[2] Fossil-fuel producing and exporting countries have responded in different ways. Colombia halted the issuance of new oil exploration contracts when leftist president Gustavo Petro came to power in 2022; Petro furthermore made use of the tools of industrial policy to promote environmentally friendly investment (Osborn 2023). Meanwhile, Mexican president Andrés Manuel López Obrador, also left leaning, instead leaned into the state-owned oil company Pemex as a motor for decidedly old-school economic development (Morales 2024).

The Neo-Developmentalist State, finally, must aggressively pursue multidimensional inequality reduction. The conventional economic rationale for state intervention has generally looked askance at efforts to reduce inequality and poverty, under the guise of protests that equity comes at the cost of increased inefficiency. More recent empirical research by IMF economists, reviewed in chapter 9, however, demonstrated that higher levels of income inequality lead to lower levels of economic growth. This complicates the "equity-efficiency tradeoff" thinking and provides an instrumental rationale for public action to reduce inequality, in addition to the intrinsic ethical rationale. Moreover, among the principal empirical findings of Thomas Piketty's groundbreaking research is that, in the absence of concerted public action to restrain it, economic inequality (especially that between labor and capital income) will tend to increase over time. For all these reasons, in addition to the considerable political, social, and moral arguments opposed to inequality, the Neo-Developmentalist State will need to redouble its efforts and experimentation in pursuit of lower levels of economic inequality.

The Neo-Developmentalist State as described most definitely has its roots in the possibilist experiments of the twenty-first century; but the ideal sketched here has not been fully embodied anywhere, not in Lula's Brazil, or the Concertación's Chile, nor Pepe Mujica's Uruguay. But the achievements of these and other governments can, if properly analyzed, provide signposts for states to move ever closer to the ideal. In no realm will the Neo-Developmentalist State be more urgently needed than in the still-sputtering energy transition to combat and adapt to global climate change: This requires overcoming conventional market failures associated with negative externalities, industrial policy led by state action to direct resource allocation and modify incentives, and coordination among stakeholders as described above.

The third and final cross-cutting theme that the first twenty-five years of this century raises when considering the next seventy-five years: Latin America requires new models of social cohesion. I understand social cohesion to be the "knitted warmth" that binds people in a community together, that provides acceptable levels of mutual trust and trust in institutions of governance.[3]

Too many Latin Americans, in the countryside and in the city, feel a sense of insecurity, perhaps a sense that the knitted warmth between people has ravelled. That insecurity is closely related to economic inequality; those with lower, or more precarious incomes, perhaps intermittently employed in the informal economy, are poorly equipped to confront life's—and the economy's—vicissitudes. Increasingly, that insecurity is related to violence: to being exposed to the threat of violence in the household, in the street, and in the nation at large. And the threat of economic ruin or physical violence is closely related to the phenomenon of marginalization, of exclusion from participation in the decisions that determine the political and economic life of the citizen, her household, and the wider community. That bespeaks a deficit of social cohesion; and reconstructing, or constructing from scratch, the knitted warmth between people requires new models of social cohesion.

In many important ways, the pursuit of higher levels of social cohesion is linked to the establishment and improvement of a Neo-Developmentalist State (and vice versa). This is most clearly seen in the case of improved fiscal policy making extensively detailed in chapter 10. Many of the means with which governments can increase citizens' economic security lie in the realm of government expenditures. This starts with social-assistance schemes (to raise the incomes of the poorest, as with many conditional cash transfer programs) and social-insurance schemes (to offset declines in earnings occasioned by unemployment, ill health, or retirement from the labor force). Social assistance and social insurance have occupied much of the attention of policy makers in Latin America in this century, to be sure, though most existing schemes are still regarded to be inadequate for the needs of citizens. To this must be added the list of spending priorities in the areas of health and education, as well as to finance the imperatives of a Neo-Developmentalist industrial policy.

Addressing the inadequacy of such schemes in turn calls for reform of the revenue side of fiscal policies: tax reform. This has proven to be among the most stubborn areas in Latin American policy. As we saw in chapter 10, tax-to-GDP ratios in Latin America average slightly under two-thirds of the level in OECD countries: 21.7 percent versus 34.1 percent. (The Latin American average is nevertheless higher than in Asia-Pacific economies [19.8 percent] and African economies [16 percent].)[4] It is not only a matter of increasing the quantity of tax revenues, of course; it is also important to improve their quality, in terms of the mix of taxes and the bases on which they are assessed. In order to marshal the resources needed to address the damage wrought by economic inequality and insecurity, governments will need more revenue, through a mix of sources more reliant on progressive income taxes and less reliant on regressive consumption taxes. Some version of this problem is faced by countries at all income levels, but the resistance to reform has been particularly obdurate in Latin America.

Indeed, as we discussed in chapter 10, well-functioning fiscal policy, politically, is a demonstration of reasonably high levels of social cohesion. That is, a reasonably well-functioning structure of tax revenues and public expenditures is a form of social contract. In exchange for publicly provided goods and services—such as education and health care—citizens opt not to evade their taxes massively and will even support political parties who suggest broader tax revenues (provided those are viewed as progressive and fair). Conversely, a poorly functioning fiscal structure is a sign of a damaged or broken social contract. Poorly funded, low-quality public services do not inspire citizens to pay their taxes or support politicians who would raise tax revenues—which sets in motion a vicious circle, in which inadequate resources further diminish the quality of publicly provided goods and services, and further diminish tax morale.

Nevertheless, broad tax reforms have been vanishingly rare in Latin America. It is striking that during the April 2024 televised debate among the three candidates for the Mexican presidency, focusing on economic issues, both leading candidates assured voters that it would not be necessary to reform the tax system to finance the ambitious new programs they laid out. This seems almost mathematically impossible, but the very mention of tax reform was adjudged electorally untenable: either because the high-income and high-wealth citizens likely to be disproportionately affected by such changes would vigorously and successfully oppose such efforts, or because the level of voters' trust in fiscal institutions was so low that such a proposal would only be met with suspicion. Or both.

Though tax-to-GDP ratios in Latin America lag those in the rich economies, there is nevertheless a similar sense of state penury even in the latter, as the ambition of the "social state" grows more rapidly than tax revenues. In such a situation, it is perhaps not surprising that proposals for wealth taxes on the largest fortunes, even a coordinated global wealth tax, have appeared on the policy agenda in many rich countries (Thomas Piketty devoted a chapter in *Le capital au XXIe siècle* to the matter of the global wealth tax; Piketty 2013, ch. 15). Wealth would extend the tax base beyond its current reach in most countries and promises to generate substantial public revenue. Of course, the wealth tax is precisely the kind of proposal whose opponents are likely to be well organized, well resourced, and uniquely motivated to thwart the measure. Given the comparatively high rates of wealth concentration in Latin America (refer to fig. 8.6), it seems only a matter of time before the wealth tax is discussed there as well, though at present there is little active policy dialogue regarding aggressive wealth taxation in the region.[5]

Note that all of this discussion regarding fiscal policy and social cohesion has largely to do with redistributive public finance: using taxes, transfers, and public expenditures to widen the gap between people's market income and disposable income. The logic of redistribution does not seek radically to reorganize the economic and political life of a society (even though redistributive measures may create incentives for firms and households to change their behavior in non-trivial ways). But building and rebuilding social cohesion surely requires more than redistribution.

Yale University philosophy professor Martin Hägglund draws a useful distinction between social democracy and democratic socialism. By the former, he means politics and policies to redistribute income generated in capitalist economies; this is meant to ensure greater equity in the division of the system's output. The latter, in contrast, refers to reorganization of the economy itself. Democratic socialism, in this view, seeks greater equity in the process of production, including in the critical decisions about what economists call resource allocation. The rhetoric regarding revolutionary politics will be familiar to Latin Americans of earlier generations well-versed in persistent debates pitting revolution against gradual reform, or market against state prevalence in economic affairs (key #4 from chapter 1). A version of Hägglund's argument—which comes down squarely in favor of democratic socialism as he defines it—was made by Che Guevara, who discounted forms of communism that were merely a "method of redistribution" rather than a "revolutionary morality." "Economic socialism without communist morality does not interest me," Che wrote. "We fight against misery, but at the same time we fight against alienation" (Tablada Pérez 1987, 174–75).[6]

Che's distinction remains a valuable one, even if separated from its perhaps dated ideological context. More and more ambitious machinery to effect income redistribution through tax and transfer may be necessary to reduce misery, but it will not be sufficient to eliminate alienation, or the sense of marginalization and mistrust that too many Latin Americans likely feel regarding the societies in which they live.

Are there models for more participatory economic and political life? It turns out that there are. Mexican social anthropologist Martha Areli Ramírez Sánchez, in a 2024 interview, said, "Zapatismo is still an option" (Cortés Hernández 2024). She was referring to the Chiapas-based guerrilla movement led by the EZLN (the Zapatista Army for National Liberation) that vaulted onto the global stage on 1 January 1994, on the day that the North American Free Trade Agreement entered into effect; on that date, Zapatista guerrillas battled Mexican troops and took control of a number of communities in Chiapas, including, for a time, the city of San Cristóbal de las Casas.[7]

Though the military phase of the Zapatista uprising lasted only days, thirty years later, Zapatista communities continue to govern themselves with decentralized, deliberative modes of democratic practice. Ramírez Sánchez did not mean to say that such a model—including armed rebellion—might be adopted by Mexican society at large, but rather that Zapatista strategies of social and symbolic actions continued to be viable means of resistance and political action for Indigenous peoples in a globalizing world. I wonder, though, if some of the considerable sympathy expressed for the Zapatistas beyond Indigenous communities, in Mexico and elsewhere, might be sparked by curiosity and even longing regarding their participatory practices, to combat, as Che put it, alienation as well as misery.

How to connect experiments in democratic autonomy in the Lacandon jungle to national politics and economics? A related current in the Andes attempts to make that connection. In this century, a number of writers and activists have developed the concepts of sumak kawsay from Quechua or suma qamaña from Aymara, variously translated into Spanish as "buen vivir" (good living) or "vivir bien" (living well); these contributions seek to sketch an alternative indicator of well-being, not based on GDP or its rate of growth (Acosta 2020; Paz Rada 2020). These concepts were explicitly incorporated into the new constitutions introduced in Bolivia and Ecuador by the governments of Evo Morales and Rafael Correa, respectively. Proponents of these new (or newly rediscovered) bases for social well-being, however incipient their translation to national practice, argue that they move us beyond "alternative development models" to "alternatives to development."[8]

Such topics take us, arguably, far beyond considerations of central bank independence, restructuring of public debt, accelerating growth of total factor productivity, or even moving the Gini coefficient down a couple points. But I introduce Zapatismo, sumak kawsay, suma qamaña, and related examples and concepts, because I think they point in the direction of more participatory economic and political life, and the infusion of private lives with more public meaning than either neoliberalism or old-school Developmentalism could, and because economic success in the remainder of this century would do well to use these and other materials to reweave the knitted warmth between people, to increase social cohesion.

I will close by turning our attention once again to the chronic fatalism and resignation that plagues long-time observers of Latin America and the Caribbean, within the region and beyond. The multiple social, political, and economic problems that beset the region are too big and too interwoven, say the pessimists, to make any kind of dent. That analysis, however, can be seen from a different perspective with the help of some basic economic logic. It could be that many Latin American societies are embroiled in a multiple-equilibria problem. The pessimists' case argues that the negative processes are mutually reinforcing; a broken social contract limits tax revenues, which in turn constrains the quality and quantity of public expenditures, driving disillusionment with democracy, and so on. That's the bad equilibrium. But a good equilibrium, with reasonably good publicly provided goods and services, supported by reasonably progressive and fair taxes, inspiring greater support for democratization, could also exist in principle.

The challenge is jumping from the bad to the good equilibrium. As in our discussion of the Neo-Developmentalist State, this is a coordination problem that might require a sort of "big push" across several domains of action. Given the particular historic inadequacy of fiscal policy in the region, and the promising innovations witnessed in recent decades, further fiscal action will be a privileged arena for attention in the effort to move to the high-social-cohesion equilibrium. States can leverage the incipient institutional improvements to make mutually reinforcing strides in this vision of Neo-Developmentalism, including industrial policy that addresses market failures, builds new opportunities, and raises productivity. From the left-populist countries, we can study what worked and what did not in harnessing the power of social movements; such experiences, after all, represent the most salient examples of attempts explicitly to activate forms of participatory politics so critical to social cohesion.

My argument is that the genuine half or full steps forward chronicled here represent sufficient institutional and historical improvements—if duly recognized and soberly analyzed—upon which to base further, broader strides forward. My hope is that historians in the not-too-distant future will say of this century, this time, that Latin America's prospects brightened.

Notes

Introduction

1. The article bears this title in the print edition of the *Journal* (Luhnow 2019); the title of the online version, to my chagrin, expresses the same fatalism—"Latin America Hangs on to its Economic Gloom"—but less dejectedly and with less poetry.
2. The PDSB's roots lie in the social-democratic left, and the party formed in opposition to the military dictatorship. During the popular presidential terms of Fernando Henrique Cardoso, former cepalino and High Developmentalist—labels that will be introduced and explained in chapter 2—the party came to embrace economic policy positions more consistent with right-wing political parties. As such, by 2006, it is probably more accurate to label the PDSB as center-right.
3. Goldman Sachs, *Emerging Markets Strategy*, 7 November 2002; Citigroup, *Global Economic Outlook and Strategy*, 23 August 2006, cited in OECD (2008, box 3.4).
4. This summary follows the version of events reported in the 6 July 2013 issue of *Folha de São Paulo*, accompanying an editorial by Marcelo Coelho (2013), who noted that for the first time, the protests revealed opposition to the left-wing Partido de Trabalho (PT) government that could not be credibly written off as "right-wing coup plotters."

Chapter One

1. Gurría Lacroix reviews the many depictions that Diego Rivera rendered of Hernán Cortés, in the course of which the conquistador becomes more sickly, decrepit, and venal, as Rivera's immersion in Mexico's history deepens: "Diego's mural work is the visual objectification of a socialist idea embodied in the History of Mexico and in the current life of the Mexican social classes" (Gurría Lacroix 1971, 74).
2. A further frontier of colonialism has been important in critiques by Latin American theorists of development: *internal colonialism*, denoting the processes of exclusion and marginalization of Indigenous populations by national governments and other powerful domestic actors. Pablo González Casanova (1963) and Rodolfo Stavenhagen (1981) are but the tip of a deep bibliographic iceberg on internal colonialism.
3. An updated account of Kay's argument is provided by Ojeda Medina and Villarreal Villamar (2020).

4. At a tricontinental conference in Havana in 1966, Che gave an address encouraging Third World leaders to resist US imperialism; the speech was entitled, "Create two, three, many Vietnams."

5. Bethell (2010) shows that the earliest usage of the term "América Latina" in fact predates Chevalier; a handful of Spanish American journalists, writers, and politicians—some of them resident in Paris, to be sure—used the expression before Chevalier in the 1850s.

6. When I first started compiling comparative data for this book in 2019, Venezuelan national income data were included, with some missing years, in the World Bank's invaluable World Development Indicators (WDI) database. By mid-2023, much of the Venezuelan data had disappeared from the WDI. In response to an enquiry to the World Bank, I was informed that the WDI "database includes data provided by official country sources. When official data are missing, we may use estimates, provided there is quite a consensus on the numbers among different agencies (W[orld] B[ank], IMF, UNSD). This is not the case for Venezuela, and the high level of uncertainty in these cases prevent us from publishing any estimates." In chapters 3 and 4, I use the data I extracted in 2019 so that Venezuela's experience can be compared to the other LAC-7 countries, even though this introduces slight inconsistencies with data discussed in this chapter and extracted in 2023. Elsewhere, I use IMF data—which include estimates for Venezuelan indicators for more recent years—for LAC-7 comparisons. In the meantime, Venezuela's national income has fallen so precipitously that it may no longer be among the top seven economies of the region.

7. The OECD's *Latin American Economic Outlook* for 2019 includes a useful overview of development challenges in the Caribbean small states, comparing their fortunes to those of the larger Latin American economies (OECD/CEPAL/CAF/EU 2019, ch. 6).

8. In addition to the LAC-19 countries, the World Bank aggregate includes the following economies: Antigua and Barbuda, Aruba, the Bahamas, Barbados, Belize, the British Virgin Islands, the Cayman Islands, Curaçao, Dominica, Grenada, Guyana, Haiti, Jamaica, Puerto Rico, Sint Maarten (Dutch part), St. Kitts and Nevis, St. Lucia, St. Martin (French part), St. Vincent and the Grenadines, Suriname, Trinidad and Tobago, the Turks and Caicos Islands, the Virgin Islands (United States).

9. The sum of the GDP figures for the LAC-19 countries accounts for about 91 percent of the WDI Latin America and the Caribbean (LCN) aggregate's economic size, though the magnitude of this proportion may be overstated because GDP data are missing for many of the smaller Caribbean economies in the WDI. The LAC-19 countries account for about 92 percent of the total *population* of the LCN aggregate in the WDI, and for what it's worth, population numbers are less likely than GDP numbers to be missing in this database (World Bank, n.d.).

10. These figures are taken from the World Bank's WDI dataset, and measure gross domestic product expressed in constant 2015 US dollars. For Latin America and the Caribbean, figures are missing for a number of smaller Caribbean economies, and more seriously from a quantitative standpoint, for Venezuela.

Chapter Two

1. "La croissance économique est la religion du monde moderne." (Cohen 2024, 21).
2. This is meant to be an economics book for non-economists. To be sure, I hope that economists will read and be stimulated by my argument, but I do not want non-specialists to be dissuaded by arcane or technical language. As such, several economic concepts and models will be introduced throughout the story and will be presented in a way that does not presume specialized vocabulary or knowledge. Readers well versed in the definitions and measurement of economic growth may wish to skip this section and proceed to the next section of this chapter, entitled "High Developmentalism in Theory and in Practice."
3. More recently, economists have argued that the appropriate comparative measure is national income per *working age adult*, rather than per person. Japan's anemic 0.8 percent average growth of income per capita over the period 1990–2019 is little more than half of the 1.5 percent growth experienced on average by the United States over the same years. But Japan's more rapidly ageing population, with a concomitant increase in the retired share of the total, means that its working age adult population grew more slowly than that of the United States; growth of national income per working-age adult was in fact more rapid in Japan than in the United States (Zumbrun 2023). The case for using the working-age adult population as the denominator of the income variable is made by Fernández-Villaverde, Ventura and Yao (2024). This distinction is most stark in cases of mature economies—like Japan—where ageing populations drive average income and income per working-age adult apart. The practical impact of this adjustment is less likely to be meaningful in Latin American and Caribbean economies over most of the span of the years being studied in this book.
4. A 2021 *Wall Street Journal* editorial, lambasting inequality researchers including Thomas Piketty, opined: "Largely missing from [their] analysis is any sense of absolute scale. Were such data included, they would show that the global pie has grown apace, especially in recent decades, leaving most people with a bigger piece . . . Instead of examining what causes the pie to expand, Mr. Piketty is building a career out of arguing over how politicians should slice and redistribute it." (*Wall Street Journal* 2021).
5. King writes: "What is freedom? It is, first, the capacity to deliberate or weigh alternatives. 'Shall I be a lawyer or a doctor?' 'Shall I be a Democrat, Republican or Socialist?' 'Shall I be a humanist or a theist?' Moment by moment we go through life engaged in this strange conversation with ourselves. Second, freedom expresses itself in decision. The word 'decision,' like the word 'incision,' involves the image of cutting. Incision means to cut in, decision means to cut off. When I make a decision, I cut off alternatives, and make a choice. The existentialists say we must choose, that we are choosing animals, and that if we do not choose, we sink into thinghood and the mass mind. A third expression of freedom is responsibility. This is the obligation of the person to respond if he is questioned about his decisions. No one else can respond for him. He alone must respond, for his acts are determined by the totality of his being." To these three Kingian expressions of freedom, I would add a fourth item, a condition for freedom that comes from King's April 1963 "Letter from Birmingham Jail," perhaps the second most well-known sentence that Dr. King would utter: "We are caught in an inescapable network of mutuality, tied in a single garment of destiny."

The excellent book by Hägglund (2019) develops the nonlibertarian ideal of freedom from a political philosophy point of view and is fundamentally inspired by King.

6. What follows is a considerably simplified explanation of the CEPAL view of the declining terms of trade, and one based on the consequences of Engel's law (see below). As Rodríguez (1980, ch.2) points out in his history of CEPAL's economic contributions, the version included in the 1949 CEPAL report relies on asymmetric changes in the terms of trade during business cycles in the global economy, amplified by differences in labor's bargaining power in the Center and in the Periphery. Rodríguez finds elements of the Engel-inspired version included herein in subsequent elaborations by Prebisch (1951, 1959).

7. Calcagno (2023) traces the emergence of industrialization in Prebisch's thinking. Eatwell (1987), Bruton (1989) and Franko (2019, ch. 3), analyze the rationales for, and performance of, ISI.

8. Rivera-Quiñones (2018), Ojeda Medina and Villarreal Villamar (2020), and Bringel and Echart Muñoz (2020) assess the trajectory of dependency theory, including its utility as a critical framework today.

9. The synthesis over time between the once-opposed cepalinos and dependentistas calls to mind an episode in the work of Argentinian author Jorge Luis Borges. In "Los Teólogos," Borges recounts a long-ago ecclesiastical dispute between the orthodox Aurelian and the heretic John of Pannonia. In the fullness of eternal time, God confuses the bitter rivals, considering them a single person: "Perhaps it could be said that Aurelian spoke with God and that God was so little interested in religious differences that he took him for John of Pannonia. This, however, would suggest a confusion of the divine mind. It is more correct to say that in Paradise, Aurelian knew that for the unfathomable divinity, he and John of Pannonia (the orthodox and the heretic, the hater and the hated, the accuser and the victim) formed a single person." So too the long embattled cepalinos and dependentistas are today enjoined in our twenty-first-century memory.

10. See the essay "The Master's Tools Will Never Dismantle the Master's House" in her collection *Sister/Outsider* (1984).

11. Later in his life, Prebisch reflected on his contributions in a World Bank publication (Prebisch, 1984). For a comprehensive overview of CEPAL's contributions in its early existence, refer to Rodríguez (1980). See also the tribute to Prebisch in the *Revista de la CEPAL / CEPAL Review* 75 (December 2001), marking the centenary of his birth and emphasizing the continuing relevance of his contributions.

12. The Mexican economist Everardo Elizondo, a former central bank official, tweeted wryly in 2020, "Un lector de mis artículos periodísticos me calificó de 'neoliberal.' No, gracias. Liberal, a secas, está bien. A mi edad, nada tengo de 'neo.'" ["A reader labelled me 'neoliberal.' No, thank you. Just liberal is fine. At my age, there's nothing 'neo' about me."]

13. More broadly, and in a similar vein, the question of "policy incoherence" would become a major concern to European members of the OECD in the 2000s: they worried that their trade policies vis-à-vis developing economies (which often restricted agricultural imports from poor countries), counteracted their aid policies (which invested in agricultural export capacity in poor countries) (Dayton-Johnson and Katseli, 2006).

14. The parallels between modern economic theory and religious faith entered more broadly into some corners of public debate during the twenty-first century, and even earlier. A noteworthy milestone in this intellectual history was the argument by famed Harvard theologian Harvey Cox that reading the *Wall Street Journal* resembled reading the Bible or St. Augustine. See Foucart (2024) for an extensive discussion. There are two strands to this economics/religion debate of relevance to the arguments in this book. The first is the tendency, noted earlier in this chapter, to confuse the instrumental value of growth—the good things that growth makes possible—for an intrinsic value: growth is good in and of itself and its pursuit ought not to be questioned. The second is the patronizing attitude toward lay people who cannot understand the subtlety of religious or economic doctrine—because they cannot read Latin, say, or they do not understand the mathematical techniques used—and are instructed merely to have faith in the workings of the dogma.

15. Bancomer was subsequently acquired by BBVA and is now part of BBVA México.

16. Cited in Carvalho (2018, 75).

Chapter Three

1. Refer back to chapter 2 for an overview of the definition and significance of average income or GDP per capita.

2. See Coronil (2011) on the 2002 coup; Weisbrot (2011) places this episode in the longer-term context of Venezuela's economic performance during the Chávez years.

3. Chudnovsky and López (2007, ch. 8) provide a useful synthesis of varied analyses of the gradually-to-suddenly phase of the economic downturn, while Lewis (2009, ch. 9) recounts the political dimension of the crisis. IMF (2003) likewise narrates the economic story, and critically evaluates the IMF's role in the crisis and its aftermath. Kiguel (2015), finally, connects the 2001/2002 crisis with earlier Argentinian financial debacles.

4. The literature on the China-Latin America economic relationship in the twenty-first century is extensive. A useful place to start is Gallagher (2012); a more exhaustive and up-to-date overview is Wise (2020).

5. The 2012 IMF study by Shaun Roache found that China's effect on commodity prices was smaller and shorter-lived than that of the United States; specifically, he analyzed shocks in economic activity and their impact on world prices.

6. Cuba's exports to China exploded from 5.2 percent of the total in 2003, to 30 percent in 2006 and 51 percent in 2007, driven almost entirely by nickel matte. Cuba's case is quantitatively unusual and as such has been removed from fig. 3.6 for ease of visual observation.

7. After a pause in new bilateral trade agreements lasting more than a decade, China signed FTAs with Ecuador and Nicaragua, both in 2023.

8. The soybean is 83 percent flour and 17 percent oil; once the oil is extracted, the remaining residue is soybean cake, meal, or pellets, with an elevated vegetable protein concentration that makes these by-products good fodder for factory farming (Turzi 2017).

9. I owe the inspiration for the discussion in the two preceding paragraphs to a stimulating conversation with Edgardo Ayala Gaytán of Tec de Monterrey, for which I am grateful.

10. This thumbnail sketch of *chavismo* draws in part upon Cheatham and Roy (2023).
11. This is not to suggest that the United States withdrew entirely from older forms of political influence peddling in the region. See Black (2005), who enumerates the ways, old and new, that US interests continued to create obstacles for democratic and left-leaning political forces in the Western Hemisphere.

Chapter Four

1. I made some of these points in an editorial I wrote for the Buenos Aires daily *Clarín:* "El efecto jazz y la economía latinoamericana," 6 October 2008. There I was more concerned with demonstrating that had economic management more closely resembled the ethos of a jazz ensemble, the world would not have gotten into the mess we were in.
2. The bibliography, research and otherwise, on the global financial crisis is vast but inconclusive; a useful starting place is Alan Blinder's (2013) narrative account. Jean Tirole's (2015) chapters on finance and the crisis are analytically very lucid. This chapter draws heavily upon the Macroeconomic Overview chapters of the OECD *Latin American Economic Outlook* reports for 2010 and 2011 (OECD 2009, 2010).
3. While the global financial crisis was underway, my colleague and coauthor Javier Santiso repeatedly reminded audiences that it constituted a *cognitive* crisis.
4. The IMF's *Balance of Payments Statistics Yearbook* is the *locus classicus* of all things balance of payments.
5. Sometimes the power asymmetry plays out in complicated and unexpected ways. In August 2019, a World Bank tribunal ordered Colombia to repay Glencore some $19 billion of a fine the government had levied against the company for underpaying royalties, but not the $575 billion in damages sought by the Swiss firm (Reuters 2019a).
6. These figures, from the World Bank's World Development Indicators database, represent both country aggregates (LCN and OECD) as tabulated by the Bank.
7. The concept of the sudden stop is most closely associated with the Argentinian economist Guillermo Calvo of Columbia University, who has studied the phenomenon extensively; see, for example, Calvo et al. (2004).

Chapter Five

1. Cited by Timiraos and Fairless (2023).
2. Some readers have cautioned that "Hurricane Season" is not an ideal metaphor for the story told in this chapter. Hurricanes, they remind me, are more than a metaphor for shocks for Latin American countries in the Caribbean and Central America, including Mexico, where hurricanes are very literal meteorological shocks. But hurricanes, typhoons, tsunamis, and windstorms are *not* endemic to most of the landmass of Latin America, though other types of natural disasters occur, notably earthquakes. This chapter's title is not intended to limit our attention to hurricane-prone Mexico, Central America, and the Caribbean. An overview of the typology of natural disasters—actual, not metaphorical—and their relation to economic development is provided in Dayton-Johnson (2004, 2006), which explores the concepts of

exposure, vulnerability, and resilience, concepts used metaphorically in this chapter and elsewhere in this book. Schwartz (2016), meanwhile, traces the interrelationship between vulnerability to hurricanes and socio-economic history in the Caribbean. "Hurricane Season" also alludes to the 2017 novel *Temporada de huracanes*, by Mexican writer Fernanda Melchor, which mixes actual hurricanes in the fictitious Veracruz locale, with social hurricanes, mostly related to violence, at the household and community level. Melchor's narrative gift at depicting people in the midst of natural and social disasters speaks very powerfully to social scientists and invites us to extend our perspective beyond our usual disciplinary domains.

3. The path of OECD average income is not shown in fig. 5.1; as the levels of OECD income per capita are so much higher than the economies depicted in the graph, it would make it difficult to differentiate among the data in the other countries and country groups.

4. All average income figures in this chapter are expressed in constant 2017 US dollars, adjusted for purchasing power parity, and found in the World Bank's World Development Indicators.

5. The full set of graphics for all seven variables are available to readers upon request.

Chapter Six

1. The Latin American aggregate downturn in 2020—extracted from the World Bank's World Development Indicators database—is −7.37 percent, as noted. The country-by-country comparisons in figs. 6.2 and 6.3 suggest, however, that the regional downturn should be larger (i.e., more negative). Most of the larger LAC-7 economies contracted more sharply than −7 percent, as did most of the smaller economies. I suspect that this is owing to the absence of the Venezuelan number in the WDI database (I extracted Venezuela's growth measure from the IMF WEO database). Leaving Venezuela out of the weighted average for all Latin American growth in 2020 would tend to underestimate the aggregate number, as Venezuela would otherwise be among the larger (and thus more heavily weighted) economies, and its shrinkage was the largest in the region.

2. Though the exchange was memorable, I cannot remember the program nor the date—and my Google searches have been in vain. Perhaps Tuesta will correct me if I have misremembered or misattributed the statement to him.

3. The OECD measure of middle class in this report proved somewhat controversial, and indeed the report uses the more neutral term "middle sectors"—like the Italian notion of the *ceto medio*. Tying the definition to the median income as the report does means that countries with lower median incomes will have objectively poorer middle classes than those with higher median incomes; that is, this is a *relative* measure of the middle class rather than an *absolute* measure (Dayton-Johnson 2015). Absolute measures of the middle class, intended to be equivalent in Switzerland and Swaziland, include Homi Kharas's "global middle class," households with daily incomes between ten and one hundred US dollars (accounting for purchasing power parity), as well as Dadush and Ali's "car index": you're middle class no matter what country you live in if you own a car (see Cárdenas, Kharas and Henao, 2015; Dadush and Ali 2012). Thomas Piketty (2013, ch.7), meanwhile, proposes an

asymmetric relative measure: middle-class households in a country are those with incomes between the fiftieth and ninetieth percentile of the income distribution.

4. OECD/CAF/EU 2021, ch. 1, figs. 1.1 and 1.2.

5. These paragraphs draw upon the late 2020 summary prepared by the Steering Group of the OECD LAC Regional Programme (OECD 2020).

Chapter Seven

1. The numbers cited here measure annual growth in the so-called *GDP deflator*, an alternative inflation indicator. Measured GDP in an economy may grow from one year to the next for one or both of two reasons: output might have increased, or the price of many goods may have increased. The GDP deflator is the factor by which *nominal* GDP is reduced to strip out the effects of inflation in increasing the GDP number; what is left is *real* GDP, and any increase year to year is solely attributable to increases in output. Growth in the GDP deflator for an economy is therefore a measure of growth in prices: inflation. Numbers cited are taken from the World Bank's World Development Indicators dataset.

2. The origins of twentieth-century inflation and hyperinflation in Latin America are complex and contested. The contributors to the volume edited by Kehoe and Nicolini (2021) argue compellingly that many of the inflationary episodes are driven by persistent government deficits in the region, although other factors, some domestic, some external, contributed to these outbreaks.

3. See Rodríguez (1980, ch. 6) and Fajardo (2022, ch. 3) for overviews of the structuralist conception of inflation in Latin America. The characterization of Noyola's "synthesis" model is due to Fajardo (2022, 83).

4. A canonical example of not only central bank independence but of monetary dominance is provided by the US Federal Reserve System under the leadership of Paul Volcker, while Ronald Reagan was president. Reagan and his Republican-controlled Congress ushered in massive tax cuts, reducing government revenues, as well as an arms buildup, increasing government expenditures. This served to increase the government budget deficit precipitously. The Fed under Volcker refused to accommodate the fiscal expansion with increased money supply, instead raising interest rates and thereby causing a sharp recession in economic activity.

5. There is no authoritative definition of hyperinflation, though a frequently cited one from the early days of monetarist economics is that of Cagan (1956), who sets the threshold at 50 percent inflation monthly, which is in excess of 12,000 percent annually. I have been a little looser, and refer to some three-digit annual inflation rates as hyperinflationary in this chapter. Note that the IMF inflation numbers we use here measure the end-of-year percentage increase in prices in the country in question, and may therefore mask shorter-lasting within-year peaks, some of which can be truly astronomical.

6. See his comments on Buera and Nicoloni (2021).

7. This account of Venezuelan inflation draws from the excellent case study by Iyer and Rodríguez (2021), which judiciously draws upon both official and independent data sources, and from the overview of Venezuelan fiscal and monetary policy history by Restuccia (2021), including commentary by Bocola and Perri.

Chapter Eight

1. These figures are from Oxfam (2016, ch. 3); see also the discussion on Mariano Turzi's concept of the "Soybean Republic" in chapter 3. Delgado and Pereira Leite (2022), meanwhile, provide a related critique of the "agribusiness pact" in Brazil. To the extent that Delgado and Pereira Leite's criticism is informed by a pessimism that the "pacto do agronegócio" can generate innovation, I would encourage readers to read their article alongside the considerably more bullish report by the Inter-American Development Bank coordinated by Ghezzi et al. (2022), about which we'll have more to say later in the chapter.

2. Before plunging into ISIC's dizzying typology of output "divisions," it is instructive to review an equally dizzying critique by Argentinian author Jorge Luis Borges of all attempts to create any kind of typology. In a short piece (is it fiction? non-fiction? some kind of mix?) called "El idioma analítico de John Wilkins" (1952), Borges avers that any such enterprise is subject to "ambiguities, redundancies and deficiencies." He recalls the taxonomy of types of animals provided in an almost certainly fictitious Chinese encyclopedia entitled the "Celestial Emporium of Benevolent Knowledge." On those remote pages it is written that animals are divided into (a) those that belong to the Emperor, (b) embalmed ones, (c) those that are trained, (d) suckling pigs, (e) mermaids, (f) fabulous ones, (g) stray dogs, (h) those that are included in this classification, (i) those that tremble as if they were mad, (j) innumerable ones, (k) those drawn with a very fine camel's hair brush, (l) others, (m) those that have just broken a flower vase, (n) those that resemble flies from a distance. To their considerable credit, statisticians in the world's statistical agencies and authorities, collaborating over the decades with the United Nations, have produced in the ISIC Rev. 3.1 a typology of economic activities that is immeasurably more internally consistent and comprehensive than the apocryphal encyclopedia's typologies of all types of animals. There is nevertheless in the ISIC something of the apparent incommensurability between categories seemingly broad ("those that are trained") and picayune ("those that have just broken a flower vase"). Thus, the ISIC Rev. 3.1 includes Division 29 (manufacture of "machinery and equipment") as well as Division 18 ("manufacture of wearing apparel; dressing and dyeing of fur"), the latter distinct from Division 17 ("manufacture of textiles").

3. And the "dyeing of fur."

4. This example is based on a wonderful exercise in Debraj Ray's excellent development economics textbook (Ray 1998, Appendix A1, exercise 8).

5. Rodrik (1996) notes President Park's absence of scruples about "protecting property rights," one of the ten tenets of the Washington Consensus. Alice Amsden's *Asia's Next Giant: South Korea and Late Industrialization* (1989) is a classic account of the politics and economics of South Korea's extraordinarily successful industrialization.

6. As Ray (1998) points out, any equilibrium in which a Brazil-like Government threatens to LIFT the tariffs regardless of Industry's action is not subgame perfect. Subgame perfect equilibria must be Nash equilibria in every subgame; in the subgame in which Industry does not invest, LIFTing the tariff is not a best response by Government, so its action cannot be part of a Nash equilibrium in that subgame. Given the configuration of

payoffs in the Korea version of the game, in contrast, Government *is* better off LIFTing the tariff in that subgame.

7. The Carso telecoms group would subsequently be absorbed into Carlos Slim's Grupo Carso conglomerate, which is invested in a wide range of activities, some of which include industrial and manufacturing activities.

8. Cemex's global expansion seemed to follow me around the world. The company's mixer trucks seemed ubiquitous when I was an exchange student in Mexico in the 1980s. Later, when I worked at the OECD Development Centre, the Centre's offices were located on the Île Saint-Germain in the middle of the Seine, and I would often walk (or travel by commuter train) past the sizeable riverside Cemex installations nearby in Paris's fifteenth arrondissement. I moved from the OECD to the Middlebury Institute in Monterey, only to find myself just a couple of exits along Highway 1, south of Cemex's sand mine on the Pacific in nearby Marina, which has stopped the removal of sand, in an agreement with the California Coastal Commission, but is still selling its inventory of mined sand and has yet to begin restoration of the dunes at the site.

Chapter Nine

1. The noted Harvard economic historian Jeffrey Williamson takes issue with the interpretation that the roots of Latin American economic inequality lie in the colonial era (Williamson 1999; Williamson 2015). With the aid of painstakingly estimated Gini coefficients from a variety of places around the world going back as far as 1491, Williamson shows that income inequality was similar or lower in the Iberian colonies than elsewhere. Latin American inequality became unusually high during the Belle Époque commodity boom, and did not decline in the mid-twentieth century, unlike most rich countries. For Williamson, Latin American exceptionalism emerged during the twentieth century, when its politics failed to redistribute. Diego Sánchez-Ancochea derives a different story from Williamson's data: "... it is clear that in Latin America institutions and policies were organized in favor of the powerful from early on: huge *latifundios*, underinvestment in primary education, and restrictive voting rights were the norm across the region." That is, the institutional roots of redistributive failure in the twentieth century could extend backward into the past (Sánchez-Ancochea 2021, 24). Diego Castañeda Garza's (2024) lucid history of economic inequality in Mexico tells a similar story: Mexico is unequal because it is stingy with redistribution, and its institutional history makes it stingy. Chapter 10 will illustrate that a large component of the difference in Gini coefficients between Latin American and European countries is attributable to the failure of fiscal redistribution in the former.

2. Italian statistician Corrado Gini developed his eponymous index in a series of papers in Italian in the 1910s. Kuan Xu (2003) provides a useful and thorough overview of the first eighty years of the Gini coefficient's development and interpretation. As for computed Gini coefficients, economist Branko Milanovic, among the most productive analysts of inequality, has compiled the so-called "All the Ginis" database, currently housed at the World Bank's data site: https://datacatalog.worldbank.org/dataset/all-ginis-dataset. See

also Ray (1998, ch. 6) for an overview of the Gini coefficient alongside other economic measures of income inequality.

3. Note also that the Gini coefficient could be calculated to measure the dispersion in wealth across households; indeed, the Gini coefficient could be computed for just about any quantifiable and measurable variable: the inequality in height levels among all the people on your subway car, or in the café or library where you are reading this right now.

4. Piketty (2013, 487–97) provides some general commentary on the relationship between minimum wages, productivity, institutions, and inequality. Moreno-Brid, Garry and Krozer (2016), meanwhile, provide background on trends in minimum wages in Latin America, and point out that prior to the 2019 Mexican reform, Mexico's minimum wage was among the lowest in the region.

5. The merging of different types of data from different sources is controversial. Kharas and Seidel (2018) argue against the practice—and cite other authors who support their view. They support the use of only household survey data and show that broad conclusions about trends in the distribution of global income can be completely reversed based on which type of dataset is used.

6. A similar logic to that of the Tavares-Serra model is expounded by CEPAL pioneer Celso Furtado in his analysis of Brazil (Furtado 1972; 1974), and in the passages on Brazil in the mid-twentieth century in Tulio Halperín Donghi's magisterial history of Latin America (Halperín Donghi 1969)—as well as in my memories of Prof. Halperín's undergraduate lectures at Berkeley in the 1980s.

7. Much of the material in this and the following section draws from Dayton-Johnson (2018). The theoretical research on the retarding effects of inequality on economic growth flourished in the 1990s, and the empirical literature addressing the same question continued for somewhat longer. Roland Bénabou (1996) provides both an authoritative overview of this literature, as well as one of the most important contributions to it. Diego Sánchez-Ancochea (2021), meanwhile, has written a highly readable synthesis of the causal links between high inequality and poor development performance in Latin America.

Chapter Ten

1. Fishlow was in the midst of a productive tenure in the department of economics at Berkeley at the time he wrote his paper on the Latin American state, the same time that I was a graduate student there in the 1990s, during which time I worked for him one summer as a research assistant. During his Berkeley years, and given his prestige and influence in Latin America, Fishlow attracted a large coterie of Latin American PhD seekers, for whose presence I was warmly grateful as they provided me with invaluable orientation regarding Latin American economics, and the social network of Fishlow's former students in Latin America has been a vital intellectual community for me in the decades since.

2. Of course, some of the elements of the Washington Consensus had less to do with market liberalization and focused instead on macroeconomic stability, especially items 1–3 in table 2.1; these were closely related to capable fiscal and monetary policies. As chapter 2 noted, items 1–4 in table 2.1 had more to do with IMF recommendations, while the

liberalization items numbered 5–10 were more closely aligned with World Bank recommendations.

3. An alternative is to express the fiscal balance as a share of GDP. This, however, masks important differences among economies. As we will see below, the size of the state—as measured by the ratio of tax revenues to GDP—has been almost half as large in Latin American countries as in OECD member countries during the twenty-first century. As such, it makes more sense in the present context to compare the fiscal balance to total government revenues, especially if one wants to compare between OECD and Latin American economies. Consider a simple numerical example. Suppose a Latin American economy has government revenues equal to 15 percent of GDP, and government spending equal to 20 percent of GDP. Then its fiscal balance is equal to –5 percent of GDP, but –33.3 percent of government revenue. If an OECD economy, meanwhile, has government revenues equal to 30 percent of GDP and government spending equal to 35 percent of GDP, then its fiscal balance is also equal to –5 percent of GDP, but only –16.7 percent of government revenue. Gavin and Perotti (1997) argue that the fiscal balance-to-government revenue ratio better captures an economy's ability to meet its debt repayment obligations. Gavin and Perotti include extensive summary statistics for fiscal variables for the period 1970–1995; OECD (2008, ch. 2) updates all the Gavin and Perotti indicators through 2006.

4. Lustig, Martínez-Pabon, and Pessino (2023), in a recent analysis of Latin American fiscal policy, find that such systems are generally progressive, though their progressivity—and thus their contribution to reducing inequality—has not improved over time. Counterintuitively, they find that in many Latin American economies, indirect taxes are in fact progressive: this is so because so many low-income households acquire many goods in the informal sector, and are therefore beyond the reach of indirect taxation. Those who pay indirect taxes, therefore, are likely to be higher-income households.

5. These arguments are developed at greater length in OECD (2008), chapter 1.

6. Gavin and Perotti (1997) demonstrate statistically that Latin American fiscal policy (both surpluses and spending) was markedly more procyclical than in rich countries over the period 1968–1995.

7. Rhymes with "brains," Richard Salvucci, the noted economic historian of Mexico, used to tell his students.

8. See Tornell's comments at the end of Gavin and Perotti (1997) for a compact and intuitive overview, and the many references to his work throughout that paper. See also Eslava (2012), especially section 2.

9. This illustrative example partly—but only approximately—resembles Chile's actual fiscal history over the last several decades. Caputo and Saravia (2021) survey the principal trends in Chilean fiscal and monetary policy since 1960, and they emphasize neither the role of copper prices, nor of procyclical fiscal surpluses. The importance of fiscal deficit pressures, particularly in the 1960s and 1970s, is nevertheless roughly consistent with the illustrative fable recounted in this chapter. My fable leaves aside the important complication of exchange rate policies, which were critical to understanding macroeconomic crises in the first decade of the military dictatorship that seized power in 1973.

10. The history and impact of Chile's fiscal rule is recounted by Andrés Velasco, the finance minister who bears much of the credit for its success, together with Eric Parrado, former chief research economist at the IDB (Velasco and Parrado 2012).

11. More details can be found in the IMF Fiscal Rules Dataset (Davoodi et al. 2022*a*).

12. Carranza (2012) candidly recounts the experience of fiscal reforms, including public debt administration.

13. These figures are computed, as in figs. 10.1 and 10.2, based on total government revenues and expenditures as a share of GDP for the Latin America and the Caribbean aggregate from the IMF's October 2023 World Economic Outlook database. This aggregate appears to include as many as 33 Latin American and Caribbean economies, and to be a simple unweighted average of countries (that is, giant Brazil and tiny Saint Lucia have an equal effect on the average). The values for 2023 are forecasts. The unweighted average of the eighteen Latin American countries differs slightly. The budget balance-to-government revenues ratio comes in higher, at −13.9 percent for the 1999–2023 period; for just the LAC-7, the average is −15.7 percent. The average budget balance-to-government revenues for the Milagrinho years is −3.4 percent for the LAC-18 and +0.8 percent for the LAC-7.

Chapter Eleven

1. Refer to the many works by these authors in the exhaustive overview by Bardhan (2016).

2. An excellent example of a historical analysis of state autonomy in Latin America is the late Nora Hamilton's classic 1982 work on the nationalization of foreign oil companies by Mexican president Lázaro Cárdenas in 1938, appropriately titled *The Limits of State Autonomy*.

3. Public goods have two characteristics that private goods do not: they are nonrival in consumption, meaning that my consumption does not lessen its availability to you; and they are nonexcludable, meaning that once they've been produced or supplied, it is not feasible to prevent others from consuming it. These elements of economic vocabulary might be confusing: "private" doesn't mean that these are goods supplied by the private sector, nor does "public" mean that they originate necessarily in the public sector. In addition to national security, lighthouses and public education are sometimes offered as examples. Nobel laureate Elinor Ostrom devoted her career to researching what she called common-pool resources, goods which are rival in consumption but nonexcludable; these include community forests and pasturelands, small-scale irrigation systems, and inshore fisheries. Ostrom (1990) describes the kind of institutions that have been developed by societies to manage these hybrid private-public goods.

4. These concepts are explained in many economics textbooks. I have borrowed here from a report that I wrote many years ago on the rationale for state support for arts and culture—notoriously a sector which fails to meet most or all of the four Arrow-Debreu assumptions (Dayton-Johnson 2000). That report provides more discussion of these concepts.

5. There are more or less orthodox currents of economics that argue that an imperfect

state might nevertheless make the allocation of resources *less* socially optimal despite its best intentions. Such conclusions arise from economists of the Public Choice school, associated with George Mason University professor and Nobel laureate James Buchanan. This kind of thinking is also reflected by the dramatic change in antitrust policy in the United States during the Reagan administration, which abandoned anti-monopoly cases and allowed the formation of monopolies, arguing that there were benefits of their scale that exceeded the negative consequences of imperfect competition.

6. When Javier Santiso and I coedited the *Oxford Handbook of Latin American Political Economy* (2012), we celebrated these scholar-practitioners by asking some of them to contribute chapters on the perspective of possibilist policy making.

7. It's not that Latin American countries did not have pacts with the private sector at all. Saragoza (1988), for example, analyzes the process of rapprochement between the Monterrey-based industrial elite and the post-revolutionary Mexican state, a pact that underlay that country's high-growth "stabilizing development" model (Solís 1981). Rather, the Latin American development pacts were less successful over the long run in securing the productivity gains needed to sustain them than their East Asian counterparts.

8. Correa, like many of the possibilist politicians and policy makers, has a doctorate in economics from a top US university: he studied with the venerable Brazil expert Werner Baer at the University of Illinois, Urbana-Champaign. Correa lays out the principal lines of his development strategy and accomplishments in a 2019 article, published after he left power—and indeed after he exiled himself to Belgium to escape a corruption conviction in Ecuador that he argues was politically motivated (Correa 2019).

9. See Bull and Rosales (2023), and Cheatham and Roy (2023), on the degradation of the political situation and the hardening of the Venezuelan regime.

10. In addition to garnering electoral support for the PT, Bolsa Família transfers led to complex political changes at the local level. Frey (2019) provides an ingenious statistical analysis to show that Bolsa Família weakened the political power of local mayors, who engaged in less clientelist solicitation of the local poor, and instead increased the provision of local public goods, including health care and education spending. A fascinating variation on this experience is analyzed by de Janvry, Gonzalez-Navarro and Sadoulet (2014); they find that land-titling in rural Mexico weakened peasants' dependence upon local politicians, and farmers who benefited were likely to switch their electoral allegiance away from the political party that granted their rights and toward the right-wing opposition party.

11. Argentina's political history is especially complicated, if not at times impenetrable. The changes to the Peronist movement since Peron's death, and particularly since the Menem presidency, are critical to an understanding of the intersection of politics and economics in Argentina, a country that has had more than its share of economic and political crises during the period covered in this study. Murillo and Zarazaga (2020) provide an overview of the state of Peronism today, including the factions within the movement, and their relationship to reprimarization and other economic problems; Semán (2020) provides a radical critique of the Kirchners' incapacity to better manage the forces unleashed by Chinese demand for soybeans and other commodity exports. Levitsky (2003) and McGuire

(1997), meanwhile are excellent references for understanding the changes inside the Peronist movement since Perón's death; while Souroujon (2023) and Teubal (2004) review the Menem presidency and its aftermath.

12. A good introduction to the IDB's policy-making process framework is provided by Tommasi and Scartascini (2012); IDB (2005) is a fundamental text in this literature. Juliana Londoño Vélez, Sebastián Nieto-Parra, and I attempted to combine the schools of thought into a single framework, and to provide an overview of many of the reform experiences (Dayton-Johnson, Londoño Vélez, and Nieto-Parra 2011).

13. Reidl et al. (2023), in addition to providing a rigorous quantitative account of democratic backsliding globally, also includes an excellent synthesis of the voluminous research literature on the subject.

Chapter Twelve

1. According to Bardhan, this may require, as probably occurred in many successful East Asian examples, that States "assur[e] some form of 'cooperation-contingent rent' that will accrue to the latter in exchange for playing a role in the state coordination efforts" (Bardhan 2016, 881).

2. These estimates are cited and discussed in Palacios and Guzmán Ayala (2023).

3. The social-science literature on social cohesion (and the related topic of "social capital") is vast. Dayton-Johnson (2001) provides a review of the various perspectives to be found in that literature. Dayton-Johnson (2003) meanwhile, includes a game theory model that illustrates the ways in which self-interested economic agents might be more likely to cooperate in the presence of earlier "investments" in social cohesion than in the absence of those investments. The latter paper also references "knitted warmth," a quotation from *The Mountain and the Valley*, a 1954 novel by the Canadian author Ernest Buckler. Buckler describes the decline in social cohesion in a rural Nova Scotia village: "How this place had aged, with change ... How the knitted warmth between its people had ravelled, until each was almost as alone in his own distraction now as the city people were." And, yes, it turns out that "ravel" is a synonym for "unravel."

4. These are 2021 data for Latin America and Asia, and 2020 data for Africa (OECD 2023, fig. 1).

5. Of course, there are taxes on wealth and property (as opposed to incomes or transactions) in many jurisdictions, Latin American countries among them. But these are partial and piecemeal and provide relatively little revenue to the fisc (a public treasury or exchequer). Darío González of the intergovernmental Inter-American Center of Tax Administrations summarizes the wealth taxes in Latin American countries in a technical note that concludes that a global wealth tax is "necessary" in Latin America and the Caribbean (González 2023).

6. "El socialismo económico sin moral comunista no me interesa. Luchamos contra la miseria, pero al mismo tiempo luchamos contra la alienación ... Si el comunismo descuida los hechos de conciencia puede ser un método de repartición, pero deja de ser una moral revolucionaria."

7. Carlos Tello Díaz's *La rebelión de Las Cañadas* is both quite critical of, and sympathetic to, the Zapatistas and remains a perceptive and readable history of the movement (Tello Díaz 1995). Sylvia Marcos's recent, rich anthology of the role of women in the Zapatista story is one among many excellent examples of books that demonstrate that our understanding of the movement, its potential, and its aims is still far from complete (Marcos 2023).

8. In this connection, I am inspired by the example of the French economists' collective Les économistes atterrés—"appalled economists"—to rethink the economic bases of social cohesion in a European context by asking "What do we really need?" (Économistes atterrés 2022).

References

Principal Data Sources

INTERNATIONAL MONETARY FUND

Balance of Payments and International Investment Position Statistics (BOP/IIP), https://data.imf.org/?sk=7a51304b-6426-40c0-83dd-ca473ca1fd52.
Balance of Payments Statistics Yearbook, Part 1: Country Tables, various years.
Primary Commodity Database, https://www.imf.org/en/Research/commodity-prices.
World Economic Outlook Databases, https://www.imf.org/en/Publications/SPROLLs/world-economic-outlook-databases#sort=%40imfdate%20descending.

OBSERVATORY FOR ECONOMIC COMPLEXITY

https://oec.world/.

WORLD BANK

World Development Indicators, https://databank.worldbank.org/source/world-development-indicators.
World Integrated Trade Solution, https://wits.worldbank.org/.

WORLD INEQUALITY LAB, WORLD INEQUALITY DATABASE

https://wid.world/.

Bibliography

Acosta, Alberto. 2020. "De las teorías de la dependencia al buen vivir. Reflexionando para salir de la trampa del 'Desarrollo.'" In Tahina Ojeda Medina and María Villarreal Villamar, eds., *Pensamiento crítico latinoamericano sobre desarrollo*, 11–27. Madrid: Los Libros de la Catarata/Instituto Universitario de Desarrollo y Cooperación.
Acosta-Ormaechea, Santiago, Gustavo Adler, Ilan Goldfajn, and Anna Ivanova. 2022. "Latin America Faces a Third Shock as Global Financial Conditions Tighten." *IMF Blog* (13

October), https://www.imf.org/en/Blogs/Articles/2022/10/13/latin-america-faces-a-third-shock-as-global-financial-conditions-tighten, accessed 10 January 2024.

Acosta-Ormaechea, Santiago, Isabela Duarte, and Samuel Pienknagura. 2022. "Productivity in Latin America and the Caribbean: Recent Trends and the COVID-19 Shock." Background paper for the October 2022 *Regional Economic Outlook: Western Hemisphere*. Washington, DC: International Monetary Fund.

Adato, Michelle, and John Hoddinott, eds. 2010. *Conditional Cash Transfers in Latin America*. Washington, DC: International Food Policy Research Institute.

Adler, Gustavo, Nigel Chalk, and Anna Ivanova. 2023. "Latin America Faces Slowing Growth and High Inflation Amid Social Tensions." *IMF Blog* (1 February), https://www.imf.org/en/Blogs/Articles/2023/02/01/latin-america-faces-slowing-growth-and-high-inflation-amid-social-tensions, accessed 10 January 2024.

Alacevich, Michele. 2021. "In Praise of Possibility." *Aeon* (3 August), https://aeon.co/essays/from-probable-to-possible-the-ideas-of-albert-o-hirschman, accessed 15 February 2024.

Alberola, Enrique, Iván Kataryniuk, Ángel Melguizo, and René Orozco. 2017. "Fiscal Policy and the Cycle in Latin America: The Role of Financing Conditions and Fiscal Rules." *OECD Development Centre Working Paper* No. 336. Paris: OECD Publishing, https://doi.org/10.1787/3c20eec1-en.

Alesina, Alberto, and Dani Rodrik. 1994. "Distributive Politics and Economic Growth." *Quarterly Journal of Economics* 109(2): 465–90. https://doi.org/10.2307/2118470.

Alesina, Alberto, and Guido Tabellini. 1990. "A Positive Theory of Fiscal Deficits and Government Debt." *Review of Economic Studies* 57: 3 (July), 403–414.

Alesina, Alberto, and Roberto Perotti. 1996. "Income Distribution, Political Instability, and Investment." *European Economic Review* 40(6): 1203–28.

Alfaro, Laura, Sebnem Kalemli-Ozcan, and Vadym Volosovych. 2008. "Why Doesn't Capital Flow from Rich to Poor Countries? An Empirical Investigation." *Review of Economics and Statistics* 90 (2): 347–368.

Amsden, Alice H. 1989. *Asia's Next Giant: South Korea and Late Industrialization*. Oxford and New York: Oxford University Press.

Appendino, Maximiliano, Ilan Goldfajn, and Samuel Pienknagura. 2022. "Latin America Hit By One Inflationary Shock On Top of Another." *IMF News* (15 April), https://www.imf.org/en/News/Articles/2022/04/15/cf-latin-america-hit-by-one-inflationary-shock-on-top-of-another, accessed 10 January 2024.

Arrow, Kenneth J. 1951. "An Extension of the Basic Theorems of Classical Welfare Economics." *Berkeley Symposium on Mathematical Statistics and Probability*, Vol. 2: 507–532.

Arrow, Kenneth J. 1962. "The Economic Implications of Learning by Doing." *The Review of Economic Studies* 29(3): 155–173.

Avendaño, Rolando, and Jeff Dayton-Johnson. 2015. "Central America, China, and the US: What Prospects for Development?" *Pacific Affairs* 88 (4): 813–847.

Bai, Xiwen, Jesús Fernández-Villaverde, Yiliang Li, and Francesco Zanetti. 2023. "The Causal Effects of Global Supply Chain Disruptions on Macroeconomic Outcomes: Evidence and Theory." Unpub. ms., University of Pennsylvania.

Banerjee, Abhijit V., and Andrew F. Newman. 1993. "Occupational Choice and the Process of Development." *Journal of Political Economy* 101(2): 274–298.

Bardhan, Pranab. 2016. "State and Development: The Need for a Reappraisal of the Current Literature." *Journal of Economic Literature* 54(3): 862–892, http://dx.doi.org/10.1257/jel.20151239.

Bardhan, Pranab. 2022. *A World of Insecurity: Democratic Disenchantment in Rich and Poor Countries.* Cambridge, MA, and London: Harvard University Press.

Bargain, Olivier, and Ulugbek Aminjonov. 2021. "Poverty and COVID-19 in Africa and Latin America." *World Development* 142 (June), https://doi.org/10.1016/j.worlddev.2021.105422, accessed 23 May 2024.

Barnett, Steven. 2014. "China: Size Matters." *IMF Blog* (26 March), https://blogs.imf.org/2014/03/26/china-size-matters/, accessed 16 February 2020.

Bénabou, Roland. 1996. "Inequality and Growth." *NBER Macroeconomics Annual* 11: 11–92.

Benhabib, Jess, and Aldo Rustichini. 1996. "Social Conflict and Growth." *Journal of Economic Growth* 1(1): 125–142.

Berr, Éric, and Luiz Carlos Bresser Pereira. 2018. "Du développementisme classique au nouveau développementisme." In *L'Économie post-keynésienne : Histoire, théories et politiques*, edited by Éric Berr, Virginie Monvoisin and Jean-François Ponsot, 413–427. Paris: Éditions du Seuil.

Berr, Éric. 2017. *L'intégrisme économique.* Paris: Éditions Les Liens Qui Libèrent.

Bethell, Leslie. 2010. "Brazil and 'Latin America.'" *Journal of Latin American Studies* 42(3): 457–486.

Bhagwati, Jagdish N. 1984. Comment on Prebisch (1984), 197–204.

Black, Jan Knippers. 2002. "Exorcising the Ghost of Pinochet." *Revista Europea de Estudios Latinoamericanos y Del Caribe / European Review of Latin American and Caribbean Studies*, no. 73: 105–11. JSTOR, http://www.jstor.org/stable/25675991, accessed 16 February 2024.

Black, Jan Knippers. 2005. "The Empire Strikes Out?: Western Hemisphere Lessons in Empire-building and Maintenance." *Journal of Developing Societies* 21(3–4): 281–299.

Blanchard, Olivier J., and Ben S. Bernanke. 2023. "What Caused the US Pandemic-Era Inflation?" *NBER Working Paper* No. 31417 (June). Cambridge, Mass.: National Bureau of Economic Research.

Blinder, Alan S. 2013. *After the Music Stopped: The Financial Crisis, the Response, and the Work Ahead.* New York: Penguin.

Borges, Jorge Luis. 2011. *Obras completas*, 4 volumes. Buenos Aires: Editorial Sudamericana.

Bringel, Breno, and Enara Echart Muñoz. 2020. "Imaginarios sobre el Desarrollo en América Latina: Entre la emancipación y la adaptación al capitalismo." In Tahina Ojeda Medina and María Villarreal Villamar, eds., *Pensamiento crítico latinoamericano sobre desarrollo*, 55–73. Madrid: Los Libros de La Catarata / Instituto Universitario de Desarrollo y Cooperación, Universidad Complutense.

Bruton, Henry. 1989. "Import Substitution." In Hollis Chenery and T.N. Srinivasan, eds., *Handbook of Development Economics*, vol. 2, 1601–44. Amsterdam: Elsevier.

Buera, Francisco J., and Juan Pablo Nicolini. 2021. "The History of Argentina." In Timothy J.

Kehoe and Juan Pablo Nicolini, eds. *The Monetary and Fiscal History of Latin America, 1960–2017*, 45–69, with comments by Guillermo Calvo, 71–74, and Andrew Powell, 75–80. Minneapolis, MN, and London: University of Minnesota Press.

Bull, Benedicte, and Antulio Rosales. 2023. "How Sanctions Led to Authoritarian Capitalism in Venezuela." *Current History* 122 (841): 49–55, https://doi.org/10.1525/curh.2023.122.841.49.

Cabot, Diego. 2023. "Déficit fiscal, una adicción de la que la Argentina nunca pudo salir." *La Nación* (17 December).

CAF [CAF Development Bank for Latin America and the Caribbean]. 2022. *Desigualdades heredadas: El rol de las habilidades, el empleo y la riqueza en las oportunidades de las nuevas generacion, Reporte de Economía y Desarrollo 2022*. Caracas: Corporación Andina de Fomento.

Cagan, Phillip. 1956. "The Monetary Dynamics of Hyperinflation." In Milton Friedman, ed., *Studies in the Quantity Theory of Money*, 25–117. Chicago: University of Chicago Press.

Calcagno, Adriana. 2023. "How Industrialization Became the Core of Raúl Prebisch's Thought." *Journal of the History of Economic Thought* 45(4): 625–46. https://doi.org/10.1017/S1053837222000670.

Calvo, Guillermo A., Alejandro Izquierdo, and Luis-Fernando Mejía. 2004. "On the Empirics of Sudden Stops: The Relevance of Balance-Sheet Effects." NBER Working Paper No. 10520, Cambridge, MA: National Bureau of Economic Research.

Campos-Vazquez, Raymundo M., and Gerardo Esquivel. 2023. "The Effect of the Minimum Wage on Poverty: Evidence from a Quasi-Experiment in Mexico." *Journal of Development Studies* 59(3): 360–80, doi:10.1080/00220388.2022.2130056.

Caputo, Rodrigo, and Diego Saravia. 2021. "The History of Chile." In Timothy J. Kehoe and Juan Pablo Nicolini, eds., *A Monetary and Fiscal History of Latin America, 1960–2017*, 199–230; with discussion by Sebastián Edwards, 231–242. Minneapolis, MA, and London: University of Minnesota Press.

Cárdenas, Mauricio, and Eduardo Levy Yeyati. 2011. "Commentary: Curbing Success in Latin America." Washington, DC: The Brookings Institution (14 April), https://www.brookings.edu/articles/curbing-success-in-latin-america/.

Cárdenas, Mauricio, Homi Kharas, and Camila Henao Arbelaez. 2015. "Latin America's Global Middle Class: A Preference for Growth over Equality." In Jeff Dayton-Johnson, ed., *Latin America's Emerging Middle Classes: Economic Perspectives*, International Political Economy Series, 51–69. Houndmills, Basingstoke: Palgrave Macmillan.

Carey, Lachlan. 2023. "Green Industrial Strategy," *Phenomenal World*, 20 May, https://www.phenomenalworld.org/analysis/green-industrial-strategy/.

Carranza, Luis. 2012. "Politics of Fiscal Reforms in Peru." In Javier Santiso and Jeff Dayton-Johnson, eds. *The Oxford Handbook of Latin American Political Economy*, 43–67. New York: Oxford University Press.

Carvalho, Laura. 2018. *Valsa brasileira: Do boom ao caos econômico*. São Paulo: Todavia.

Casanova, Lourdes. 2009. *Global Latinas: Latin America's Emerging Multinationals.* Fountainebleau/Houndmills, Basingstoke: INSEAD Business Press/Palgrave Macmillan.

Casanova, Lourdes, Jeff Dayton-Johnson, Nils Olaya Fonstad, and Sukriti Jain. 2016. "Innovation in Emerging Markets: The Case of Latin America." In Jerry Haar and Ricardo Ernst, eds., *Innovation in Emerging Markets*, International Political Economy Series, 72–86. Houndmills, Basingstoke: Palgrave Macmillan.

Casanova, Lourdes, and Matthew Fraser. n.d. *From Multilatinas to Global Latinas: The New Latin American Multinationals (Compilation Case Studies).* Washington, DC: Inter-American Development Bank.

Casanova, Lourdes, and Henrique B. Renck. 2015. "Business Sector Responses to the Rise of the Middle Class." In Jeff Dayton-Johnson, ed., *Latin America's Emerging Middle Classes: Economic Perspectives*, International Political Economy Series, 150–172. Houndmills, Basingstoke: Palgrave Macmillan.

Casey, Michael. 2004. "China Builds Trade Ties with South America." *Wall Street Journal* (19 November), https://www.wsj.com/articles/SB110081955662978642, accessed 2 March 2024.

Cason, Jeffrey W., and Sunder Ramaswamy. 2003. "An Introduction to the Debates." In Sunder Ramaswamy and Jeffrey W. Cason, eds., *Development and Democracy: New Perspectives on an Old Debate*, 3–16. Hanover, NH, and London: Middlebury Bicentennial Series in International Studies, Middlebury College Press, published by University Press of New England.

Castañeda Garza, Diego. 2024. *Desiguales: Una historia de la desigualdad en México.* Mexico City: Debate/Penguin Random House.

Castro, Lucio. 2012. "Variedades de primarización, recursos naturales y diferenciación: el desafío de Sudamérica en la relación con China." *Apuntes: Revista de Ciencias Sociales* 39(71): 61–98.

CEPAL [Comisión Económica para América Latina y el Caribe]. 1949. *El desarrollo económico de América Latina y algunos de sus principales problemas.* Lake Success, NY: Comisión Económica para América Latina de las Naciones Unidas.

CEPAL [Comisión Económica para América Latina y el Caribe]. 2018. *Medición de la pobreza por ingresos: actualización metodológica y resultados*, Metodologías de la CEPAL, N° 2 (LC/PUB.2018/22-P). Santiago: Economic Commission for Latin America and the Caribbean, United Nations.

CEPAL [Comisión Económica para América Latina y el Caribe]. 2021. *Panorama Social de América Latina 2020* (LC/PUB.2021/2-P/Rev.1). Santiago: Economic Commission for Latin America and the Caribbean, United Nations.

Cheatham, Amelia, and Diana Roy. 2023. "Venezuela: The Rise and Fall of a Petrostate." New York: Council on Foreign Relations, https://www.cfr.org/backgrounder/venezuela-crisis, accessed 13 May 2024.

Chinn, Menzie D., and Hiro Ito. 2006. "What Matters for Financial Development? Capital Controls, Institutions, and Interactions." *Journal of Development Economics* 81:1, 163–192, dataset available at https://web.pdx.edu/~ito/Chinn-Ito_website.htm.

Chudnovsky, Daniel, and Andrés López. 2007. *The Elusive Quest for Growth in Argentina*, Houndmills, Basingstoke: Palgrave Macmillan.

Clark, Patrick, and Antulio Rosales. 2023. "Broadened Embedded Autonomy and Latin America's Pink Tide: Towards the Neo-Developmental State." *Globalizations* 20, no. 1: 20–37. doi:10.1080/14747731.2022.2032986.

CNN Chile. 2013. "Bachelet: (Hugo Chávez) siempre fue un gran amigo y gran colega." CNN Chile, March 6, 2013, https://www.youtube.com/watch?v=dQBRCGN3Cm4.

Coatsworth, John H. 1978. "Obstacles to Economic Growth in Nineteenth-Century Mexico." *American Historical Review* 83(1): 80–100.

Coelho, Marcelo. 2013. "Manifestações expõem o fato de que o poder não muda." *Folha de São Paulo* (6 July), http://www1.folha.uol.com.br/cotidiano/2013/07/1307302-opiniao-manifestacoes-expoem-o-fato-de-que-o-poder-nao-muda.shtml, accessed 1 March 2024.

Cohen, Daniel. 2024. *Une brève histoire de l'économie*. Paris: Éditions Albin Michel.

Collier, Paul. 2015. "Development Economics in Retrospect and Prospect." *Oxford Review of Economic Policy* 31(2): 242–258.

Coronil, Fernando. 2011. "State Reflections: The 2002 Coup against Hugo Chávez." In Thomas Ponniah and Jonathan Eastwood, eds., *The Revolution in Venezuela: Social and Political Change under Chávez*, The David Rockefeller Center Series on Latin American Studies, 37–66. Cambridge, MA, and London: Harvard University Press.

Correa, Rafael. 2019. "L'Équateur, un nouvel imaginaire politique. Le développement comme processus politique." *Mondes en Développement* 2019/4, no. 188, 107–126.

Cortés Hernández, Alberto Elihú. 2024. "El zapatismo sigue siendo una opcion: especialista IBERO" (interview with Martha Areli Ramírez Sánchez). Mexico City: Universidad Iberoamericana, https://ibero.mx/prensa/el-zapatismo-sigue-siendo-una-opcion-especialista-ibero, accessed 1 May 2024.

Coutinho, Luciano, João Carlos Ferraz, André Nassif, and Rafael Oliva. 2012. "Industrial Policy and Economic Transformation." In Javier Santiso and Jeff Dayton-Johnson, eds., *The Oxford Handbook of Latin American Political Economy*, 100–132. Oxford and New York: Oxford University Press.

Crenshaw, Kimberlé. 2014. *On Intersectionality: Essential Writings*. New York: The New Press.

Criales, José Pablo. 2024. "Javier Milei se enfrenta a una inflación anual en Argentina del 211,4%, superior a la de Venezuela." *El País* (11 January), https://elpais.com/argentina/2024-01-11/argentina-cierra-2023-con-una-inflacion-del-2114-y-supera-a-venezuela.html, accessed 7 March 2024.

Dadush, Uri, and Shimelse Ali. 2012. "In Search of the Global Middle Class: A New Index." *The Carnegie Papers: International Economics*. Washington, DC: Carnegie Endowment for International Peace.

Daude, Christian. 2010. "Innovation, Productivity and Economic Development in Latin America and the Caribbean." OECD Development Centre *Working Papers* 288. Paris: OECD Publishing.

Daude, Christian, Jeff Dayton-Johnson, and Ángel Melguizo. 2013. "Legitimidad fiscal y protestas en la calle: sobre Brasil y América Latina." Vox.LACEA, Latin American and Caribbean Economic Association, https://vox.lacea.org/?q=cambios_politica_fiscal_brasil, accessed 19 April 2024.

Daude, Christian and Eduardo Fernández-Arias. 2010. "On the Role of Productivity and Factor Accumulation in Economic Development in Latin America and the Caribbean." OECD Development Centre *Working Papers* 290. Paris: OECD Publishing.

Daude, Christian, Hamlet Gutiérrez and Ángel Melguizo. 2015. "Political Attitudes of the Middle Class: The Case of Fiscal Policy." In Jeff Dayton-Johnson, ed. *Latin America's Emerging Middle Classes: Economic Perspectives*, International Political Economy Series, 186–204. Houndmills, Basingstoke: Palgrave Macmillan.

Daude, Christian, and Ángel Melguizo. 2012. "Taxation and Democracy in Latin America." In Javier Santiso and Jeff Dayton-Johnson, eds. *The Oxford Handbook of Latin American Political Economy*, 532–556. New York: Oxford University Press.

Davoodi Hamid R., Paul Elger, Alexandra Fotiou, Daniel Garcia-Macia, Xuehui Han, Andresa Lagerborg, W. Raphael Lam, and Paulo Medas. 2022b. "Fiscal Rules and Fiscal Councils: Recent Trends and Performance during the Pandemic." *IMF Working Paper* No. 22/11. Washington, DC: International Monetary Fund.

Davoodi, Hamid R., Paul Elger, Alexandra Fotiou, Daniel Garcia-Macia, Andresa Lagerborg, W. Raphael Lam, and Sharanya Pillai. 2022a. *Fiscal Rules Dataset: 1985–2021*. Washington, DC: International Monetary Fund.

Dayton-Johnson, Jeff. 2000. "What's Different About Cultural Products? An Economic Framework." Report prepared for the Strategic Research and Analysis unit of the Department of Canadian Heritage, Government of Canada. https://publications.gc.ca/collections/collection_2010/pc-ch/CH4-150-2010-eng.pdf.

Dayton-Johnson, Jeff. 2001. *Social Cohesion and Economic Prosperity*. Toronto: James Lorimer.

Dayton-Johnson, Jeff. 2003. "Knitted Warmth: The Simple Analytics of Social Cohesion." *Journal of Behavioral and Experimental Economics* (formerly *Journal of Socio-Economics*) 32(6):623–645.

Dayton-Johnson, Jeff. 2004. "Natural Disasters and Adaptive Capacity." OECD Development Centre *Working Paper* No. 237. Paris: OECD Publishing.

Dayton-Johnson, Jeff. 2006. "Natural Disaster and Vulnerability." OECD Development Centre *Policy Brief* No. 29. Paris: OECD Publishing.

Dayton-Johnson, Jeff. 2008a. "El efecto jazz y la economía latinoamericana." *Clarín* (6 October): 17.

Dayton-Johnson, Jeff. 2008b. "Taxes and Spending in Latin America: First Stability, Now Development." *Policy Insights*, no. 77 (October). Paris: OECD Development Centre.

Dayton-Johnson, Jeff. 2008/2009. "Is Fiscal Policy Back? An Emerging Market Perspective." *OECD Observer*, no. 270/271 (December 2008/January 2009), 10–11.

Dayton-Johnson, Jeff. 2015. "Making Sense of Latin America's Middle Classes." In Jeff Dayton-Johnson, ed. *Latin America's Emerging Middle Classes: Economic Perspectives*, International Political Economy Series, 1–31. Houndmills, Basingstoke: Palgrave Macmillan.

Dayton-Johnson, Jeff. 2018. "Shaking Up Governance and Inequality in South America: A Political-Economy Account." In Pía Riggirozzi and Christopher Wylde, eds. *Handbook of South American Governance*, 321–333. London and New York: Routledge.

Dayton-Johnson, Jeff, and Louka T. Katseli. 2006. "Migration, Aid and Trade: Policy Coherence for Development." OECD Development Centre *Policy Briefs* No. 28. Paris: OECD Publishing, https://doi.org/10.1787/206328060646.

Dayton-Johnson, Jeff, Juliana Londoño Vélez, and Sebastián Nieto-Parra. 2011. "The Process of Reform in Latin America: A Review Essay." OECD Development Centre Working Papers No. 304. Paris: OECD Publishing, https://doi.org/10.1787/5kg3mkvfcjxv-en.

De Ferranti, David, Guillermo E. Perry, Francisco H.G. Ferreira, and Michael Walton. 2004. *Inequality in Latin America: Breaking with History?* Washington, DC: World Bank.

de Janvry, Alain, Marco Gonzalez-Navarro, and Elisabeth Sadoulet. 2014. "Are Land Reforms Granting Complete Property Rights Politically Risky? Electoral Outcomes of Mexico's Certification Program." *Journal of Development Economics* 110, 216–225, https://doi.org/10.1016/j.jdeveco.2013.04.003.

de la Fuente Lora, Gerardo. 1994. "El pensamiento económico latinoamericano." *Problemas del Desarrollo*, vol. 25, no. 98, 55–93.

De Rosa, Mauricio, Ignacio Flores, and Marc Morgan. 2020a. "Inequality in Latin America Revisited: Insights from Distributional National Accounts." *Issue Brief* 2020/09. Paris: World Inequality Lab.

De Rosa, Mauricio, Ignacio Flores, and Marc Morgan. 2020b. "Inequality in Latin America Revisited: Insights from Distributional National Accounts." *Technical Note* N° 2020/02. Paris: World Inequality Lab.

De Sousa Pinto, Ana Estela. 2020. "América Latina é o atual epicentro da pandemia, diz OMS." *Folha de São Paulo* (23 May), p. B1.

Debreu, Gérard. 1959. *Theory of Value: An Axiomatic Analysis of Economic Equilibrium*, a Cowles Foundation Monograph. New Haven, CT, and London: Yale University Press.

Delcas, Marie. 2011. "Pour le président colombien, Juan Manuel Santos, 'l'Amérique latine offre tout ce dont le monde a besoin.'" *Le Monde* (22 January), https://www.lemonde.fr/ameriques/article/2011/01/22/pour-le-president-colombien-juan-manuel-santos-l-amerique-latine-offre-tout-ce-dont-le-monde-a-besoin_1469091_3222.html, accessed 7 March 2024.

Deléchat, Corinne, and Leandro Medina. 2020. "What is the Informal Economy?" *F&D: Finance & Development* (December). Washington, DC: International Monetary Fund.

Delgado, Guilherme C., and Sergio Pereira Leite. 2022. "O agro é tudo? Pacto do agronegócio e reprimarização da economia." *Revista Rosa*. Hors-série number of Volume 6. revistarosa.com.

DeYoung, Karen. 2014. "Obama moves to normalize relations with Cuba as American is released by Havana." *Washington Post* (17 December), https://www.washingtonpost.

com/world/national-security/report-cuba-frees-american-alan-gross-after-5-years-detention-on-spy-charges/2014/12/17/a2840518-85f5-11e4-a702-fa31ff4ae98e_story.html, accessed 23 January 2024.
Dubé, Ryan. 2016. "Odebrecht Bribery Scandal Shakes Up Latin America." *Wall Street Journal* (22 December).
Dubé, Ryan, and Anthony Harrup. 2023. "Rates Fall in Latin America." *Wall Street Journal* (18 August), p. A8.
Duff-Brown, Beth. 2022. "How Has Africa Largely Evaded the COVID-19 Pandemic?" reporting on the research of Tofunmi Omiye, *Stanford Health Policy News* (27 April), https://healthpolicy.fsi.stanford.edu/news/how-has-africa-largely-evaded-covid-19-pandemic-0, accessed 1 January 2024.
Easterly, William. 2001. "The Middle Class Consensus and Economic Development." *Journal of Economic Growth* 6(4): 317–35. http://www.jstor.org/stable/40216047.
Eatwell, John. 1987. "Import Substitution and Export-Led Growth." In John Eatwell, Murray Milgate, and Peter Newman, eds., *The New Palgrave Dictionary of Economics*. London: Palgrave Macmillan, https://doi.org/10.1057/978-1-349-95121-5_1141-1, accessed 10 May 2024.
Économistes atterrés, les. 2022. *De quoi avons-nous vraiment besoin?* Paris: Éditions Les Liens Qui Libèrent.
Elizondo, Carlos, and Javier Santiso. 2012. "Killing Me Softly: Local Termites and Fiscal Violence in Brazil and Mexico." In Javier Santiso and Jeff Dayton-Johnson, eds. *The Oxford Handbook of Latin American Political Economy*, 457–502. New York: Oxford University Press.
Ellingwood, Ken, and Tracy Wilkinson. 2012. "Enrique Peña Nieto wins Mexico's presidency, early results show." *Los Angeles Times* (2 July), https://www.latimes.com/nation/la-xpm-2012-jul-02-la-fg-mexico-presidential-election-20120702-story.html, accessed 1 March 2024.
Engbom, Niklas, and Christian Moser. 2022. "Earnings Inequality and the Minimum Wage: Evidence from Brazil." *American Economic Review* 112 (12): 3803–47.
Eslava, Marcela. 2012. "The Political Economy of Public Spending and Fiscal Deficits: Lessons for Latin America." In Javier Santiso and Jeff Dayton-Johnson, eds. *The Oxford Handbook of Latin American Political Economy*, 503–531. New York: Oxford University Press.
Evans, Peter B. 1995. *Embedded Autonomy: States and Industrial Transformation*. Princeton, NJ: Princeton University Press.
Fajardo, Margarita. 2022. *The World That Latin America Created: The United Nations Economic Commission for Latin America in the Development Era* (Harvard Historical Studies 192). Cambridge, MA, and London: Harvard University Press.
Fajnzylber, Fernando. 1983. *La industrialización trunca de América Latina*. Mexico City: Nueva Imagen.
Feierherd, Germán, Patricio Larroulet, Wei Long, and Nora Lustig. 2023. "The Pink Tide and Income Inequality in Latin America." *Latin American Politics and Society* 65(2): 110–44, https://doi.org/10.1017/lap.2022.47.

Fernández-Arias, Eduardo, and Nicolás Fernández-Arias. 2021. "The Latin American Growth Shortfall: Productivity and Inequality." *UNDP LAC Working Paper* No. 04. Background Paper for the UNDP *LAC Regional Human Development Report* 2021. New York: United Nations Development Programme.

Fernández-Villaverde, Jesús, Gustavo Ventura, and Wen Yao. 2024. "The Wealth of Working Nations." Unpub. ms., Dept. of Economics, University of Pennsylvania.

Ffrench-Davis, Ricardo. 2016. "Progresos y retrocesos del desarrollo económico de Chile en los gobiernos de la Concertación: 1990–2009." *El Trimestre Económico* 83 (329): 5–34, https://doi.org/10.20430/ete.v83i329.190.

Fishlow, Albert. 1990. "The Latin American State." *Journal of Economic Perspectives* 4(3), Summer 1990, 61–74.

Foucart, Stéphane. 2024. "Le libéralisme, une forme de théologie où le marché est érigé en dieu tout puissant." *Le Monde* (22 March).

Franko, Patrice. 2019. *The Puzzle of Latin American Economic Development*, fourth edition. Lanham, MD: Rowman & Littlefield.

Frey, Anderson. 2019. "Cash Transfers, Clientelism, and Political Enfranchisement: Evidence from Brazil." *Journal of Public Economics* 176, August, 1–17. https://doi.org/10.1016/j.jpubeco.2019.05.002.

Friedman, Milton. 1962. *Capitalism and Freedom*. Chicago: University of Chicago Press.

Furtado, Celso. 1972. *Análise do 'modelo' brasileiro*. Rio de Janeiro: Editora Paz e Terra.

Furtado, Celso. 1974. *O mito do desenvolvimento econômico*, Rio de Janeiro: Editora Paz e Terra.

Gallagher, Kevin P. 2012. "A Catalyst for Hope: China's Opportunity for Latin America." In Javier Santiso and Jeff Dayton-Johnson, eds., *Oxford Handbook of Latin American Political Economy*, 333–363. New York: Oxford University Press.

Gallagher, Kevin P., and Amos Irwin. 2017. "China's Economic Statecraft in Latin America: Evidence from China's Policy Banks." In Margaret Myers and Carol Wise, eds., *The Political Economy of China-Latin America Relations in the New Millennium: Brave New World*, 50–68. New York and London: Routledge.

Gallón, Natalie. 2020. "Bodies are being left in the streets in an overwhelmed Ecuadorian city." CNN (3 April), https://www.cnn.com/2020/04/03/americas/guayaquil-ecuador-overwhelmed-coronavirus-intl/index.html, accessed 23 January 2024.

Galor, Oded, and Joseph Zeira. 1993. "Income Distribution and Macroeconomics." *Review of Economic Studies* 60(1): 35–52.

Gavin, Michael, and Roberto Perotti. 1997. "Fiscal Policy in Latin America." *NBER Macroeconomics Annual* 12, 11–72.

Ghezzi, Piero, Juan Carlos Hallak, Ernesto Stein, Romina Ordoñez, and Lina Salazar, coords. 2022. *Competing in Agribusiness. Corporate Strategies and Public Policies for the Challenges of the 21st Century*, Latin American and Caribbean Microeconomic Report. Washington, DC: Inter-American Development Bank.

Goldin, Claudia, and Lawrence F. Katz. 2007a. "Long-Run Changes in the Wage Structure: Narrowing, Widening, Polarizing." *Brookings Papers on Economic Activity* 38(2): 135–167.

Goldin, Claudia, and Lawrence F. Katz. 2007b. "The Race Between Education and Technology: The Evolution of U.S. Educational Wage Differentials, 1890 to 2005." *NBER Working Paper* No. 12984. Cambridge, MA: National Bureau of Economic Research.

Goldin, Claudia, and Lawrence F. Katz. 2008. *The Race Between Education and Technology.* Cambridge, MA, and London: Harvard University Press.

González Casanova, Pablo. 1963. "Sociedad plural, colonialismo interno y desarrollo." *América Latina: Revista del Centro Latinoamericano de Investigaciones en Ciencias Sociales* 6(3): 15–32.

González, Darío. 2023. "Imposición al Patrimonio Global: hacia una mayor equidad del sistema tributario latinoamericano." Panama City: Centro Interamericano de Administraciones Tributarias, https://www.ciat.org/ciatblog-imposicion-al-patrimonio-global-hacia-una-mayor-equidad-del-sistema-tributario-latinoamericano/, accessed 6 May 2024.

Goodman, J. David, and William K. Rashbaum. 2020. "N.Y.C. Death Toll Soars Past 10,000 in Revised Virus Count." *New York Times* (14 April).

Gurría Lacroix, Jorge. 1971. *Hernán Cortés y Diego Rivera* (Serie Historia Moderna y Contemporánea, 10). Mexico City: Instituto de Investigaciones Históricas, Universidad Nacional Autónoma de México.

Gwynne, Robert N. 1986. "The Deindustrialization of Chile, 1974–1984." *Bulletin of Latin American Research* 5(1): 1–23, https://doi.org/10.2307/3338781.

Haber, Stephen, and Victor Menaldo. 2012. "Natural Resources and Democracy in Latin America: Neither Curse nor Blessing." In Javier Santiso and Jeff Dayton-Johnson, eds., *The Oxford Handbook of Latin American Political Economy*, 367–380. New York: Oxford University Press.

Hägglund, Martin. 2019. *This Life: Secular Faith and Spiritual Freedom.* New York: Pantheon Books.

Halperín Donghi, Tulio. 1969. *Historia contemporánea de América Latina.* Madrid: Alianza Editorial.

Hamilton, Nora. 1982. *The Limits of State Autonomy: Post-Revolutionary Mexico.* Princeton, NJ: Princeton University Press.

Harris, Pedro. 2021. "La protección de la naturaleza en Ecuador y Bolivia—Una subjetivación común, pero diferenciada." Asesoría Técnica Parlamentaria, N° SUP: 132263. Santiago: Biblioteca del Congreso Nacional de Chile (October), https://obtienearchivo.bcn.cl/obtienearchivo?id=repositorio/10221/32696/1/Informe.pdf, accessed 7 March 2024.

Hausmann, Ricardo, and Dani Rodrik. 2003. "Economic Development as Self-Discovery." *Journal of Development Economics* 72(2): 603–633, https://doi.org/10.1016/S0304-3878(03)00124-X.

Hines, Sarah T. 2022. *Water for All: Community, Property, and Revolution in Modern Bolivia.* Berkeley, CA, and London: University of California Press.

Hines, Sarah T. 2024. "Dispossession and Redistribution: Social Struggle over Water in Bolivian History." In Rossana Barragán and Carmen Soliz, eds., *Natural Resources in Dispute: Lessons from Bolivia*, Diálogos Series. Albuquerque, NM: University of New Mexico Press.

Human Rights Watch. 2008. *A Decade Under Chávez: Political Intolerance and Lost Opportunities for Advancing Human Rights in Venezuela*. New York, NY: Human Rights Watch. https://www.hrw.org/report/2008/09/18/decade-under-chavez/political-intolerance-and-lost-opportunities-advancing-human.

IDB [Inter-American Development Bank]. 2005. *The Politics of Policies*, Economic and Social Progress in Latin America 2006 Report. Washington, DC, and Cambridge, Mass.: Inter-American Development Bank, and David Rockefeller Center for Latin American Studies, Harvard University.

IEA/IFC [International Energy Agency/International Finance Corporation]. 2023. *Scaling up Private Finance for Clean Energy in Emerging and Developing Economies*. Paris and Washington, DC: International Energy Agency and International Finance Corporation of the World Bank Group.

IMF [International Monetary Fund]. 2003. *The Role of the IMF in Argentina, 1991–2002*, Issues Paper/Terms of Reference for an Evaluation by the Independent Evaluation Office (IEO). Washington, DC: International Monetary Fund (July).

IMF [International Monetary Fund]. 2008. *Balance of Payments Statistics Yearbook, Part 1: Country Tables*. Washington, DC: International Monetary Fund.

IMF [International Monetary Fund]. 2021. *Regional Economic Outlook Western Hemisphere: A Long and Winding Road to Recovery*. Washington, DC: International Monetary Fund (October).

IMF [International Monetary Fund]. 2022. *Regional Economic Outlook Western Hemisphere: Navigating Tighter Global Financial Conditions*. Washington, DC: International Monetary Fund (October).

IMF [International Monetary Fund]. 2023a. *Annual Report on Exchange Arrangements and Exchange Restrictions: Overview 2022*. Washington, DC: International Monetary Fund.

IMF [International Monetary Fund]. 2023b. *Regional Economic Outlook Western Hemisphere: Securing Low Inflation and Nurturing Potential Growth*. Washington, DC: International Monetary Fund (October).

INSEAD/OECD. 2011. *InnovaLatino: Impulsando la Innovación en América Latina*. Madrid/Barcelona: Fundación Telefónica/Editorial Ariel.

Ito, Hiro and Menzie D. Chinn. 2023. "Notes on the Chinn-Ito Financial Openness Index 2021 Update." Unpub. ms., Portland State University, https://web.pdx.edu/~ito/Readme_kaopen2021.pdf.

Iyer, Lakshmi, and Francisco Rodríguez. 2021. "Hyperinflation in Venezuela," case study. Keough School of Global Affairs, University of Notre Dame. doi:10.7274/r0-z7wm-f385.

Jenkins, Rhys. 2008. "Measuring the Competitive Threat from China for Other Southern Exporters." *The World Economy* 31(10): 1351–66.

JHU [Johns Hopkins University Coronavirus Resource Center]. 2023. coronavirus.jhu.edu, accessed January 2024.

Jütting, Johannes, and Juan Ramón de Laiglesia, eds. 2009. *Is Informal Normal? Towards More and Better Jobs in Developing Countries*. Paris: OECD Publishing.

Kay, Cristóbal. 1991. "Reflections on the Latin American Contribution to Development Theory." *Development and Change* 22, 31–68.

Kehoe, Timothy J., and Juan Pablo Nicolini, eds. 2021. *A Monetary and Fiscal History of Latin America, 1960–2017*. Minneapolis, MN, and London: University of Minnesota Press.

Keynes, John Maynard. 1936. *The General Theory of Employment, Interest and Money*. London: Macmillan.

Kharas, Homi, and Brina Seidel. 2018. "What's Happening to the World Income Distribution? The Elephant Chart Revisited." *Global Economy & Development Working Paper* 114. Washington, DC: The Brookings Institution.

Kiguel, Miguel A. 2015. *Las crisis económicas argentinas: Una historia de ajustes y desajustes*. Buenos Aires: Editorial Sudamericana.

King, Martin Luther, Jr. 1967. *Where Do We Go from Here? Chaos or Community*. Boston: Beacon Press.

Klemm, Alexander, Andre Meier, and Sebastián Sosa. 2014. "Taper Tantrum or Tedium: How U.S. Interest Rates Affect Financial Markets in Emerging Economies." *IMF Blog* (22 May), https://www.imf.org/en/Blogs/Articles/2014/05/22/taper-tantrum-or-tedium-how-u-s-interest-rates-affect-financial-markets-in-emerging-economies, accessed 7 March 2024.

Krauss, Clifford. 2001. "Reeling from Riots, Argentina Declares a State of Siege." *New York Times* (20 December), https://www.nytimes.com/2001/12/20/world/reeling-from-riots-argentina-declares-a-state-of-siege.html, accessed 7 March 2024.

Kremer, Michael, Jack Willis, and Yang You. 2022. "Converging to Convergence." *NBER Macroeconomics Annual* 36: 337–412.

Kuznets, Simon. 1955. "Economic Growth and Income Inequality." *American Economic Review* 45(1): 1–28.

Lagarde, Christine. 2015. "Lifting the Small Boats," Address at Grandes Conférences Catholiques, Brussels (17 June). www.imf.org/external/np/speeches/2015/061715.htm, accessed January 2017.

Lahart, Justin. 2024. "How Supply-Chain Snarls Made Everyone Wrong on Inflation." *Wall Street Journal* (4 January).

Larrouqué, Damien. 2019. "Au-delà de la distinction entre politiques d'État et politiques de gouvernement, une réflexion sur le *policy making* et ses évolutions en Amérique latine." *Mondes en développement*, no. 188: 33–50. https://doi.org/10.3917/med.188.0033.

Latinobarómetro. 2023. *Informe 2023: La recesión democrática en América Latina*. Santiago, Chile: Corporación Latinobarometro.

Lesser, Barry. 1991. "When Government Fails, Will the Market Do Better? The Privatization/Market Liberalization Movement in Developing Countries." *Canadian Journal of Development Studies / Revue canadienne d'études du développement* 12(1): 159–172, DOI: 10.1080/02255189.1991.9669427.

Levitsky, Steve. 2003. "From Labor Politics to Machine Politics: The Transformation of Party-Union Linkages in Argentine Peronism, 1983–99." *Latin American Research Review* 38(3): 3–36.

Levy Yeyati, Eduardo. 2022. "Can Anyone Stop Argentina's Great Unraveling?" *Americas Quarterly* (1 August).

Levy Yeyati, Eduardo. 2023. "Can Argentina's Time Bomb Be Defused?" *Americas Quarterly* (16 March).

Lewis, Paul H. 2009. *The Agony of Argentine Capitalism: From Menem to the Kirchners.* Santa Barbara, CA: Praeger.

Lewis, W. Arthur. 1954. "Economic Development with Unlimited Supplies of Labour." *The Manchester School* 22(2): 139–191, https://doi.org/10.1111/j.1467-9957.1954.tb00021.

Lewis, W. Arthur. 1964. *Jamaica's Economic Problems.* Kingston, Jamaica: Gleaner Co. (cited in Lewis, 1984).

Lewis, W. Arthur. 1984. "Development Economics in the 1950s." In Gerald M. Meier and Dudley Seers, eds., *Pioneers in Development*, 119–137. Washington, DC, and New York: World Bank/Oxford University Press.

López-Calva, Luis Felipe, and Nora Lustig, eds. 2010. *Declining Inequality in Latin America: A Decade of Progress?* Washington, DC: Brookings Institution Press.

Lorde, Audre. 1984. *Sister/Outsider: Essays and Speeches.* Berkeley, CA: Crossing Press.

Lucas, Robert E., Jr. 1990. "Why Doesn't Capital Flow from Rich to Poor Countries?" *American Economic Review (Papers and Proceedings)* 80(2): 92–96.

Luhnow, David. 2019. "Latin America's Prospects Dim, Again." *Wall Street Journal* (26 August), p. A2.

Lustig, Nora, Luis Felipe López-Calva, and Eduardo Ortiz-Juárez. 2013. "Deconstructing the Decline in Inequality in Latin America." *Policy Research Working Paper* 6552. Washington, DC: The World Bank.

Lustig, Nora, Valentina Martínez-Pabon, and Carola Pessino. 2023. "Fiscal Policy, Income Redistribution, and Poverty Reduction in Latin America." *IDB Working Paper Series* 1530. Washington, DC: Inter-American Development Bank.

Marcos, Sylvia. 2023. *Una poética de la insurgencia zapatista.* Mexico City: Akal.

Martínez, Carlos, Efren Lemus, and Óscar Martínez. 2023. "Régimen de Bukele desarticula a las pandillas en El Salvador." *El Faro* (3 February), https://elfaro.net/es/202302/el_salvador/26691/R%C3%A9gimen-de-Bukele-desarticula-a-las-pandillas-en-El-Salvador.htm, accessed 22 April 2024.

Mathieu, Edouard, Hannah Ritchie, Esteban Ortiz-Ospina, Max Roser, Joe Hasell, Cameron Appel, Charlie Giattino, and Lucas Rodés-Guirao. 2021. "A global database of COVID-19 vaccinations." *Nature Human Behaviour* 5, 947–953. https://doi.org/10.1038/s41562-021-01122-8, accessed 23 May 2024.

Mazzucato, Mariana, and Dani Rodrik. 2024. "Industrial Policy with Conditionalities: A Taxonomy and Sample Cases." London and Cambridge, Mass.: Institute for Innovation and Public Purpose, University College London, and The Reimagining the Economy Project, Harvard University (April).

McGuire, James W. 1997. *Peronism Without Perón: Unions, Parties, and Democracy in Argentina.* Stanford, CA: Stanford University Press.

McKoy, Jillian. 2022. "Morgue Data Reveal Africa's High COVID-19 Death Toll," reporting on the research of Christopher Gill and Lawrence Mwananyanda. *BU School of Public Health* (14 June), https://www.bu.edu/sph/news/articles/2022/morgue-data-reveals-true-covid-19-death-toll-in-africa/, accessed 23 May 2024.

McLeod, Darryl, and Nora Lustig. 2010. "Inequality and Poverty Under Latin America's New Left Regimes." *Department of Economics Discussion Paper* Series No. 2010:13 (December), Fordham University, https://archive.fordham.edu/ECONOMICS_RESEARCH/PAPERS/dp2010_13_mcleod_lustig.pdf, accessed 15 February 2024.

Melchor, Fernanda. 2017. *Temporada de huracanes.* Mexico City: Random House; English translation 2020. Hurricane Season, translated by Sophie Hughes. New York: New Directions.

Mella, Carolina. 2024. "Noboa logra una victoria rotunda en la pregunta clave de una consulta para enfrentar la espiral de violencia en Ecuador." *El País* (21 April), https://elpais.com/america/2024-04-22/noboa-logra-una-victoria-rotunda-en-la-pregunta-de-una-consulta-para-enfrentar-la-espiral-de-violencia-en-ecuador.html, accessed 22 April 2024.

Milanovic, Branko. n.d. All the Ginis dataset, https://datacatalog.worldbank.org/dataset/all-ginis-dataset, accessed 14 July 2020.

Mineo, Liz. 2021. "From Bad to Worse in Latin America" (interview with Alisha Holland). *The Harvard Gazette* (27 July), https://news.harvard.edu/gazette/story/2021/07/how-the-pandemic-has-affected-latin-america/, accessed 2 January 2024.

Ministry of Foreign Affairs, China. 2004. "Foreign Minister Li Zhaoxing Comments on the Fruitful Results Of President Hu Jintao's Trip to Latin America." Beijing: Ministry of Foreign Affairs of the People's Republic of China (26 November), https://www.fmprc.gov.cn/eng/wjb_663304/zzjg_663340/gjs_665170/gjsxw_665172/200411/t20041126_597071.html, accessed 2 March 2024.

Moleiro, Alonso. 2024. "Venezuela, el país en el que una inflación de 193% puede ser una buena noticia." *El País* (8 January), https://elpais.com/america/2024-01-09/venezuela-el-pais-en-el-que-una-inflacion-de-193-puede-ser-una-buena-noticia.html, accessed 23 May 2024.

Morales, Isidro. 2024. "Mexico's Next Leader Has an Energy Problem," *Foreign Policy,* 29 May, https://foreignpolicy.com/2024/05/29/mexico-presidential-election-economy-energy-pemex-cfe-amlo-sheinbaum-usmca/.

Moreno-Brid, Juan Carlos, Stefanie Garry, and Alice Krozer. 2016. "Minimum Wages and Inequality in Mexico: A Latin American Perspective." *Revista de Economía Mundial* 43, 113–129.

Murillo, María Victoria, and S. J. Rodrigo Zarazaga. 2020. "Argentina: Peronism Returns." *Journal of Democracy* 31(2), 125–136. Project MUSE, https://doi.org/10.1353/jod.2020.0026.

Nación, La. 2008. "Cristina lo bautizó el 'efecto jazz.'" *La Nación* (24 January), https://www.

lanacion.com.ar/economia/cristina-lo-bautizo-el-efecto-jazz-nid981428, accessed 7 October 2019.
Nazaryan, Alexander. 2020. "'They know how to keep people alive': Why China's coronavirus response is better than you think." *Yahoo News* (13 March), https://news.yahoo.com/they-know-how-to-keep-people-alive-why-chinas-coronavirus-response-is-better-than-you-think-211702070.html, accessed 1 January 2024.
Nessi, Hernan. 2024. "Argentina annual inflation tops 211%, highest since early 90s." *Reuters* (11 January), https://www.reuters.com/markets/argentina-annual-inflation-tops-211-highest-since-early-90s-2024-01-11/, accessed 7 March 2024.
Nieto-Parra, Sebastián, and Javier Santiso. 2012. "Revisiting Political Budget Cycles in Latin America." In Javier Santiso and Jeff Dayton-Johnson, eds. *The Oxford Handbook of Latin American Political Economy*, 557–584. New York: Oxford University Press.
OECD [Organisation for Economic Co-operation and Development]. 2007. *Latin American Economic Outlook 2008*. Paris: OECD Publishing.
OECD [Organisation for Economic Co-operation and Development]. 2008. *Latin American Economic Outlook 2009*. Paris: OECD Publishing.
OECD [Organisation for Economic Co-operation and Development]. 2009. *Latin American Economic Outlook 2010*. Paris: OECD Publishing.
OECD [Organisation for Economic Co-operation and Development]. 2010. *Latin American Economic Outlook 2011: How Middle-Class Is Latin America?* Paris: OECD Publishing.
OECD [Organisation for Economic Co-operation and Development]. 2020. *COVID-19 en América Latina y el Caribe: Panorama de las respuestas de los gobiernos a la crisis*. Paris: OECD Publishing.
OECD [Organisation for Economic Co-operation and Development]. 2021. *OECD Economic Outlook*, Volume 2021 Issue 2.
OECD [Organisation for Economic Co-operation and Development]. 2023. *Revenue Statistics in Asia and the Pacific*. Paris: OECD Publishing.
OECD [Organisation for Economic Co-operation and Development]. n.d. "Colombia's path towards OECD accession." https://web-archive.oecd.org/2020-04-29/531972-colombia-accession-to-the-oecd.htm, accessed 7 March 2024.
OECD/CAF/EU [Organisation for Economic Co-operation and Development/CAF Development Bank of Latin America and the Caribbean/European Union]. 2021. *Latin American Economic Outlook 2021: Working Together for a Better Recovery*. Paris: OECD Publishing.
OECD/CEPAL/CAF/EU [Organisation for Economic Co-operation and Development/ Comisión Económica para América Latina y el Caribe/ CAF Development Bank for Latin America and the Caribbean/ European Union]. 2019. *Latin American Economic Outlook 2019: Development in Transition*. Paris: OECD Publishing.
OECD/CIAT/IDB/CEPAL [Organisation for Economic Co-operation and Development, Inter-American Center of Tax Administrations, Inter-American Development Bank and Comisión Económica para América Latina y el Caribe]. 2023. *Revenue*

Statistics in Latin America and the Caribbean 2023. Paris: OECD Publishing, https://doi.org/10.1787/a7640683-en.

Ojeda Medina, Tahina, and María Villarreal Villamar. 2020. "Orígenes y evolución del pensamiento crítico latinoamericano sobre desarrollo." In Tahina Ojeda Medina and María Villarreal Villamar, eds. *Pensamiento crítico latinoamericano sobre desarrollo,* 29–51. Madrid: Los Libros de La Catarata / Instituto Universitario de Desarrollo y Cooperación, Universidad Complutense.

Osborn, Catherine. 2023. "How Oil-Rich Colombia is Trying to Go Green," *Foreign Policy,* 7 November, https://foreignpolicy.com/2023/11/07/colombia-petro-oil-industrial-policy-green-economy-energy-transition/.

Ostrom, Elinor. 1990. *Governing the Commons : The Evolution of Institutions for Collective Action.* Cambridge and New York : Cambridge University Press.

Ostry, Jonathan D., Andrew Berg, and Charalambos G. Tsangarides. 2014. "Redistribution, Inequality and Growth." *IMF Staff Discussion Note* SDN/14/02. Washington, DC: International Monetary Fund.

Oxfam. 2016. *Desterrados: Tierra, poder y desigualdad en América Latina.* Nairobi: Oxfam Internacional.

Palacios, Luisa, and Juan José Guzmán Ayala. 2023. "Financing the Energy Transition in Latin America and the Caribbean: An Incomplete Puzzle." New York: Center on Global Energy Policy, School of International and Public Affairs, Columbia University, https://www.energypolicy.columbia.edu/publications/financing-the-energy-transition-in-latin-america-and-the-caribbean-an-incomplete-puzzle/.

Parker, Dick. 2007. "Chávez and the Search for an Alternative to Neoliberalism." In Steve Ellner and Miguel Tinker Salas, eds., *Venezuela: Hugo Chávez and the Decline of an "Exceptional Democracy",* 60–74. Lanham, MD: Rowman & Littlefield.

Parker, Susan W., and Petra E. Todd. 2017. "Conditional Cash Transfers: The Case of Progresa/ Oportunidades." *Journal of Economic Literature* 55(3): 866–915.

Paz Rada, Eduardo. 2020. "Posdesarrollo y *sumak kawsay.*" In Tahina Ojeda Medina and María Villarreal Villamar, eds., *Pensamiento crítico latinoamericano sobre desarrollo,* 87–104. Madrid: Los Libros de la Catarata/Instituto Universitario de Desarrollo y Cooperación.

Persson, Torsten, and Guido Tabellini. 1994. "Is Inequality Harmful for Growth?" *American Economic Review* 84(3): 600–21. http://www.jstor.org/stable/2118070.

Persson, Torsten, and Lars E. O. Svensson. 1989. "Why a Stubborn Conservative Would Run a Deficit: Policy with Time-Inconsistent Preferences." *Quarterly Journal of Economics* 104(2): 325–45. JSTOR, https://doi.org/10.2307/2937850, accessed 15 January 2024.

Piketty, Thomas. 2013. *Le Capital au XXIe siècle.* Paris: Éditions du Seuil; also 2014. *Capital in the Twenty-First Century,* translated by Arthur Goldhammer. Cambridge, MA, and London: The Belknap Press of Harvard University Press.

Prebisch, Raúl. 1951. *Problemas teóricos y prácticos del crecimiento económico, serie conmemorativa del XXV aniversario de la CEPAL.* Santiago, Chile: Comisión Económica para América Latina, reprinted 1973.

Prebisch, Raúl. 1959. "Commercial Policy in the Under-Developed Countries." *American Economic Review (Papers and Proceedings)* 49(2): 251–273.
Prebisch, Raúl. 1981. *Capitalismo periférico: crisis y transformación*. Mexico City: Fondo de Cultura Económica.
Prebisch, Raúl. 1984. "Five Stages in My Thinking on Development." In Gerald M. Meier and Dudley Seers, eds., *Pioneers in Development*, 175–191. Washington, DC, and New York: World Bank/Oxford University Press.
Presidencia de la Republica del Ecuador. n.d. "Presidente Correa explica en Harvard cómo liberó al Ecuador del poder financiero." https://www.presidencia.gob.ec/presidente-correa-explica-en-harvard-como-libero-al-ecuador-del-poder-financiero/, accessed 16 April 2024.
Pritchett, Lant. 1997. "Divergence, Big Time." *Journal of Economic Perspectives* 11(3): 3–17.
Quenan, Carlos, and Velut, Sébastien, eds. 2014. *Les enjeux du développement en Amérique latine: Dynamiques socioéconomiques et politiques publiques*, second edition. Paris: Agence Française de Développement.
Ranis, Gustav, and John C.H. Fei. 1961. "A Theory of Economic Development." *American Economic Review* 51(4): 533–65, http://www.jstor.org/stable/1812785.
Ray, Debraj. 1998. *Development Economics*. Princeton, N.J.: Princeton University Press.
Reidl, Rachel Beatty, Paul Friesen, Jennifer McCoy, and Kenneth Roberts. 2023. "Democratic Backsliding, Resilience, and Resistance." *World Politics* 75(2), 1–28.
Restuccia, Diego. 2021. "The History of Venezuela." In Timothy J. Kehoe and Juan Pablo Nicolini, eds. *A Monetary and Fiscal History of Latin America*, 495–524, with comments by Luigi Bocola, 525–7, and Fabrizio Perri, 529–35. Minneapolis, MN, and London: University of Minnesota Press.
Reuters. 2019a. "Glencore awarded just $19 million by tribunal in Colombia lawsuit" (27 August), https://www.reuters.com/article/us-glencore-colombia/glencore-awarded-just-19-million-by-tribunal-in-colombia-lawsuit-idUSKCN1VI01N, accessed 19 October 2019.
Reuters. 2019b. "Key Events for the Fed in 2013: The Year of the 'Taper Tantrum.'" Reuters (11 January), https://www.reuters.com/article/idUSKCN1P52A8/, accessed 7 March 2024.
Ricardo, David. 1817. *On the Principles of Political Economy and Taxation*. London: John Murray.
Rivera-Quiñones, Miguel A. 2018. "Dependency Theory and South American governance in post-neoliberal times." In Pía Riggirozzi and Christopher Wylde, eds. *Handbook of South American Governance*, 45–55. London and New York: Routledge.
Roache, Shaun K. 2012. "China's Impact on World Commodity Markets." IMF Working Paper No. 2012/115, Washington, DC: International Monetary Fund.
Rodríguez, Octavio. 1980. *La teoría del subdesarollo de la CEPAL*. Mexico City: Siglo XXI Editores.
Rodrik, Dani. 1996. "Understanding Economic Policy Reform." *Journal of Economic Literature* 34:1, 9–41. *JSTOR*, http://www.jstor.org/stable/2729408, accessed 2 February 2024.

Rodrik, Dani. 2015. "Premature Deindustrialization." *NBER Working Paper* 20935. Cambridge, MA: National Bureau of Economic Research.

Rohter, Larry. 2004. "China Widens Economic Role in Latin America." *New York Times* (20 November), https://www.nytimes.com/2004/11/20/world/asia/china-widens-economic-role-in-latin-america.html, accessed 2 March 2024.

Rohter, Larry. 2005. "With New Chief, Uruguay Veers Left, in a Latin Pattern." *New York Times* (1 March), https://www.nytimes.com/2005/03/01/world/americas/with-new-chief-uruguay-veers-left-in-a-latin-pattern.html, accessed 1 March 2024.

Rouquié, Alain. 2010. *À l'ombre des dictatures. La démocratie en Amérique latine*. Paris : Albin Michel.

Sabel, Charles F., Eduardo Fernández-Arias, Ricardo Hausmann, Andrés Rodríguez-Clare, and Ernesto Stein. 2012. *Export Pioneers in Latin America*. Washington, DC: Inter-American Development Bank.

Saint-Upéry, Marc. 2008. *Le rêve de Bolivar : Le défi des gauches sud-américaines*. Paris : La Découverte.

Sánchez-Ancochea, Diego. 2021. *The Costs of Inequality in Latin America: Lessons and Warnings for the Rest of the World*. London: I.B. Tauris.

Santiso, Javier. 2005. *Amérique latine : Révolutionnaire, libérale, pragmatique*, Collection CERI/Autrement. Paris: Sciences Po/Éditions Autrement; English translation 2006. *Latin America's Political Economy of the Possible: Beyond Good Revolutionaries and Free Marketeers*, translated by Cristina Sanmartín and Elizabeth Murry. Cambridge, MA, and London: MIT Press.

Santiso, Javier. 2008. "La emergencia de las multilatinas." *Revista de la CEPAL* 95, 7–30.

Santiso, Javier. 2013. *The Decade of the Multilatinas*. Cambridge, UK: Cambridge University Press.

Santos, Juan Manuel. 2011. "Intervención del Presidente Santos en el Foro Económico Internacional América Latina y el Caribe." Bogotá: Presidencia de la República de Colombia, http://wsp.presidencia.gov.co/Prensa/2011/Enero/Paginas/20110124_03.aspx, accessed 7 March 2024.

Saragoza, Alex M. 1988. *The Monterrey Elite and the Mexican State, 1880–1940*. Austin, TX, and London: University of Texas Press.

Schorr, Martín. 2023. "Democracia, economía y captura del Estado." *Nueva Sociedad* 308 (November/December), 88–98.

Schwalb, Álvaro, and Carlos Seas. 2021. "The COVID-19 Pandemic in Peru: What Went Wrong?" *American Journal of Tropical Medicine and Hygiene* 104(4): 1176–8.

Schwalb, Álvaro, Eleonora Armyra, Melissa Méndez-Aranda, and César Ugarte-Gil. 2022. "COVID-19 in Latin America and the Caribbean: Two years of the pandemic." *Journal of Internal Medicine* 292(3): 409–27.

Schwartz, Stuart B. 2016. *Sea of Storms: A History of Hurricanes in the Greater Caribbean from Columbus to Katrina*. Princeton, NJ: Princeton University Press.

Semán, Ernesto. 2020. "Argentina: A Tentative Case for Democratic Populism." NACLA, https://nacla.org/news/2020/01/29/argentina-democratic-populism-peronism, accessed 16 April 2024.

Sen, Amartya. 1995. *Inequality Reexamined*. Cambridge, MA, and London: Harvard University Press.
Sen, Amartya. 1999. *Development As Freedom*. New York: Oxford University Press.
Solís, Leopoldo. 1981. *La realidad económica mexicana: retrovisión y perspectivas*, 11th revised edition. Mexico City: Siglo XXI Editores.
Solow, Robert M. 1956. "A Contribution to the Theory of Economic Growth." *Quarterly Journal of Economics* 70(1): 65–94.
Solow, Robert M. 1957. "Technical Change and the Aggregate Production Function." *Review of Economics and Statistics* 39(3): 312–320.
Souroujon, Gastón. 2023. "When Peronism Met the New Right. The Menem Administration (1989–1999). Between Neoliberalism and Neopopulism." In Gisela Pereyra Doval and Gastón Souroujon, eds., *Argentina's Right-Wing Universe During the Democratic Period (1983–2023)*. London: Routledge.
Stampini, Marco, and Leopoldo Tornarolli. 2012. "The Growth of Conditional Cash Transfers in Latin America and the Caribbean: Did They Go Too Far?" Policy Brief No. 185. Washington, DC: Inter-American Development Bank, https://publications.iadb.org/handle/11319/1448.
Stavenhagen Rodolfo. 1981 [1965]. "Siete tesis equivocadas sobre América Latina." In Rodolfo Stavenhagen, *Sociología y subdesarrollo*, 15–84. Mexico City: Nuestro Tiempo ediciones.
Stein, Ernesto, and Lorena Caro. 2017. "Ideology and Taxation in Latin America." *Economia: Journal of the Latin American and Caribbean Economic Association* 17(2): 1–27, https://www.jstor.org/stable/90004156.
Stein, Stanley J., and Barbara H. Stein. 1970. *The Colonial Heritage of Latin America: Essays on Economic Dependence in Perspective*. New York: Oxford University Press.
Svampa, Maristella. 2013. "Consenso de los Commodities y lenguajes de valoración en América Latina." *Nueva Sociedad* 244 (March/April), 30–46. http://nuso.org/articulo/consenso-de-los-commodities-y-lenguajes-de-valoracion-en-america-latina/.
Svampa, Maristella. 2019. *Las fronteras del neoextractivismo en América Latina. Conflictos socioambientales, giro ecoterritorial y nuevas dependencias*. Guadalajara: Centro Maria Sibylla Merian de Estudios Latinoamericanos Avanzados en Humanidades y Ciencias Sociales (CALAS), Universidad de Guadalajara.
Tablada Pérez, Carlos. 1987. *El pensamiento económico de Ernesto Che Guevara*. Havana: Ediciones Casa de las Américas.
Tavares, Maria da Conceição, and José Serra. 1971. "Além da estagnação: uma discussão sobre o estilo de desenvolvimento recente do Brasil." Reprinted in Ricardo Bielschowsky, org. 2000. *Cinqüenta anos de pensamento na CEPAL*, vol. 2, 589–608. Rio de Janeiro: United Nations Economic Commission for Latin America & Conselho Federal de Economia (COFECON)/Editorial Record.
Taylor, Lance. 1997. "Editorial: The Revival of the Liberal Creed—The IMF and the World Bank in a Globalized Economy." *World Development* 25(2): 145–152.
Tello Díaz, Carlos. 1995. *La rebellion de Las Cañadas. Origen y ascenso del EZLN*. Mexico City: Cal y Arena.

Teubal, Miguel. 2004. "Rise and Collapse of Neoliberalism in Argentina: The Role of Economic Groups." *Journal of Developing Societies* 20(3–4): 173–188. https://doi.org/10.1177/0169796X04050957.

Thorp, Rosemary. 2012. "A Historical Perspective on the Political Economy of Inequality in Latin America." In Javier Santiso and Jeff Dayton-Johnson, eds., *The Oxford Handbook of Latin American Political Economy*, 149–167. Oxford and New York: Oxford University Press.

Tigres del Norte, Los. 2001. *Uniendo fronteras*. FonoVisa SDCD 6145, compact disc.

Timiraos, Nick, and Tom Fairless. 2023. "The Outlook: Fed's Effect on Inflation Subject to Debate." *Wall Street Journal* (31 July), p. A2.

Tirole, Jean. 2015. *Économie du bien commun*. Paris: Presses Universitaires de France.

Tollefson, Jeff. 2021. "Illegal Mining in the Amazon Hits Record High Among Indigenous Protests." *Nature*, vol. 598 (7 October), 15–16.

Tommasi, Mariano, and Carlos Scartascini. 2012. "How (Not) to Produce Effective Policies? Institutions and Policymaking in Latin America." In Javier Santiso and Jeff Dayton-Johnson, eds., *Oxford Handbook of Latin American Political Economy*, 263–284. New York: Oxford University Press.

Turzi, Mariano. 2011. "The Soybean Republic." *Yale Journal of International Affairs* 6: 59–68.

Turzi, Mariano. 2017. "The Agropolis: South America, China, and the Soybean Connection." In Margaret Myers and Carol Wise, eds., *The Political Economy of China-Latin America Relations in the New Millennium: Brave New World*, 170–188. New York and London: Routledge.

UNCTAD [United Nations Conference on Trade and Development]. 2020. *External debt sustainability and development, Note by the Secretary-General*, A/75/281, United Nations General Assembly, Seventy-fifth Session. New York: United Nations.

United Nations Statistical Commission. 2022. *ISIC Rev. 3.1: International Standard Industrial Classification of All Economic Activities* (Updated: 21.02.2002). New York: United Nations.

Vaca, Mery. 2009. "Bolivia Promulga Nueva Constitución." BBCMundo.com (7 February), http://news.bbc.co.uk/hi/spanish/latin_america/newsid_7877000/7877041.stm, accessed 7 March 2024.

Valencia, Oscar, and Carolina Ulloa-Suárez. 2022. "Numerical compliance with fiscal rules in Latin American countries." *IDB Working Paper* No. 1345. Washington, DC: Inter-American Development Bank.

Velasco, Andrés, and Eric Parrado. 2012. "The Political Economy of Fiscal Policy: The Experience of Chile." In Javier Santiso and Jeff Dayton-Johnson, eds. *Oxford Handbook of Latin American Political Economy*, 68–99. New York: Oxford University Press.

Velez, Patricia. 2009. "UDPATE 2-Peru wins third investment grade rating." Reuters (16 December), https://www.reuters.com/article/peru-ratings-moodys/udpate-2-peru-wins-third-investment-grade-rating-idUSN1611592020091216, accessed 21 June 2020.

Volpi, Jorge. 2009. *El insomnio de Bolívar: Cuatro consideraciones intempestivas sobre América Latina en el siglo XXI*. Buenos Aires: Debate/Editorial Sudamericana.

Vyas, Kejal, and Ryan Dube. 2021. "In Venezuela, Covid-19 Data Is a State Secret, but Citizens See Many Deaths." *Wall Street Journal* (2 June).
Wall Street Journal. 2021. "About All Those Pandemic Billionaires." *Wall Street Journal* (December 8).
Weisbrot, Mark. 2011. "Venezuela in the Chávez Years: Its Economy and Influence on the Region." In Thomas Ponniah and Jonathan Eastwood, eds., *The Revolution in Venezuela: Social and Political Change under Chávez* (The David Rockefeller Center Series on Latin American Studies), 193–224. Cambridge, MA, and London: Harvard University Press.
Williamson, Jeffrey G. 1999. "Real Wages, Inequality, and Globalization in Latin America Before 1940." *Revista de Historia Económica/Journal of Iberian and Latin American Economic History* 17 (special number): 101–142. doi: 10.1017/S0212610900002287.
Williamson, Jeffrey G. 2015. "Latin American Inequality: Colonial Origins, Commodity Booms or a Missed Twentieth-Century Leveling?" *Journal of Human Development and Capabilities* 16(3): 324–341. https://doi.org/10.1080/19452829.2015.1044821.
Williamson, John. 1990. "What Washington Means by Policy Reform." In John Williamson, ed., *Latin American Adjustment: How Much Has Happened?* Washington, DC: Peterson Institute of International Economics.
Wise, Carol. 2012. "Tratados de libre comercio al estilo chino: los TLC Chile-China y Perú-China." *Apuntes: Revista de Ciencias Sociales* 39(71): 161–88.
Wise, Carol. 2020. *Dragonomics: How Latin America Is Maximizing (or Missing Out on) China's International Development Strategy*. New Haven, CT, and London: Yale University Press.
Wise, Carol, and Margaret Myers. 2017. "Introduction: Political Economy of China-Latin America Relations in the 21st Century." In Margaret Myers and Carol Wise, eds., *The Political Economy of China-Latin America Relations in the New Millennium: Brave New World*, 1–18. New York and London: Routledge.
World Bank. n.d. *World Bank Country and Lending Groups*, https://datahelpdesk.worldbank.org/knowledgebase/articles/906519-world-bank-country-and-lending-groups, accessed 27 June 2023.
Xu, Kuan. 2003. "How Has the Literature on Gini's Index Evolved in the Past 80 Years." *Department of Economics Working Paper*, Halifax, NS: Dalhousie University, http://dx.doi.org/10.2139/ssrn.423200.
Yu, Yongzhen. 2011. "Identifying the Linkages between Major Mining Commodity Prices and China's Economic Growth—Implications for Latin America." *IMF Working Paper* No. 2011/086. Washington, DC: International Monetary Fund.
Zumbrun, Josh. 2023. "Data Tweak Shifts How We View Growth." *Wall Street Journal* (December 23/24).
Zweig, Jason. 2019. "The Intelligent Investor: The Case for Commodities." *Wall Street Journal* (23/24 November), p. B2.

Index

ALBA, 72
Alckmin, Geraldo, 3
Alesina, Alberto, 183
Alessandri, Jorge, 157
Allende, Salvador, 157, 221
Arévalo, Bernardo, 72
Argentina, 2, 3, 55, 149; central bank, 31, 57, 139, 220; Convertibility Plan, 57; Covid-19 in, 116; currency board, 57; democratic transition in, 223; diversification of trading partners, 100; economic crisis (2001), 1; economic recovery (2003), 56–57; economic crisis of 2023, 8; fiscal balance in, 194, 204; inequality in, 171, 174, 178, 180, 181; inflation in, 130, 134, 138–40; Peronist social movements, 227–28, 263n11; public debt, 208; possibilist and left-populist aspects of Kirchner governments, 227–8
Arrow, Kenneth: learning-by-doing model, 41; welfare theorems, 216–18
Aylwin, Patricio, 71
average income. *See* per capita income

Bacha, Edmar, 53
Bachelet, Michelle, 71, 202
balance of payments, 78–82; and transmission of economic shocks, 82–88. *See also* current account; capital/financial account
bananas, 63
Bardhan, Pranab, 231, 239–40, 263n1

BBVA, 160
Bernanke, Ben, 6, 133–34
Bethell, Leslie, 21
Bhagwati, Jagdish, 37
Biden, Joseph R., 236, 238
Blanchard, Olivier, 133–34
BNDES, 239
Bolívar, Simón, 23
Bolivia, 4, 147, 149; Cochabamba water conflict, 226; Constitution of 2009, 4, 246; electoral business cycles, 204; Framework of Mother Earth and Integrated Development to Live Well law, 4; neoextractivism in, 150; non-tax revenues, 198; Rights of Mother Earth law, 4; social movements, 226
Bolsa Família, 10, 174; and clientelism, 227
Bolsonaro, Jair, 8, 20, 231
Borges, Jorge Luis, 252n9, 257n2
Brazil, 2, 149; as part of Latin America, 21; bank recommendations regarding public debt, 3; Caipirinha effect, 4, 47, 84; Covid-19 in, 111; deforestation of Amazon Basin, 8; democratic transition in, 223; electoral business cycles, 204; fiscal balance in, 194; hyperinflation in the twentieth century, 130; industry and manufacturing in, 153; inequality in, 177; minimum wage increase, 174–75; nationwide protests against transport price increases 2013, 6–7;

Brazil (continued)
    "PIBaço", 95; possibilism, 223; protests (2013), 6–7, 230, 249n13. See also Bolsa Família; Workers Party (Brazil)
Bresser Pereira, Luiz Carlos, 238
Brubeck, Dave, 76
Bukele, Nayib, 231

Calderón, Felipe, 20
Calvo, Guillermo, 138, 254n7 (chap. 4)
Canada, 133, 188, 223, 239
capital, definition, 39
capital flows, 39, 57, 68, 102, 125. See also sudden stops
capital goods, 155
capital market imperfections and inequality, 183
capital/financial account, 79; direct investment, 81; measures of exposure, 89; measures of resilience, 100–108; portfolio investment, 85–86
Caputo, Luis, 138
Cárdenas, Lázaro, 19
Cárdenas, Mauricio, 148, 220
Cardoso, Fernando Henrique, 35, 220, 238
Carranza, Luis, 5, 207, 220, 235
Carvalho, Laura, 9
Casanova, Lourdes, 161
Castro, Fidel, 19, 71
Castro, Lucio, 239
Castro, Raúl, 7
Cavallo, Domingo, 2
Cemex, 160
Center-Periphery framework, 32–37, 151, 158; contemporary relevance, 236–37
Central America, commodity exports during Milagrinho, 63
central banks: independence, 136; monetary policy tools available to, 136; responses to twenty-first century inflation, 132–33
CEPAL, 31, 135, 146, 151, 192. See also *El desarrollo económico de la América Latina y algunos de sus principales problemas*; Prebisch, Raúl
Chávez, Hugo, 20, 70–71, 140
Chicago boys, 19, 157, 198; as forerunner of Washington Consensus, 221
Chile: Chile Solidario, 10, 174; Concertación, 71, 185; Covid-19 in, 122; deindustrialization in, 153, 157–58; democratic transition in, 223; fiscal balance in, 194; fiscal rule, 202–3; income redistribution, 185; inequality in, 171–72, 178; mining revenue, 198; possibilism, 221–22; reserve changes during Jazz Effect, 88
China Development Bank, 68
China, 2, 18; Center-Periphery framework and, 237; competition with Latin American exporters in third-country markets, 62, 65; convergence to OECD countries, 58; Covid-19 in, 117; economic growth of, 58, 96; Fiscal Responsibility Law, 202; global commodity prices and, 60; industrialization, 10, 60, 146; inequality levels, 170; policy banks, 68; trade relations with Latin American countries, 2, 67, 254n7; typology of impact on Latin American economies, 66–67; visit of Hu Jintao to Latin America (2004), 2
Chinn-Ito Index, 100–103
Citigroup, 132
Clark, Patrick, 225
Clinton, Bill, 47
coffee, 63
Cohen, Daniel, 26, 28, 45
Coleman, Ornette, 76
Collier, Paul, 48
Colombia: accession to OECD, 5; balance of payments of, 78–84; central bank, 82; Covid-19 in, 116; halting of new oil exploration, 241;

Liberal-Conservative political rivalry, 71; neoextractivism in, 150; non-tax revenues, 198; remittances, 81
colonial heritage (key #1), 16–17
Colosio, Luis Donaldo, 46
Comisión Económica para América Latina y el Caribe. *See* CEPAL
commodities, 2, 10, 18, 145; key #3, 18, 32; and Chinese growth, 60; Commodity Consensus, 147, 179; Commodity Pessimism, 34, 146; commodity-related exports compared with Asia and Africa, 148–9. *See also* bananas; commodity prices; coffee; copper; iron ore; mining; nickel; oil; sisal; soybeans; sugar
commodity prices: during Covid-19, 125, 132; during Hurricane Season, 96; during Milagrinho, 60–61; energy prices, 61; metals prices, 61; soybean prices, 61
conditional cash transfers, 175, 234. *See also* Bolsa Família; social transfers
convergence, 38; in China, 58; of Latin American economies, 68–70, 92–93
coordination failures, 239
copper, 61, 202
CORFO, 162
Coronavirus Response Center at Johns Hopkins University, 112, 113, 115
Correa, Rafael, 20, 226–27
Cortés, Hernán, 15–16
Costa Rica: high-tech exports, 162; inequality in, 172; democratic consolidation, 230
Coutinho, Luciano, 220, 239
Covid-19, 7–8, 111–27; case-fatality rates, 112; economic growth and, 119–21; fatality counts, 115; fatality rates, 115; health care systems and, 116; impact on poverty, 124–27; inflation and, 131–32; informality and, 122–25; Latin American experience, 114–18; mortality indicators and, 112–16; policy responses to, 125–27; record keeping capacity and, 118; unemployment and, 116; vaccination progress, 121–22

Cuauhtémoc brewery, 155, 160
Cuba, 2, 9, 19, 221, 224, 230; normalization of relations with US, 7
current account 79, 81; current transfers and workers' remittances, 81, 85; income balance, 81; measures of exposure, 83, 98; measures of resilience, 97–100; trade balance, 81
current account deficit, as measure of financial/capital account exposure, 98–100

Daude, Christian, 163–65
de la Rúa, Fernando, 1, 139
Debreu, Gérard, 216–18
debt. *See* debt crises; debt sustainability; public debt
debt crises: Argentina (2001), 2; Latin America (1982), 41–42
debt maturity, 107–8
debt sustainability, 103, 205
declining terms of trade, 33, 146
deindustrialization, 153–54, 234; premature deindustrialization, 150–51. *See also* industry; manufacturing
democracy: and development, 215; and possibilism, 230; public support for, 230–33
democratic socialism, 244–45
dependency theory, 35
desarrollismo. *See* High Developmentalism
desenvolvimentismo. *See* High Developmentalism
Desmond, Paul, 76
devaluation, as self-fulfilling prophecy, 46
development: as process of self-discovery, 238–39; defined, 29. *See also*

development pacts; economic growth
development pacts: comparing possibilist and left-populist states, 228; coordination failures and, 240; defined, 225; High Developmentalist, 225; MAS in Bolivia, 226
developmentalism. *See* High Developmentalism
Díaz, Porfirio, 182
Dimon, Jamie, 91
Dominican Republic, 85, 94, 100
Dutch Disease, 34, 146

ECLAC. *See* CEPAL
Economic Commission for Latin America and the Caribbean. *See* CEPAL
economic governance, 235
economic growth: defined, 26; interpreting graphs of, 54; long-term global trends in, 27; as religion, 26; in twentieth-century Latin America, 38; in twenty-first century Latin America, 59–60; qualifiers to, 29; vs. development, 29–31, 145. *See also* convergence; national income
Ecuador, 7–8, 147; constitution, 246; development pacts, 226–27; external debt, 227; manufacturing and industry, 153; oil/gas revenues, 198; social movements, 227
El desarrollo económico de la América Latina y algunos de sus principales problemas, (1949 CEPAL report), 31, 83
El Salvador, 231
electoral business cycles, 204
embedded autonomy, 225
Embrapa, 162
European Central Bank, and 2021–24 inflation, 133
Evans, Peter, 225
Export-Import Bank of China, 68

exports' contribution to growth, 83, 98, 99
external indebtedness, 103–8

factor accumulation, 164
Fajardo, Margarita, 36, 256n3 (chap. 7)
Fajnzylber, Fernando, 35, 154–58, 225, 239
Federal Reserve System, 6, 91; and 2021–2024 inflation, 132–33
FEMSA, 160
Fernández, Alberto, 48, 139
Fernández Arias, Eduardo, 163–65
Fernández de Kirchner, Cristina, 3, 139
financial/capital account, 79, 81; measures of exposure and resilience, 98
fiscal dominance, 137
fiscal policy, 10, 104, 136, 191–212; components, 193; countercyclical vs. procyclical, 199–202; and economic development, 199; fiscal legitimacy and fiscal violence, 210; fiscal surplus as share of government revenues, 194, 212, 260n3; improvements during twenty-first century; inequality and; "less-is-more" conception, 198–99; as social contract, 209–10; stabilization conception, 199. *See also* fiscal dominance; fiscal rules; tax
fiscal rules, 203, 229; compliance with, 203; diminished procyclicality and, 203–4
Fishlow, Albert, 42, 192
Folha de São Paulo, 249n13
FONTAR, 163
Fortune magazine Global 500 listing, 159
Fox Quesada, Vicente, 6
France: inequality levels, 170
Frei Montalva, Eduardo, 157
Frei Ruíz Tagle, Eduardo, 71
Friedman, Milton, 30, 157
Furtado, Celso, 35

game theory, 156

García, Alan, 5, 207
Garcia, Marco Aurélio, 219, 220
Gini coefficient: defined, 169; evolution in Latin America, 171–72; international comparisons, 170; Latin America vs. Europe, 210–11; principle of transfers and, 169–70
Glencore, La Jagua mine, 81
global financial crisis. *See* Jazz Effect
Goldin, Claudia, 174
Goldin/Katz "race between education and technology," 174–75
Goldman Sachs, 3
Great Depression (1930s), 28
gross domestic product, real vs. nominal, 26. *See also* national income
gross national income. *See* national income
growth. *See* economic growth
Grupo Monge, 161
Guayaquil, Ecuador, Covid-19 emergency in, 7–8, 127
Guevara, Ernesto "Che," 20, 245, 250n4
Guidotti-Greenspan rule, 107–8
Gwynne, Robert, 157

Hägglund, Martin, 244–45
Hausmann, Ricardo, 238
Haya de la Torre, Victor Raúl, 19
Herfindahl-Hirschman Index of Export Concentration, 98, 100
High Developmentalism, 19–20, 31–37, 135, 146, 182, 192, 218
high-tech exports, as indicator of innovation, 162
Hirschman, Albert O., 220
Holland, Alisha, 117
Honduras: coup (2009), 72; Covid-19 in, 116, 124; manufacturing and industry in, 153
Hong Kong, industrialization, 155
Hu Jintao, 2
Humala, Ollanta, 137
Hurricane Season: Latin American economic growth during, 92–95; changes in balance of payments exposure and resilience, 108–9
hyperinflation: defined, 257n5; twentieth century hyperinflations in Latin America, 137, 140–41

import substituting industrialization (ISI): 34, 156; economic growth and, 39–40; policies to promote ISI, 35; "spontaneous ISI," 83
income taxation, 185, 197
index of competitive threat, 66
Indigenous support for political movements, 73, 226
industrial policy, 236; and Neo-Developmentalist State, 238
Industrial Revolution, 28. *See also* industrialization
industrialization, 28; truncated, 154–57, 225, 239. *See also* China; deindustrialization
industry: definition, 151; value added, 152; vs. manufacturing, 151–52
inequality, 167–189: colonial legacy and, 258n1; data limitations, 168, 176–77; decline in Latin America, 170–176, 234; evolution during twenty-first century, 178; impact on economic growth, 183–86; income, 169–79; intrinsic vs. instrumental value, 181–82; key #2, 17–18; landholding, 179; measures, 169, 177; total factor productivity and, 164; wealth, 179–81, 234. *See also* Gini coefficient; inverted-U hypothesis
inflation, 8, 129; CPI, 129; defined, 129; GDP deflator, 256n1; interpretations of, 2021–2022; monetarist vs. structuralist schools, 135–36. *See also* hyperinflation
Inflation Reduction Act, 238

informal economy, 117, 122, 164; Covid-19 and, 122–25; defined, 122; prevalence, 123
innovation, 162
INSEAD, 162
InnovaLatino project, 162, 165
insecurity, 231, 241
Inter-American Development Bank, 163, 229, 239
interest rates, and monetary policy, 136
International Monetary Fund, 6, 8, 37, 42, 47, 88, 184
International Standard Industrial Classification of All Economic Activities (ISIC Rev 3.1), 151–53
inverted-U hypothesis, time path of inequality, 187; vs. Piketty's evidence, 188
investment, defined, 39
invisible hand, 216
iron ore, 61

Jamaica, bauxite industry in, 34
Jazz Effect (global financial crisis), 10, 75–90; comparative economic impact, Latin America and OECD, 75–78; as described by Cristina Fernández de Kirchner, 3, 75; Free Jazz phase (collapse of income/trade), 76, 85–88; Take Five phase (liquidity crisis), 76, 84–85
Johns Hopkins University, Coronavirus Response Center at, 112

Katz, Lawrence F., 174
Kay, Cristóbal, 19
Keynes, John Maynard, 199–200, 208
King, Martin Luther, Jr., 30, 251n5
Kirchner, Cristina. See Fernández de Kirchner, Cristina
Kirchner, Nestor, 72
Korea, Republic of (South Korea): credibility of state, 157; development pacts, 225; industrialization, 155; R&D in, 162; and Washington Consensus, 44
Kremer, Michael, 69
Kubitschek, Juscelino, 19
Kuznets, Simon, 187. See also inverted-U hypothesis

Lagarde, Christine, 184
Lagos, Ricardo, 71, 202
Latin America and the Caribbean: countries included, 20–23; diversity of (key #5), 20; phases of economic growth, 40, 48; size of combined gross domestic product, 22–23; size of combined population, 23; weakness of state in, 191–92. See also individual countries
Latin American Economic Outlook (OECD report series), 99, 123, 140, 148, 209, 250n7, 254n2
Latinobarómetro, 230, 235
Lehman Brothers, 76, 85
Levy Yeyati, Eduardo, 139, 148
Lewis, W. Arthur, 34, 186; model of economic development, 186–87. See also inverted-U hypothesis
Li Zhaoxing, 2
liberalism, economic, 215
López Calva, Luis Felipe, 170, 173–75
López Obrador, Andrés Manuel, 5, 20, 72, 241
Lorde, Audre, 36
Los Tigres del Norte, 23
Lost Decade, 45, 92
Lucas, Robert: model of global capital flows, 39
Lugo, Fernando, 72
Lula (Luiz Inácio Lula da Silva), 3, 9, 20, 71, 137, 219
Lustig, Nora, 170, 173–75, 218

Macri, Mauricio, 48, 139

Maduro, Nicolás, 71, 72, 140, 224
manufacturing, 151; value added, 152; vs. industry, 151–52
maquiladoras, 162
Mariátegui, José Carlos, 19
market vs. state (key #4), 193, 245
Menem, Carlos, 72, 139, 228
Mercosur, 67
Mexico, 17; central bank, 70; competition with China in third-country markets, 65; concentration of trading partners, 100; Covid-19 in, 113, 114, 116; devaluation (1994), 45–47; inequality in, 171, 175, 178; minimum wage, 175; NAFTA and, 45, 65, 70, 223, 226; neoextractivism in, 150; 1990s political reforms, 70; presidential debates, April 2024, 243–44; remittances, 81; stabilizing development, 262n7; Zapatista uprising, 245. *See also* North American Free Trade Agreement (NAFTA); Progresa/Oportunidades/Prospera (Mexico); tequila effect
middle classes, 123–24, 161, 256n3 (chap. 6)
Milagrinho 54–73; economic growth rates during, 55–56; origin of name, 53
Milanović, Branko, 259n2
Milei, Javier, 8, 138, 232
military dictatorships, 19, 73, 223
mining, 8; and government revenue, 198
Mirelles, Henrique, 137
Modi, Narendra, 231
monetary dominance, 137, 256n4 (chap. 7)
monetary policy, 136. *See also* interest rates; quantitative easing
Monterrey, Mexico: early industrialization in, 155; industrial élite and development pact, 262n7
Moody's, 4
Morales, Evo, 4, 20, 72
Moreno, Lenin, 7–8

Mujica, José "Pepe," 2, 9, 72
multilatinas, 159–62, Global Latinas, 161
multiple equilibria, and coordination failure, 246–47

NAFTA. *See* North American Free Trade Agreement
national income, 23; as "pie", 28; real vs. nominal, 26. *See also* per capita income
natural resource curse, 34, 149
Neo-Developmentalist State, 226, 236, 237–42
neoextractivism, 150
neoliberalism, 218, 237, 246: and Commodity Consensus, 147; and Washington Consensus, 43, 69, 192, 226, 237; view of Brazilian PT, 219, 223
New York Times, 3
Nicaragua: electoral business cycles, 204
nickel, 61
Noboa, Daniel, 231
non-tax revenues: defined, 194; Latin America vs. OECD countries, 198
North American Free Trade Agreement (NAFTA), 45, 65, 70, 223, 226
Noyola, Juan, 35, 135

Obama, Barack, 7
Odebrecht scandal, 235
OECD, 53; Colombia's accession, 5; group of economies, 10, 23, 27, 38–39, 55, 58–59, 68, 76–78, 88–89, 119, 162, 194–98, 204, 210, 233, 235, 243; organization: 5, 65, 123, 204, 230, 256n3 (chap. 6). *See also Latin American Economic Outlook*
oil, 42, 131, 140, 150, 160, 240, 261n2; and energy transformation, 240–41; and government revenues, 140–41, 198; and natural resource curse, 34, 149–50
open market operations, 136

Oportunidades. *See* Progresa/Oportunidades/Prospera (Mexico)
Organisation for Economic Co-operation and Development. See OECD
Ortega Saavedra, Daniel, 72
Oxfam, 179
OXXO, 161

Palacio Nacional (Mexico City), Diego Rivera murals, 15–16
PAN (Mexico), 6, 223
Panama: non-tax revenues, 198
Paraguay, 149; Covid-19 in, 115–16; democratic transition in, 223
Park Chung Hee, 157
patents, as indicator of innovation, 162
PDSB (Brazil), 249n5
PDVSA, 56, 140
Pemex, 241
Peña Nieto, Enrique, 5–6, 70
per capita income, definition, 26, 251n3
Pérez, Carlos Andrés, 71
Perón, Juan Domingo, 19, 228
Peronism. *See* Argentina.
Peru, 55; Covid-19 in, 116; fiscal balance, 194; hyperinflation in the twentieth century, 130; inequality in, 178, 181; mining revenue, 198; neoextractivism in, 150; public debt, 4, 207; and ratings agencies, 4–5, 207; remittances, 81; reserve changes during Jazz Effect, 88; restructuring of public debt, 4
Petro, Gustavo, 72, 241
petroleum. *See* oil
Piketty, Thomas, 27, 176, 187, 188, 241, 244, 251n4
Piñera, Sebastián, 72
Pink Tide, 2, 58, 70–73; camps within Pink Tide, 219; and democratic consolidation, 73; and income redistribution, 184–85
Pinochet Ugarte, Augusto, 19, 71, 157

policy reform: political economy vs. policy-making process schools, 228–29; waves of reform, 229
Pontificia Universidad Católica de Chile, 157
populism, 19
Portugal, 16–17
possibilism, 10, 73, 220, 235; Chile as exemplary case, 220–21; Neo-Developmentalist State and, 238; possibilists vs. left-populist governments, 214; pragmatism of, 220
Prebisch, Raúl, 31–33, 37,192, 218, 236, 252n11; model of declining terms of trade, 32–33, 252n6
presidencialismo, 229
PRI (Mexico), 5–6, 223
primary products. *See* commodities
Progresa/Oportunidades/Prospera (Mexico), 10, 175
Prospera. *See* Progresa/Oportunidades/Prospera (Mexico)
PT. *See* Workers Party (Brazil)
public debt, 194, 205–8; and Neo-Developmentalist State, 238
public goods, 261n3
public spending, 199–202, 243; voracity effect, 201; see also electoral business cycles, social transfers

quantitative easing, 6, 96, 136

Ramírez Sánchez, Martha Areli, 245
raw materials. *See* commodities
R&D, as indicator of innovation, 162
redistributive public finance and inequality, 183–85
reform vs. revolution (key #4), 18–20
remittances, 81, 83, 85, 99
reprimarization, 8, 10, 146–49, 225, 228, 234
reserve requirements, 136
reserves: and Jazz Effect transmission to Latin American countries, 88;

and short term external debt, 90, 107n8. *See also* balance of payments; Greenspan-Guidotti rule
resilience, 89
Ricardo, David, 18, 32
Rio de Janeiro, 7, 21
Rivera, Diego, 15–16
Rodrik, Dani, 44, 150–51, 184, 238, 239
Rohter, Larry, 3
Rosales, Antulio, 225
Rouquié, Alain, 222
Rousseff, Dilma, 9, 20, 47; impeachment of, 72–73, 95

Salinas de Gortari, Carlos, 226
Santander, 160
Santiso, Javier, 10, 160, 210, 220, 238. *See also* possibilism
Santos, Juan Manuel, 5; Paris "Latin American Decade" speech (2011), 5, 53, 211
São Paulo, 7, 20
São Paulo Forum, 72, 219
Schorr, Martín, 138–39
Selic, 106
Sen, Amartya, 30
Serra, José, 182
Singapore, industrialization, 155
Singer, André, 47
sisal, 19
skill premium, 10; defined, 173; and labor income inequality, 173–75
Smith, Adam, 216
social cohesion, 236, 241–46, 263n3
social conflict and inequality, 183
social democracy, 218–19, 244–45, 249n5
social security contributions, 197
social transfers: in possibilist vs. left-populist states, 227; social assistance, 242; social insurance, 243
Solow, Robert, 38
soybeans, 61, 149; soybean cake and soybean oil, 254n8; "Soybean Republic," 67–68

Spain, 16–17, 23, 82; multinational firms as model for *multilatinas*, 160
special drawing rights, 88
state: autonomy, 215, 261n2; characteristics favoring economic effectiveness, 215; development pacts, 225; embedded autonomy, 225; intervention in economy, 192, 215–18; state policies vs. government policies, 209, 214, 226. *See also* market vs. state (key #4)
Stein, Barbara, 16–17
Stein, Stanley, 16–17
structural transformation, 145–65, 218. *See also* commodities; industrialization; reprimarization
sudden stops, 57, 89, 107, 125, 201, 208, 254n7 (chap. 4)
sugar, 19
suma qamaña, 29–30, 246
sumak kawsay, 29, 246
Sustainable Development Goals, 236, 241
Svampa, Maristella, 147

Taiwan: development pact in, 225; diplomatic relations with Latin American countries, 63–64; industrialization, 155; and Washington Consensus, 44
Taper Tantrum, 6
tariffs, 35, 41, 45, 83, 151, 155–57, 209
Tavares, Maria da Conceição, 35, 182
Taylor, Lance, 44
tax: composition, Latin America vs. OECD, 195–98; direct vs. indirect, 197; evasion, 193, 209–10, 243; regressive vs. progressive forms of, 197, 261n4, 261n13; tax morale, 210, 243; tax reform, 243; tax-to-GDP ratios, Latin America vs. OECD, 194–95, 243; wealth tax, 244. *See also* non-tax revenues
Telefónica, 160

Temer, Michel, 9
tequila effect, 47
terms of trade, 33, 61. *See also* declining terms of trade
Thorp, Rosemary, 18, 167; "embeddedness of inequality", 168; "functionality of inequality", 181
total factor productivity, 163–65
trade liberalization, 32, 43, 70, 151, 229
trade openness, 83, 97, 98, 103, 108
Trinidad and Tobago, oil/gas revenues, 198
Trump, Donald J., 231, 236
Tuesta, David, 121
Turzi, Mariano, 67

Ukraine, Russian invasion of, 132
United Kingdom, 17
United Nations, 236
United Nations Statistical Commission, 151
United States, 17, 23, 42, 67, 71, 82–83, 89; Cold War policies toward Latin America, 7, 20, 73; as epicenter of Jazz Effect, 75; inequality levels, 170; shift of foreign policy after September 11, 2001, terrorist attacks, 73. *See also* Federal Reserve System
University of Chicago, 157
Uribe, Álvaro, 20
Uruguay, 2, 149; democratic transition in, 223; inequality in; pragmatism of Frente Amplio government, 2

value added, 152
Vázquez, Tabaré, 2, 72
Velarde, Julio, 137
Velasco, Andrés, 235; and Chile's fiscal rule 202

Venezuela: attempted coup (2002), 55–56, 71; authoritarianism, 71; Bolivarian Missions, 71; Caracazo, 71; Covid-19 in, 115; development pact, 226–27; economic crisis and recovery 2002–03, 56; fiscal balance in, 195; Human Rights Watch and, 71; inflation in, 134, 140–41; Liberal-Conservative political rivalry, 71; natural resource curse and, 149; non-tax revenues, 198; oil and politics, 56, 71, 227; public debt, 208; social movements, 227
Viteri, Cynthia, 7
Volcker, Paul, 256n4 (chap. 7)
Volpi, Jorge, 23

Wall Street Journal, 1, 115, 145, 251n4
Washington Consensus, 19, 42–47, 70, 151, 157; elements of, 43; stabilization and, 44; structural adjustment and, 44; neoliberalism and, 43, 192
wealth, vs. income, 168
welfare theorems (Arrow-Debreu), 216
Williamson, Jeffrey G., 258n1
Williamson, John, 43
Workers Party (Brazil), 3, 20, 71
World Bank, 37, 42, 167, 241
World Development Indicators, 176, 250n6, 251n9, 255n1 (chap. 6)
World Health Organization, 111
World Inequality Lab, 176, 180–81
World Trade Organization, 2, 67
Wuhan, China, 111

Zapatistas, 245
Zedillo Ponce de León, Ernesto, 47
Zelaya, Manuel "Mel," 72